Manchester Medieval Sources Series

series advisers Rosemary Horrox and Janet L. Nelson

This series aims to meet a growing need among students and teachers of medieval history for translations of key sources that are directly usable in students' own work. It provides texts central to medieval studies courses and focuses upon the diverse cultural and social as well as political conditions that affected the functioning of all levels of medieval society. The basic premise of the series is that translations must be accompanied by sufficient introductory and explanatory material, and each volume, therefore, includes a comprehensive guide to the sources' interpretation, including discussion of critical linguistic problems and an assessment of the most recent research on the topics being covered.

also available in the series

Mark Bailey *The English Manor c. 1200–c. 1500*

Malcolm Barber and Keith Bate *The Templars*

Simon Barton and Richard Fletcher *The world of El Cid: Chronicles of the Spanish Reconquest*

Andrew Brown and Graeme Small *Court and civic society in the Burgundian Low Countries c. 1420–1520*

Samuel K. Cohn, Jr. *Popular protest in late-medieval Europe: Italy, France and Flanders*

Trevor Dean *The towns of Italy in the later Middle Ages*

P. J. P. Goldberg *Women in England, c. 1275–1525*

Rosemary Horrox *The Black Death*

Anthony Musson and Edward Powell *Crime, law and society in the later middle ages*

I.S. Robinson *Eleventh-century Germany: The Swabian Chronicles*

I.S. Robinson *The papal reform of the eleventh century: Lives of Pope Leo IX and Pope Gregory VII*

Michael Staunton *The lives of Thomas Becket*

Craig Taylor *Joan of Arc: La Pucelle*

Elisabeth van Houts *The Normans in Europe*

David Warner *Ottonian Germany*

Diana Webb *Saints and cities in medieval Italys*

HISTORY AND POLITICS IN LATE CAROLINGIAN AND OTTONIAN EUROPE

Manchester University Press

MedievalSources*online*

Complementing the printed editions of the Medieval Sources series, Manchester University Press has developed a web-based learning resource which is now available on a yearly subscription basis.

MedievalSources*online* brings quality history source material to the desktops of students and teachers and allows them open and unrestricted access throughout the entire college or university campus. Designed to be fully integrated with academic courses, this is a one-stop answer for many medieval history students, academics and researchers keeping thousands of pages of source material 'in print' over the Internet for research and teaching.

titles available now at MedievalSources*online include*

Trevor Dean *The towns of Italy in the later Middle Ages*

John Edwards *The Jews in Western Europe, 1400–1600*

Paul Fouracre and Richard A. Gerberding *Late Merovingian France: History and hagiography 640–720*

Chris Given-Wilson *Chronicles of the Revolution 1397–1400: The reign of Richard II*

P. J. P. Goldberg *Women in England, c. 1275–1525*

Janet Hamilton and Bernard Hamilton *Christian dualist heresies in the Byzantine world, c. 650–c. 1450*

Rosemary Horrox *The Black Death*

Graham A. Loud and Thomas Wiedemann *The history of the tyrants of Sicily by 'Hugo Falcandus', 1153–69*

Janet L. Nelson *The Annals of St-Bertin: Ninth-century histories, volume I*

Timothy Reuter *The Annals of Fulda: Ninth-century histories, volume II*

R. N. Swanson *Catholic England: Faith, religion and observance before the Reformation*

Elisabeth van Houts *The Normans in Europe*

Jennifer Ward *Women of the English nobility and gentry 1066–1500*

Visit the site at *www.medievalsources.co.uk* for further information and subscription prices.

HISTORY AND POLITICS IN LATE CAROLINGIAN AND OTTONIAN EUROPE

The *Chronicle* of Regino of Prüm and Adalbert of Magdeburg

selected sources translated and annotated with an introduction
by Simon MacLean

Manchester University Press

Copyright © Simon MacLean 2009

The right of Simon MacLean to be identified as the author of this work has been asserted by him in accordance with the Copyright, Designs and Patents Act 1988.

Published by Manchester University Press
Altrincham Street, Manchester M1 7JA, UK
www.manchesteruniversitypress.co.uk

British Library Cataloguing-in-Publication Data is available

ISBN 978 0 7190 7134 8 *hardback*
ISBN 978 0 7190 7135 5 *paperback*

First published by Manchester University Press in hardback 2009

This edition first published 2017

The publisher has no responsibility for the persistence or accuracy of URLs for any external or third-party internet websites referred to in this book, and does not guarantee that any content on such websites is, or will remain, accurate or appropriate.

Printed by Lightning Source

For Pia
21 June 2005

CONTENTS

Series editor's foreword	*page* ix
Acknowledgements	xi
Abbreviations	xiii
Genealogies	xv
Maps	xix

Introduction
Regino's world and career	1
Regino as historian	8
Date and design	9
Book I: themes and sources	18
Book II: themes and sources	29
Adalbert of Magdeburg	53
On this translation	58

Regino of Prüm's *Chronicle*
Book I	61
Book II	121

Adalbert's Continuation   232

Bibliography	273
Index	296

SERIES EDITOR'S FOREWORD

Of all the earlier medieval works of historiography, the *Chronicle* of Regino of Prum is among those that have remained longest, and for students of the period most frustratingly, untranslated. This work is puzzling: the structure and function of its earlier sections (1 AD to 741, and 742–814), its author's purposes, its context, and its intended audience, are all more or less inscrutable. Now Simon MacLean has met the need and risen to the challenge of translating not just the *Chronicle*'s more familiar (long-)ninth-century section (to 906) but the earlier sections too, adding into what becomes a tremendous bargain the *Continuation* by Adalbert of St-Maximin, archbishop of Magdeburg, who offers a distinctive take on events down to 967, that final entry being especially significant. Between them, these chroniclers give access to unique information; more interesting still, to particular concerns and readings of times and regions otherwise not, or hardly, documented by other writers. Ideally qualified to unravel their mysteries is Dr Simon MacLean, an expert decoder of early medieval historiography whose own research-focus has extended from the later ninth century to include the tenth. As ever with volumes in the Manchester Medieval Sources series, scholarship is put at the service of a wide readership, and the introduction and annotation supply so much invaluable background material and thought-provoking commentary that scholars engaging, as they increasingly often are these days, with the late-Carolingian and post-Carolingian periods will make this a first port-of-call. Who, we find, but Regino offers the wherewithal to deconstruct the modern paradigm of the Carolingian Empire's 'decline and fall'? Who but Regino explains the formation of a regional entity in what modern economic historians call 'the blue banana', *alias* Lotharingia? Who but Adalbert reveals the near-panoptic vision of the early Ottonian regime? Simon MacLean's translation offers an entrée to revelatory understandings by these writers of their own worlds, and hence to those worlds themselves. This is the book for students (and they include teachers) seeking enlightenment on what can never again be called the darkest phase of the Dark Ages.

Janet L. Nelson
King's College London

ACKNOWLEDGEMENTS

I am indebted to various institutions and individuals for help in the preparation of this book. Several people were kind enough to read and comment on large chunks of the introduction and translation, and their feedback improved the final product no end: Stuart Airlie, David Ganz, Matthew Innes, Jinty Nelson, Julia Smith and David Warner. For their willingness to check long sections of the translation and discuss at length the hard bits I thank Rosalind MacLachlan, Peter Maxwell-Stuart and Steve Robbie. Bill North's correspondence about Adalbert was immensely helpful, as was his unpublished English translation of the continuation which he was kind enough to send me. At various stages of the project I benefited enormously from discussions with many colleagues in St Andrews, and I am particularly grateful to Michael Bentley for his advice at an early stage in the proceedings. It is a privilege to work with such a dedicated and supportive group of medievalists. In funding a year of research leave in 2006–7, the School of History at the University of St Andrews and the Arts and Humanities Research Council provided support essential to the book's completion. At Manchester University Press, Emma Brennan and Alison Welsby have been unfailingly efficient and helpful. All those mentioned are responsible for vastly improving the quality of the book you are holding; for any misjudgements and stupid blunders that remain, responsibility is mine alone. Last but by no means least, I would like to record a special thank-you to Claire for her patience and strength; and another to Naomi for proving to me that there are indeed more than enough hours in the day.

ABBREVIATIONS

AA	Annales Alamannici
AAng	Annales Engolismenses
AASS	Acta Sanctorum
AB	Annals of St-Bertin, trans. Nelson 1991
AF	Annals of Fulda, trans. Reuter 1992
AF(B)	Annals of Fulda, Bavarian continuation
AF(M)	Annals of Fulda, Mainz continuation
AFont	Annales Fontanellenses
AH	Annales Hildesheimenses
AL	Annales Laubacenses
AnnAug	Annales Augienses
AP	Annales Prumienses
ARF	Annales Regni Francorum
ASA	Annales Sancti Amandi
ASC	Anglo-Saxon Chronicle
ASGM	Annales Sangallenses Maiores
AV	Annales Vedastini
AX	Annales Xantenses
BM	Böhmer and Mühlbacher, *Regesta Imperii*
BO	Böhmer and Ottenthal, *Die Regesten des Kaiserreichs*
BZ	Böhmer and Zielinski, *Die Regesten des Regnum Italiae*
DA	*Deutsches Archiv für Erforschung des Mittelalters*
D(D)	Diploma(s) of:
	P Pippin III (ed. Mühlbacher)
	L Lothar I (ed. Schieffer)
	L2 Lothar II (ed. Schieffer)
	LG Louis the German (ed. Kehr)
	K Karlmann of Bavaria (ed. Kehr)
	AC Arnulf of Carinthia (ed. Kehr)
	CIII Charles III the Fat (ed. Kehr)
	Z Zwentibald (ed. Schieffer)

	LC	Louis the Child (ed. Schieffer)
	HI	Henry I (ed. Sickel)
	OI	Otto I (ed. Sickel)
DTR	Bede, *De Temporum Ratione*	
GD	*Gesta Dagoberti*	
GSR	*Gesta sanctorum Rotonensium*	
LHF	*Liber Historiae Francorum*	
LP	*Liber Pontificalis* (trans. Davis 1992, 1995 and 2000)	
MGH	Monumenta Germaniae Historica	

      AA   Auctores antiquissimi

      Capit 2 Capitularia regum Francorum vol.2, ed. A. Boretius and V. Krause (Hanover, 1890)

      SRG   Scriptores rerum Germanicarum in usum scholarum separatim editi

      SRG NS Scriptores rerum Germanicarum, Nova series

      SRL   Scriptores rerum Langobardicarum

      SRM   Scriptores rerum Merovingicarum

      SS   Scriptores

MUB   Beyer (ed.), *Urkundenbuch*

RGS   Widukind of Corvey, *Rerum Gestarum Saxonicarum*

1 The Early Carolingians (*simplified*)

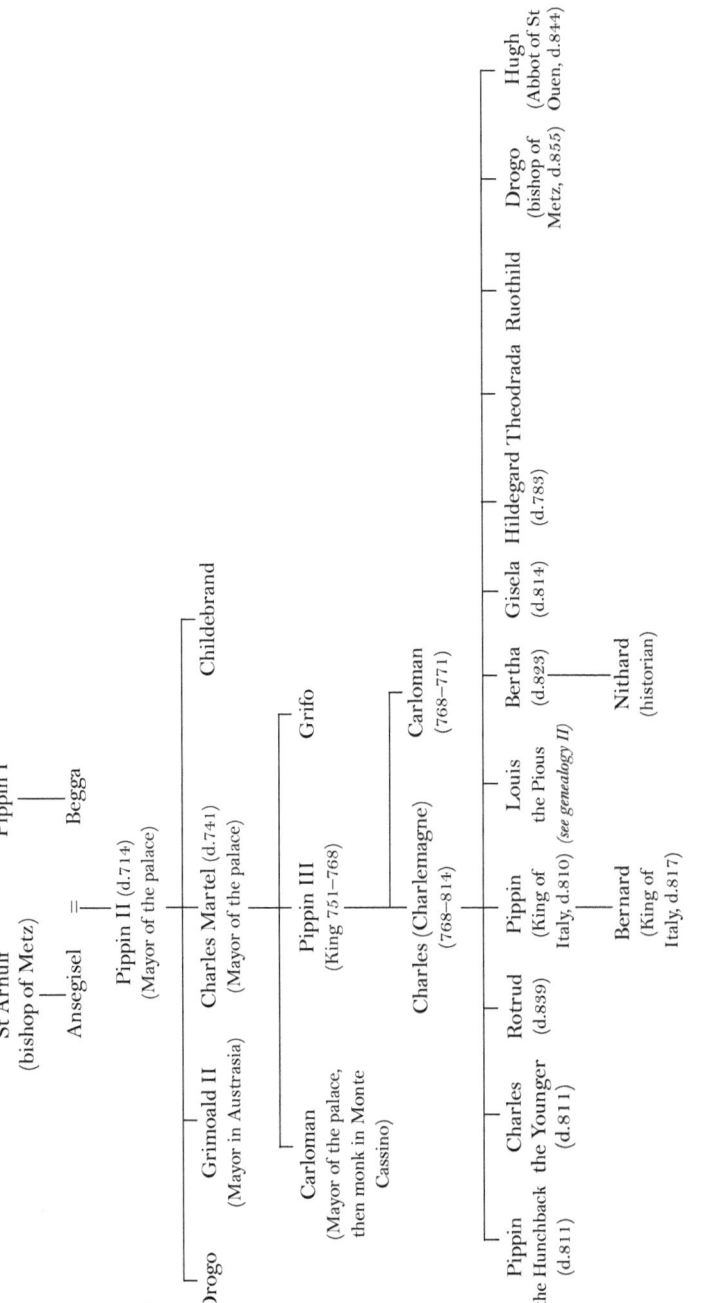

2 The Carolingian Kings *(ninth and tenth centuries) (simplified)*

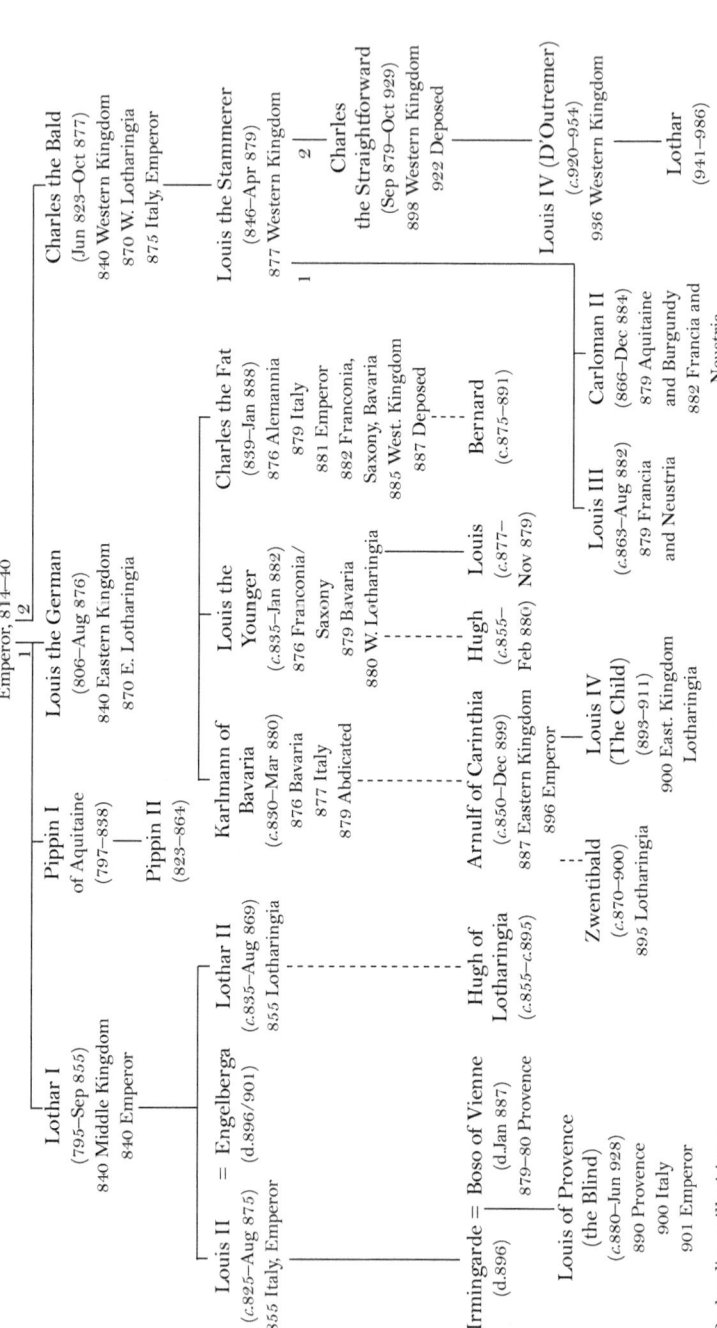

3 The Ottonians/Liudolfinger

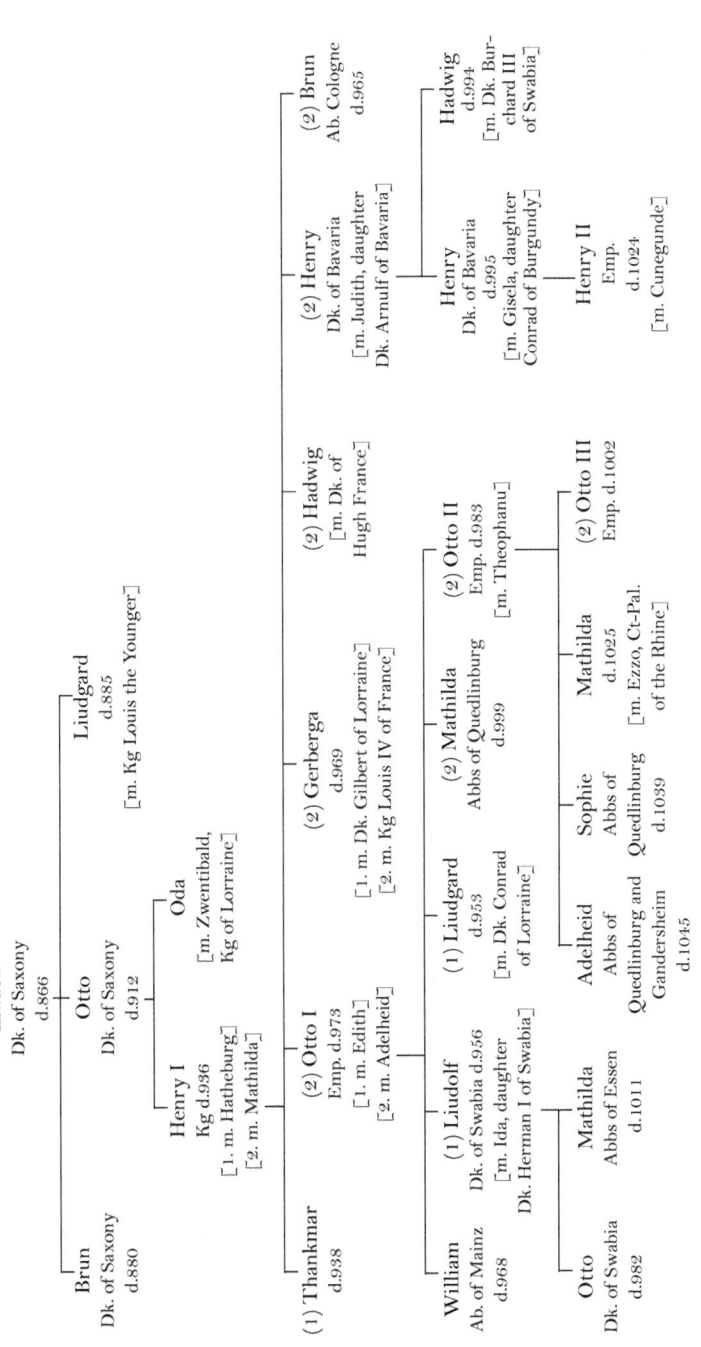

Source: T. Reuter, *Germany in the Early Middle Ages, 800–1056*, London and New York, 1991, p. 337.

4 The Robertians

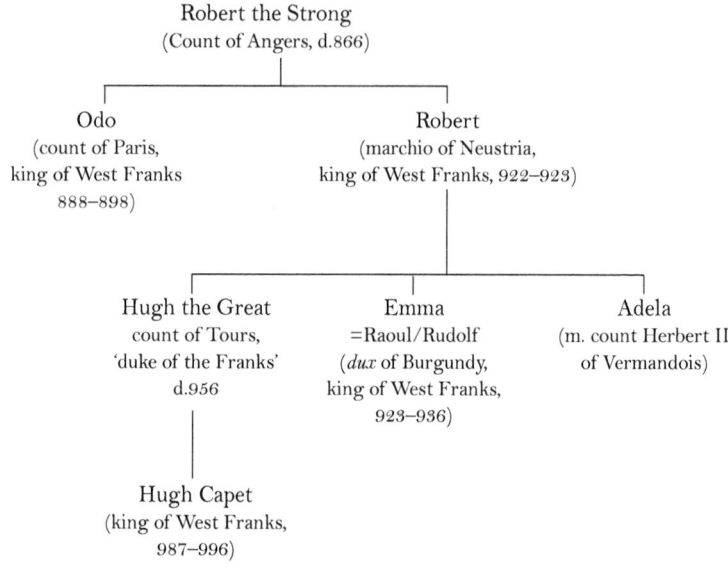

5 The Conradines

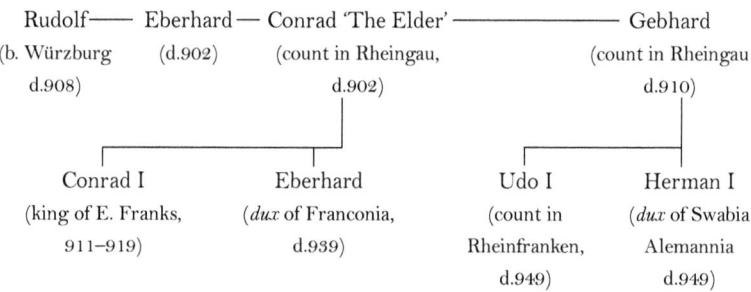

xviii

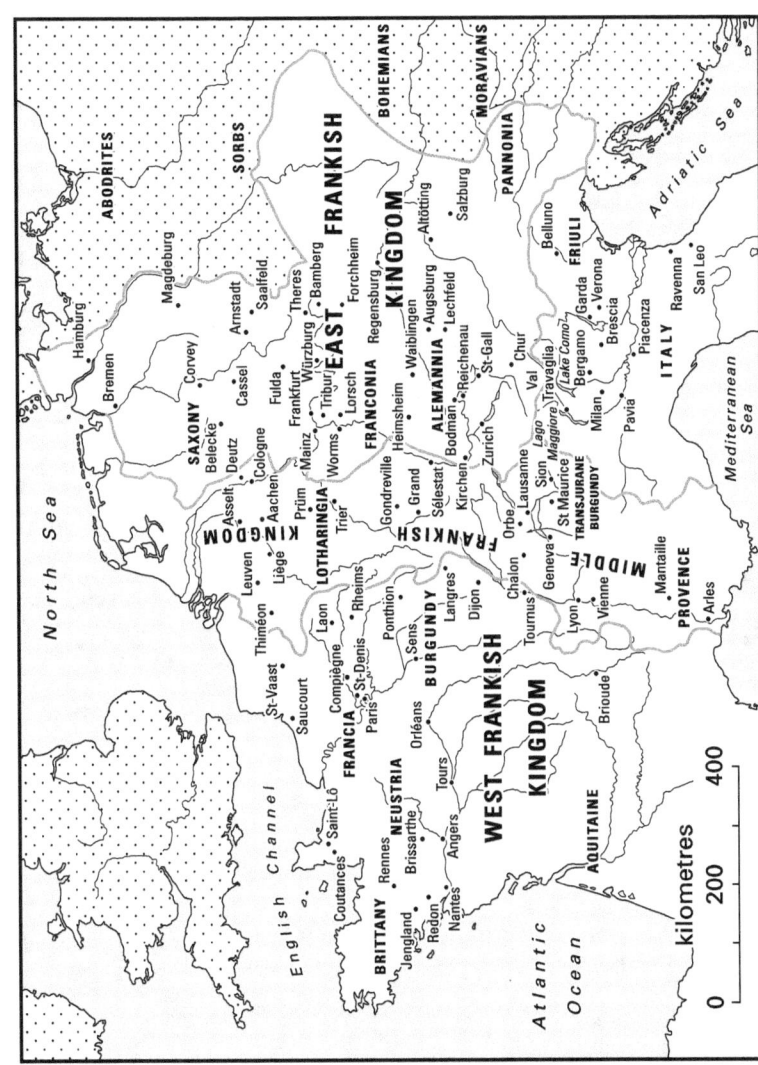

1 Late Carolingian/early Ottonian Europe

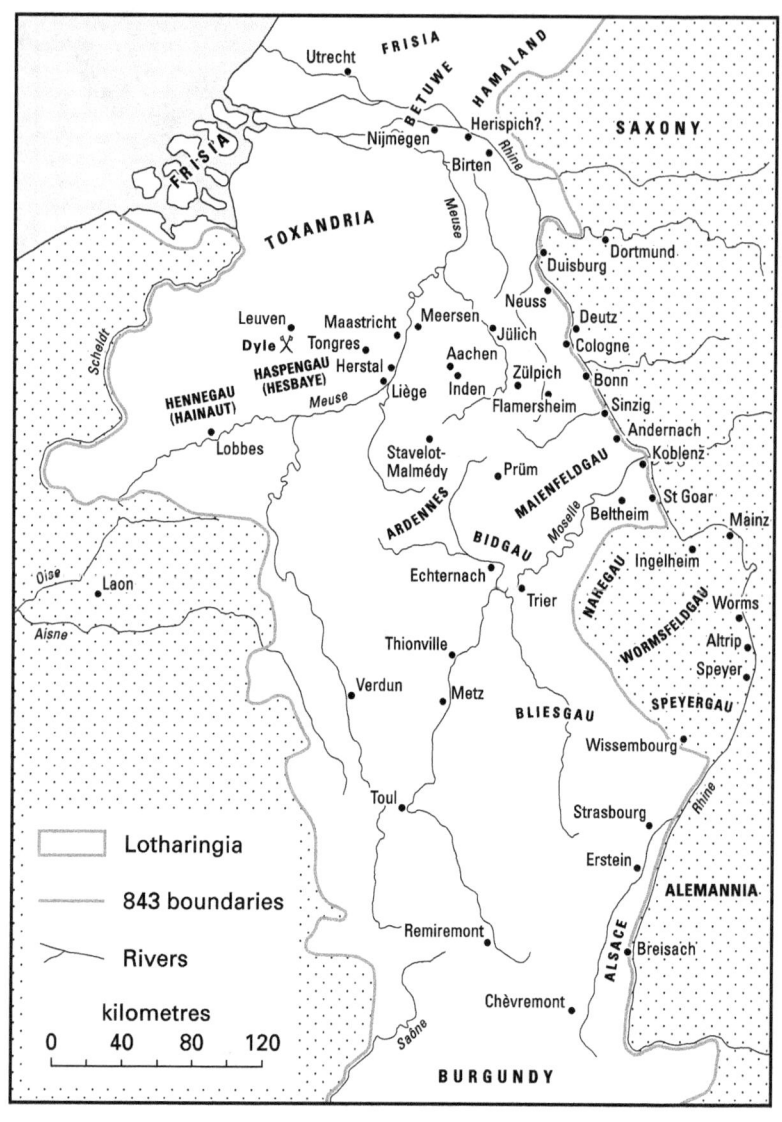

2 Lotharingia

INTRODUCTION

Regino's world and career

The career, mental world and writings of Regino, abbot of Prüm (d.915), were all defined by the Carolingian empire and, more particularly, by its end. The Carolingians were the second great ruling dynasty of the Franks, one of the barbarian peoples which had taken up the reins of power in the Roman provinces at the end of the fifth century. Their predecessors, the Merovingians, had rapidly expanded their dominions out from their heartlands in north-eastern Gaul and maintained a successful dynastic hegemony that endured for some 250 years. The Carolingians were an aristocratic family from the eastern regions of the Frankish realm who by around 700 had come to control the crucial political office of mayor of the palace (in effect, second to the king); and the greatest of the mayors, Charles Martel, after whom posterity named the family, entrenched its position through military aggression in the decades before his death in 741. In 751 Charles's son Pippin III seized the throne for himself. For more than a century thereafter, the Carolingians maintained an unbroken (though not unchallenged) monopoly on royal power. Pippin's son Charlemagne (Charles the Great, 768–814) was the hero of the story, expanding the empire's territory to an area of some one million square kilometres through relentless campaigning and ruthless political manoeuvring, and having himself crowned emperor in Rome on Christmas Day 800. After 840, the existence of multiple heirs meant that the empire was divided and subdivided several times. Such division was part and parcel of Frankish politics, and the empire retained its hegemonic character thanks to the close family relationships of its rulers. However, a realm sustained by dynastic ideology depended for its continued existence on the capacity of the ruling dynasty to keep reproducing itself. A series of unexpected royal deaths and barren marriages in the 870s and 880s caused the political fabric to begin unravelling, and in winter 887–8 the deposition and death without heir of Emperor Charles III 'the Fat', sole ruler of the empire and the only legitimate adult male Carolingian left, shattered the dynasty's claims to hegemony. The territory they had ruled split into several smaller kingdoms, most of them fought over by would-be kings drawn from rival aristocratic families, none of them powerful enough to impose their will decisively on the others. Although these kingdoms retained a sense of belonging to a common Frankish world, and all were modelled on the legacy of Charlemagne, the empire's territorial and dynastic coherence was gone. This post-imperial era of political instability was the age of Regino of Prüm.[1]

Regino the abbot was a victim of this instability: the defining moment of his career came in 899 when he was ejected from Prüm during a violent struggle for control of Lotharingia, the middle Carolingian kingdom that stretched south from the Low Countries to the edge of Provence. But Regino the historian and scholar was heir not just to a legacy of conflict and violence, but also to a rich cultural heritage. Driven by an intense sense of mission and Christian obligation, and encouraged by the (as they saw it) providential success of their territorial expansion, the Carolingians fostered a surge in the study, copying and production of texts. A sense of the importance of this development, which is with justification termed a 'Renaissance' by historians, is imparted by the fact that some 7,000 manuscripts survive from the ninth century, compared to around 1,800 for the previous eight combined.[2] Among the many strands of this dynastically-sponsored phenomenon, the writing and re-writing of history loom large. The elites of the Carolingian age not only keenly devoured classical and biblical history, but also saw to the composition of a panoply of contemporary historical works. Several major sets of annals inspired by the *Royal Frankish Annals*, a work associated with the court of Charlemagne, together with a variety of ruler-biographies, lesser annals and widescreen universal chronicles, not to mention commentaries on biblical and classical history, make possible for us the detailed reconstruction of Carolingian politics and the analysis of ninth-century historical sensibilities.[3] Regino's *Chronicle*, dedicated to Bishop Adalbero of Augsburg in the year 908, was the last work of its kind for several decades, and as such its author can be regarded as the last great historian of the Carolingian Empire.

In another sense, though, Regino is better understood as its first.

---

1 For the political history of the Carolingian empire see McKitterick 1983; Riché 1993; Costambeys, Innes and MacLean forthcoming; on its disintegration see MacLean 2003a; Airlie 2006b. For overviews of Regino's career and work see Hlawitschka 1975; Schmitz 1989; Wattenbach, Levison and Löwe 1990: 897–904; Schneidmüller 1990; Hartmann 2003.

2 Brown 1994: 34. On the Carolingian Renaissance more generally see the essays collected in McKitterick 1994 and McKitterick 1995.

3 See now McKitterick 2004; McKitterick 2006.

INTRODUCTION

Writing in the aftermath of the empire's disintegration, he was the first author to look back over its entire course and to chart its fall as well as its rise. This privileged position allowed him, unlike annalists who wrote up their texts yearly or in chunks of years, to take on the persona of a 'master narrator', building into his narrative carefully crafted themes and morals, and describing events with 20/20 hindsight. The end of the story was already known to both author and audience, and because of this Regino's work can, and should, be read as an ironic history of Carolingian politics.[4] Yet the scope of his text was not limited to the lifespan of the empire. The *Chronicle* is divided into two books. The first, subtitled 'On the times of the Lord's incarnation', begins with the incarnation of Christ (Regino was the first major historian to do so) and proceeds as far as the death of Charles Martel in 741, while the second ('On the deeds of the kings of the Franks') takes the story from the death of Charles Martel through to 906. The text is a valuable resource for the historian in two related ways. Firstly, Regino offers us a warehouse of material with which to analyse the method and thought-world of a working Carolingian historian. Although it has been largely dismissed as a work of naïve compilation, Book I's assemblage of excerpts from older sources forms, as we shall see, an essential part of Regino's narrative about the deeds of Frankish kings, Roman emperors and Christian heroes; while Book II's deployment of stories learned at the feet of the monastic elders offers us a window into the mentality and identity of the community of Prüm itself. Secondly, the *Chronicle*'s independent – and in the later stages eyewitness – account of Frankish political history from 818 until 906 makes it one of the four major narrative sources (along with the *Annals* of Fulda, St-Bertin and St-Vaast) for the history of the second half of the ninth century.

But Regino was more than an eyewitness: he was a participant. If the end of the empire dominated Regino's historical perspective, this is partly because its consequences intersected with the dramatic events of his own career, which by his account was dominated by his deposition in 899. His family background and early career are obscure. According to a tradition recorded in a sixteenth-century source Regino came from an aristocratic family based at Altrip near Speyer, which is usually accepted as plausible because Prüm held important estates there.[5] Thanks to the survival in charters and memorial books of several lists of Prüm monks

---

4 These are the insights of Airlie 2006a.
5 Hlawitschka 1975: 12; Airlie 2006a: 113.

from the abbacy of Ansbald (860–886), Regino may have left a further impression in the documentary record: two monks named Reginhardus are listed among the community, and it seems likely that one of them was the future abbot, 'Regino' being an abbreviation.[6] Both of these figures were upwardly mobile in the lists' ordering of names, suggesting that Regino's rise to seniority was gradual but steady. By 892 he had become sufficiently prominent and respected to be elected abbot by his fellow monks in accordance with the freedom of election they were guaranteed by royal charters of 884 and 891.[7] Paradoxically, kings' guarantees of freedom and protection carried with them the implicit expectation of influence over the monastery.[8] Regino acknowledged this reciprocity unquestioningly in the account of his own succession in the *Chronicle*, implying, even as he underlined the regularity and propriety of the election, that the approval of the east Frankish king Arnulf had been sought.

Arnulf's interest was more than perfunctory, for Prüm was one of the region's most politically important institutions. Although located in a rural part of the Ardennes, it was close to key Frankish royal centres like Metz, Trier and Aachen, and its rise to prominence was intimately connected with that of the Carolingian dynasty. Founded in 721 by the noblewoman Bertrada, it was refounded in 752 by her granddaughter, also Bertrada, and her husband Pippin, the first Carolingian king. A decade later, Pippin renewed his links to the house with a spectacular gift of lands.[9] Subsequent generations of Carolingians continued to shower the abbey with patronage, repeatedly confirming its enjoyment of royal protection and immunity from dues and services. The monastery also enjoyed physical proximity to the ruling dynasty. Among several kings who visited were Charles the Bald, who, briefly incarcerated there during the rebellions of 830–834, reportedly regarded himself as an 'alumnus', and the Emperor Lothar I, one of the abbey's most generous patrons, who became a monk there shortly before

---

6 Tellenbach 1988: 413; though Schleidgen 1977: 1–2 is sceptical about the identification. Werner 1997: 10–20 argues on the basis of his name that Regino was related to the Robertian family of King Odo of west Francia (888–898), but his case lays a lot of weight on fragile similarities of name and does not explain what purpose a pro-Robertian bias in the *Chronicle* would have served at the time of its composition. See also below, pp. 38–9.

7 D CIII 100; D AC 92; Wisplinghoff 1999: 440–1.

8 Rosenwein 1999.

9 DD P 3 and 16; Zielinski 1989: 102–9; Airlie 2006a: 114–15.

INTRODUCTION 5

his death in 855 and was then buried in the monastery.[10] That said, Prüm was not an exclusively royal institution. None of its abbots were members of the Carolingian family, nor laymen drawn from among its prominent supporters, two features commonly found in the history of monasteries associated with the Frankish kings. The monk-lists contain many names characteristic of the region's most prominent aristocratic kindreds, and the inmates had formidable political connections, illustrated by the fact that several of them went on to become high-profile bishops.[11] Local elites, not just kings and emperors, were ostentatious benefactors of the monks.[12] A survey of the monastery's lands and dues (sometimes known in the literature as a polyptyque or Urbar) commissioned after Viking attacks in 882 and 892, and probably completed under Regino's supervision in 893, reveals that by the end of the ninth century Prüm controlled around 1,700 estates inhabited by an estimated 16,000–20,000 people, mainly in Lotharingia. This total does not include extensive possessions in and around Brittany, which were not counted in the survey. These resources, along with the size of the central community – perhaps 100 monks and ancillaries – suggest what made Prüm one of the empire's most economically and politically important institutions.[13] Although we know little about his actual tenure as abbot, the very fact of his promotion to leadership of such an establishment tells us something about Regino's talent, standing and connections.[14] That in the later 890s he was entrusted with the custody of the blinded rebel Hugh, son of King Lothar II, confirms his ongoing closeness to the kingdom's political centre.[15]

The tentacles of the political world, then, did not stop dead at the walls of Carolingian monasteries, and in 899 one reached in and grabbed Regino by the throat. Political instability in Lotharingia had escalated since the death of Charles the Fat in 888. The aristocratic elite was repeatedly convulsed by a series of high-profile murders and an almost

10 See below, p. 32.
11 Haubrichs 1979: 50.
12 Hennebicque 1981.
13 Figures from Kuchenbuch 1978: 46–9, 57–8; Haubrichs 1979: 38–40. See *Das Prümer Urbar* for the full text; Wisplinghoff 1999 argues against Regino's involvement but the evidence seems unambiguous.
14 Wisplinghoff 1999: 447 points to charters whose linguistic similarities to sections of the *Chronicle* may suggest that they were his work. More generally he argues that Regino was regarded as a failure as abbot, though the evidence is all indirect: see further below, p. 50.
15 See below, 885.

continuous fight for the middle kingdom between the rulers and would-be rulers of west and east Francia, Odo, Arnulf and Charles the Straightforward (or Simple).[16] Although Arnulf (a bastard, but the only one of the immediately post-888 rulers whose father had been a Carolingian king) managed to impose a dynastic settlement in 895 through the installation as king of his illegitimate son Zwentibald, the latter's capriciousness (which was in part a frustrated response to the deep factionalisation of Lotharingian politics) continued to undermine prospects for stability.[17] When Arnulf fell gravely ill in 899 a plan was hatched to remove Zwentibald and replace him with his half-brother Louis IV 'the Child', aptly named since he was then aged only five or six. Regino's career seems to have become collateral damage in the execution of this plan. He was removed from Prüm against his will and replaced by Richar, brother of two prominent local nobles named Gerard and Matfrid (often referred to by historians as the Matfridings). Unfortunately, the precise circumstances and causes of this event are unclear because someone, possibly Regino himself, erased the section of the *Chronicle* that described them.[18] The abbot fled to the nearby city of Trier, where he was favourably received by Archbishop Ratbod (d.915) and placed in charge of the monastery of St-Martin, a very much lesser responsibility than Prüm. Favoured insider turned embittered outsider, he remained there until his death in 915.[19]

Despite his precipitous and stomach-churning drop in status, Regino was not content simply to stew in his own juices: his three major scholarly works all belong to this period of exile in Trier. Aside from the *Chronicle* he also composed a treatise on music, *De harmonica institutione*, together with a book of liturgical chants (or 'tonary'). Dedicating his efforts to Ratbod, his purpose was to improve the quality of chant in the churches of the diocese.[20] The text is a crucial early witness to the development of modes in Western liturgical music.[21] It also seems to have had played a major role in Regino's construction of his own

---

16 I use the epithet 'Straightforward' to emphasise the positive connotations of the Latin *simplex*: Schneidmüller 1978. Regino manifestly considered it a positive royal attribute; for arguments to the contrary see Koziol 2006a: 238, n. 14

17 For a nuanced interpretation of Zwentibald's reign see Innes 2001: 430–3.

18 See below, 892, 899, pp. 47–51 and MacLean forthcoming for further discussion.

19 Part of Regino's epitaph survives: see Kurze's edition of the *Chronicle*, p. vi. A text written nearly a century later also remembers him as a worthy abbot of St-Martin: *De abbatia Sancti Martini*.

20 Kurze prints the dedicatory letter in his edition of the *Chronicle*, xviii–xix.

21 Hüschen 1962; Bernhard 1979; Boncella 1995; Boynton 1999.

public persona at St-Martin: an ivory probably produced there under his supervision explicitly compared his achievements with those of Pope Gregory the Great (d.604), who was reputed to have introduced music to the Roman church.[22] A section of the ivory showing an abbatial figure perhaps intended to represent Regino himself is reproduced on the front cover of this book. The other work was a handbook of canon law for episcopal visitations composed at the request of Ratbod and dedicated to Archbishop Hatto of Mainz (d.913) after 906 (the date of the latest material included). This compilation, known as *De synodalibus causis*, consisted of some 900 excerpts from church councils and other legal authorities organised into two parts, one aimed at priests and the other at the behaviour of the laity. Organised thematically and framed with lists of questions for the user to ask when travelling round his diocese, this was apparently a volume designed for bishops' practical use and for the training of priests. Accordingly, some of the procedures described (those concerning penance, for example) seem to reflect contemporary practice in the archdiocese of Trier. *De synodalibus causis* was hugely influential, surviving in 11 manuscripts and passing into the mainstream of Western canon law via its influence on the eleventh-century canonist Burchard of Worms.[23]

Regino's work on music and canon law were serious intellectual endeavours composed with practical application in mind. However, the dedication of his three texts to Adalbero, Hatto and Ratbod also points to less obvious intentions. Ratbod was, as we saw, Regino's patron and benefactor, and Adalbero and Hatto were leading figures in the east Frankish church. More importantly, these men were among the main backers of Louis the Child's regime. Adalbero and Hatto had baptised Louis in 893 and remained closely involved in the young ruler's upbringing.[24] Louis's charters refer to Adalbero as his *nutritor* ('nourisher' / 'upbringer' – in the sense of 'foster-father' or 'godfather').[25] The three men's political connections were strengthened by shared background (all were about the same age and came from the same region of the empire, Alemannia), and after 900 they formed the core of something like a regency council. Their closeness to the king and to each other is clearly illustrated by a charter from 908 in which Hatto and Adalbero

---

22 Sanderson 1982; the ivory is also reproduced by Goldschmidt 1914: no. 153.
23 See Hartmann's introduction to Regino, *De synodalibus causis*; Kéry 1999: 128–33; Hamilton 2001: 25–50.
24 AF 893: 125.
25 DD LC 4, 9, 65.

intervened with Louis to secure a royal favour for Ratbod.²⁶ Such interventions are often the best indication we have of who was 'in' and 'out' at court. By dedicating his work to such figures, and flattering them directly and indirectly, Regino doubtless hoped to remind them of his abilities and to re-establish his broken links with the kingdom's leading lights.²⁷ Dark references in his prefatory letters to the dangers of modern times and his fears about offending important people seem to represent not just conventional rhetoric, but also an author brooding on the rocky path of his own career and the political instability with which it was enmeshed.²⁸ These troubles haunted the story of dynastic rise and fall in the *Chronicle*, to which we now turn.

Regino as historian

The *Chronicle* is one of the most important sources for late Carolingian history. As such it is frequently cited and often attracts scholars' approval for its colourful anecdotes and independent judgements. These virtues prompted the nineteenth-century historian Ernst Dümmler to venture the opinion that it deserved to be ranked among the greatest of all medieval chronicles.²⁹ In the modern literature, on the other hand, Regino is generally celebrated less as a historian than for the great influence of his other works, and Dümmler's admiration is not reflected by the relatively meagre attention the *Chronicle* has received as a work of historiography. Aside from the dissection of individual passages sifted for their information on aspects of political history, concentrated discussion has generally focused fairly narrowly on two areas: the text's problematic manuscript transmission and the extent of Regino's debt to classical authors. Both these issues will be considered below. However, more recent interpreters of the *Chronicle*, particularly Stuart Airlie, Hans-Werner Goetz and Rosamond McKitterick, have drawn attention to the shape of the work as a whole and highlight the need for its readers to consider broader themes and structures.³⁰ Only by understanding the complete text (including the oft-dismissed first book) can

26 D LC 59. For discussion see Offergeld 2001: 518–641; Airlie 2006a: 111–12.
27 In addition to the explicit flattery of the texts' prefatory letters, all three men are given favourable mentions in the *Chronicle*: see 883, 887, 891, 895, 899.
28 Particularly in the prefaces to the *Chronicle* and *De synodalibus causis*. All three prefaces are published by Kurze in his edition of the *Chronicle*, pp. xviii–xx, 1–2.
29 Dümmler 1888: 657.
30 Goetz 1999: 191–2, 204, 223; McKitterick 2006: 30–3, 38–42; Airlie 2006a.

we properly understand its parts. Taking its cue from this insight, the purpose of the following discussion is to highlight some of the key features of the *Chronicle* as a work of history. As well as presenting my own interpretation of the text, my intention is to help readers place Regino in his historiographical context and to identify areas of interest for further research.

Date and design

Dating the Chronicle

The final text is easily dated thanks to Regino's preface, which reveals that he dedicated the work to Adalbero in 908, but it is more difficult to be certain about when he started writing and how long it took him. These issues take on significance in light of evidence that the text was revised after completion. A substantial passage in the annal for 892 explaining Regino's ejection from Prüm was erased at some point; and the fact that the last entry in the text is 906 rather than 908 has led to speculation that its two final annals were likewise excised. Reconstructing the process of composition and censorship therefore becomes an important preliminary task for the historian wishing to understand the vicissitudes of Regino's career and the impact that these may have had on the shape and content of his text.

In 1959 Karl-Ferdinand Werner advanced an intricate and well-documented case that the *Chronicle* was in preparation for many years before 908. Werner argued that charter material from Angers whose narrative content resembles Regino's discussion of certain events in Brittany must have drawn on the historian's preparatory notes, made whilst on a mission to Prüm's estates in the far west before he became abbot in 892.[31] Although this ingenious argument continues to influence some historians, a thorough manuscript study by Wolf-Rüdiger Schleidgen established beyond doubt that the Angers fragment was based on the text of the *Chronicle* and not the other way round.[32] In the absence of Regino's autograph manuscript, we therefore have to fall back on the relatively sparse internal dating evidence. This tends to point towards a date of composition relatively close to 908, and thus to a much shorter writing-up process than that envisaged by Werner. Allusions in two entries, 885 and 888, make it clear that King Zwentibald

---

31 Werner 1959a.
32 Schleidgen 1977: 14–16, 109–11. Werner 1997 implicitly draws on his earlier theory.

(d.900) was already dead at the time they were written. A reference to the murder of Count Herbert of Vermandois in the 818 annal confirms this but does not narrow the window any further because the killing cannot be dated more precisely than 900–908. In the entries for 874 and 892 Regino explicitly mentions that two *duces*, Alan of Brittany and Burchard of Thuringia respectively, were still alive at the time of writing. Burchard is known to have died on 3 August 908.[33] Alan's death is recorded under 907 by the *Annales Rotonenses*, but given that this source is not absolutely contemporary we cannot rule out the possibility that he was still alive in 908: charter evidence does not confirm that his successor was in place before November of that year.[34]

Strictly speaking, these considerations allow us to conclude no more than that the part of the *Chronicle* covering the years 818–906 must have been composed in the period 900–908. However, informed speculation might take us further. Three points can be made here. First, Dümmler drew attention to surprising errors of chronology at the end of the text – most notably, the murder of Archbishop Fulk of Rheims is placed in 903 instead of 900 – which, he argued, are best explained by supposing that Regino was writing some years after the memories of these events had faded.[35] Secondly, thematic links between the pre- and post-818 parts of the *Chronicle*, to be discussed below, would suggest that the work was conceived as a single piece. Finally, the fact that Regino's accounts of royal marriage and divorce in the *Chronicle* show similarities to some of the legal material he compiled in *De synodalibus causis* might imply that he was working on the two texts at around the same time: as already mentioned, the latter was completed no earlier than 906.[36] Complete certainty is not possible, but the likelihood is that Regino, although he may have been thinking about it for some time, did not write out his history much before 908.

Genre and design

As mentioned, the Carolingian era witnessed a surge of interest in the reading of old histories and the writing of new. This activity encompassed a variety of formal genres, among which Regino's *Chronicle* is

---

33 Dümmler 1888: 657, n. 3; Offergeld 2001: 561.
34 Pettiau 2004: 173–4.
35 Dümmler 1888: 657, n. 3.
36 For one such similarity see the account of the divorce of Charles the Fat and Richgard under 887.

INTRODUCTION   11

usually classified as a universal or world chronicle.³⁷ The father of this genre was the early fourth-century bishop and scholar Eusebius of Caesarea, whose chronicle was made known in the west through its translation (into Latin) and continuation by St Jerome. The Eusebius-Jerome text had a profound impact on subsequent historiographers, and was widely known in the Carolingian period. Regino of Prüm, as far as we know, was not among its readers.³⁸ He was, on the other hand, a connoisseur of the Anglo-Saxon monk Bede's so-called 'Greater Chronicle', originally composed as chapter 66 of his great treatise on chronology, *De temporum ratione* ('On the reckoning of time', 725), though sometimes transmitted as a separate work. World chronicles like those of Eusebius-Jerome and Bede were characterised by the breadth of their chronological and geographical sweep, and their attempt to synthesise the histories of numerous peoples. They were also deeply Christian works informed by eschatological concerns (that is, by issues surrounding the age of the world and its prospective end) and thus by the desire to align earthly events with sacred time and God's plan for his creation.³⁹ Accordingly, all but two of the 28 Christian world chronicles before *c.*950 catalogued in the standard analysis by Anna-Dorothee von den Brincken began with the Creation itself. The exceptions were Eusebius-Jerome, who began with the birth of Abraham, and Regino, the first major historian to open his work with the Incarnation of Christ.⁴⁰

Regino's singularity in this fundamental respect forces us to consider the genre of his work carefully. The Frankish elite in the eighth and ninth centuries were avid readers of Eusebius-Jerome, Bede and other late antique world chroniclers, but produced only a handful of texts modelled on them, the most notable examples being the histories by Claudius of Turin (*c.*814), Frechulf of Lisieux (*c.*830) and Ado of Vienne (*c.*870), as well as the anonymous 'Chronicle of 741'.⁴¹ Regino's self-conscious use of Bede, his widescreen coverage of peoples and places and his concern with Christian history justify the bracketing of his work with these Carolingian chronicles, although he seems not to have

---

37 McKitterick 2004 offers the broadest definition of historical genres.
38 Although he refers to Eusebius in his entry for 405–12.
39 Allen 2003; McKitterick 2006: 9–22.
40 Von den Brincken 1957: 252 (table 3); cf. McKitterick 2006: 9. Obviously, I count Eusebius-Jerome as a single text.
41 A full study of these would be welcome: McKitterick 2006: 22–33 provides a good starting point.

known any of them.⁴² Structure and design mattered to these authors. Although the considerable body of sources surviving from the early Middle Ages does not yield any abstract discussions of the nature of historical writing after that of Isidore of Seville in the seventh century, that Carolingian historians reflected seriously on matters of genre is not in doubt.⁴³ Several statements by Regino (particularly in the preface, at the end of Book I, and just before the entry for 818) confirm that he had a clear idea of what he was doing and that his work's structure was carefully plotted.

That said, historical genres were flexible.⁴⁴ For all that Regino, Ado and the others wrote self-consciously in the tradition of earlier authorities, the differences between the Carolingian universal histories are arguably as significant as their similarities. Regino's decision to begin with the Incarnation rather than the Creation was, as noted, exceptional. Allied to this was his attempt to assign AD dates (whose popularity had increased during the ninth century) to all the events in his text, something that concerned the other chroniclers little or not at all. In terms of form this attempt gives the *Chronicle* a kind of hybrid appearance, a narrative history compressed into the format of contemporary annals.⁴⁵ Regino is also much more interested than the others in recent history. Frechulf's work ended some 200 years before his own day and Ado's information on the ninth century, though often important, is relatively sparse.⁴⁶ Claudius, meanwhile, was primarily concerned with establishing the place of Old Testament chronology in the framework of sacred history – a polemical contribution to the branch of scholarship known as computus.⁴⁷ Universal histories were also characterised by their suitability for locating the specific within the context of world history and sacred time. The format thus provided a vehicle for the claims of a particular people to a special place in God's plans for the world, a role taken by the English in Bede's text and the Franks in that of the 741 chronicler.⁴⁸ Ado, meanwhile, used the genre

42 Boschen 1972: 218 suggests that Regino knew Ado's *Chronicle*, but the evidence is not direct.
43 On early medieval historiographical theory see Deliyannis 2003b; Goffart 2005; and more generally Goetz 1985. On Carolingian historians' reflection on their own work see Simon 1958; Simon 1959; Ganz 2005a.
44 Deliyannis 2003 provides a useful survey of prior research.
45 These genres were normally regarded as distinct: Ganz 2005a.
46 Von den Brincken 1957: 120–8; Allen 2003: 39–42.
47 Allen 1998. For an accessible discussion of computus see Borst 1993: 3–4, 16–23.
48 Rabin 2005; McKitterick 2006: 23–8.

INTRODUCTION

in part to project the saints' cults of his diocese into the distant past and thus furnish its sacred geography (and his own episcopal authority) with a kind of deep historical legitimacy.[49] Regino's purposes do not conform straightforwardly with those of his Carolingian predecessors. Although, as we shall see, he was interested in the history of the Franks, he arranged it along a decidedly un-triumphal and somewhat ambiguous trajectory. Nor was he out to provide an explicit historical underpinning for the power of the churches of Prüm or Trier. Prüm's foundation, its royal privileges and the deeds of its luminaries like the mid-ninth-century scholar Wandalbert and the high-profile abbots Marcward and Eigil go largely unmentioned.[50] Although Regino was very much *of* Prüm, his chronicle was not *about* Prüm. Meanwhile, it was left to Adalbert, Regino's posthumous editor and continuator, to interpolate vignettes about the great bishops and saints of Trier.

Even more striking than all this is Regino's decision not to use either of the two eschatological frameworks within which almost all universal histories were constructed: the four empires or the six ages.[51] These models furnished historians with a means of conceptualising and organising sacred time, and relating earthly events to God's ultimate plan for his creation. Each pointed teleologically toward the end of the world, the coming of Antichrist and the Day of Judgement. The four empires, popularised above all by Jerome, was based on an exegetical reading of Nebuchadnezzar's dream in the book of Daniel and organised history according to the dominion of four 'world empires'. The last of these, usually identified as the Roman, was seen as the bulwark against the coming of Antichrist. The end of the Western empire in the fifth century did not kill off this idea; instead, it encouraged authors in the ninth and tenth centuries to reformulate the Frankish realm as a metaphorical continuation of Rome. The six ages of the world were developed as a tool for Christian historians by St Augustine and transmitted into the historiographical canon via Isidore of Seville and Bede. Augustine picked up on a reading of the Genesis story in which each day of

---

49 Borst 1993: 47; McKitterick 2006: 29–30.
50 As an example see the *Revelatio Stephanae Papae* reproduced under 753, whose reference to Bertrada, wife of King Pippin, provided Regino with a golden opportunity to mention the monastery's founder, her grandmother, and highlight its royal connections. He turned this opportunity down, even though Pippin and Bertrada are known to have been commemorated at Prüm in association with the foundation: Haubrichs 1979: 75, 81–2. There are occasional exceptions to this rule, such as the reference to St Goar at 517–537. Further study of Regino in the context of Prüm's literary culture, building on Haubrichs 1979, would nonetheless repay the effort.
51 The literature is vast, but see Allen 2003 for a concise discussion.

creation was interpreted as a millennium and recast it as an allegory for six ages of sacred history. Because the sixth age in Augustine's scheme was inaugurated by the birth of Jesus Christ, the current 'millennium' was regarded as the last before the beginning of the end times. It was partly to confound simplistic understandings of this concept – and to reinforce the orthodoxy that the real date of the End was unpredictable – that the likes of Bede were so concerned in their chronicles to establish the age of the world.

By the Carolingian period these two metanarratives had become authoritative and were adopted and adapted by numerous writers – in works of universal history, the six ages had become 'virtually obligatory'.[52] Not unreasonably, then, Regino's decision to start with the Incarnation has been interpreted as evidence that he was an adherent of this model, and that his was an orthodox Augustinian history of the world's sixth age.[53] The six-ages scheme was certainly current at Prüm: it figured prominently in Wandalbert's martyrology, written there and sent to Emperor Lothar I in 848–849, and in the chronicle of Ado, who had spent time at the monastery before becoming archbishop of Vienne.[54] Yet there is room for doubt in Regino's case. His division of the *Chronicle* into two books seems to disrupt the unity of the presumed sixth age, especially as the reference in the title of the first book to the 'times of the Lord's Incarnation' is undercut by the second's declared focus on 'the deeds of the kings of the Franks'. Even more worthy of note is Regino's deliberate alteration of a line in his very first quotation from Bede in the 1–15 entry. Where Bede wrote that 'Jesus Christ, the son of God, hallowed the sixth age of the world by his coming', Regino simply has 'Jesus Christ the son of God was born'. This contraction implies that Regino consciously suppressed Augustine's historical scheme, not because he denied its validity, but because it was not at the forefront of his mind when he was structuring his work.[55]

This does not mean that the *Chronicle* should be shifted to the other end of the spectrum and interpreted as following the conventions of secular historiography. Regino has acquired a reputation among modern scholars as a neo-classicist with a peculiarly secular conception of history driven by the forces of *fortuna* ('luck' or 'fortune'). There is no doubt that the abbot's deployment of the language of fortune was

---

52 Allen 2003: 38.
53 Von den Brincken 1957: 131.
54 Haubrichs 1979: 60.
55 The six ages also play a secondary role in Frechulf's chronicle: Allen 2003: 39–41.

INTRODUCTION

strongly influenced by Justin's *Epitome* (usually dated to the second century AD) of the *Philippic History* by Pompeius Trogus, and perhaps also by the work of the sixth-century philosopher Boethius.[56] As Max Manitius surmised, Regino must have had a copy of Justin on his desk as he wrote.[57] However, the extent of this influence has been overplayed.[58] The number of direct citations is limited in the context of the whole work, and the deployment of imagery influenced by ancient historians was in any case far from unusual in Carolingian historiography. Early medieval historians found classical models useful as counterpoints to the Bible for framing discussions of secular events, but the ubiquity of such borrowings means we have to be very wary of extrapolating from them an entire historical philosophy.[59] The lists of martyrs that stud Regino's Book I hardly fit with the idea that he saw history as a mainly secular affair, and at its end he explicitly stated that one of his purposes had been to 'make known specifically the triumph of the saints, martyrs and confessors, and where and under which kings they secured the crown of glory'. In any case, it is very clear that Regino's conception of *fortuna* was a Christian one. A pre-battle speech put into the mouth of the Breton leader Wrhwant in 874 defines *fortuna* as an expression of God's will: 'Let us test the forces of fortune with the enemy, for our salvation does not rest in numbers, but rather in God.'[60] The deposition of Emperor Charles the Fat is described in 887 in terms of *fortuna* in a passage seen as crucial by those who contend that Regino's concepts of history and politics were heavily classical. But when in 888 the same events are described again, Regino casts them in explicitly Christian terms: Charles, we are told here, was being tested by God. In these and other examples, God himself is the main actor, and the rulers in question mere subjects and vectors – the extent to which they submitted themselves to divine will/*fortuna* was the benchmark against which Regino judged them.

The generic features of Christian universal or secular classical histories evidently offer only limited assistance in understanding the form and intentions of the *Chronicle*. To develop a more constructive concept of his work, we need to pay attention to Regino's own statements about

56 Löwe 1973b; Kortüm 1994.
57 Manitius 1900.
58 As pointed out by Hlawitschka 1975: 24–5; Goetz 1999: 195–6; Airlie 2006a: 119–21.
59 See also Innes 1997a.
60 Kortüm 1994 argues that this passage carries Boethian overtones.

what he was doing. The first of these comes in the preface, which takes the form of a dedicatory letter to Adalbero. Here, Regino positions himself implicitly but clearly as a historian of a people (the Franks) by comparing himself to historians of 'other peoples' like the Hebrews, Greeks, and Romans. His assertion that there was an absence of writings about 'our times' rings true to the extent that the Carolingian period did not produce many new Frankish 'ethnic' histories, and in this respect too Regino was an unusual author. More surprisingly, for someone whose career was spent in major political and cultural centres like Prüm and Trier, Regino's statement about the lack of sources lays bare his ignorance of the numerous contemporary annalistic and biographical histories. There was a Christian subtext here too: 'our times' may have carried a double meaning, referring to the whole period since the Incarnation as well as to the present day.

Regino's next self-reflective comment appears at the very end of Book I:

> We have therefore brought this [narrative], beginning with the very year of the Lord's incarnation, up to this point so that, because the following little book set out by our humble self reveals the times and deeds of rulers according to the same incarnation years, likewise it may show the main points of what was done by each ruler, and when and where; and also make known specifically the triumph of the saints, martyrs and confessors, and where and under which kings they secured the crown of glory. Therefore where the first finishes let the second consequently begin, and where the second starts let the first be assigned its conclusion.

This passage confirms the preface's allusion to the importance of sacred as well as secular events. It also seems to suggest that the *Annales Regni Francorum* (*ARF*, 'Royal Frankish Annals'), which Regino began Book II by copying out, were the model for Book I: the narrative up to this point had been organised by incarnation years *because* that is how 'the following little book' (the *ARF*) was set out. The *ARF* thus sits at the centre of Regino's work and functions as the pivot around which its two halves swing. By the end of the ninth century the *ARF*, whose composition and distribution were associated with the court of Charlemagne, had acquired considerable authority in the Frankish historiographical canon.[61] Regino's explicit acknowledgement of its importance to the structure of his *Chronicle* suggests that his concern with AD dating was more political than eschatological: it signalled his intention to provide a back-story for the Carolingian kings of the Franks, arranged in the

---

61 Reimitz 2006.

same idiom as the authoritative version of their rise to power. At the same time, AD dating implicitly endowed those rulers with a privileged position in the broader course of Christian history by linking their reigns with Christ's kingdom.[62]

In view of these considerations it would be misleading to single out (as historians have been inclined to do) one aspect of the *Chronicle* as its sole defining feature: debates over whether it is best categorised as universal or ethnic, sacred or secular, ancient or contemporary history can mislead, because all of these labels have some validity simultaneously. A more inclusive definition of historiographical genre may serve us better. Karl-Ferdinand Werner identified broad similarities between a wide range of early medieval texts whose formal variety was overridden by their generic contemporary labelling as 'historiae'. This categorisation reflects a perception that the shared features of 'histories' were more important than their differences.[63] What these narratives – patterned on the fourth-century work of Orosius – had in common above all was the admonition of rulers. Through exemplary stories, attributions of sin and the interpretation of omens and signs as manifestations of divine will, historical texts provided kings with lessons in the leadership of a chosen people and the responsibilities involved in guiding it toward salvation – in this respect their ultimate model was the Old Testament.[64]

Regino's work, like many from the Carolingian period, comfortably meets this definition. Carolingian authors frequently dedicated their works to rulers. Commentaries on biblical history sent to kings and empresses during the ninth century were intended in part to illuminate contemporary politics through example and parallel.[65] In 844 Lupus of Ferrières sent Charles the Bald a 'very brief summary of the deeds of the [Roman] emperors' in order that, he told him, 'you may readily observe from their actions what you should imitate or what you should avoid'.[66] Fifteen years earlier Frechulf of Lisieux had addressed the second book of his chronicle to the Empress Judith for the education of the same king, her then 6-year-old son, so that he might 'see in these [histories] as in a mirror what should be done and what should be

---

62 We should also note the growing currency of AD dating in the formulas of late-ninth-century royal charters.
63 Werner 1987; Werner 1990.
64 See also Allen 2003: 35–7; Pizarro 2003: 55–6; Ganz 2005b: 42–3.
65 De Jong 2000; De Jong 2001; McKitterick 2004: 235–44.
66 Lupus, *Letters*, no. 37: 160–5 (Regenos 1966: 55).

avoided ... Enlightened by the deeds of the emperors, the triumphs of the saints, and the teachings of magnificent doctors, he will discover what to do cautiously and what to avoid shrewdly'.[67] Regino surely had something similar in mind when in 908 he dedicated the *Chronicle*, packed with good kings, bad kings and examples of God's judgement, to the godfather of King Louis the Child.[68] Louis was growing up and had to be educated. Males of the Frankish elite underwent an important rite of passage at age 15, receiving a sword and military belt as symbols of their transition to manhood, and 908 was the year of Louis's fifteenth birthday.[69] What better occasion to present him with an opportunity to reflect on the reigns of his ancestors and other great kings of past ages, and to absorb from their deeds lessons about rulership, character and sin?

Book I: themes and sources

Until recently, the first book of the *Chronicle* was largely ignored by historians eager to get to the goldmine of contemporary information in Book II, and sometimes even sneered at as a work of plagiarism made up from a random selection of cut-and-pasted source material: Hubert Ermisch's spiky dismissal of Regino's 'promiscuous' use of sources can stand as an emblem for this appraisal.[70] Regino himself certainly did not see the first part of his text as a formality to be disposed of before arriving at the main event, the Carolingian era: his preface implored readers to copy out the whole work intact, and in the passage quoted above from the end of Book I he explicitly connected its two halves. Evidently, the author conceptualised the *Chronicle* as an organic whole. A further disservice was done to his vision by the editorial practices of the *Monumenta Germaniae Historica*, under whose auspices the standard modern edition by Friedrich Kurze appeared in 1890. The MGH house style of printing excerpts from older works using smaller print than that employed for medieval authors' original material can be useful, but a side-effect is the implicit diminution of the significance of huge

---

67 Frechulf, *Histories*: 435–7; the translation is from Dutton 2004: 255–6.
68 Haubrichs 1979: 70; Airlie 2006a: 111–12. For Adalbero as Louis's godfather (*nutritor*) see above, n. 25.
69 Le Jan 2000: 284–5. I am grateful to Eric Goldberg for pointing out to me the potential significance of Louis's age.
70 Ermisch 1872, cited by McKitterick 2006: 31–2. A more accessible summary of Ermisch's work is provided by Kurze 1890. Positive re-evaluations of Book I are offered by Sonntag 1987: 87–120; Goetz 1999: 191–2, 204, 223; McKitterick 2006: 30–3, 38–42.

INTRODUCTION

chunks of works like the *Chronicle*. It also disguises the extent to which writers like Regino might have reworded and paraphrased their sources in significant ways, rather than simply reproducing them uncritically. Whether or not changes were made, we have to remember that excerpting and collecting alone involved numerous critical decisions about what to include and what to leave out. The sum of these decisions created a new text; the act of compilation itself articulated an independent authorial voice.[71] First and foremost, commemoration of past events was seen as an activity worthy in itself – history, being true, was its own virtue.[72] No work of history, however, is politically neutral. As a master narrator writing long after the events he described, Regino knew all along where his story was going to end, and cut and pasted his sources accordingly. If we squint hard enough at pixellated textual mosaics such as that presented by Regino's Book I, coherent pictures can emerge. It is with these considerations in mind that all of Book I has been translated in this volume.

Book I is built around excerpts from six major narrative sources:

- the Bible
- Bede's 'Greater Chronicle', chapter 66 of *De Temporum Ratione* (*DTR*), a history of the world from the Creation to the ninth year of the Byzantine emperor Leo III – that is, AD 725[73]
- Paul the Deacon's *Historia Langobardorum* ('History of the Lombards'), covering events up to the reign of King Liutprand, d.744, and written sometime in the period 787–799, probably before 796[74]
- the *Liber Historiae Francorum* (*LHF*, 'Book of the History of the Franks'), c.727, a much-copied work based on the *Histories* of Gregory of Tours (d.594)[75]
- the *Gesta Dagoberti* (*GD*, 'Deeds of Dagobert'), a biography of King Dagobert I (629–639) written at St-Denis in the 830s, perhaps by Abbot Hilduin, who was closely associated with Prüm and may have ended his life there[76]

---

71 The individuality of Frechulf's chronicle compilation is picked out by Allen 2003: 39–42.
72 Ganz 2005a.
73 Wallis 2004.
74 Pohl 1994; Chiesa 2000.
75 Gerberding 1987; Fouracre and Gerberding 1996.
76 McKitterick 2004: 214.

- the *Annales Sancti Amandi* (*ASA*, 'Annals of St-Amand'), a set of short annals covering the early eighth century; Regino appears to have had access to a Prüm edition that differs somewhat from surviving versions.[77]

Throughout Book I Regino leans heaviest on Bede and Paul, the most chronologically extensive of his sources, with the others coming on-stream to illuminate specific periods. A seventh major narrative, the *Liber Pontificalis* (*LP*, 'Book of the Pontiffs', a serial biography of the papacy), is used more sparingly.[78] The early part of the first book is also punctuated by extensive lists of martyrs from the influential *Martyrology* by Ado, archbishop of Vienne and sometime monk at Prüm.[79] Beyond these, Regino also referred periodically to a wide range of hagiography, mostly of northern Frankish provenance, and on a couple of occasions to the great Spanish canon-law collection known as the *Hispana*. In most cases it is not possible to compare Regino's text with the actual books he used. The abbot may have taken some manuscripts with him when he was exiled in 899: one Trier manuscript, a major collection of monastic texts evidently composed in Prüm, has been plausibly identified as an item of his luggage.[80] It would also be worth investigating parallels between the dossier of sources used by Regino and the many compilations of historical material known to have circulated in the Carolingian period.[81] To date, though, the monastery's library has had to be reconstructed backward, by inference from the sources cited in the *Chronicle* and other works composed by its denizens.[82]

Book I is structured in direct imitation of Bede's 'Greater Chronicle', which organised events according to spans of time defined by the reigns of Roman, and then Byzantine, emperors. As he went, Regino translated Bede's AM dates (*Anno Mundi*, years since the Creation) into AD (*Anno Domini*, years since the Incarnation). To ease this task he assumed that all months were 30 days long, that for the purposes of calcula-

---

77 Boschen 1972: 85–95, 186–95; Haubrichs 1979: 31.

78 It should be noted that since Bede used the *LP* and both of them were used by Paul, it is not always possible to determine which was Regino's main source in any given instance.

79 Dubois 1978.

80 Haubrichs 1979: 91–2.

81 For example the compilations described by McKitterick 2004: 33–6, 277, whose blend of sources was not dissimilar to that of the *Chronicle*. See also now Diesenberger 2006.

82 Haubrichs 1979: 89–95. Kurze 1890 discusses Regino's possible manuscript sources in detail.

INTRODUCTION

tion all regnal years began on 1 January and ended on 30 December, and that each emperor took over directly from his predecessor with no interregnum. Regino kept remaindered months and days to one side, inserting them into the chronology when he had enough to make up a full year. Despite its obvious limitations, this method should not have knocked him too far out of orbit; indeed, his implicit acceptance of a level of inaccuracy suggests that he was more interested in creating a broadly correct relative chronology than in fixing events with absolute precision. Unfortunately, his attempt foundered on some basic errors. Regino is frustratingly inconsistent in his arithmetical approach, so that sometimes he includes the final year of a span in his calculation (as when Theodosius's 11 years are given as 339–349), but sometimes he does not (for instance Arcadius and Honorius, whose 13 years come out as 350–363). More catastrophically, he made several straightforward mistakes: Domitian's 15-year reign is rendered as AD 85–90, and similar howlers are not hard to find. By the time he approached the end of Book I Regino was aware that his chronology was several decades behind, and tried to catch up by converting Bede's last entry, the nine years of Leo III (Regino did not consider the possibility that Leo may still have been reigning when Bede stopped writing) into the AD span 655–718.[83] He then tried to check his calculations by totalling Bede's imperial reigns since the birth of Christ and the papal reigns since St Peter from the *Liber Pontificalis*. He got both sums wrong.

It is easy for us, privileged as we are to live in the age of the digital watch and the calculator, to lampoon Regino's clumsy arithmetic. But before we conclude that his project 'fundamentally failed', we need to acknowledge the nature and difficulty of the task he set himself.[84] As the first major chronicler to attempt a complete AD chronology for world history, Regino had meagre precedents on which to draw.[85] His main sources provided few prominent landmarks: Bede's chronicle contains only two AD dates, Paul the Deacon's history only one.[86] Regino knew his starting and finishing points: respectively the birth of Christ in what

---

83 Regino must have been aware of being off-course by the time he wrote his 510–516 entry, where he conspicuously does not include the passage from Paul specifying the date as 568.
84 The judgement is that of Borst 1993: 48.
85 Regino's novelty is established by the discussions of precedents and parallels in von den Brincken 1957: 128–33, 229–40 and Sonntag 1987: 98–109.
86 Sonntag 1987: 95–6. Regino did not know Bede's *Ecclesiastical History*, which was influential in spreading the popularity of AD dating. He had probably read Bede's theoretical discussion of incarnation years in chapter 47 of *DTR*.

he decided was AD 1 (the 42nd year of Octavian Augustus as specified by Bede) and the death of Charles Martel in 741 (the first entry in the *ARF*). Filling the space in between was a massive chronological jigsaw puzzle in which the placement of only two other pieces was known: 568 (the Lombards' arrival in Italy according to Paul the Deacon); and 716 (which according to Bede fell in the reign of Anastasius II). Even these triangulation points were not secure, for Regino, probably relying on his version of the *ASA* or another set of Prüm annals, seemingly thought that Charles Martel's era began in 716 – Anastasius' reign, according to Bede – while Paul's work contradicted this by associating Charles's accession instead with Leo III. Thus when he reached Anastasius' reign in, according to his calculations, 650–653, he realised how far out he was and began adding the Frankish annalistic material on Charles's reign. The resulting chronology is odd and plainly wrong, but it should not be dismissed as a product of dull thinking or unreflective plagiarism. Instead, Regino's cumbersome but logical solution reflects the intractability of the conundrum: how to reconcile two conflicting but equally authoritative sources.[87] Indeed, this 'error' may give a further insight into his thinking. Regino's unapologetic readiness to stretch Charles Martel's reign out over nearly a century, which he must have known was wrong, seems to confirm that he was above all concerned with correctly establishing a *relative* chronology; and the relative chronology (the order of events) could be correct even if the absolute chronology (the dating of events) was wrong. In this respect he was different from Bede and other universal historians who, with eschatological concerns in mind, needed to establish the precise dates of major events in order to work out the age of the world.

Which is not to say that dates did not matter to him: far from it, as his method reveals. Regino started each entry with Bede's imperial span (translated into AD) and then combed his sources for events that could be associated with the relevant emperor. This method is made explicit in the entry for 144–156, where Regino apologises for being unable to work out where to place certain martyrdoms because the names Lucius and Antoninus were borne by more than one emperor, and his source (Ado) did not specify which was which. Although the scaffolding of Book I was Bede's, Regino was no slavish copier of the 'Greater Chronicle', omitting, for instance, almost all its material on events in Britain. At several points within the narrative itself we also glimpse Regino

---

87 See 655–718, n. 398; Boschen 1972: 191–2; Sonntag 1987: 114–16. It is not, however, altogether clear why Charles's succession was mentioned in 642–7, the reign of Justinian and Tiberius.

engaging critically with his sources, and even 'correcting' them. In his entry for AD 45–58 he showed his working by comparing the information found in the Bible, the *LP* and Bede in order to establish the timing of Paul's second journey to Jerusalem. In the same entry, Regino's apparent error in dating Herod's death to AD 47 can be explained more satisfactorily as the logical conclusion of a series of deductions based on other material he knew, and suggests that he was not afraid to reject information that he found in Bede. Regino also inserted himself into the text as editor. This is exemplified in 642–647, where he adds the signposts 'while this was happening in the east' and 'as we set out', and avoids a continuity error by cutting out a cross-reference to a prior mention of Charles Martel from the middle of a lengthy quote from Paul the Deacon. Elsewhere we can observe him cutting and pasting his sources for particular reasons: in 498–509, for instance, he chops up sections of the *LHF* in order to create a clear account of the fates of King Clothar's sons, making discreet additions and alterations to emphasise the negative consequences of Charibert's marital misdemeanours.[88] These adaptations, and others like them, reveal Regino to have been a self-conscious compiler who evaluated, appropriated and organised his source material in the service of his own narrative.

The narrative itself can and should be sifted for consistent themes. Regino's view of Rome and the empire is an important starting point here. In moving seamlessly from a chronology defined by the reigns of emperors to one defined by the reigns of Frankish kings, several ninth-century texts appropriated Bede's 'historical map' to provide an imperial past for the Carolingian dynasty to inherit.[89] Ado's *Chronicle* pulls off this trick, as do various abbreviated continuations of the 'Greater Chronicle'.[90] It would not be implausible to explain the design of Regino's history in the same way. Certainly, he was careful to omit in his entry for 397–404 Bede's statement about the death of Aetius: 'With him fell the Western realm, and to this day it has not had the strength to be revived.'[91] However, it is equally striking that Regino omits most of the explicit celebrations of imperial power and greatness he came across in Bede and Paul the Deacon: Gaius's appointment of Herod Agrippa (45–58); the conquests and construction projects of Vespasian and Titus (83–84); Commodus's invasion of Germany (144–156); the

---

88 See also below, pp. 27–8.
89 For the idea of a 'historical map' see McKitterick 2006.
90 Goetz 1999: 194; Garipzanov 2005.
91 Wallis 2004: 222.

games held to celebrate 1,000 years of Rome (198–203); and the imperial coronation of Tiberius (510–516) to name a few. Regino was no starry-eyed gazer at the splendour of emperors. Two comments from Book II further undercut imperial Rome's ideological usefulness to the Carolingians.[92] In 842 Regino refers to the city as being 'venerated by all the Holy Church with a certain special status because of the presence of the apostles Peter and Paul', and states that it was 'formerly called the mistress [*domina*] of the lands of the earth because of the undefeated power of the name of Rome'. Contrast this with the obituary of Pope Nicholas I in 868: 'He commanded kings and tyrants, and exercised authority over them as if he were the lord of the lands of the earth.' The verbal similarities between the two suggest that Regino had a clear sense of the distance of the past as far as the eternal city was concerned: Rome was once an imperial centre, but now its aura was emphatically apostolic.[93]

Rather than sprinkling neo-Roman glitter on the Carolingians, Regino's purpose was if anything to apostolicise the character of the empire, ancient and modern. A heavy stress on the careers of Peter and Paul in 45–58 establishes this thread, which culminates with the same two saints ordaining the rise of the Carolingians in the *Revelatio Stephani Papae* inserted under 753. Book I's long lists of martyrs point in the same direction (for example 189–191, 242–262, 295–309, 310–313). Roman martyrs were usually placed at the head of the lists, establishing the city's identity as a place of glorious persecution rather than a centre of secular power. Compilation of these litanies was more than just an exercise in chronology, for they formed part of the identity of the Christian church itself. Later in Regino's narrative, the persecution of martyrs is replaced by the persecution of churchmen. We meet several rulers distinguished by their unjust persecution of popes and bishops, such as Theoderic the Ostrogoth (450–458), Justinian II (612–631) and Philippicus (648–649), a theme continued in Book II by the lengthy account of Lothar II's conflict with Pope Nicholas I. Strikingly, in some instances where Bede explicitly gave emperors credit for their support and defence of the church (370–396, 405–412, 450–458), Regino silently edited his account to shift agency to the pope. In 459–497 Paul the Deacon's reference to Justinian's great Catholicism is dropped in order to set up a discussion of the popes exiled in his reign. In 263–294

---

92 On which see also von den Brincken 1957: 132–3; McKitterick 2006: 35–45.

93 I take the concept of the 'distance of the past' from Magdalino 1999. Papal supremacy over the churches is also mentioned in 538–545. On ideas about Rome in this period see now Smith 2005.

INTRODUCTION 25

credit for services to Christianity is withheld even from Constantine the Great, with Regino's praise going instead to Pope Sylvester – it was left to Adalbert, the *Chronicle*'s continuator, to improve the text's account of the celebrated emperor. The effect of these subtle emphases is to undermine the legitimacy of Rome and the empire as a source of secular power, and to stress instead its papal and apostolic character.[94] This ideological tendency could partly reflect the monastic culture of Prüm itself, whose strong Roman imprint was enhanced by the translation of relics from the holy city in 844.[95] More generally it must tell us something about Regino's views, made explicit in Book II's account of Lothar II's reign, on the limits of secular power and the respect owed by rulers to popes.[96]

These considerations take shape amid a range of broader concerns. As mentioned already, Regino in his preface implicitly positions himself as a historian of the Franks. Accordingly, the content of Book I is overwhelmingly and unsurprisingly Frankish, with his sources' information on other peoples, such as Bede's on the Anglo-Saxons and Irish, omitted systematically.[97] The exception to this is the history of the Lombards, furnished from Paul's *Historia*, which had more contemporary relevance given the Carolingians' incorporation of Italy into the Frankish empire after 774. Franko-Lombard relations figure prominently and information on internal Lombard politics is usually excluded. Still, Regino was interested enough in non-Frankish invasions of Italy to discuss the Goths and Vandals in 350–363 and to dwell on the campaigns of Narses in 498–509. He was certainly keen to neutralise Paul's general characterisation of the Franks as enemies.[98]

Regino's view of Frankish history was not, then, ethnically airtight. He was careful to mention the advance of Christianity through the conversion of peoples like the English (546–571) and the Persians (572–574), who were otherwise of little interest to him. This suggests that Regino's sense of himself as the historian of a people did not efface his subscription to St Augustine's view of history as progress toward universal

---

94 There are exceptions to this observation, for example the role ascribed to the emperor in the conversion of the Persian ruler in 572–574 and praise for Tiberius in 510–516. Barbarian kings are also usually seen as persecutors, and popes their enemies (e.g. 421–449).

95 Herbers 1998; Smith 2000: 326–9; and in general Haubrichs 1979.

96 He was, of course, no proto-Gregorian: see also the story in 869 in which the king's right to influence episcopal elections is underlined.

97 For examples see 370–396, 397–404, 413–420.

98 Bullough 1986; cf. McKitterick 2004: 60–83.

conversion.[99] His interest in the obliteration of various heresies also fits into this conception. With this in mind it is interesting that the Franks' first step onto the *Chronicle*'s historical stage only comes with their baptism, together with that of their king Clovis in the entry for 421–449. By keeping them in reserve until this point, Regino subverted the structure of his source, the *LHF*, which opened with an origin myth associating the Franks with the Trojans.[100] In emphasising the significance of the baptism, Regino also plays down the *LHF*'s stress on the derivation of Clovis's power from Emperor Anastasius, and implicitly prunes Anastasius's own status by ending his entry with Bede's report of his death by thunderbolt (for support of Eutychius's heresy). Still, in view of his self-definition as a historian of his people, we should take seriously the possibility that Regino intended the earlier parts of his narrative to serve as a metaphorical pre-history for the Franks that replaced the *LHF*'s Trojan myth. The opening phase of Book I, based mainly on the Bible, told the story of Judea and its rulers, followed by the era of persecutions. This narrative represented a kind of universal origin story about the suffering of the Christians and the formation of their church in which the Franks were given a special role signified by their baptism. By incorporating the baptism of the Franks as an epochal event in the formation of a universal Christian identity, Regino implicitly used it to open a new chapter in the story of a blessed people on their journey toward salvation.[101]

Nevertheless, Regino was not in the business of providing the Frankish kings of his own era with straightforward historical comfort. Not only did he decline the opportunity to graft Carolingian authority onto the imperial power of late antique Rome and Byzantium, he also opted not to use Book I to deliver a historical legitimisation of Frankish territorial hegemony. Such a purpose would have been well served by the inclusion of Paul the Deacon's description of King Clothar's mastery of the Saxons and Thuringians (498–509) or the *GD*'s accounts of Breton submission to Frankish power (612–631): Regino ignored both. What's more, individual Frankish rulers were open to criticism in the same way as other secular leaders. In the entries for 510–516 and 517–537 he included a series of parables about wealth and rulership from which King Guntram and Emperor Tiberius emerge with credit, in contrast

---

99 On the early medieval reception of Augustine's historical models see now Rabin 2005: 25–8.
100 The 'Chronicle of 741' also incorporated the Franko-Trojan origin legend: McKitterick 2006: 23–8.
101 The role of the church in Frankish self-perception is illuminated by de Jong 2006.

to the avaricious King Chilperic. In the moral economy of Regino's text, purity of motive and the inner qualities of rulers mattered more than narrower political allegiances.

At the same time, it is clear that some of Book I's stories about good and bad rulers were filtered through a particular dynastic lens. Regino's voice is heard particularly clearly in matters dealing with royal marriage and divorce, and the associated issue of legitimate succession. In the 498–509 entry he reworded the *LHF* to condemn the marital misbehaviour of King Charibert and show him losing his life and kingdom as a result, while the idea of legitimate birth as a prerequisite for legitimate kingship is also alluded to in 510–516 and 538–545.[102] These concepts were wholly anachronistic for the Merovingian period, and the vocabulary used by Regino was plainly resonant of the disputes associated with the ninth-century divorce case of Lothar II, which is treated at length in Book II. As a religious professional and scholar of canon law, Regino may well have been convinced that legitimate marriage was proper, and its own justification. However, his treatment of royal marriages also helps to articulate a dynastic narrative by highlighting the legitimate power of successive Merovingian rulers. The Merovingians, rather than the emperors, are presented as the Carolingians' real predecessors. Their failures are often excused: for example in 517–537 Regino subtly shifts the blame for a Frankish military defeat from Childebert to Maurice, the emperor. For every Charibert there is a Dagobert I, who, his problematic marital arrangements airbrushed out, is presented as a kind of proto-Carolingian through use, in preference to the *LHF*, of the ninth-century *Gesta Dagoberti*. At the end of 510–516 Dagobert's status is flagged up by Regino in advance of his birth in a dynastic statement that encompasses three generations (Chilperic – the 'great king' Clothar – Dagobert) and starts with Chilperic correcting his questionable personal life by 'recognising' his wife – again, the vocabulary of marital rectitude is the hinge. Later (546–571), the narrative associates Dagobert with the Carolingian progenitor Arnulf of Metz and in 612–631 makes a point of pairing his son with Pippin II, Charles Martel's father, thus fusing together the lines of the Merovingians and proto-Carolingians.[103] Regino does not overplay his hand, and in 635–641 leaves out passages of Paul the Deacon's warm praise for Arnulf. It is interesting nonetheless that his desire to stress the legitimacy of the

---

102 I hope to discuss Regino's view of queenship, marriage and dynasty more fully elsewhere.
103 Regino's appreciation of Arnulf's Carolingian identity is clear from his 880 entry.

Carolingian dynasty did not lead him to denigrate Merovingian power, a strategy employed in earlier histories like the *Annales Mettenses Priores* and Einhard's biography of Charlemagne.[104] Instead, by celebrating the descent of legitimate Frankish kingship through a particular branch of the Merovingian family and then associating those kings, identified by the correctness of their marital arrangements, with Arnulf and Pippin, Regino stressed the continuity of royal power in a way that has parallels in some of the ninth century's less famous grand narratives.[105]

This dynastic narrative culminated in 655–718 with the reign of Charles Martel, whose death, as we have seen, was the intended endpoint of Book I. The brief accounts of Charles's wars taken from the *ASA* create an image of relentless Frankish expansion that is all the more effective for their terseness. Regino interleaves the Frankish conquests with stories from Paul's *Historia* about the Lombard king Liutprand becoming a spiritual father to Charles's son Pippin and sending aid to the Franks against a Saracen invasion. The purpose of these stories is surely to elevate not Liutprand's reputation but Charles's. Paul's extended discussion of Liutprand's great military prowess (the endpoint of the *Historia*) is ignored, and Regino adds a line stating that the Lombard king's territorial gains came at the expense of the pope, thus undermining their legitimacy. Charles, meanwhile, is implicitly elevated to the status of a king, sharing in rituals of royalty via his son and receiving military help from Liutprand at the snap of his fingers. At the same time we read about the Byzantine Emperor Leo III's persecution of the church and descent into heresy. Charles is given the same status as Leo and Liutprand, and in the implicit comparison he is presented as the most virtuous and powerful of the three. By making his death the endpoint of the 'times of the Lord's incarnation', Regino asserted the legitimacy of Charles Martel's moral and dynastic authority. These themes were consummated at the start of Book II in the *Revelatio Stephani Papae* (753) which made explicit the notion that the foundations of Carolingian power were the dynasty's dedication to protection of the church of Rome and the apostolic endorsement that came with it. Charles Martel and his family were the rightful heirs to the power of the Franks inaugurated by the baptism of Clovis and confirmed by conquest. The church, persecuted by emperors, kings and heretics since the days of Octavian, had finally found its rightful defenders.

---

104 Fouracre 2005.
105 For an example of the blending of Merovingian and Carolingian history see the second abbreviation of Bede discussed by Garipzanov 2005: 291. Cf. Story 2005: 76–9.

Book II: themes and sources

Sources: written and oral

If the theme of Frankish history was implicit to the structure of Book I, in Book II ('On the deeds of the kings of the Franks') it became explicit. The centrepiece for Regino was the *ARF*, included in its entirety for the period 741–813, setting the tone and format for what was to come. After 818, the *Chronicle* becomes an original work of contemporary history and must be seen in the context of Regino's stated aim of addressing historians' 'unbroken silence concerning our own times'. For him, the events of the distant past as recorded in authoritative texts were certain, while recent history was unsure, foggy and disputed. This seeming paradox – an inversion of modern appreciations of history – was partly a result of the puzzling lack of written sources apparently available to Regino. He relied on a handful:

- the *Annales Regni Francorum* (*ARF*, 'Royal Frankish Annals') were, as already discussed, a key text for Regino and were reproduced in their entirety for the period 741–813, where his copy evidently broke off.[106] Regino made grammatical improvements and added clarificatory glosses (for example in 806, glossing Nijmegen as 'in Batua'). The desire to improve led him to make some errors, for instance in 796 where he misunderstood a reference to the Avar fortress known as the Ring and rendered it as the name of an Avar leader. Regino's editorial changes were made with a lot of care – when the Ring comes up again, clearly as a place, Regino eliminates the line from the text so as not to confound his earlier interpretation. An eclipse described in *ARF* 807 as having occurred in the previous year is moved by Regino into 806. He adds various signpost phrases like 'while this was happening in Italy …'. Occasionally, especially toward the end of the *ARF* section, he summarises rather than copying exactly. Other than the long stories inserted under 746 and 752 Regino makes only one noteworthy addition to his source, a gloss on the death of Gerold of Bavaria in 799: 'one can read about him in the Vision of Wetti, which lists him among the martyrs' (a reference to Heito of Reichenau, *Visio Wettini*, c. 27). Because the *ARF* text is reproduced so faithfully and is available in existing English translations, it would be superfluous to include all of this section of the *Chronicle* in the present book.[107]

---

106 One group of ARF manuscripts stopped in 813: see McKitterick 2004: 20, 111–13.
107 For a complete translation see Scholz and Rogers 1972 and (revised version only) King 1987.

- the *Revelatio Stephani Papae* ('Vision of Pope Stephen'), inserted into the *ARF* under 753. The text was written (like the *GD*) before 835 at St-Denis and became widely known thereafter.[108] Its presence at Prüm may plausibly be connected with Hilduin, abbot of St-Denis, who was closely associated with the monastery in the middle of the ninth century and may have died there.[109]
- a set of annals known as the *Older Annals of Prüm* (*AP*) offered short notices concerning the deaths of abbots and kings, which provided Regino with some chronological landmarks. Unfortunately the text does not survive and has to be reconstructed hypothetically from later sources which were based on it. Regino's last use of the *AP* seems to be in 898.[110]
- Justin's *Epitome* of the Philippic History by Pompeius Trogus, written most probably in the second century, and a major influence on early medieval historiography.[111] Regino cited Justin explicitly in 889, more surreptitiously in other entries such as 888, and elsewhere recycled imagery from the *Epitome* which he had evidently internalised.[112]
- Paul the Deacon's *Historia* is likewise cited in 889 and informs imagery used by Regino in 873 and perhaps elsewhere.
- traces of other ancient authors including Curtius and Virgil have been identified in the text, suggesting that Regino had internalised their imagery.[113]
- a dossier of letters relating to the divorce case of Lothar II (855–869). Pamphlets of such material are known to have been circulated during the dispute.[114]

Although several well-qualified nineteenth-century scholars went over the text with a fine-tooth comb, it is always possible that additional citations from these and other sources may yet be identified. By far the most significant source in Book II after 818 was, however, the infor-

---

108 Stoclet 2000: 720–2.
109 Haubrichs 1979: 50.
110 Boschen 1972. The footnotes to the translation indicate Kurze's identification of passages from *AP*, though it should be noted that Boschen is sceptical about some of them.
111 Werner 1990 discusses Justin's medieval influence.
112 Manitius 1900. On Regino and Justin see also above, pp. 14–15.
113 Manitius 1900.
114 Cf. *AB* 863, 864: 106–10, 113–16; *AF* 863: 50–1.

mation Regino gleaned by listening to what he calls in his preamble to the 818 entry 'the stories of the elders'. The word translated here as 'elders' is *seniores* – the same word used in Charles the Straightforward's charter of immunity for Prüm in 919 to describe the members of the community whose counsel the king would seek before approving an abbatial election.[115] That the elders in question were primarily those of Prüm rather than of Trier (where, as we have seen, Regino was writing) seems to be put beyond doubt by the *Chronicle*'s numerous stories linked to Breton affairs: these clearly reflect the interests of Regino's first monastery, which had extensive landholdings in Brittany, rather than his second, which did not.[116] That Regino's historical consciousness carried a deep Prüm imprint even after his exile is not surprising given his long association with the monastery – the 892 entry makes it abundantly clear that he was still brooding on his expulsion. In any case, Prüm and Trier were intimately connected by the religious and political life of the region, so it is very likely that Regino remained in touch with at least some of the Prüm *seniores* after 899.[117]

As a self-conscious historian, Regino was careful to keep his audience informed about his methodology, and acknowledged the shift in his use of sources after 818 by quoting Jerome: 'Things we have seen are told in one way, and those we have heard in another: those things we know better, we also explain better.' For twenty-first century readers it is worth stressing that Regino was not seeking here to justify his use of oral traditions as opposed to written texts. The distinction drawn is between the things he had learned and the things he had seen for himself – in the former category might be put both written and spoken material. The authority of the written word was not as superior to that of the spoken in the early Middle Ages as it is today. Historians like Notker of St-Gall, Regino's contemporary, sometimes prioritised oral traditions even when they had a text available covering the same events, while documents produced in court during land disputes usually had to be vouched for by the locals with the longest memories: in law as in history, oral traditions informed texts, and vice versa.[118] The extent

---

115 MUB 162 and discussion by Wisplinghoff 1999: 442–3. Regino also referred to the elders as *patres*.

116 The assumption made by historians including Chédeville and Guillotel 1984 that Regino must have had lost annalistic sources for his Breton stories is neither necessary nor likely, since the stories are much more detailed than those found in most contemporary annals, particularly those that do survive from the far west.

117 For the connections see Haubrichs 1979.

118 Fentress and Wickham 1992; Innes 1998; van Houts 1999.

to which these two modes of communication intertwined must be kept in mind – stories deriving from oral tradition made the same claim to truth in a text like the *Chronicle* as those based on written sources. A considerable amount of material in Book II can be interpreted as deriving from stories current in late ninth-century Prüm. A story about Carloman, brother of Pippin III, who abdicated his worldly power to become a monk at Montecassino, was inserted by Regino into the *ARF* under 746, and does not appear to depend directly on a written source.[119] It is not out of the question that this Carloman was talked about in central Italy – when Abbot Marcward of Prüm journeyed to Rome in the year 844, he must have brought back traditions as well as relics – but the ultimate source is of course unknowable.[120] Its currency in Regino's Prüm might be easier to explain. The monastery had become temporary home and last resting place to several Carolingian kings and princes. Pippin the Hunchback, Charlemagne's eldest son, had been imprisoned there after his rebellion in the 790s, as recalled a century later by Regino's contemporary Notker of St-Gall.[121] A generation after Pippin, the young Charles the Bald was incarcerated at Prüm during the troubles of the 830s, and reportedly remembered the experience as educational, thinking of himself as an 'alumnus' of the monastery.[122] In 855 Lothar I, one of Prüm's greatest benefactors, voluntarily became a monk and died there; and at some point after 895 his grandson Hugh, blinded for an earlier rebellion, was also tonsured and buried within its walls.[123] The presence of these elite figures must have left an imprint on the community's collective memory, and the fact that the *Chronicle* contains several narratives about rulers who became monks (746, 855, 868, 870, 885) suggests – if Regino can be taken as representative of the monks – that this aspect of its history played an important role in the community's sense of itself as a place with close connections to royalty.[124] This function was certainly important to the brothers of Regino's day: the abbot had tonsured Hugh of Lotharingia in person. This alone might explain the contemporary relevance of stories like the one about Carloman, and one wonders if such stories, as well as

---

119 On Carloman's abdication see Krüger 1973. Regino calls him king, though he was only mayor of the palace.
120 On the relics see Herbers 1998; Smith 2000.
121 Notker, *Gesta Karoli*, II.12: 72–4.
122 Lupus, *Letters*, no. 83: 68–9 (Regenos 1966: 102–3).
123 Below, 855 and 885.
124 See also Airlie 2006a: 114–15.

INTRODUCTION

telling us something about the brothers' communal identity, could have functioned as exemplary mirrors for fallen rulers like Hugh: the narrative turns on how Carloman's inherent royalty was made apparent only through his acceptance of humility, utter debasement and self-denial. At the same time, the Carloman story works as a kind of commentary on or parable about aspects of the Benedictine Rule, to which it silently refers at several points.[125] The ex-ruler's inner nobility is established in part by his exemplary adherence to the Rule's strictures; that he is seen to be superior in this respect to the monks of Monte Cassino, the very home of Benedictine monasticism, adds an overtone of Frankish superiority to the tale. This works within the *Chronicle*'s bigger picture by underlining the implications of the relics of Benedict having been moved to Francia (reported by Regino under 612–631).

Regino's recounting of the Battle of Jengland (851, misdated to 860) also has the ring of a monastic memory. Unlike the *Chronicle*'s other stories set on the Breton frontier, here the Bretons are faceless and nameless and function as foils to illuminate the cowardice of the story's main character, Charles the Bald. This implies that it was a narrative passed down from the *seniores* rather than one drawn from contemporary contacts in the west, where Charles's posthumous stock was rather higher. Such a version of the battle fits well with the probable political atmosphere of Prüm at the time of the battle, when tension between Lothar I and Charles was palpable. A source survives that tells us something about how the monks first learned of the engagement at Jengland. Lupus, abbot of Ferrières in west Francia, had witnessed the battle and wrote to Marcward of Prüm late in 851 referring sarcastically to the defeat as 'the most magnificent festivities'.[126] The letter gives no further details, but does mention the courier to whom its delivery had been entrusted, and who surely passed on further details. Whatever mechanisms of gossip and memory reformed the Jengland story into the shape recorded in the *Chronicle*, this letter at least enables us to appreciate the role of personal networks in transmitting oral traditions around the empire: Marcward was a friend of Lupus and himself an alumnus of Ferrières, as was his successor Eigil. Monastery walls were porous and bonds of family and friendship were not cut off abruptly at the edges of the precinct.

A monastery's corporate connections could also create conduits for the transmission of stories. The links articulated by the cult of saints

125 Borst 1973: 528–31, and below, 746, n. 11 for details.
126 Lupus, *Letters*, no. 83: 68–9 (Regenos 1966: 102–3).

were naturally important here, especially for an institution like Prüm with a strong interest in importing relics. Regino's remarkably detailed knowledge of political events in southern Italy during the reign of Louis II (871, 872) tallies neatly with his community's liturgical interest in St Priscus of Capua – the *Chronicle*'s account of Louis's siege of that city may reflect active late ninth-century contacts there, along which relics of and stories about the saint may also have travelled.[127] However, perhaps even more important in the process of information gathering was Prüm's extensive property base. Several stories in Book II match up with these interests. The fight between the men of King Odo and Archbishop Fulk of Rheims as they passed through the Rhineland (895) was widely known – a similar account is found in the *Annals of St-Vaast* – but Regino's version contains some unique details, including the fact that Count Adalung, killed in the engagement, was buried at Beltheim. It is surely not a coincidence that Prüm had landed interests at Beltheim.[128] The *Chronicle*'s coverage of the battles fought against the Vikings by King Arnulf on the Rivers Geul and Dyle (891) is uniquely detailed. Prüm monks may have been present: Arnulf's renewal of the monastery's right to free election was issued en route to the Dyle, and the charter had probably been drawn up in-house and taken to him for approval.[129] Significantly, though, Prüm also had important properties in the vicinity, at Gewelesdorf.[130] Our main source for these landholdings is the Prüm estate survey whose surviving version was completed in 893 under Regino's supervision. Research into the construction of this document has revealed the enormous logistical effort that underpinned it: several panels of commissioners were despatched throughout the middle kingdom on lengthy circuits, representing the work of many months if not years.[131] What looks to us like a dry administrative document was the product of a massive effort of collective memory. With this in mind it is unthinkable that the monastery's agents and estate managers did not share stories about recent political events after long days spent auditing peasants and pigs.

The mentality fostered by this major project must have renewed the monks' sense of connectedness with their far-flung properties and subordinates. In this context the *Chronicle*'s stories about Breton affairs make

127 Haubrichs 1979: 120.
128 *Das Prümer Urbar*: 248.
129 D AC 92; Wisplinghoff 1999: 440–1.
130 *Das Prümer Urbar*: 244.
131 Kuchenbuch 1978: 12–27; *Das Prümer Urbar*: 132–6.

more sense.¹³² A number of these suggest local knowledge, including the miraculous death of the sinful Breton leader Nominoë at the hands of a ghostly bishop of Angers (862) and the siege of Angers by the Vikings (873) which casts another Breton leader, Salomon, as its hero. A third, the long parable of Wrhwant and Pacsweten (874), also looks like a narrative with western roots. The story about the conflict between Alan and Judicael under 890 seems to have been a direct sequel to the 874 narrative (which finishes by glancing forward to their rivalry) and it may be that they originated as a single account rearranged by Regino into separate annals. Equivalent stories are known to have circulated in contemporary Brittany.¹³³ The subject matter was different, though one point of common interest is provided by the sixth-century Bishop Melanius of Rennes, who is mentioned approvingly by both Regino (874) and the late ninth-century Breton *Deeds of the Saints of Redon*.¹³⁴ Prüm's properties in and around the Breton territories (Rennes, Angers and elsewhere) were long-standing and extensive.¹³⁵ These lands were not audited in 893, but we know that members of the community retained active interests in them. Writing in 862, Lupus celebrated Prüm's recovery of some of its western estates and expressed the hope that he would henceforth be in more regular contact with Abbot Ansbald 'as a result of [his agents'] trips there and back through our place'.¹³⁶ The liturgical priorities of Prüm were also oriented heavily to the far north-west, whence many of its main saints' cults originated.¹³⁷ It is not impossible that Regino visited Brittany himself, though there is no direct evidence that he did.¹³⁸ Rather than hypothesising an exotic research trip (which, had it taken place, we might expect Regino to have mentioned in one of his methodological asides), it seems more likely that stories from the Breton frontier travelled along the networks upon which the monastery's interests rested. Although we do not have a Lupus to inform us directly about Prüm's western connections after his letter to

---

132 The argument sometimes made that these stories derived from written sources, or from a visit made by Regino to the west, is not supported by the evidence: Schleidgen 1977: 14–16, 109–11.

133 For example *GSR* I.7: 126–31.

134 *GSR* I.1: 110.

135 For details see Brunterc'h 1983: 47–53; Chédeville and Guillotel 1984: 206; Willwersch 1989: 86–91; Smith 1992: 56–7, 131, 146.

136 Lupus, *Letters*, no. 116: 166–9 (Regenos 1966: 132–3). A later source suggests that representatives of Prüm were at Angers in 888; Wisplinghoff 1999: 457.

137 Boschen 1972: 68; Haubrichs 1979: 54, 104–6, 110–12, 123–5.

138 See above, nn. 31, 32.

Ansbald in 862, these networks had not become fossilised by Regino's day. Important relics were translated to Prüm from the Pays de Retz (near Nantes) in the later ninth century.[139] While the exact origin of purportedly contemporary synodal material from Nantes incorporated in *De synodalibus causis* is debatable (it may rather have derived from an episcopal capitulary), a late ninth-century north-western provenance remains plausible.[140] We also have a vernacular poem on St George composed at Prüm in the 880s in whose text Poitevin influences were detected by Wolfgang Haubrichs.[141]

The monks' productive relationships with far-off estate managers and distant friends among the secular and monastic elites of west Francia and Italy demonstrate the persistence of trans-imperial economic, cultural and political links during the last years of Carolingian hegemony, and indeed after the dynastic rupture of 888. They should not, however, blind us to Prüm's role in a much more local political landscape. All monasteries, including the greatest royal houses, had close ties with the regional aristocracy of their own hinterlands, and Prüm was no exception. Charter witness lists show members of the local secular elite actively involved in the transaction of the monastery's business. The same families acted as the abbey's benefactors, providing lands to swell its resources and sons to replenish its brotherhood.[142] The benefits ran both ways, the benefactors deriving social prestige from their ostentatious generosity and spiritual benefits from the monks in the form of prayer and commemoration. The depth of the abbey's influence on its constituency is illustrated by the emulative piety of the local worthies who founded family monasteries dedicated to Prüm cults.[143]

It would be surprising if such associations had not left a mark on the shape of a text like the *Chronicle* and, on close inspection, the influence of several Prüm benefactors can be detected in its pages. One aristocratic figure, Eberhard, is mentioned in no fewer than three of Regino's entries: 881 (Eberhard Saxo, son of Count Meginhard, is captured by the Vikings and ransomed by his mother Evesa); 885 (Eberhard, having been deprived of possessions by the Viking leader Godafrid, helps engineer his murder); and 898 (Eberhard is himself murdered and his command is given to his brother Meginhard). Although not a

139 Haubrichs 1979: 126–7, 171 (discussing St Lupianus).
140 Hartmann 1989: 385–7; Hartmann 2004.
141 Haubrichs 1979: 131–6.
142 Kuchenbuch 1978: 25–6; Hennebicque 1981; Tellenbach 1988.
143 Haubrichs 1979: 131–45.

INTRODUCTION 37

regular cast-member in the major narrative sources for the late ninth century, Eberhard was a considerable figure. Count of Hamaland in Frisia, with an additional responsibility for overall coastal defence in the area, his family's extensive landholdings also comprised interests further south in the heartlands of Lotharingia.[144] Some of these may have left a mark in the Prüm estate survey. Because the information was not directly relevant to its purpose, very few donors were named in this document, and those that were presumably had a special relationship with the monastery – we know this to be true of the one donor who has been identified, the Madalwin who gave fourteen manses before signing up as a monk in the 840s.[145] One of the other named benefactors was a certain Meginhard, who was remembered for having given four manses at Duisburg.[146] Meginhard was also the name of Eberhard's father and of the brother who succeeded him in 898, and Duisburg lay within the compass of their interests.[147] If Meginhard the donor was a member of the Hamaland comital family, this would explain the otherwise incongruous discussion of their affairs in the *Chronicle*. Eberhard's prominent role in the murder of Godafrid in 885 – he was instructed to provoke a fight by loudly denouncing his mistreatment at the hands of the Scandinavians – suggests, by the same token, that the *Chronicle*'s elaborate account may have derived from him or one of his relatives. In view of this it is interesting that Regino reports the first sign of Godafrid's expansionary ambitions to have been an attack in the previous year on Duisburg.

Regino's glowing report gave Eberhard bonus points for having landed the first blow on Godafrid, chief ally of Lothar II's rebellious son Hugh. Another digressionary narrative connected to Hugh's rising reflects less well on its protagonists. In 883 Regino reports:

> About this time Lothar's son Hugh killed Count Wigbert, who had been close to him since his youth. A few days after that, he deceitfully ordered the murder of Bernarius, a noble man who was most faithful to him, because he was captivated by the beauty of his wife, whom he married without delay. The woman was called Friderada. Before she was joined to Bernarius, she had been married to Engelram, a powerful man; she bore him a daughter who was later taken in marriage by Count Richwin, and whom the same count ordered to be beheaded for committing a disgrace.

144 Van Winter 1980; Althoff 1992: 166–85.
145 Wisplinghoff 1999: 453.
146 *Das Prümer Urbar*: 242.
147 The absence of a comital or ducal title is explained if this was Eberhard's brother, who was not promoted to office until 898.

Engelram was count in Frisia and Charles the Bald's former chamberlain. The other characters in this narrative, which spans two generations, are harder to identify, but some Prüm links can be dimly discerned. A Bernarius who would have been about the right age is found among the local aristocracy witnessing a charter transacting Prüm business in 865.[148] Richwin was probably the count of Verdun active in the years either side of 900.[149] He is mentioned in two of Zwentibald's charters from the 890s, in one of them intervening for the church of Trier.[150] A Richwin is also mentioned in a document of 943 as a former benefice holder of Prüm.[151] It is probably now impossible to recover precisely what Regino's deadpan retelling of these shocking events was meant to signify, but if we accept the main characters' association with Prüm and Trier it can be read as a local – or personal – angle on the political turmoil surrounding the rebellion of Hugh.

Some higher-profile friends of Prüm can also be identified. Robert the Strong, count of Angers, was probably connected to the monastery on two fronts. While his official role gave him influence over Prüm's interests in Anjou, his family background in the Rhineland meant he was also plugged into political networks much further east. Among its many connections, his family counted associations with Prüm: indeed, there is evidence suggesting that the monastery's landholdings in both areas aided the transfer of Robert and his followers to the western kingdom in the 830s.[152] This relationship may have informed Regino's praise of Robert's qualities in 861 and his spectacular account in 867 of the count's heroic death at the Battle of Brissarthe (actually 866). Another eastern source, the *Annals of Fulda*, also mentions Robert's death in 867: 'He was, so to speak, a second Macchabeus in our times, and if all his battles which he fought with the Bretons and Northmen were fully described they would be on the same level as the deeds of Macchabeus.'[153] This implies that stories about Robert were circulating in the Rhineland soon after the count's death and (since he and the annalist misdated it identically) it is presumably on one of these, kept alive by Robert's eastern relatives, that Regino drew in compiling his account of Brissarthe. The *Chronicle*'s evident enthusiasm for Robert

148 MUB 103; cf. Kuchenbuch 1978: 350.
149 Hlawitschka 1968: 196; Hlawitschka 1969: 54, 126.
150 DD Z 3, 27.
151 MUB 181.
152 Haubrichs 1979: 47–9.
153 *AF* 867: 57.

and his son Odo (whose kingly qualities are surreptitiously raised above those of his rivals in 888 by means of a carefully deployed quote from Justin) need not, therefore, be attributed solely to factional partisanship on Regino's part, far less to the historian's being a member of the family himself.[154] If he was not primed to incorporate favourable stories about Robert and Odo because of their family's past relationship with Prüm, he may have had in mind their even closer association with the monastery of Lorsch, numbered among whose recent abbots was none other than his would-be patron Adalbero of Augsburg. Its present proprietor was another, Hatto of Mainz.[155]

Two final figures might have owed their good write-ups in the *Chronicle* to Prüm connections. One is Boso, the count of Vienne who attempted to usurp the throne of west Francia in 879–880. Although he was partially and temporarily successful, Boso's power was more or less crushed within a year, and consequently he received general condemnation from the Carolingian press.[156] Regino is the puzzling exception to this, extolling Boso's virtues in 877 and 879 and portraying him as a victim of persecution at the hands of the Carolingians Louis III and Carloman II, whose own legitimacy he implicitly questioned in 878. He was also favourable to Boso's son Louis 'the Blind' of Provence, sometime emperor and king of Italy. It is hard to read Regino's attitude as a result of straightforward political partisanship for Louis, since the latter's power was slipping at the time the *Chronicle* was being written, and was effectively ended by his blinding in 905 (another event about the precise circumstances of which Regino is surprisingly well informed). The idea that Regino was simply more objective than other writers does not really satisfy either.[157] More significant surely is the fact that Boso's family were major benefactors of Prüm. Around 840 the count's uncle Richard had donated the estate of Villance for the good of his soul, and included his brother Bivin, Boso's father, in the gift's narrative. The significance of the grant is reflected in the fact that confirmations were sought from both Lothar I and Lothar II, and that in the 893 estate survey it was classified as one of Prüm's most important properties.[158] The second major figure is Salomon, generally cast as a

---

154 As argued by Werner 1997.
155 On the Robertians and Lorsch see Innes 2000.
156 Airlie 2000; MacLean 2001.
157 Staab 1998: 380.
158 D L 68; D L2 23; MUB 102–3; *Das Prümer Urbar:* 89–91, 200–8. On Villance's significance in the monastic estate see also Devroey 1976: 428–33.

villain in Carolingian sources but not in the *Chronicle* (especially 873). Regino's positive view of the Breton leader did not follow automatically from his knowledge of Breton stories – he was more than capable of adapting and omitting material that did not fit his purposes, as we have seen. Probably more important in securing the abbot's approval was the fact that Salomon was remembered as a friend of Prüm, having issued a comprehensive privilege of immunity covering the monastery's western lands at a crucial juncture in 860.[159]

Their generosity preserved in the monastic archive and their names regularly invoked in the monks' prayers, the reputations of the likes of Richard, Salomon and Meginhard lived on in the social memory of the community, controlled and mediated by the *seniores*.[160] Thus it was that they survived in a form capable of resurfacing in a text like the *Chronicle*, where they reflected well on their successors, descendants and relatives like Boso and Eberhard. Some of these descendants and relatives may even have been literally present in the cloisters: among the lists of monks surviving from the abbacy of Ansbald (860–886) we find both a Richard and a Meginharius.[161] The version of the past we encounter in the pages of the *Chronicle* may thus conceivably have been one that was shared by groups within the community with some of its lay benefactors. Regino's retelling of stories involving those benefactors and their families served to align monastery and author with the interests of members of the local elite in ways that mattered to them, even though it is usually impossible for us to reconstruct the precise contours of their relationships.[162]

Memory is of course selective, and material heard was just as susceptible to editorial manipulation as material read. The absence in the *Chronicle* of stories praising Lothar I, Prüm's most ostentatious benefactor (and remembered as such in other texts from the monastery), is a striking and puzzling indication of this – the account of Pippin I's career in the 853 entry hints that Regino had an ambivalent attitude to Lothar. Here we should also bear in mind that the denizens of monasteries like Prüm, with its far-flung connections and brotherhood drawn from the ranks

---

159 MUB 95; Smith 1992: 131. The charter survives from Prüm rather than Redon.

160 Gifts of land were sometimes accompanied by stipulations that the benefactor be commemorated with an annual feast. For the example of Ercanfrida and St-Maximin see Nelson 1995; Innes 2001: 429.

161 Tellenbach 1988.

162 Further examples may also be found: cf. Archbishop Hermann of Cologne, complimented by Regino in 890, who had close family ties with Prüm (MUB 120 and Kuchenbuch 1978: 350).

of rival aristocratic families, need not have subscribed to a single and agreed version of political history. Regino's emphases and omissions may well have resulted from a now-obscure debate about history and monastic identity that, prompted by wider political events, raged within the cloister. In the course of such arguments, social memories could be activated and deactivated consciously or by unspoken understanding. Stories about old friends like Salomon and Robert might not have mattered to all of the monks all of the time, but may have become newly relevant because of the contemporary reputations of their successors like Alan and Odo, both of whom are openly praised in the *Chronicle*. In the hands of a skilled historian like Regino, such stories could also be used instrumentally – by recalling their families' Prüm connections and writing their deeds into the history of the Frankish world, the former abbot may have hoped to win sympathy for his own plight from the movers and shakers of the early tenth-century elite.

Narrative and episode

The stories that Regino learned from oral traditions were not mechanically transcribed into the *Chronicle* any more than the written sources of Book I were thoughtlessly copied word for word. The need to take into account the knowledge of their audiences meant that early medieval authors could not simply make things up, expect tendentious interpretations to be accepted unquestioningly or ignore uncomfortable facts, but there is no doubt that Regino shaped the structure and content of Book II with a firm authorial hand – decisions about what to include and exclude were made with a clear concept of the work's overall shape in mind.[163]

In his preamble to the 'original' section of the *Chronicle* which begins in 818, Regino divides the remainder of Book II into three sections: the times of Louis the Pious (814–840); the times of Emperor Lothar and his brothers (840–*c*.875); and 'our own times', apparently referring to the period covered by his own career (direct references to which begin in 892). Of these three periods, written sources play a major role only in the second. The most surprising aspect of this is Regino's professed ignorance of the reign of Louis the Pious, about which he 'included very little because [he] neither found written texts, nor heard from the elders [*seniores*] anything that was worth committing to memory'. Yet the widely read biography of Louis by Thegan had been written in Trier, and the emperor's archchaplain Hilduin of St-Denis had been closely

163 On audience expectation see Althoff 2001.

associated with the community at Prüm before his death. Although we could simply take Regino at his word, it is not impossible that his reticence was born of discretion in view of the troubles of Louis's reign. The story about Pippin I recorded under 853 certainly hints that he knew more about Louis than he let on. The shape of this vignette also seems to point back to the circle of Archbishop Drogo of Metz, Louis's half-brother and close adviser, in whose entourage another biography of the emperor by the 'Astronomer' may have been written.[164]

However disingenuous Regino's claim about Louis, his threefold periodisation served to shape a finely tuned blend of narrative and episode. The *Chronicle*'s grand narrative is the story of the rise and fall of the Carolingian dynasty.[165] Most of the rising is done before 818, as we have seen: Book I's documentation of the dynasty's ascent is made explicit in the apostolic endorsement of the *Revelatio* (753) and climaxes in the *ARF*'s authoritative glorification of Charlemagne's reign and conquests.[166] Thereafter, the theme was decline and fragmentation, a stark contrast with Book I's narrative of incremental unification (of church, peoples and dynasty). After 818, as Stuart Airlie aptly puts it, 'the dynasty is always already falling' in Regino's text.[167] The tone is set in the 818 annal itself, where events divided by nearly a century are collapsed into a single brief narrative, thereby connecting the death of one Carolingian with the post-888 era in which Carolingian authority itself was dying.[168] This kind of flash-forward authorial artifice was essential to the *Chronicle*'s narrative drive, and Regino's imposition on Book II of a central storyline is what distinguishes it above all from the ninth-century annals which it superficially resembles. The decline-and-fall script culminates in the 888 entry itself, where Regino presents the death without heir of Charles the Fat as the end of an era. It was only sensible, given that he was attempting to woo members of the court circle of Louis the Child, that he tried his best to overcome the implications of his own logic by characterising Arnulf, Louis's father, as the last heir to the empire. However, the fact that he makes this case in the entry for 880 means that it is subsequently buried by the crisis of 888, in which it becomes implicitly clear that Arnulf is in truth *not* the sole heir to the dynasty's power. Regino's emphasis on the resonances of the

164 Tremp 1988.
165 Airlie 2006a, on whose insights this paragraph depends.
166 The *ARF*'s tendentiousness and ideological programme are explored by Becher 1993; Airlie 1999; McKitterick 2004: 120–55.
167 Airlie 2006a: 126.
168 Airlie 2006a: 127–8 and *passim*.

king's name, shared with the semi-legendary Carolingian progenitor St Arnulf of Metz, smacks of special pleading; and even that argument was little more than a caveat embedded within a mini-narrative of the dynasty's dwindling. From Regino's vantage point decades later, everything was crushed by the inevitable weight of dynastic history moving toward its known outcome.

If the heroes of this story were rulers like Charles Martel and Charlemagne, the villain was unquestionably Lothar II (855–869). As a young man, Lothar had had a relationship with a noblewoman called Waldrada who bore him a son named Hugh and two daughters. In late 855 he put Waldrada aside and married Theutberga, an aristocrat whose family connections brought him control of some of the major routes to Italy. The aim was clearly to establish his influence in the south of Lotharingia at the start of his reign. Early in 860, when his need for this influence had declined and it was becoming clear that his marriage was barren, Lothar divorced Theutberga at a synod in Aachen, using against her as justification a litany of sexual accusations including incest, sodomy, conception through witchcraft, and abortion. The pope became involved and attempted to overrule the divorce, asserting that Theutberga was the king's legitimate wife, while Lothar's uncles tried to manipulate the situation in order to keep him married lest his return to Waldrada reactivated the royal claims of Hugh. After years of diplomacy, acrimony and outrage, things seemed to be going Lothar's way in 867 when Pope Nicholas I, his implacable opponent, died. Even rosier prospects presented themselves in 869 when the new pope, Hadrian II, offered Lothar absolution, but the king's death during his return trip from Rome meant that his political resurrection was short-lived.[169]

For Regino, as for other writers, Lothar's death was a clear sign of God's displeasure at his immoral and disobedient conduct, and the 869 entry depicts it as a sort of ordeal which the king fails by taking communion with an impure heart. More than this, however, Regino sees wider consequences in Lothar's disgrace, interpreting Nicholas's letter of 866 as a curse on his whole kingdom and seeing its fulfilment in the rebellion of Hugh in 883:

> Thus almighty God was enraged at the kingdom of Lothar and began to act against and to utterly destroy the strength of that same kingdom by increasing disasters of such a kind that the prophecy of the most holy Pope Nicholas, and also the curse which he had pronounced over this kingdom, was fulfilled.[170]

169 The best discussion of the divorce is Airlie 1998.
170 See also 856 ('the greatest ruin resulted from this union, not only for him, but also

The kingdom in question was Lotharingia, the middle kingdom, inside whose frontiers Regino's own turbulent career played out. But the curse, in Regino's telling, also reverberated west of the Meuse and east of the Rhine. In his description of the fading fortunes of the Carolingians under 880, Regino referred to the 'sterility of their wives'. Sterility had been discussed in one of the papal letters quoted by Regino in 866 as a sign of sin rather than of infertility. As far as the former abbot of Prüm was concerned, Lothar's disgrace had brought a curse not just on his kingdom but on his whole family: the tragedy of Lotharingia was knitted seamlessly into the tragedy of the Carolingian dynasty.

Regino's enthusiastic insistence on the correctness of the pope's position against Lothar II should not be construed as the constitutional ranting of the proto-Gregorian (in 869, after all, he firmly asserted the right of kings to influence episcopal appointments), nor the finely tuned professional analysis of the canon lawyer.[171] Rather, it is characteristic of the early medieval historian's view of sin and divine favour as key factors in politics. For the edification and instruction of Louis the Child, the story of Lothar II functioned not simply as part of a grand historical narrative, but also as an episode with its own exemplary message. In fact, Book II is replete with such episodes. These are carefully constructed and often sacrifice chronological precision for the sake of forming complete mini-narratives: thus, for example, the entire career of the Carolingian prince Carloman is inserted as part of a digression in the entry for 870, while in 865 the deaths of Archbishops Gunther and Theutgaud (Lothar's right-hand men) were mentioned well before their time in order to illustrate the consequences of their actions.

Most of these tales concern kings and princes, and are presumably intended to be cautionary or exemplary. Alongside the political consequences of Lothar's sinfulness Regino placed the parable of the Breton leader Wrhwant, who won battles against the odds by placing his trust in God (874) and the deeds of the Christ-like Bulgar king Boris-Michael whose humility and piety led him to become a monk (868). Many other paradigmatic moral stories of a type common in contemporary histories stud both books of the *Chronicle*.[172] It is noticeable that these tales

---

for his whole kingdom') and 867 ('even then it was becoming clear that God was opposed not only to Lothar, because of his hard and impenitent heart, but also to his entire kingdom').

171 The niceties of canon law were less significant in driving the divorce case than competing views of authority: Kottje 1983; cf. Bauer 1994.

172 Royal virtues praised by Regino are catalogued by Hlawitschka 1975: 23–4; Kortüm 1994: 505.

are not necessarily arranged to support a specific territorial claim or a particular line of kings. Few of Regino's Carolingians were uniformly good or bad. Charles the Bald is shown as a coward in 860 but held up in a positive light against Lothar II in 866; Lothar himself gets at least provisional credit for helping his brother against the Saracens (Muslims) in 867; and even though he was Louis the Child's great-grandfather and otherwise one of Regino's favourite kings, Louis the German is openly criticised at the end of the 866 entry for the ambition and avarice that led him to invade his brother's kingdom.

Such vacillation could be taken as a sign that Regino's text was more ad hoc and less patterned than modern historians might like to believe.[173] On close inspection, though, we can discern a consistent system of values running through Regino's depictions of rulership. He measured the actions of kings explicitly against the purity of their motivations. Regino's primary interest was their inner character – his regular royal obituaries stress personal qualities over material achievements. Stories such as those about Louis the German's silent endurance of dislocated ribs (870) and the Christian stoicism of Charles the Fat, resolute in the face of ruin (888), turn on the kinds of men they were. Above all, success and failure were defined according to rulers' willingness to submit themselves to God's will: worldly and heavenly rewards and punishments followed from there. Regino was not offering Louis the Child a to-do list of kingly glories (subdue the Slavs, become emperor, be generous to the church and so on) so much as a series of assertions about what kind of man (hard and fair) made a good king and which motives (humility and restraint) should guide kingly action. This value system is particularly clear in the *Chronicle*'s several stories about kings who renounced the world to become monks, discussed earlier in the context of the monastery's long history of sheltering or imprisoning former rulers.[174] The stories of Carloman (746) and Boris-Michael (868) turn precisely on the contrast between the protagonists' inner life and outward behaviour: in different ways, these men's essential kingliness was confirmed rather than negated by their patient endurance, pure motives and almost monastic sensibilities. Another Carloman (870) provided a clear counter-example. Having been ordained into religious orders, his desire for a throne inspired him to lead an uprising against his father that gained him a comparison with the apostate emperor Julian, and Regino explicitly linked his fate (blinding) with the falseness

---

173 See in general Morse 1991.
174 See above, pp. 32–3.

of his motives. The same, implicitly, was true of Lothar II's son Hugh, whose blinding and tonsuring were reported with relish by Regino, his final jailer (885).[175]

Another striking theme in Book II is warfare (especially 860, 871, 873, 874, 876, 890, 891). Early medieval historical works are notoriously reticent about the mechanics of battle, preferring to dwell instead on its causes and outcomes and the moral lessons to be drawn therefrom.[176] Regino's relatively detailed accounts of battles are therefore as unexpected as they are valuable. Naturally, he did not refrain from explaining their outcomes in moral terms, so his descriptions of warfare were congruent with contemporary historians' broader purpose of interpreting divine judgements on the deeds of powerful men. We could nonetheless also see them as having a more practical instructional purpose. As far as Regino's intended audience at the court of Louis the Child would have been concerned, there was an elephant in the room: the Battle of Bratislava (or Pressburg) which had been fought in 907. This engagement between the Bavarians and Hungarians ended in unequivocal defeat for the former, claimed the lives of several leading aristocrats and led to a fundamental reconfiguration of the high nobility.[177] In 908, another Hungarian raid laid the eastern kingdom low, and the casualties included some of the nobles praised by Regino in the latter stages of his text.[178] One wonders if the desire to avoid mentioning these disastrous events was one reason that Regino tactfully ended his work in 906. It may also be more than coincidence that the one extended piece of explicit source-criticism undertaken by Regino in Book II concerns the Hungarians. In the 889 entry he digresses into an analysis of their origins and way of life, concluding that they must be the same people as the Scythians he had read about in the works of Justin and Paul the Deacon. Although he quoted the relevant passages directly, he silently edited them in a way that suggests an attempt to make them fit what he knew of the present-day Hungarians. The endpoint of his discussion turns to Hungarian modes of warfare. After stating that 'their way of fighting is all the more dangerous in that other peoples are not used to it', Regino offers an explicit comparison with Breton tactics, which were similar in most key respects and which had been described in detail

---

175 Cf. also 853, where a king's dissolution is linked to his having been prevented entering the religious life; and 855 (Lothar's deathbed conversion).
176 Halsall 2003: 1–6.
177 Reuter 1991: 129–30; Hiestand 1994; Bowlus 2006: 83–4.
178 For details see the footnotes to 907 and 908.

INTRODUCTION

in earlier parts of the *Chronicle*. The Hungarians/Scythians – nomadic shaven-headed cannibalistic blood-drinkers – might be culturally alien, but they were militarily familiar and, like the Bretons, beatable. The generals of Louis the Child and his successors gradually started to get on top of the Hungarians thereafter, and it is hardly likely that their success was attributable to intense strategy sessions spent poring over Regino's accounts of the Battle of Jengland (860) or the Siege of Angers (873). We might nevertheless see in his attempt to educate the young king in the finer points of warfare the response of a scholarly armchair general to a new threat whose raids were getting slightly too close for comfort.

Regino as eyewitness

As we have seen, Regino clearly distinguished his approach to events he had merely heard or read about from his approach to those he had witnessed. Although he must have been old enough to have personal memories from before 870, it is only in the 892 entry that the character of the *Chronicle* starts to reflect this clearly. From this point on the affairs of the middle kingdom's aristocracy become much more prominent than the deeds of kings per se, but events are described much more tersely than before and until the very last entry there are no more extended anecdotes. Properly contextualised, the *Chronicle*'s account of events between 892 and 906 provides crucial insights into Lotharingian politics after the end of the empire. Competition for power was articulated by two major feuds whose details were clearly of interest to Regino, particularly as Trier lay at the heart of the troubles. His text's change in tone reflects the fact that he saw himself as sitting at the eye of the storm. It was certainly a conscious decision: in both the 892 entry and the preface to the whole work he states his intention to keep his commentary on his own fate to a minimum. The reasons given – fear of causing offence to 'certain people who are still alive' and the desire to avoid accusations of verbosity and self-obsession – suggest that Regino saw discretion as the better part of valour.

This discretion means that his own role in events – important for establishing the nuances of the *Chronicle* – remains enigmatic, primarily because a section of text including a detailed account of the abbot's ejection from Prüm was erased from the 892 entry. What remains tells us that the alleged culprits were Gerard and Matfrid, regional aristocrats of some influence whose brother, Richar, was Regino's 'hateful successor'. The Matfridings, as historians know the family, were involved in the murky political feud sparked off by the murder in 892 of Megingoz, a very powerful noble and lay-abbot of St-Maximin in Trier, whose connections had enabled him to build up a position as a royal middleman in Lotharingia. In 896 Alberic, his murderer, was himself killed by count Stephen, an associate of Gerard and Matfrid; and he in turn fell victim to an assassin's arrow while evacuating his bowels in 901. King Arnulf's contribution to the turmoil was to try to establish his illegitimate son Zwentibald as the main authority in the kingdom, and after several false starts he eventually (895) managed to have him installed as king. Zwentibald's reign was turbulent, in no small part due to his capricious and aggressive style of rule, though royal heavy-handedness was to some extent inevitable given the thorough faction-alisation of regional politics.[179] In 896/897 a group of counts including Stephen, Matfrid and Gerard was dispossessed by the king, forcing Arnulf to step in and broker a reconciliation; and in 898 Zwentibald ejected Reginar ('his most faithful and only counsellor' according to Regino) from court, whereupon Reginar took up with other disaffected figures and proceeded to make further trouble for the regime by joining up with Charles the Straightforward, newly made king of west Francia. Charles invaded Lotharingia in the course of that year, and Prüm was one of his stopping-off points. Things came to a head in 899 when a peace-summit of sorts was held at St-Goar, a monastery dependent on Prüm, involving leading aristocrats from the courts of Arnulf and Charles. Regino refers to secret talks held at this meeting in which the king (presumably meaning Zwentibald) was not involved. Historians have generally assumed that these talks produced an agreement among the other parties that Louis the Child would succeed in Lotharingia, and perhaps included a plot to do away with Zwentibald, who was killed the following summer by Gerard, Stephen and Matfrid.[180]

The *Chronicle* offers tantalising clues as to Regino's involvement in these shenanigans: Charles's visit to Prüm in 898, the St-Goar summit of 899, and the 898 entry's peculiar description of Reginar's deposition. The excisions from the 892 entry have, however, drawn the most attention. Who mutilated the *Chronicle*? Was it Adalbero, the bishop of Augsburg, taking literally the historian's request for feedback? Could it have been the historian's enemies, embarrassed by what he had written? The continuator, Adalbert? Or was it Regino, the mild-

179 Innes 2001: 430–3.
180 On all these events see for example Beumann 1966/7; Hlawitschka 1968: 158–84; Ewig 1980: 187–200; Innes 2000: 222–34; M Hartmann 2002; MacLean forthcoming.

mannered abbot, himself? All have been suggested without a satisfactory consensus being reached.[181] The mechanisms of manuscript transmission make the first two options inherently implausible: it is hard to see why Adalbero would have crossed out one section of the text before seeing to the distribution of the rest; and even harder to envisage, amid the retributive murders of the 890s and 900s, the abbot's history-loving enemies taking revenge for presumed insults by wielding a vicious editorial pen. The fact that the excisions affect all manuscripts proves that the censorship took place very early in the transmission process and certainly before the text was received by Adalbert (whose revisions feature only in one group of manuscripts). The most likely candidate is thus Regino himself.[182] No autograph original versions of major historical works survive before that of Richer of Rheims in the late tenth century; but from that manuscript and many that follow, the phenomenon of authors returning to edit and rewrite sections of their own work is widely attested.[183]

More problematic still is the original structure of the 892 annal. Kurze misleadingly published two sections in his edition that never appeared together in any manuscript:

- the sentence: 'However, I did not remain in that position for very long because at the instigation of my rivals I had to put up with Richar, the brother of Gerard and Matfrid, becoming the hateful successor to my job' only appears in Kurze's 'A' manuscripts.

- the rest of the paragraph ('I pray ... and oppose me') including the obliterated lines only appears in Kurze's 'B' manuscripts.

Kurze's assumption that the 'A' group represents the version of the *Chronicle* edited, interpolated and continued by Adalbert, while the 'B' version is closer to Regino's original text, was not based on a thorough examination of all the manuscripts but was subsequently vindicated by Otto Prinz's detailed linguistic comparison.[184] This opens up the possibility that the text's identification of the Matfridings as Regino's persecutors was one of Adalbert's interpolations rather than part of the original work. There is no doubt that a long section of text was

---

181 For some key discussions see in addition to the works cited in the previous note Hümpfner 1924; Levison 1926; Lintzel 1937; Prinz 1973; Schleidgen 1977: 88–96.

182 Lintzel 1937 pointed out that the 899 entry's stress on the need for restraint contradicts the 892 entry's statement about the need to spell things out in great detail, suggesting that Regino had indeed had a change of heart while writing.

183 Glenn 2004; van Houts 2006.

184 Prinz 1973; endorsed by Schleidgen 1977: 90–1.

removed, because the following paragraph, securely Regino's, refers back to it. If we attribute to Adalbert the line about the Matfridings, then it might follow that they were the subject of the excised section. Regino, scared of offending his still-powerful foes, thought twice about accusing them directly and deleted his rant; Adalbert, writing long after the matter had cooled down, restored them to their original place in the text, albeit more briefly than had Regino.

While it makes perfect sense for Adalbert to have omitted the now-senseless mutilated passage (we know he was a careful editor), there are reasons for doubting the rest of this reconstruction. In the first place, one wonders how Adalbert, writing seven decades later, would have known that the Matfridings were to blame, or why it would have mattered to him enough to mention. Secondly, none of Adalbert's other editorial interventions are written in the first person. Indeed, where he referred explicitly to Regino at the start of his continuation he did so in the third person – there was no attempt to pretend that the entire text was the work of a single author. Thirdly, the 899 entry also contains an implicit but clear reference to Richar's succession having been the result of hostile action: if the excised section in 892 had contained accusations against the Matfridings that Regino decided were too direct to remain, then why did he not give the 899 entry the same treatment? Taking all this into account, the most likely author of the sentence mentioning the Matfridings in 892 is also Regino. Had this line originated as a marginal note added to the autograph manuscript at the same time as the excisions were made, that would explain why it was not transmitted uniformly; such, at any rate, was the fate of other lines entered in the margins of the *Chronicle*'s earlier sections.[185]

From all this it follows that even more powerful forces than those represented by the Matfridings were connected with Regino's deposition. Recently, Erich Wisplinghoff has argued that the abbot's foes were internal rather than external, and that he lost his job thanks to incompetence.[186] Though far from impossible, the case depends on arguments from silence and on the presumption that regular ecclesiastical procedures would have operated during his deposition – hardly a necessary assumption in a time of such extreme political upheaval that the assassination of a king was being contemplated. In any case, as we have seen, the worlds of the monastic community and the political world overlapped: a man named Matfrid had recently held the senior rank of

185 Cf. 517–537, n. 267; 605–611, n. 340.
186 Wisplinghoff 1999: 439–63.

praepositus (prior), and the brotherhood contained other men with names characteristic of the same family.[187] Of whom, then, was the abbot afraid enough for him to remove their names from his text? In the opinion of many historians, Charles the Straightforward fits the bill best because of the *Chronicle*'s sympathetic treatment of his erstwhile rival Odo; others see Regino as a partisan of Reginar, and Zwentibald as his nemesis.[188] Still further reconstructions are possible – the text's allusiveness and innuendo invite the reader to make up his or her own mind.[189] That Regino's history of the world should boil down to a history of his own people and their rulers, and ultimately to an account of his own troubles is, however, wholly characteristic of Carolingian historiography.[190]

Conclusion

Medieval manuscripts were not so much published impersonally like modern books as written for the consumption of specific groups. Consequently, texts could be powerfully shaped by the perceived expectations of their audiences.[191] Imagining Regino's primary audience as the inner circle around Louis the Child gives us a good fit between the subject matter of the *Chronicle* and its presumed readers (or listeners), and reinforces our confidence in an interpretation of Book II as a work of thematic coherence composed by a master narrator in full control of his material. Yet at the same time we have encountered Regino as a furtive character, anxious about the contents and distribution of his work. The abbot had an awareness born of experience of the dangers of raising his head above the parapet, and his expressions of disquiet in the preface and the latter sections of the text remind us that he was an outsider, and as such could not completely control who read or heard his work, nor be sure that what he wrote would not cause offence to the wrong people. In the small world of the elite, history was not simply a neutral scholarly discipline but also a medium of political argument. The tension inherent in Regino's position simmered just below the

---

187 Tellenbach 1988; Wisplinghoff 1999: 446. The coup may nonetheless have been justified with accusations of poor leadership against Regino, as a now-lost letter seemingly suggested: Wattenbach, Levison and Löwe 1990: 903. The document naming Matfrid as *praepositus*, MUB 120, is dated to 886 by Kuchenbuch 1978: 25–6.

188 See for example von den Brincken 1957: 129; Hlawitschka 1975: 14–15; Haubrichs 1979: 74.

189 MacLean forthcoming offers a new hypothesis.

190 On personal detail as a feature of universal histories see McKitterick 2006: 14–19.

191 Innes 1998: 14.

Chronicle's surface, and should not be forgotten even as we admire his magisterial control of sources and narrative.

Regino's individuality – the particular criteria he used to gather and select sources, his crafting of overarching and episodic narratives, and his grinding of political axes – presents us with as many problems as answers. The remarkable gaps in his knowledge (not least the Louis the Pious- and Lothar I-shaped gaps) are hard to explain. Was he disingenuous about what he knew; did his reduced circumstances mean he had restricted library access; or was the Frankish elite's familiarity with texts like Thegan's biography of Louis, even in the place where it had been written, in fact more limited than historians have argued? Analogous doubts pertain to what he did know: it remains difficult to judge the extent to which Regino edited and reformulated what he learned from the *seniores*. We know that some of what he tells us is untrustworthy. His use of oral sources led to some fairly significant chronological mistakes, for instance his merging of two phases of Viking activity in the 853 entry. Even his own memory of comparatively recent events seems not to have been completely reliable, if that is how we understand his misdating of Archbishop Fulk's murder.

But we should not be over-sceptical about Regino's skill and value as a historian. Where he had written sources, we know that he checked them, clearest in his regular use of the lost Prüm annals. Where we can compare his information with that provided by other, often more contemporaneous, sources, he usually turns out to be a reliable informant, at least from about 870 onward. For a clear example we can cite the terms of surrender reportedly agreed between Adalgis and Louis II in the 871 entry, described in very similar terms by Hincmar of Rheims in the *Annals of St-Bertin*, a source which Regino did not know. Other verifiable reports are not hard to find: Charles the Younger's mutilation and Louis the German's accident at Flamersheim (both 870), the locust attack of 873, the death and unorthodox burial of Charles the Bald in 877 and the Battle of Thiméon in 879, to name a few, all closely resemble reports in other annalistic works. Rather than hypothesising a common written source for these stories, we can see them as fragments of a communal conversation in which members of the Frankish elite engaged each other. Although that conversation was fractured and its details often contested, the close relationship they had with their audiences imposed certain expectations on historians and restricted the extent to which they could invent or ignore. Regino belonged to an elite that was partly defined by its shared historical knowledge. His work is as eloquent a testimony to that elite's common cultural assumptions as is his career to the political conflicts that divided it.

Adalbert of Magdeburg

One important reason for the comparative lack of scholarly interest in Regino's *Chronicle* is that there are no modern Lotharingians to claim it as their own. By contrast, the much shorter continuation by Adalbert of Magdeburg (sometimes referred to as Adalbert of St-Maximin in Trier) enjoys a place in the canon of works relating to the history of the earliest German *Reich* and consequently has received considerably more attention. In view of this imbalance, what follows will attempt no more than to introduce the continuator and his work in the most general terms. Adalbert lived in a quite different political world to Regino's. Where the abbot of Prüm was haunted by the decline of one empire, Adalbert told the story of another's rise. Members of the Carolingian family staggered through the tenth century wielding intermittent and generally compromised royal power in west Francia, but in the east their line died with Louis the Child in 911. The kingship then passed to Conrad I (911–918), leading representative of the noble family known as the Conradines, whose rise to prominence under Arnulf and Louis was documented in the last part of Regino's *Chronicle*. As king, Conrad was forced to rely heavily on his connections and resources in his family's power bases (the Rhineland and Lotharingia), meaning that he was unable to extend his authority as effectively across the other regions of the kingdom.[192] In this respect he epitomised Regino's description of the post-888 kings as men equal in 'descent, authority and power ... none so outshone the others that the rest deigned to submit to his rule'. His reign exacerbated a tendency already discernible in the east Frankish kingdom for the operation of regional politics to take place with diminishing reference to the political centre, and for those regions or 'duchies' (Saxony, Bavaria, Swabia/Alemannia, Franconia and Lotharingia) to develop increasingly independent political traditions. Thus when Conrad's successor, Henry I of Saxony, was chosen by an election of regional leaders (*duces*, singular *dux* – 'dukes') after the king had died without heir, his prospects did not look much better. Writing in the late 960s, however, Adalbert knew that Henry, in 918 mere *dux* of Saxony, was the father of what would turn out to be a new line of great kings: the Ottonians.

192 Goetz 1980; Goetz 2006.

Henry I's success was based on his recognition of the regionalised nature of his kingdom. By establishing ties of *amicitia* ('friendship') with the leading nobles, he performed the role of king as a first among equals, a style best illustrated by Adalbert's entry for 931, where he is depicted travelling round the residences of the leading men to gain and keep their approval. The platform that Henry thus built for himself enabled him to have his son Otto recognised as his successor some years before his own death in 936. Otto I's long reign (936–973) cemented the dynasty's reputation and created the conditions for his own descendants to continue the line into the eleventh century. Two of Otto's achievements define his reputation in both tenth-century sources and modern historiography: his decisive victory over the Hungarians at the Lech in 955, and his conquest of Italy and coronation as emperor in Rome in 962. Still, as Adalbert's detailed accounts of the rebellions of 938/939 and 952/953 make clear, he did not have it all his own way, as rivals for the crown periodically emerged from within the dynasty as well as from the ranks of the ducal families.

The high Ottonian period of the mid-tenth century also witnessed a revival of historiography, exemplified by the work of the three major authors who wrote about the rise of the dynasty. The first of these was Liutprand of Cremona, whose *Antapodosis* ('Tit-for-Tat'), a history of European politics from 888 until around 950, and *Historia Ottonis* ('History of Otto'), a focused account of events surrounding Otto's imperial coronation, were both written in the earlier 960s. The second was Widukind of Corvey, whose *Rerum Gestarum Saxonicarum Libri Tres* ('Three Books of the Deeds of the Saxons') was written during the 960s and subsequently continued to 973. The third was Adalbert, who most probably wrote his continuation to the *Chronicle* in 967/968. These authors broke an east Frankish historiographical silence that had endured more or less intact since Regino stopped writing. The coincidence of their activity with Otto's imperial coronation is striking, though the extent to which the new histories filtered a dynastic ideology consciously developed at court is now rightly disputed.[193]

Adalbert, like Liutprand, was an actor on the highest political stage as well as a historian. Adalbert's family origins are not known with certainty.[194] Arguments that he was a Conradine are based on little more than the fact that his name was common in that family and that his history was concerned with their deeds. Neither fact makes the case

---

193 Körntgen 2001.
194 For what follows see Frase 1990: 12–14; Kölzer 1997; Zeller 2006.

compelling. There is slightly more substance to the idea that he was related to the founding family of the abbey of Borghorst, one of the leading noble kindreds of Saxony, though the main source for this association is very late.[195] His career began at the monastery of St-Maximin at Trier, a house with close connections to the Ottonian dynasty (and where, perhaps, he became familiar with the *Chronicle*). It was from Trier that he was plucked by Otto I's brother Archbishop William of Mainz and dispatched as missionary bishop to the Rus'. Although he offers few details other than recording his displeasure at this turn of events, Adalbert's reference to this mission in his 961 entry is important for establishing his authorship of the continuation. Although unsuccessful, his undertaking of missionary duties gained him favour at court, where he worked as a notary in the entourages of Otto I and his recently crowned heir Otto II. Adalbert is usually identified with the notary known as Liudolf A, who drafted several charters in the royal chancery (writing office) in the mid-950s, but Wolfgang Huschner has recently advanced compelling arguments that he was instead a different scribe, Liudolf H, active between 963 and 980. His frequent appearances in this capacity involved him in many of the high political events of the day, and placed him at the heart of both Ottos' entourages over a sustained period.[196] In 966 Adalbert became abbot of Wissembourg, a prominent royal monastery in Alsace, and performed well enough that two years later he was appointed first archbishop of the new see of Magdeburg, the establishment of which had been a pet project of Otto I. He held this post until his death in 981.[197]

It was at Wissembourg in 967/968 that Adalbert most probably composed his continuation of Regino's chronicle.[198] Although anonymous, its intermittent references to Wissembourg, St-Maximin and Adalbert's own career establish his authorship beyond reasonable doubt, not to mention the fact that its endpoint coincides with his move to Magdeburg. It is also clear that he carefully edited Regino's original text, updating the Latin to what he saw as more correct forms.[199] Because manuscripts survive which do not depend on Adalbert's edition of the *Chronicle*, we can be certain that he did not amend the text significantly.

195 Althoff 1978; cf. Karpf 1985; Nightingale 2001: 211–12, 224.
196 Huschner 2003: 658–85.
197 On Adalbert's career as archbishop see Claude 1972: 114–35; Kölzer 1997: 13–16.
198 The older view that the text was written in two drafts, the first ending in 939, is not supported by the manuscript evidence: Frase 1990: 24–43; Nass 1996: 262–3.
199 Prinz 1973.

He was, however, most likely the person responsible for inserting stories relating to the saintly heroes of Trier under 263–294, 295–309, 397–404 and 459–497, and for adding clarificatory glosses to passages in 853 and 892. Adalbert used few written sources for the continuation. The brief early entries were based on some minor annalistic works from Alemannia. Historians have also identified similarities between parts of Adalbert's work and parts of Liutprand's, principally the passages surrounding Conrad I's deathbed scene in 919 and the invitation for Otto to enter Italy in 960.[200] The comparisons reveal a general congruence that may be significant, though arguments for verbal similarity are not particularly convincing.[201] Philippe Buc's suggestion that Liutprand and Adalbert used a common source to construct their accounts of Conrad's death provides the best solution to the problem.[202] Other similarities are most likely to be interpreted in the context of both authors' membership of Otto's court circle: both were involved with the chancery and may have known each other as early as 958, while Liutprand is explicitly mentioned by Adalbert in his 965 entry.[203] More generally, both had access to, and helped to shape, the elite's collective historical memory.

Placed alongside the barbed humour of Liutprand's histories and the sweeping scope of Widukind's, Adalbert's text can seem dry and factual. Even the facts are not always reliable, since there are several clear chronological errors in the earlier part of the work. An older generation of historians, led by Martin Lintzel, therefore readily dismissed the continuation's value.[204] Recent evaluations have been kinder. Adalbert's chronological errors are hardly surprising given that he did not have many written sources to hand: we cannot judge by the standards of modern historiography his coverage of events some four decades before he wrote. We also need to appreciate that Adalbert, like Regino, was a master narrator, a teller of a story leading up to a known end – Otto II's visit to Rome at Christmas 967. The text thus presented dynastic history as a developmental process leading up to this point. The narrator's presence is reinforced by entries like that for 910: 'Count Gebhard died, leaving behind his two sons Udo and Hermann. They were still children, and later became famous and notable in Francia.' The

200 Lintzel 1933; Hauck 1974.
201 Frase 1990: 50–6.
202 Buc 2004.
203 Huschner 2003: 596–8, 682–5.
204 Lintzel 1961a.

mid-tenth-century audience was here openly invited to read contemporary significance into long-past events. Adalbert's description of the Ottonians' rise was thus knowing; he could offer detailed accounts of the rebellions against Otto himself, safe in the knowledge that the end of the story was understood by his audience. The memory of opposition to the ruling house could be neutralised by incorporating it into a narrative of perseverance and ultimate triumph, at the same time ensuring that past acts of faithlessness would not be forgotten. Otto I's allies were extolled by Adalbert, his actual and potential rivals (like Conrad I's brother Eberhard) undermined.[205] Above all, the continuation carefully presented the Saxon kings as peacemakers and their enemies and rivals as violators of peace.[206]

Unfortunately, Adalbert does not offer any explicit comments on his methodology or his understanding of his work. In its own way, however, this silence gives us an insight into his concept of history, for it suggests that the abbot of Wissembourg saw his work as a seamless continuation of Regino's, with his predecessor's stated aims and justifications taken to stand implicitly for the additions. His adoption of Regino's annalistic format and his conscientious editing of Books I and II imply that Adalbert envisaged the *Chronicle* plus the continuation as a single composite text (though without pretending that it was the work of a single author). At least once, in the 911 entry, he cross-referenced to events recounted by Regino which he assumed his readers had already read about. Adalbert's statement in the same entry that Conrad I succeeded 'because the royal line had failed' shows him picking up on one of the *Chronicle*'s main themes and extending its thread into his own text.[207] The implication was that Regino's story of dynastic decline was not yet finished: the Ottonians would rise where the Carolingians had fallen. Even more than a passing-on of dynastic status, Adalbert's use of ethnic terminology suggests that he was describing a wider process of *translatio imperii* in which the Saxon kings were characterised as true heirs to the destiny of the Franks. His appropriation of Regino's chronicle thus stood for the larger attempts of the Saxons to appropriate the Frankish past.[208]

Adalbert's impetus for writing was probably the hegemonial position achieved by Otto I in the 960s. Crowned emperor in Rome, confirmed

205 Zeller 2006: 143.
206 Hauck 1974; Frase 1990.
207 Airlie 2006a.
208 Zeller 2006.

as ruler of Italy and possessed of informal influence over west Francia after becoming stepfather-in-law to its young king in 965, Otto could justifiably be portrayed as a ruler with a genuinely imperial sphere of influence. Adalbert's carefully calibrated implications of Ottonian superiority over powerful figures south of the Alps and west of the Rhine should be interpreted in this light.[209] Such status deserved a historical underpinning, with its place fixed in the course of Christian history. It may, however, be no accident that the culmination of this history was the visit to Rome of Otto II, into whose entourage the abbot's career had intermittently taken him. Implicitly, Otto's inheritance of his father's hegemony was confirmed. Was Otto II himself perhaps part of the audience envisaged for the extended version of the *Chronicle*? He would certainly have been flattered by the place reserved for him in Adalbert's vision of historical development. But flattery was not the only aim. Otto was still a pliable youth, 12 or 13 years old at the time of writing. Adalbert may have thought that, like Louis the Child before him, Otto was ready to be instructed and edified by what history had to teach kings about the responsibilities of power.

On this translation

All the translations in this book are based on the standard edition of the *Chronicle* and its continuation by Friedrich Kurze (1890). Like many nineteenth-century editions, this is now regarded as in need of revision. Serious doubts about Kurze's method were raised by Wolf-Rüdiger Schleidgen in a major study published in 1977. Two points in particular gave cause for concern. First, Kurze consulted only 7 of the 30 known manuscripts in person; and secondly, his criteria for establishing relationships between manuscripts were not sound.[210] Schleidgen demonstrated that Kurze's grouping of the manuscripts into two transmission groups, A and B, was too simplistic, although the assumption that the A texts and not the B were edited by Adalbert was later vindicated by the linguistic analysis of Otto Prinz and accepted by Schleidgen.[211] While many of the surviving manuscripts are early (22 date from the tenth to twelfth centuries), at least one generation of lost manuscripts lies between the earliest witnesses and the archetype. This means that the B version, although not adapted by Adalbert, may

209 Zeller 2006: 147–50.
210 Schleidgen 1977: 7–13; Frase 1990: 19–43.
211 Prinz 1973.

INTRODUCTION   59

also have been altered and edited in some way after it left Regino's desk. Barring the unlikely possibility that the autograph ever turns up, only a rigorous linguistic/stylistic comparison of all the manuscripts along the lines prescribed by Schleidgen will allow us to be confident that we are close to the exact form of Regino's original text.[212] Consequently, this translation and the introductory discussion based on it must be seen (like all historical research) as provisional.

All that said, we have to take some reassurance from Schleidgen's ultimate conclusion that despite the methodological problems, Kurze's efforts resulted in a basically sound text – its essential trustworthiness was presumably one reason why Schleidgen did not follow up his book with a new edition of his own.[213] Only a few passages are seriously affected by the editorial problems, in particular 892, as discussed earlier, and the lists of martyrs in the first part of Book I, whose details vary considerably between manuscripts. A modern critical re-edition remains desirable, but the likelihood is that the resultant text would be substantially similar to Kurze's. At the same time, such a re-edition would offer significant insights into the reception of the *Chronicle*, an interesting topic in its own right. As well as pointing out the bluntness of Kurze's division of the manuscripts into two groups, Schleidgen showed that the transmission of the text could best be understood in geographical terms, with groups of related manuscripts identified in the scriptoria of Lotharingia, Alemannia and Bavaria/Austria.[214] His preliminary conclusion, that knowledge of the text spread outward through the political and monastic networks articulated by the Gorze reform, would undoubtedly be worth investigating further.[215] Regino's work was excerpted and repackaged by several monastic compilers after Adalbert, and analysis of the ways in which this was done would contribute insights into perceptions of history and identity in the earlier Middle Ages more broadly.

This is the first English translation of the *Chronicle* and its continuation, other than short extracts included in anthologies.[216] Some of the texts used and excerpted by Regino, especially in Book I, have previously appeared in English, and to assist readers the footnotes duly refer to those translations. Although these were invaluable aids and there

212 Schleidgen 1977: 88–129.
213 Schleidgen 1977: 156.
214 Schleidgen 1977: 20–87.
215 Schleidgen 1977: 130–54.
216 Rau 1960 gives a German translation of Book II.

will be unavoidable similarities, the translations provided here are in all cases my own. For biblical citations I have generally preferred the New International Version. Some words whose precise meaning may be controversial (or whose standard translations are anachronistic) have been left in the Latin or (where context permits) rendered with the most neutral translation possible. These include *dux/duces* ('duke', 'leader'), *ducatus* ('command', 'duchy', 'political unit ruled by a *dux*'), *villa* ('village', 'estate', 'settlement') and *castrum* ('castle', 'stronghold'). On the whole I have tried to give a readable approximation of the original text rather than attempting to render the Latin more freely into flowing English, so to some extent the awkwardness of the prose is a conscious choice – I wanted to reproduce what Regino and Adalbert wrote, not to pre-empt readers' interpretations of what they meant. Nonetheless, translation involves interpretation and this, to say nothing of the mistakes that will inevitably remain, should deter readers from laying too much weight on any particular passage without checking the Latin original as well.

Nor can the footnotes stand in for the full critical apparatus required of a scholarly edition. Instead, they reflect the interests, knowledge, prejudices and limitations of the translator. Generally speaking, the footnotes to Book I and the non-original sections of Book II are intended to clarify the ways in which Regino used and manipulated his sources, indicating what was left out as well as what was included. Those to the independent sections of Book II and the continuation are more concerned with comparing the information given to that in other contemporary histories, identifying the people mentioned, and giving a sense of the works' value as primary sources for the ninth and early tenth centuries. Page numbers in citations of sources usually refer to Latin editions except where indicated by the list of abbreviations and the bibliography, including the three cases where a Manchester Medieval Sources translation is available (*AB*, *AF* and Thietmar, *Chronicon*). The identification of sources in most cases derives from Kurze, whose edition incorporated the work of previous historians who had combed the text. Although other sources used by Regino and Adalbert could surely be detected, we can be confident that the great majority have been found. In all aspects of its approach to the texts and authors with which it is concerned, a book like this can never be regarded as definitive; rather, it should be read as an open invitation to further research on Regino, Adalbert and Carolingian historiography more generally.

REGINO OF PRÜM'S *CHRONICLE*
BOOK I

HERE BEGINS THE PREFACE TO THE FOLLOWING WORK

To the lord Bishop Adalbero,[1] a man of the highest abilities distinguished in manifold ways through the pursuit of every type of philosophy, Regino, although the lowest of Christ's worshippers, in all things most devoted to your greatness, commits the faithful tributes of his prayers. I have entrusted to your singular discretion for examination the chronicle which I have compiled from works about our own times and those of our forefathers, so that it may be either approved or condemned by your perspicacious judgement. I have divided it into two little books, starting with the first year of the Lord's incarnation and completing the work thus begun as far as the present year, which is calculated as the 908th since the aforementioned incarnation of the Lord.[2] For it seemed to me unworthy that, since the historians of the Hebrews, Greeks, Romans and other peoples have transmitted to our knowledge through their writings the deeds done in their times, there should be such an unbroken silence concerning our own times, even though they are much more recent,[3] as if in our days human activity had ceased, or perhaps people had done nothing worthy of memory or, if deeds worth remembering have been carried out, nobody suitable could be found to commit them to writing because the scribes have slipped into inactivity through negligence.[4] So, because of this I have not suffered the times of our fathers and ourselves to pass by completely untouched, but have taken the trouble to record a few of the many things [I could have done]; and, when I come to the present day, I have restrained my pen so as not to offend certain people who are still alive: I leave

---

1 Bishop of Augsburg (887–910).
2 However, the text's last annal is that for 906. For discussion of the discrepancy see MacLean forthcoming.
3 The Latin is 'de nostris quamquam longe inferioribus temporibus': 'inferior' here could also imply the literal inferiority of the present as opposed to the glorious Christian past.
4 Complaints about learning and writing having declined from past ages are conventional in early medieval texts.

posterity to pursue these matters more fully.[5] Accept, therefore, this small present with goodwill equal to the devotion with which it is sent to you by my humble self. In conclusion I implore the reader that if he likes these words of ours, of whatever sort they may be, and wants to have them copied, he should in no way leave out this little preface, but rather should have it written out right at the front of the little book. May heavenly providence see it fitting long to preserve unharmed the glory of your greatness for the good of the many people that you will benefit.

HERE ENDS THE PREFACE

HERE BEGINS THE LITTLE BOOK ON THE TIMES OF THE LORD'S INCARNATION

1–15[6]

In the 42nd year of the reign of Caesar Octavian [Augustus], Jesus Christ the son of God was born.[7] That same night he was proclaimed by the angels and visited by the shepherds.[8] On the 8th day he was circumcised[9] and on the 13th day he was adored by the magi, who were led by a star, and praised with mystical gifts.[10] On the 40th day when he was led into the temple to be offered by his parents he was received by Simeon and recognised by Anna.[11] Afterward he was taken away into Egypt, where he remained until the death of Herod.[12]

In the year of the Lord's incarnation 2, Herod sent [soldiers] and ordered that in Bethlehem and all its surrounding areas innocent boys should have their throats cut.[13] Then he turned to arms and killed many of his family members. He killed his beloved wife Mariamne and

---

5 A reference to Regino's descriptions of his own political misfortunes during the 890s: the wording is almost identical to a key passage in the annal for 892.

6 Actually 1–14.

7 Bede, *DTR* 66: 494–5 (Wallis 2004: 194–5), who says: 'Jesus Christ, the son of God, hallowed the sixth age of the world by his coming.'

8 Luke 2: 8–20.

9 Luke 2: 21.

10 Matthew 2: 1–11; the reference to 13 days is not from this source: see Ermisch 1872: 44.

11 Luke 2: 22–38.

12 Matthew 2: 13–15.

13 Matthew 2: 16. Regino seems to have derived the date (AD 2) from Matthew's statement that Herod's order applied to all boys aged 2 and under.

BOOK I

he ordered his sons by her, Aristobulus and Alexander, strangled in Samaria.[14] Finally he put to the sword his son by Dosis, Antipater, who been the inciter of all these evil things.[15] After that he suffered a miserable death in the 6th year of the Lord's incarnation, which was the 36th of his own reign.[16]

In the year of the Lord's incarnation 7, Herod's son Archelaus ruled in Judea.[17] The Lord led Jesus back from Egypt and because of fear of the aforementioned king he turned away to the town of Nazareth in Galilee, where he lived until the time of his baptism.[18] In the 12th year of his life Jesus went up to Jerusalem and there after three days his parents found him in the temple, sitting among the teachers.[19]

In the year of the Lord's incarnation 15 Archelaus was denounced by the Jews before Augustus, and he was exiled to Vienne, a city in Gaul. The kingdom of the Jews was divided among his four brothers, Herod, Antipater, Lysania and Philip.[20] Caesar Augustus died after ruling the empire for 56 years and 6 months.[21]

16–38[22]

[Beginning] in the year of the Lord's incarnation 16, Tiberius began to reign; he reigned for 23 years.[23]

14 Bede, *DTR*, c. 66: 494 (Wallis 2004: 194). Again, Regino is not faithful to his source's chronology or wording: Bede implies this happened before Christ's birth, and states that Herod killed his sons personally.
15 Bede, *DTR*, c. 66: 494 (Wallis 2004: 194) only mentions that Antipater was Herod's son by Dosis, whom he discarded before marrying Mariamne, the great-niece of Herod's predecessor.
16 Regino calculated AD 6 from Bede's statements that Herod came to power in the eleventh year of Augustus, and that Christ was born in the forty-second: Bede, *DTR*, c. 66: 494–5 (Wallis 2004: 194–5).
17 Regino's decision that the date was 7 reveals that he calculated the reigns of rulers from the year following the deaths of their predecessors rather than, as was usually correct, from the same year.
18 Bede, *DTR*, c. 66: 495 (Wallis 2004: 195) mentions Archelaus's succession, but this could also have been derived, as was the rest of the passage, from Matthew 2: 19–23.
19 Luke 2: 41–2, 46.
20 Bede, *DTR*, c. 66: 495 (Wallis 2004: 195). The third brother was called Lysias: Regino's copy of Bede was evidently miscopied here.
21 Bede, *DTR*, c. 66: 494 (Wallis 2004: 194). Regino places this in AD 15 based on Bede's statement that Archelaus reigned for 9 years.
22 Actually 14–37.
23 Bede, *DTR*, c. 66: 495 (Wallis 2004: 196).

In the year of the Lord's incarnation 27, Pilate was sent by Tiberius to be procurator of Judea.[24]

In the year of the Lord's incarnation 30, that is the 15th of Tiberius, John went through the Jordan area preaching the baptism of repentance for the remission of sins and he baptised many people.[25] Among those he dipped in the waters of the Jordan was the redeemer of the world himself, who washed away the sins of everyone. After the baptism, the Lord withdrew to the desert and fasted for 40 days. After the fast, having defeated his assailant and in the power of the Spirit, he entered Galilee, gathered the apostles, proclaimed the kingdom of God and performed many signs and miracles.[26]

In the year of the Lord's incarnation 32, John the Baptist was beheaded in prison on the orders of Herod thanks to the trickery of Herodias.[27]

In the year of the Lord's incarnation 33, that is the 18th of Tiberius, the Lord redeemed the world by his Passion.[28] On the 40th day after his resurrection he ascended to heaven, and on the 50th he sent the consoling Spirit, and Mathias was made an apostle in the place of Judas.[29] The Lord's brother James was consecrated as bishop of Jerusalem, 7 deacons were ordained and Stephen was stoned.[30]

In the year of the Lord's incarnation 34, according to the Latins, who begin to calculate the year from January, Paul was called on from heaven by Christ while he was on his way to Damascus.[31] According to the Hebrews, who hold that the year begins in March, this happened in the 11th month of the same year as the Lord's suffering, that is 25 January.[32]

---

24 Bede, *DTR*, c. 66: 495 (Wallis 2004: 196) says that took place in the twelfth year of Tiberius.
25 Luke 3: 1–6.
26 Luke 4: 1–14 and passim.
27 Matthew 14: 3–12; Mark 6: 17–29; Luke 3: 19–20; Ado, *Martyrologium*: 293. From these sources Regino knew that this took place a year before Jesus's death.
28 Bede, *DTR*, c. 66: 496 (Wallis 2004: 196).
29 Cf. Acts 1: 6–11, 15–26.
30 Bede, *DTR*, c. 66: 496 (Wallis 2004: 196).
31 Acts 9: 1–8.
32 Paul's conversion was celebrated on this date: eg. Ado, *Martyrologium*: 70.

BOOK I

39–44[33]

[Beginning] in the year of the Lord's Incarnation 39, Gaius [Caligula] ruled for 4 years, 10 months and 8 days.[34] If, therefore, we add these 10 months to the 6 left over from the 16 years of Octavian, that makes 16 months.[35] Subtracting 4 from that leaves a full year, which it seems right to insert here.[36] Herod Agrippa was set up to rule over the Jewish people.[37]

In the year of the Lord's incarnation 44, Herod the tetrarch died destitute with Herodias in Spain. Pilate, who had passed the verdict of death in the Passion of the Lord, committed suicide.[38]

45–58[39]

[Beginning] in the year of the Lord's incarnation 45, Claudius reigned for 13 years, 7 months and 28 days.[40] We therefore add these 7 months to the 4 which are left over from earlier, making 11; and the 8 days from earlier to these 28, making 36. That makes a year and 6 days, which it seems fitting should be added to this period.[41]

In the year of the Lord's incarnation 47, John's brother James was beheaded by Herod and Peter was put in prison; that same Herod was struck down by an angel.[42] The Holy Spirit addressed the disciples in Antioch, saying: 'Set apart for me Paul and Barnabas', etc.[43] Herod's son

---

33 Actually 37–41.
34 Bede, *DTR*, c. 66: 496 (Wallis 2004: 197) says he ruled for 3 years, not 4.
35 See above, s.a. 1–15.
36 In other words, bringing the total up to 44 rather than 43. Regino here and at various other points adds extra months to a chronology that is already advancing too fast thanks to his calculation of all reigns as if they started in January and finished in December.
37 Bede, *DTR*, c. 66: 496 (Wallis 2004: 197).
38 Bede, *DTR*, c. 66: 496–7 (Wallis 2004: 197) says nothing about the chronology of these events, so it is not immediately clear why Regino placed them in the final year of Gaius's rule.
39 Actually 41–54.
40 Bede, *DTR*, c. 66: 497 (Wallis 2004: 197).
41 Regino's rudimentary approach to the lengths of years, months and reigns is again apparent.
42 Acts 12: 1–4, 20–3; Bede, *DTR*, c. 66: 496 (Wallis 2004: 197).
43 Acts 13: 1–2. The full quote reads 'Set apart for me Barnabas and Saul for the work to which I have called them.' The 'etc.' must say something about Regino's perception of his audience's knowledge.

Agrippa ruled in Judea until the Jews were overthrown.[44]

In the year of the Lord's incarnation 48, that is the 14th of the Passion and the 4th of Claudius, Paul and Barnabas went up to Jerusalem. Paul himself wrote about his visit in a letter to the Galatians: 'Then after 14 years I went up to Jerusalem with Barnabas, taking Titus as well, and with them', that is with the apostles, 'I spread the gospel that I had preached to the gentiles.'[45] Therefore in the 14th year after the Lord's Passion Paul set out with the agreement of James, Cephas and John to teach and be apostle to the gentiles.[46] Here we can review the numbers of years that Paul records. We know that the apostles Peter and Paul were killed in the 38th year after the Lord's Passion, that is the last year of Nero's reign, and that the blessed Peter sat on the episcopal throne of Rome for 25 years.[47] However, 25 plus 14 comes to 39, not 38. It therefore follows, we believe, that the blessed Peter came to Rome in the same year, the 14th after the Lord's Passion, that Paul said he went to Jerusalem, that is the 4th year of Claudius. Equally, it would not be wrong to suppose that Paul was tested to come to the faith in the same year as the Lord died.[48]

In the same year there was a very serious famine, which is mentioned by Luke, and Claudius entered Britain.[49]

In the year of the Lord's incarnation 53, Claudius expelled the troublemaking Jews from Rome.[50]

---

44 Bede, *DTR*, c. 66: 496 (Wallis 2004: 197) states that Herod Agrippa was killed by the angel and succeeded by Agrippa in the 4th year of Claudius, and that the overthrow of the Jews happened after 26 years of Agrippa: both statements should have led Regino to date these events in AD 48 according to his own internal chronology, since he places the latter event in 74. This could be a simple error on Regino's part. However, it is more likely that he deliberately ignored Bede's statements in order to make his chronology fit with the calculations described in the next annal: 72 (Peter's death in the last year of Nero) – 25 (length of Peter's pontificate) = 47. This exemplifies Regino's critical engagement with his sources.

45 Galatians 2: 1–2.

46 Galatians 2: 7–9.

47 Bede, *DTR*, c. 66: 497 (Wallis 2004: 197); *LP* (Davis 2000: 1–2).

48 Ermisch 1872 saw this passage as a prime example of Regino's befuddlement. However, Sonntag 1987: 111–14 rightly recognises that the historian here made an imaginative and valiant attempt to reconcile the information he found in Bede, the *Liber Pontificalis* and the Bible. The absolute AD chronology was still, of course, inaccurate. See also above, n. 44.

49 Bede, *DTR*, c. 66: 497 (Wallis 2004: 198) puts these events in the fourth year of Claudius.

50 Bede, *DTR*, c. 66: 497 (Wallis 2004: 198) has this in Claudius' ninth year (hence Regino's calculation of AD 53).

BOOK I   67

59–72[51]

[Beginning] in the year of the Lord's incarnation 59, Nero reigned for 13 years, 7 months and 28 days.[52]

In the year of the Lord's incarnation 61, Festus succeeded Felix as procurator and Paul was sent to Rome in chains. This was the second year of Nero's rule.[53]

In the year of the Lord's incarnation 63 the Lord's brother James was stoned to death by the Jews. Albinus succeeded Festus in the governorship of Judea, and Florus succeeded Albinus.[54]

In the year of the Lord's incarnation 70 the Master of the Soldiers Vespasian was sent with an army into Judea.[55]

In the year of the Lord's incarnation 72 Peter was crucified in Rome and Paul was beheaded.[56] The following were crowned as martyrs under the Neronian persecution: Processus and Martinianus of Rome; the 47 who were baptised by the blessed Peter and were thrust back into the custody of Mamurtinus; Torpes, Marcellus and Apuleius; the evangelist Mark of Alexandria suffered in Nero's 8th year; Nazarius and Celsus of Milan; Protasius and Gervasius under the prefect Anulinus; at Nuceria Felix with Constantia; Bishop Hermagoras at Aquileia; and the deacon Fortunatus.[57]

73–82[58]

[Beginning] in the year of the Lord's incarnation 73, Vespasian ruled for 9 years, 11 months and 22 days.[59] Adding these 11 months to Nero's 7 makes 18; and these 22 days to his 28 makes 50. That makes one year,

51 Actually 54–68.
52 Bede, *DTR*, c. 66: 497 (Wallis 2004: 198).
53 Bede, *DTR*, c. 66: 497 (Wallis 2004: 198). The second year of Nero should have been AD 60 in Regino's scheme. Bede does not specify that Paul was sent to Rome in that year.
54 Bede, *DTR*, c. 66: 497–8 (Wallis 2004: 198). According to Bede, James was killed in Nero's seventh year: in Regino's chronology, this should be AD 65, not 63.
55 Bede, *DTR*, c. 66: 497–8 (Wallis 2004: 198). It is not clear why Regino thought this was AD 70; possibly because it comes almost at the end of Bede's entry on Nero.
56 Bede, *DTR*, c. 66: 498 (Wallis 2004: 198). The detail that Paul was beheaded does not come from Bede.
57 All these martyrs were from Ado, *Martyrologium*.
58 Actually 69–79.
59 Bede, *DTR*, c. 66: 498 (Wallis 2004: 199).

7 months and 20 days: I will insert this year here.⁶⁰

In the year of the Lord's incarnation 74 the kingdom of Judea was overthrown and the temple destroyed by [Vespasian's son] Titus.⁶¹ It was during his reign that Bishop Apollinaris, sent to Ravenna by the blessed Peter, was martyred.⁶²

83–4⁶³

[Beginning] in the year of the Lord's incarnation 83, Titus reigned for 2 years and 2 months.⁶⁴

85–90⁶⁵

[Beginning] in the year of the Lord's incarnation 85, Domitian ruled for 15 years and 5 months.⁶⁶ These 5 months added to Vespasian's 7 completes a year, which we will insert here.⁶⁷

In these times the Apostle John was placed in a pot of boiling oil before the Latin Gate of Rome and then banished to the island of Patmos, where he wrote the Apocalypse.⁶⁸ Flavia Domitilla was exiled to the island of Patmos.⁶⁹ Pope Anacletus, the third after Peter, was crowned with martyrdom.⁷⁰

---

60 More evidence of Regino's wayward arithmetic: only a few days were needed to bring Vespasian up to 10, not a whole year. This method of adding extra years shows that Regino's aim was less to correlate Roman history with correct AD dates than to create a relative chronology that would fit the gap between the birth of Christ and 741, when he knew Charles Martel had died: see above, Introduction, pp. 21–2.

61 Bede, *DTR*, c. 66: 498 (Wallis 2004: 199) says that this happened in Vespasian's second year.

62 Ado, *Martyrologium*: 231–3.

63 Actually 79–81.

64 Bede, *DTR*, c. 66: 498 (Wallis 2004: 199).

65 Actually 81–96.

66 Bede, *DTR*, c. 66: 498 (Wallis 2004: 199). Wallis has 16 years.

67 A mistake: 16 years should have given Regino a span of 85–100; previously ahead of the true chronology, Regino now slips behind it.

68 Ado, *Martyrologium*: 149; Bede, *DTR*, c. 66: 499 (Wallis 2004: 200). Regino's wording and references to Rome suggest his primary source here was Ado, who added detail to the information he got from Bede.

69 Bede, *DTR*, c. 66: 499 (Wallis 2004: 200).

70 *Liber Pontificalis* (Davis 2000: 2). Anacletus was actually the second pope after Peter, as was also made clear by Ado, *Martyrologium*: 134.

90[71]

[Beginning] in the year of the Lord's incarnation 90, Nerva reigned for 1 year, 4 months and 8 days.[72]

The Apostle John was called back from exile and wrote his gospel at Ephesus.[73]

In these times there suffered at Rome Eutyches, Victorinus and Maro, and at the town of Amiterna Bishop Victorinus the brother of Severinus.[74]

91–110[75]

[Beginning] in the year of the Lord's incarnation 91, Trajan reigned for 19 years, 6 months and 15 days.[76] If these 6 months are added to Titus' 2 and Nerva's 4, we get a year which fits in here, leaving over the 28 days which were noted above.[77]

In the year of the Lord's incarnation 101, John the apostle came to rest at Ephesus.[78]

In the time of Trajan these were crowned as martyrs: Clemens the pope of Rome; Alexander, the 4th pope after Peter; Quirinus and his daughter Balbina; Sulpicius and Servilianus; the virgins Domitilla and Seraphia; Nereus and Achilleus; Ignatius bishop of Antioch; Simeon bishop of Jerusalem and son of Cleophas; Bishop Phocas in Pontus.[79]

---

71 Actually 96–98.
72 Bede, *DTR*, c. 66: 499 (Wallis 2004: 200). Note that in counting 90 as both the last year of Domitian and the first of Nerva Regino breaks his own system.
73 Bede, *DTR*, c. 66: 499 (Wallis 2004: 200).
74 Ado, *Martyrologium*: 124–5, 299–300. The first three named saints were associated with Flavia Domitilla, mentioned in the previous entry.
75 Actually 98–117.
76 Bede, *DTR*, c. 66: 499 (Wallis 2004: 200).
77 Thus Regino gives Trajan 20 full years instead of 19; the 28 days are 20 from Vespasian and 8 from Nerva.
78 Bede, *DTR*, c. 66: 499 (Wallis 2004: 200) says this was the 68th year after the Passion: 33 + 68 = 101.
79 Bede, *DTR* c. 66: 499 (Wallis 2004: 200) only lists the martyrdoms of Simeon, Ignatius and Alexander. The others are from Ado, *Martyrologium*, with some anomalies (for instance Ado says that Seraphia was martyred under Hadrian, not Trajan).

111–122[80]

[Beginning] in the year of the Lord's incarnation 111, Hadrian reigned for 11 years.[81]

In these times suffered: Pope Sistus of Rome; Getulius, Sabina and the virgin Seraphia; at the city of Messina in Apulia, Bishop Eleutherius with his mother Anthea; Quadratus and Aristides, who were held to be famous men, at Athens; Bishop Dionysius the Areopagite; Simphorosa with her 7 sons at Tiburtina, a town in Italy.[82]

123–124[83]

[Beginning] in the year of the Lord's incarnation 123, Antoninus (nicknamed Pius) ruled with his sons [Marcus] Aurelius and Lucius [Commodus] for 22 years and 3 months.[84] Justin was distinguished in philosophy. Under Bishop Pius [of Rome], Hermes wrote a book called The Shepherd.[85]

125–143[86]

[Beginning] in the year of the Lord's incarnation 125, Marcus Antoninus Verus [Marcus Aurelius] ruled with his brother Lucius Aurelius Commodus for 19 years and 1 month.[87]

In these times and those mentioned above the following were martyred: Pope Anicetus of Rome, Pope Victor, Simetrius the priest, Felicitas with 7 sons; 50 martyrs under the judge Agricola in Sebastia in Armenia minor; Concordius at Spoleto; Bishop Polycarp at Smyrna, who was a disciple of St John, likewise Germanicus and Pionius; Alexander and Gaius at Apamia; Bishop Philippus at Cortina in Crete; Bishop Carpus

---

80   Actually 117–138.

81   There are two mistakes here: 111–122 is, on Regino's way of working, 12 years; and in any case Bede, *DTR*, 66: 500 (Wallis 2004: 201) states 21. Either Regino or the scribe of the manuscript he was using misread XXI for XI.

82   Ado, *Martyrologium*. Seraphia, repeated from Trajan's reign, is this time in her correct place. The story of Quadratus and Aristides influencing Hadrian to be moderate in his prosecution of Christians is in Bede, *DTR* c. 66: 500 (Wallis 2004: 201), and so provided Regino's cue for placing these martyrs.

83   Actually 138–161.

84   This entry should thus have spanned 123–144: this must have been a simple slip of Regino's pen.

85   All this is from Bede, *DTR* c. 66: 500 (Wallis 2004: 202).

86   Actually 161–180.

87   Bede, *DTR* c. 66: 501 (Wallis 2004: 202).

BOOK I   71

at the town of Pergamon in Asia; the deacon Papirius and Justin the philosopher; Bishop Irenaeus with many others at Lyon in Gaul; Bishop Photinus at his own town and Blandina with 48 others; Epipodius and Alexander; Victor and Corona in Syria; Faustus of Milan; Marcellus in Cabillone; likewise in the territory of Cabillone, in the fortress of Trenortio, Valerian; Ptolomeus and Lucius at Alexandria.[88]

144–156[89]

[Beginning] in the year of the Lord's incarnation 144, Lucius Antoninus Commodus ruled for 13 years after the death of his father Antoninus Verus.[90] We listed above the many people who suffered in these times. However, we were not able to place these in a definite order according to the reigns of emperors because in certain passions of the saints named above the name of the emperor is recorded confusingly. Thus when something is said to have been done under Antoninus, I do not know whether this happened under Pius, Verus or Commodus. When something is said to have happened in the reign of Lucius it is ambiguous whether this took place under Aurelius, Antoninus or Commodus. Nonetheless they report that around this time Irenaeus the bishop of Lyon was martyred.[91]

157[92]

[Beginning] in the year of the Lord's incarnation 157, Aelius Pertinax ruled for 6 months.[93]

158–169[94]

[Beginning] in the year of the Lord's incarnation 158, Severus Pertinax ruled for 17 years.[95] Clement, a priest of the Church of Alexandria, and

88 Regino's information was from Ado, *Martyrologium*.
89 Actually 180–193.
90 Bede, *DTR* c. 66: 501 (Wallis 2004: 203).
91 This digression illuminates Regino's method of trying to fit Ado's martyrs into Bede's chronology. He knew from Bede *DTR* c. 66: 501 (Wallis 2004: 203) that Irenaeus lived in the time of Lucius Antoninus Commodus (thus *c.*144–156 in his own reckoning) but could not fix his martyrdom in time from Ado. However, Ado did tell him which martyrs died around the same time as Irenaeus.
92 Actually 193.
93 Bede, *DTR* c. 66: 502 (Wallis 2004: 203).
94 Actually 193–211.
95 Thus the span should have been 158–174.

the philosopher Parthenus were famous. Narcissus bishop of Jerusalem and Theophilus of Caesarea were notable at this time. Leonides the father of Origen was crowned with martyrdom, and Perpetua and Felicitas were thrown to the beasts at Carthage.[96]

170[97]

[Beginning] in the year of the Lord 170, Antoninus, surnamed Caracalla, the son of Severus, reigned for 7 years.[98]

171[99]

[Beginning] in the year of the Lord's incarnation 171, Macrinus reigned for one year.[100]

172–175[101]

[Beginning] in the year of the Lord's incarnation 172, Marcus Aurelius Antoninus reigned for 4 years.[102]

176–188[103]

[Beginning] in the year of the Lord's incarnation 176, Aurelius Alexander reigned for 13 years. Origen was famous throughout the whole world.[104]

About this time these were crowned as martyrs: Calixtus the pope of Rome; Pope Urban; the virgin Cecilia, Tiburtius and Valerianus; the priest Calepodius; the priest Asterius; the consul Palmatius with his wife and children and the senator Simplicius.[105]

---

96 Bede, *DTR* c. 66 (Wallis 2004: 204).
97 Actually 211–217.
98 Thus the span should have been 170–176. The slip may be explained by the fact that Bede lists the dates of emperors according to the final year of their reigns rather than, as Regino and most other annalists did it, according to the first. Because the subsequent reign *was* only one year, a brief mental slip into the latter mode would have made Regino list the timespan as one year rather than seven.
99 Actually 217.
100 Bede, *DTR* c. 66: 503 (Wallis 2004: 205).
101 Actually 218–222.
102 Bede, *DTR* c. 66: 503 (Wallis 2004: 205).
103 Actually 222–235.
104 Bede, *DTR* c. 66: 503 (Wallis 2004: 206).
105 Ado, *Martyrologium*; Bede only mentions Urban here.

BOOK I   73

189–191[106]

[Beginning] in the year of the Lord's incarnation 189 Maximinus reigned for 3 years.[107] At this time the following were crowned as martyrs: Pope Antheros of Rome; Pope Pontianus; the priests Panphilus and Maximus of Caesarea in Palestine.[108]

192–197[109]

[Beginning] in the year of the Lord's incarnation 192, Gordian reigned for 6 years. In Caesarea in Palestine, Origen initiated the brothers Theodore (known as Gregory) and Athenodorus into divine philosophy.[110]

198–203[111]

[Beginning] in the year of the Lord's incarnation 198, Philip ruled with his son Philip for 6 years. He was the first of all emperors to be a Christian.[112]

204–205[113]

[Beginning] in the year of the Lord's incarnation 204, Decius ruled for 1 year and 3 months.[114] Adding these 3 months to the 3 from Antoninus Pius, 1 from Marcus Antoninus and 6 from Aelius Pertinax makes a year, which is inserted here. This leaves the 1 month and 28 days listed earlier.[115]

At this time the following were crowned with martyrdom: Fabianus the pope of Rome; Pope Sixtus; the deacons Laurentius, Felicissimus and Agapetus; Abdon and Sennes; Ypolitus and Concordia; Irenaeus and

---

106 Actually 235–238.
107 Bede, *DTR* c. 66: 504 (Wallis 2004: 206).
108 Ado, *Martyrologium*; Bede mentions the two popes.
109 Actually 238–244.
110 Bede, *DTR* c. 66: 504 (Wallis 2004: 206).
111 Actually 244–249.
112 Bede, *DTR* c. 66: 504 (Wallis 2004: 206).
113 Actually 249–251.
114 Bede, *DTR* c. 66: 504 (Wallis 2004: 207).
115 Regino seems to have omitted 15 days from Trajan's reign.

Abundius; Pope Cornelius; the virgin Victoria; Miniates; Bishop Babilas of Antioch; Leacus, Tirsus and Gallinecus in the city of Apollonia; Alexander, bishop of Jerusalem; Nazanzo Trypho; in the city of Thinius in Egypt, Bishop Phileas and the tribune Philoromus together with many others; in the city of Catania in Sicily, the virgin Agatha; in Persia Polocronius bishop of Babylon and Ctesiphon; Bishop Pergen Nestor of Panphilia; in the city of Cordoba, the priest Parmenius with his associates; at Circensem Colonia, Marianus and James; in Tyre, Anatolia and Audax; in Africa, Nemesianus and Felix, Rogatianus the priest and Felicissimus with many others; Bishop Asclepiades of Antioch; Agatho and Serapion of Alexandria; Arsenius and Dioscorus with their followers.[116]

206–208[117]

[Beginning] in the year of the Lord's incarnation 206, Gallus reigned with his son Volusian for 2 years and 4 months. Origen the teacher died and was buried at Tyre.[118]

209–223[119]

[Beginning] in the year of the Lord's incarnation 209, Valerian ruled with [his son] Gallienus for 15 years.[120]

In these times were crowned as martyrs: Pope Stephen of Rome; the virgin Eugenia; Jovinus and Basileus; Pope Lucius; the virgins Basilla, Rufina and Secunda; Tertullian, Protinus and Jacintus; Pope Sixtus; Valerian; Nemesius; Simphronius and Olympius; Bishop Zeno of Verona; in the town of Tarragona in Spain, Bishop Fructuosus and the deacons Augurius and Eulogius; Marinus and Artemius in Caesarea in Palestine; in the city of Tebourba in Africa, the virgins Maxima, Donatilla and Secunda; in the village of Minatensis in the territory of Gevaudan, Privatus the bishop; at Carthage, Bishop Cyprian; Bishop Dionysius of Alexandria.[121]

---

116 Ado, *Martyrologium*, who places Phileas and Philoromus under Diocletian; Babilas of Antioch and Alexander of Jerusalem are the only martyrs mentioned by Bede at this point.

117 Actually 251–253.

118 Bede, *DTR* c. 66: 505 (Wallis 2004: 208).

119 Actually 253–268.

120 Bede, *DTR* c. 66: 505 (Wallis 2004: 208).

121 Ado, *Matyrologium*. Bede here mentions the martyrdoms of Popes Sixtus, Stephen and Cyprian of Carthage.

BOOK I 75

Bishop Theodore of Neocaesarea in Pontus, who was also called Gregory, was renowned for the glory of his virtues.[122]

224–225[123]

[Beginning] in the year of the Lord's incarnation 224, Claudius [ruled for] 1 year and 9 months.[124] Add the 4 months from Volusian to these and we get a year, which is included here, leaving a month left over.[125]

In these times suffered: Pope Felix of Rome; Marius and his wife Martha with their children; 47 soldiers who were baptised by Pope Dionysius; Cyrilla the virgin; the priest Felix and Eusebius in Tarracina in Campania.[126]

226–231[127]

[Beginning] in the year of the Lord's incarnation 226, Aurelian reigned for 5 years and 6 months.[128]

At this time were martyred: Eutychius the pope of Rome; Theodora, Basilides, Tripos and Mandalio; the sainted twins of Langres; Conon of the city of Iconio; Mames of Caesarea in Cappadocia; Agapitus in the town of Prenestina; Anastasius in the city of Salona; Symphorianus of Augsburg; Andeolus the subdeacon, in the place called Gentibus in the Vivarais; Andochius the priest, Tirsus the deacon and Felix; Benignus the priest in the fortress of Dijon.[129]

232[130]

[Beginning] in the year of the Lord's incarnation 232, Tacitus ruled for 6 months. Add the 6 from Aurelian to make up a full year.[131] That

---

122 Bede, *DTR* c. 66: 506 (Wallis 2004: 208).
123 Actually 268–270.
124 Bede, *DTR* c. 66: 506 (Wallis 2004: 209).
125 Thus Regino reckons Claudius as 2 years, starting in January and finishing in December.
126 Ado, *Martyrologium*.
127 Actually 270–275.
128 Bede, *DTR* c. 66: 506 (Wallis 2004: 209).
129 Ado, *Martyrolgium*; Eutychius is the only martyr named by Bede in Aurelian's reign.
130 Actually 275–276.
131 Bede, *DTR* c. 66: 506 (Wallis 2004: 209).

leaves Florian's 88 days, which combined with the 28 days left over from earlier makes 108 days, in other words 3 months and 18 days.[132] Adding the 2 outstanding months makes a total of 5 months and 18 days.[133]

Bishop Anatolius of Laodicea in Syria was widely renowned.[134]

233–239[135]

[Beginning] in the year of the Lord's incarnation 233, Probus reigned for 6 years and 4 months.[136] Combining these with the 6 months from Tacitus, and the 5 mentioned above, makes a year with 3 months left over.[137]

240–241[138]

[Beginning] in the year of the Lord's incarnation 240, Carus ruled with his sons Carinus and Numerian for 2 years.[139]

At this time these were crowned as martyrs: Chrysanthus and Daria in Rome; Claudius and his wife Hilaria with their children Iasone and Marus and 70 soldiers.[140]

242–262[141]

[Beginning] in the year of the Lord's incarnation 242, Diocletian along with Maximian and Constantius (and after Diocletian's death Maximian along with Severus, Galerius and Maximin) reigned for 20 years.[142]

---

132 An arithmetical slip: 88 + 28 = 116, not 108. Regino counted all months as 30 days long. Bede says that Florian reigned for 88 days after Tacitus' death.

133 See above, 204–205, 224–225.

134 Bede, *DTR* c. 66: 507 (Wallis 2004: 209).

135 Actually 276–282.

136 Bede, *DTR* c. 66: 507 (Wallis 2004: 210).

137 Regino apparently forgot that he had already used Tacitus' 6 months.

138 Actually 282–284.

139 Bede, *DTR* c. 66: 507 (Wallis 2004: 210).

140 Ado, *Martyrologium*. Chrysanthus and Daria were the focus of a major cult at Prüm, their relics having been translated there from Rome by Abbot Marcward: Haubrichs 1979: 127–30, 138–42, 154–6; Smith 2000: 326–9.

141 Actually 284–305.

142 Bede, *DTR* c. 66: 507–8 (Wallis 2004: 210–12). Regino here folds together two separate but consecutive entries from Bede.

BOOK I 77

Crowned as martyrs in this period were: Pope Gaius of Rome; Pope Marcellus; Pope Marcellinus; Cyriacus the deacon; Largus and Smaragdus; Apronianus; Papias and Maurus; Claudius and Prepedigna with their children; the priest Gabinus; Castulus; Pancratius; Artemius with his wife and daughter; Sebastian; Marcus and Marcellianus; Marcellinus the priest and Peter the exorcist; Tranquillinus, Nicostratus, his wife Zoe, Primus and Felicianus; Claudius, Castorius, Victorinus, Simphronianus; Basiliscus; Faustinus, Simplicius and Beatrix; Tiburtius the son of Chromatius; the virgin Susanna; John, Crispus, Genesius; Felix and Adauctus; Lucia, Geminianus, Sergius and Bacchus; Crisogonus; Saturninus and Sisinnius; the 4 crowned martyrs [Severus, Severianus, Carpophorus and Victorinus]; Theodore; Pontianus; Praetextatus and Thraso; Gregory the priest in Spoleto; Bishop Sabinus; the deacons Exuperantius and Marcellus; on the island of Palmaria, Anastasia; Julian and Basilissa of Antioch; in the city of Zaragoza in Spain, the deacon Vincentius; Cucufas and Eulalia the virgin in Barcelona; Felix at Girona; Juliana the virgin in Cumis; at Tyre, Bishops Tirannio, Silvanus, Pelenus and Linus with a countless multitude; Sirenus in Sirmium; Peter of Nicomedia and Lucianus the priest from Antioch; Bishop Anthimus; Pantaleon; John, Hadrian; Dorotheus and Gorgonius; Eleutherius; Irenaeus bishop of Smirna; in Palestine, in the city of Gaza, Silvanus; Victor of Milan; at Siscia in Illyricum, Bishop Quirinus; Boniface at Tarsus; Felix and Fortunatus at Aquileia; in Sicily, Vitus, Modestus and Crescentia; the virgin Lucia; Albanus in Britain; Victor at Marseilles; at Augsburg in the province of Rhaetia, Afra and her mother Hilaria; Theodota with her children at Nicaea in Bithynia; the brothers Justus and Pastor at Compluto in Spain; the deacon Euplus at Cantania in Sicily; at the town of Bergamo in Italy, Alexander; Euphemia in the town of Chalcedon; the Beneventan Bishop Januarius at Naples in Campania; Socius the deacon in Misenas; Faustus and Desiderius; Bishops Peleus and Nilus in Palestine; in Cizico, Fausta and Evilasius; Maurice of Agaune and his associates; Cyprian bishop of Antioch with Justina; Cosmas and Damianus at Egea; at the fortress of Solothurn, which is on the River Aare in Gaul, Victor; Gereo with his followers at Cologne; Taracus, Probus and Andronicus at Tarsus; at the city of Venusia, Bishop Felix of Apulia, the priests Audax and Januarius; Crispin and Crispinianus at the city of Soissons; Zenobius the priest in Sion; in the territory of Agathensus, Tiberius, Modestus and Florentia; Menas of Salutaria, the metropolitan of Phrygia, in Scythia; Romanus of Antioch; Bishop Peter of Alexandria; the virgin Crispina in the city of Colonia in Africa; in

Tuscia, the virgin Barbara; Leocadia in Spain; the virgins Eulalia and Julia in the city of Merida.[143]

263–294[144]

[Beginning] in the year of the Lord's incarnation 263, Constantine, the son of Constantius by his concubine Helena, ruled for 30 years and 10 months.[145] To these [10 months] we add the 3 left over from earlier, making one year with one month remaining.[146]

[At the time of this Constantine, peace was restored to the Churches, bishops deprived of their sees were restored, and many other things were conceded that were useful to the Christian religion. Among these was the foundation of the monastery of the servants of God at Trier, which Abbot John initiated between adjacent walls in the city with the assent of the aforesaid prince. The blessed Augustine mentions this community in his book of confessions. The holy confessor and bishop Agricius of Trier shone with great distinction; he appointed the blessed and worthy Maximin as his successor.][147]

Pope Sylvester was renowned at this time; through his very splendid diligence a synod was celebrated at the town of Nicaea by 318 fathers from all over the world.[148] The cross of our Lord Jesus Christ was found by Judas. However, we read in the Deeds of the Pontiffs of Rome [*Liber Pontificalis*] that that same cross was discovered in the reign of Constantine's father Constantius and in the Roman pontificate of Eusebius. For there it can be read: 'In his time', that is Eusebius', 'the cross of the Lord was discovered on 3 May and Judas, also known as Cyriacus, was baptized.'[149]

143 Ado, *Martyrologium*.
144 Actually 306–337.
145 Bede, *DTR* c. 66: 509 (Wallis 2004: 212).
146 Another example of Regino's inconsistency on dating: on the way he reckoned some reigns, 263–294 would be 32 years, not 31.
147 This paragraph only appears in manuscripts of Kurze's group A, so is probably to be regarded as an editorial intervention by Regino's continuator Adalbert: see above, Introduction, pp. 55–6.
148 Ado, *Martyrologium*: 39; Bede, *DTR* c. 66: 509 (Wallis 2004: 212) also mentions Nicaea (where 'the catholic faith was laid out'), but dates it as the 636th year after Alexander.
149 *LP* (Davis 2000: 14). Here we see Regino trying to reconcile two apparently conflicting sources: Ado, *Martyrologium*: 141–4 says that the cross was discovered 'under the prince Constantine by Queen Helena'. His identification of the finder as Judas (who decided where to look) rather than Helena (whose project it was) apparently reflects Regino's decision to prioritise here the *LP* (from which he quotes directly) over Ado. Since Helena was specifically mentioned in Regino's *Tonarium*, and since the cult of the cross was intensively venerated at Prüm, it is unlikely

295–309[150]

[Beginning] in the year of the Lord's incarnation 295, Constantius ruled together with his brothers Constantine and Constans for 24 years, 5 months and 13 days.[151] In this period Anastasius was sought out for punishment by Constantine and the holy bishops Servatius of Tongres and Maximin of Trier were renowned.[152] Bishop James of Nisibis was famous, the monk Anthony died in the desert and Bishop Hilary of Poitiers was recalled from exile.[153]

Pope Julius was sent into exile; Pope Liberius was carried off into exile, but once recalled he favoured the heretics. Pope Felix was deposed and put to death by the heretics.[154]

Because of his Catholic faith, Eusebius the priest was shut up in a certain room and died there after 7 months; Dionysius the bishop of Milan was condemned to exile in Cappadocia; Bishop Paul of Constantinople was strangled by the Arians.[155] Paulinus the bishop of Trier, successor to the holy Bishop Maximin, was sent into exile by Constans because of his Catholic faith and until his death was exhausted by frequent changes of exile, even beyond the pretext [that he was] a Christian. Finally he died in Phrygia, and from there was carried back to Trier.[156]

[His body was borne back to Trier and up until the present day, by divine will, it miraculously hangs in the air in a certain crypt with no support from anything.][157]

---

that the alteration of Ado's wording here has any other particular significance: see Haubrichs 1979: 164, 168.

150 Actually 337–361.
151 Bede, *DTR* c. 66: 510 (Wallis 2004: 213): Regino mistakenly calculated a span of 14 years instead of 24.
152 Anastasius may be a slip for Athanasius, mentioned by Bede as having been persecuted by the Arian heretic Constantine. Bede does not mention Servatius. The references to Anastasius and Servatius only appear in Kurze's A-group manuscripts, so they may have been added by a later editor of Regino's text, probably Adalbert: see above, Introduction, pp. 55–6.
153 Bede, *DTR* c. 66: 510 (Wallis 2004: 213–14).
154 *LP* (Davis 2000: 28–30) was Regino's source here.
155 Regino got these names from Ado, *Martyrologium*.
156 *Vita Paulini*: *AASS* Aug VI has the detail that he was the successor of St Maximin; Ado, *Martyrologium*: 294. The cult of Paulinus was intensively cultivated at Prüm: Haubrichs 1979: 176.
157 This only appears in Kurze's group A manuscripts, so is probably an addition by Adalbert: see above, Introduction, pp. 55–6.

310–313[158]

[Beginning] in the year of the Lord's incarnation 310, Julian reigned for 2 years and 8 months.[159] To these we add the 6 left over from earlier to make a year, leaving a remainder of 2 months and 18 days.[160] In his time these were crowned martyrs: Priscus the priest of Rome; the cleric Priscillian; the woman Benedicta; Pigmenius the priest; Gordianus; Demetria the virgin; John the priest; another John and Paul; Faustus and Dafrosa; Hilarinus in Ostia; Quiriacus, bishop of Jerusalem, also called Judas; Gallicanus of Alexandria; Bishop Eusebius of Vercelli; Donatus, bishop of the city of Arezzo; the priest Theodoritus in Antioch.[161]

314[162]

[Beginning] in the year of the Lord's incarnation 314, Jovian ruled for 8 months. That same ruler enquired after bishop Athanasius in courteous letters.[163]

315–326[164]

[Beginning] in the year of the Lord's incarnation 315, Valentinian ruled for 11 years with his brother Valens. Pope Damasus of Rome was renowned; Bishop Ambrose of Milan was distinguished; Bishop Hilarius of Poitiers died.[165] Athanasius of Alexandria ended his life.[166]

327–331[167]

[Beginning] in the year of the Lord's incarnation 327 Valens ruled

---

158 Actually 361–363.
159 Bede, *DTR* c. 66: 510 (Wallis 2004: 214).
160 The 6 months are left over from Constantine and Constantius; the 18 days come from Tacitus; and Regino appears to have missed out 13 days from Constantius. In this entry Regino calculates Julian's 3 years into a time-span of 4.
161 Ado, *Martyrologium*.
162 Actually 363–364.
163 Bede, *DTR* c. 66: 511 (Wallis 2004: 215). Regino does not explain why he assigns Jovian a full year.
164 Actually 364–375. Regino adds 11 to 315 to reach 326, again assigning one year too many.
165 Bede, *DTR* c. 66: 511–12 (Wallis 2004: 215–16).
166 Ado, *Martyrologium*.
167 Actually 375–378. Again, a year extra is mistakenly added to the span.

BOOK I   81

with Gratian and Valentinian, the son of his brother Valentinian, for 4 years. The Huns burst forth from their own lands against the Goths, and the Goths devastated Thrace.[168]

332–338[169]

[Beginning] in the year of the Lord's incarnation 332, Gratian ruled for 6 years with his brother Valentinian. Theodosius was made emperor by Gratian. A synod of 150 bishops was held in the Augustan city [Rome] under Pope Damasus. Theodosius made his son Arcadius his co-ruler. Maximus was made emperor in Britain: he killed the emperor Gratian at Lyon in Gaul and expelled his brother Valentinian from Italy.[170] Martin the bishop of Tours shone with the glory of the virtues.[171] Jerome was renowned as a translator of holy scripture in Bethlehem.[172]

339–349[173]

[Beginning] in the year of the Lord's incarnation 339, Theodosius, having already ruled the east for 5 years while Gratian was alive, ruled for 11 years after his death. The tyrant Maximus was killed at the fourth milestone from Aquileia.[174]

Pope Siricius ruled the Roman Church.[175]

Jerome wrote a book about illustrious men.[176]

John the hermit was famous in Egypt; he predicted that Theodosius would defeat the tyrants.[177]

---

168 Bede, *DTR* c. 66: 512 (Wallis 2004: 216).

169 Actually 378–383.

170 Bede, *DTR* c. 66: 512–13 (Wallis 2004: 216–17).

171 *Vita Martini*, c. 20 locates him in the time of Valentinian and Maximus. However, the cult of Martin had been celebrated at Prüm since its origins, so there need not be a particular textual source for this information: Haubrichs 1979: 174.

172 Ado, *Martyrologium*: 337–8, identifies the place as Bethlehem; but the wording seems to come from Bede's subsequent entry which mentions Jerome's composition of a book on illustrious men.

173 Actually 383–395.

174 Bede, *DTR* c. 66: 513 (Wallis 2004: 217), which says Maximus died at the third milestone (presumably this is no more than a slip of the pen by Regino or the scribe of his Bede manuscript).

175 *LP* (Davis 2000: 31–2).

176 Bede, *DTR* c. 66: 513 (Wallis 2004: 218).

177 Ado, *Martyrologium*: 113.

350–363[178]

[Beginning] in the year of the Lord's incarnation 350, Arcadius the son of Theodosius ruled with his brother Honorius for 13 years. The Goths entered Italy and the Vandals and Alans entered Gaul. The bodies of the prophets Habakkuk and Micah were discovered.[179]

Pope Innocent ruled the Roman Church, and after him Pope Zosimus.[180]

The holy bishop Martin crossed into heaven. Severinus bishop of Cologne and Theodorus bishop of Lucca were greatly renowned.[181] The great teacher Bishop Augustine taught divine philosophy in the Church of Hippo.[182] Pelagius the Briton impugned the grace of God.[183]

364–369[184]

[Beginning] in the year of the Lord's incarnation 364, Honorius ruled for 15 years with Theodosius the younger, his brother's son. Alaric king of the Goths captured Rome. In Honorius's 7th year, the [locations of the] bodies of the saints Stephen the protomartyr, Gamaliel and Nicodemus were revealed to the priest Lucian.[185]

Popes Boniface and Celestine ruled the Roman Church.[186]

The priest Jerome died in the 12th year of Honorius' reign at the age of 97; he had been writing books for 50 years.[187]

---

178 Actually 395–408.
179 Bede, *DTR* c. 66: 513 (Wallis 2004: 218), though Regino switches the order of these two sentences.
180 Regino presumably knew this from the *LP*.
181 Severinus was culted at Prüm: Haubrichs 1979: 105–8. There is little other evidence for the monks' particular veneration of Theodorus of Lucca.
182 The wording is clearly based on a subsequent entry from Bede, inserted here out of order: Bede, *DTR* c. 66: 516 (Wallis 2004: 220).
183 Bede, *DTR* c. 66: 513 (Wallis 2004: 218).
184 Actually 408–423. An inclusive calculation this time; but Regino accidentally misses out 10 years.
185 Bede, *DTR* c. 66: 513–14 (Wallis 2004: 218).
186 Bede mentions that Boniface lived in the time of Honorius.
187 A combination of sources is used here: Bede *DTR* c. 66: 515 (Wallis 2004: 219) for the first part; and Ado, *Martyrologium*: 338–9 for the second. However, Bede says Jerome was 91, Ado says he was 98; and Ado states that his books were written over 56 years. These variations presumably reflect scribal errors at some stage.

BOOK I   83

370–396[188]

[Beginning] in the year of the Lord's incarnation 370 Theodosius the younger, the son of Arcadius, ruled for 26 years. Valentinian the younger, son of Constantius, was made emperor at Ravenna. The people of the Vandals, Alans and Goths devastated Africa. Bishop Augustine went to the Lord amid the anguishes of those sieges. The Vandals captured Carthage and crossed to Sicily.[189]

Sixtus ruled the Roman Church.[190]

In the time of Theodosius the great Leo obtained the apostolic throne; he [Leo] wrote many things to him [Theodosius] and to the empress Pulcheria about the error of Eutychius. Flavian the bishop of Constantinople condemned Eutychius.[191]

397–404[192]

[Beginning] in the year of the Lord's incarnation 397 Marcian and Valentinian ruled for 7 years. John the Baptist revealed [the location of] his head to two monks. Germanus bishop of Auxerre and Lupus bishop of Trier were sent to Britain.[193]

[… in order to wipe out the Pelagian heresy. Germanus and Bishop Severus of Trier, a disciple of the blessed Lupus, were sent on a second journey for the same reason and through God's mercy they destroyed by miraculous signs and distinguished doctrine the heresy that had sprung forth. This Severus, who was in all things the equal of the apostles in merit, had first ministered the word of God in Germany. The saintly Lupus also had as disciples Policronius of Verdun and Alpinus of Châlons-sur-Marne, so the virtues of his followers made evident how great was the master's sanctity.][194]

188 Actually 423–450.
189 Bede, *DTR* c. 66: 516 (Wallis 2004: 219–20).
190 Sixtus is mentioned by Bede as active in the reign of Theodosius.
191 This section, in Regino's own words, refers to the disputes over the nature of Christ's divinity which were ruled on authoritatively by the Council of Chalcedon in 451. Bede's account places it in the reign of Emperor Leo rather than that of Theodosius, and identifies the emperor and Bishop Theoderet of Cyrrhus as the defenders of orthodoxy against Eutychius. By crediting the pope as the prime mover in this regard, Regino prefers the account in the *LP* to that of Bede: *LP* (Davis 2000: 39). Flavian appears in neither source. Cf. *Collectio canonum Hispaniae*, no. 37–8, 41–8. See also the next annal.
192 Actually 450–457.
193 Bede, *DTR* c. 66: 517–18 (Wallis 2004: 221–2).
194 This paragraph is inserted in manuscripts of Kurze's group A only, presumably by Adalbert, and replaces the one following: see above, Introduction, pp. 55–6.

[After this Germanus died at Ravenna.[195] Bishop Severus of Trier, Policronius of Verdun and Albinus of Châlons-sur-Marne, disciples of Saint Lupus, were renowned.][196]

Anianus bishop of Orléans was illustrious.[197]

Bishop Leo wrote to Marcian many doctrines of the faith. Anatolius the bishop of Constantinople condemned the error of Eutychius and it was argued by Pope Leo that he had wanted to subordinate to himself the churches of Antioch and Alexandria, against the council of Nicaea.[198]

The patrician Aetius was killed by Valentinian.[199] At Arles, bishop Hilary died. He was a most learned and distinguished man who had written the *vita* of his predecessor St Honoratus.[200]

405–412[201]

[Beginning] in the year of the Lord's incarnation 405, Leo reigned for 17 years.[202] Pope Leo wrote many times to this Leo.[203] Theodorus, bishop of the town of Cyrrhus, wrote an ecclesiastical history starting at the end of Eusebius' book.[204]

Pope Hilary ruled the Roman Church.

On the orders of Pope Hilary, Victorinus wrote about the revolution of the great year.[205]

---

195 Bede, *DTR* c. 66: 518 (Wallis 2004: 222).

196 *Vita Lupi*, *AASS* July VII, c. 11, contains this information. On the cult of Lupus at Prüm see Haubrichs 1979: 107–10, 172. This sentence appears only in Kurze's B manuscripts, so is presumed to be part of Regino's original work.

197 One of the west Frankish figures culted at Prüm: Haubrichs 1979: 160.

198 This section is based on *Collectio canonum Hispaniae* nos 50–1, 53, 55–9. Again, papal primacy is asserted by Regino in his choice and framing of sources: cf. 370–396.

199 Bede, *DTR* c. 66: 518 (Wallis 2004: 222). Regino omits Bede's comment that this marked the definitive end of the western empire.

200 Ado, *Martyrologium*: 148.

201 Actually 457–474. Another 10 years lost through a slip of the pen.

202 Bede, *DTR* c. 66: 518 (Wallis 2004: 222).

203 Cf. above, 397–404.

204 Bede, *DTR* c. 66: 519 (Wallis 2004: 222): however, Regino systematically omits references to Theoderet (Theodorus) and Emperor Leo condemning Eutychius and establishing the Chalcedonian positions, ascribing agency in this to the pope instead.

205 Bede, *DTR* c. 66: 519 (Wallis 2004: 222): this refers to Victorinus' paschal cycle.

BOOK I   85

413–420[206]

[Beginning] in the year of the Lord's incarnation 413, Zeno reigned for 17 years. Odoacer king of the Goths obtained control of Rome. Theoderic, also called Walager, wasted Macedonia. Huneric, the Arian king of the Vandals, having driven away more than 334 bishops, closed their churches and afflicted the people with various sufferings.[207] Pope Felix condemned Bishop Acacius of Constantinople and Bishop Peter of Alexandria. Gelasius, a prudent man, succeeded Pope Felix in the pontificate. He also condemned Acacius and Peter. After him Anastasius was made pope. He wanted to recall Acacius secretly but couldn't; he was then struck down by divine will.[208]

421–449[209]

[Beginning] in the year of the Lord's incarnation 421, Anastasius reigned for 28 years. Trasamund the king of the Vandals sent 220 bishops into exile in Sardinia.[210]

In his times, and those of Zeno, these were crowned martyrs in the Vandal persecution: in Africa Eugenius bishop of Carthage and with him more than 500 others; likewise, Abbot Liberatus, Boniface the deacon, Servius and Rusticus the subdeacons, the monks Rogatus and Septimus and the boy Maximus were first set on fire and then killed by being struck with bars. Also Marcian and Satirianus and the virgin Maxima were cruelly killed with 270 others. In addition, the bishops Papias and Mansuetus, Vultdeus, Valerian, Urbanus and Crescens, Felix and Hortolanus, and Florentian perfected the course of their lives in confession; also Dativa, Dionysia and Emilianus the doctor with many others; Bishop Valerian.[211]

Pope Symmachus governed the Roman Church and he supplied money and clothes to the bishops who had been sent into exile in Africa and Sardinia.[212] After him Hormisdas was made pope.

206 Actually 474–491. Once more, Regino loses 10 years in his arithmetic. He omits Bede's information on British matters, as he did most of the time.
207 Bede, *DTR* c. 66: 519 (Wallis 2004: 223).
208 All of this information is from *LP* (Davis 2000: 43–5); cf. *Collectio canonum Hispaniae*, no. 80.
209 Actually 491–518.
210 Bede, *DTR* c. 66: 520 (Wallis 2004: 223).
211 Ado, *Martyrologium*.
212 Bede, *DTR* c. 66: 520 (Wallis 2004: 223–4).

Clovis king of the Franks ruled in Gaul for 30 years. He killed the patrician Syagrius, expelled King Gundobad from Burgundy, made the Alemans into tributaries, and in the 15th year of his reign was baptised together with the Franks by Bishop Remigius of Rheims. Vedastus was ordained bishop of Arras by St Remigius. Mammertus, bishop of the city of Vienne, established 3 days of litanies before the Ascension of the Lord.[213]

Clovis fought with Alaric, king of the Goths, by Poitiers in Aquitaine and deprived him of his kingdom and life. Amalric the son of Alaric obtained the paternal kingdom in Spain. The Emperor Anastasius sent royal gifts to Clovis.[214]

Clovis killed Reginar, his relative and associate in the kingdom.[215] From the passing of St Martin until the death of Clovis there were 112 years.[216] His 4 sons Theoderic, Clodomer, Childeric and Clothar divided the kingdom of their father between them.[217]

The Emperor Anastasius was killed by a thunderbolt.[218]

450–458[219]

[Beginning] in the year of the Lord's incarnation 450, Justin the elder reigned for 8 years. Pope John was imprisoned in Ravenna by Theoderic king of the Goths because of his Catholic faith, and he died there. The

---

213 The information in this paragraph seems to come (drastically abbreviated) from *LHF* cc. 9, 15, 16, 19: 251, 261–7, 273–5 except the line about Vedastus, which may be drawn from *Vita Vedasti, AASS* Feb I: 782. Regino, unlike the *LHF* author, saw Clovis' baptism as the beginning of Frankish history. The phrase 'Alamannos tributarios fecit' corresponds directly with a marginal addition found only in Krusch's *LHF* manuscript B1a (see *LHF* 262 for the addition). The scribe of this manuscript (BM Arundel 375, ninth century) made other changes to the text that suggest a detailed knowledge of the Ardennes region: *LHF* 224–5. Regino also followed this manuscript's spelling of Clovis' name as Clodoveus, compared to the Chlodoveus of many others. Regino may thus have had access to this manuscript, or one related to it, in Prüm. On the manuscript see McKitterick 1989: 276.

214 *LHF* c. 17: 267–71, which says that he sent a purple cloak and crown and made Clovis consul.

215 *LHF* c. 18: 271–3. Regino summarises the whole chapter in this sentence.

216 Regino recorded Martin's death s.a. 350–363, in other words no more than 100 years before he reckoned the death of Clovis to have taken place. There is no sign that he noticed any discrepancy in his adoption of the 112-year span from the *LHF*.

217 *LHF* c. 19: 273–5, illustrating Regino's emphasis on dynastic history.

218 Bede, *DTR* c. 66: 520 (Wallis 2004: 224). By ending with Bede's judgement on Anastasius as a victim of divine disfavour (for his support of Eutychius' heresy), Regino deliberately chooses to undercut the more positive portrayal of him as the source of Clovis's authority in the *LHF*.

219 Actually 518–527.

BOOK I

same tyrant killed the patrician Symmachus.[220] He thrust Boethius, who was second to none in the liberal disciplines, into prison, where together with that very philosophy he was investigated by means of the wonderful proofs of the disputations.[221] The same Theoderic died suddenly, and Athalaric succeeded to the kingdom.[222]

Father Benedict, first in the place called Subiaco and afterward in the fortress called Monte Cassino, shone as a man with great virtue and apostolic qualities.[223] Felix and Boniface ruled the Roman Church.[224] King Sigismund of the Burgundians built a monastery of the saints of Agaune. The same man was killed by the above-mentioned sons of Clovis.[225] Theoderic with his son Theudebert and brother Clothar laid waste to Thuringia, and he killed Ermenfrid *dux* of the Thuringians at Zülpich.[226]

459–497[227]

[Beginning] in the year of the Lord's incarnation 459 Justinian, Justin's nephew through his sister, reigned for 38 years.[228]

Through the patrician Belisarius he vigorously subdued the Persians and through the same Belisarius he completely exterminated the Vandal people, captured their king Gelismer and restored all of Africa to the Roman Empire after 96 years. Once again through the power of Belisarius he triumphed over the Goths in Italy after capturing their king

220 Bede, *DTR* c. 66: 520 (Wallis 2004: 224). Bede makes Justin the champion of the Catholic faith; Regino's edited version shifts the agency to the pope. Cf. Ado, *Martyrologium*: 172.

221 This rather obtuse passage is all Regino, who may have been influenced by Boethius's *Consolation of Philosophy*: Kortüm 1994.

222 Bede, *DTR* c. 66: 520 (Wallis 2004: 224). Regino misses out some of Bede's detail, as well as the recall of the exiled bishops by the Vandal king and a reference to the glory of St Benedict.

223 Paul the Deacon, *Historia*, I.26: 73–4 (Foulke 2003: 47–8). Regino's wording is very close to Paul's. His cue for this entry must however have been Bede, *DTR* c. 66: 521 (Wallis 2004: 224), who commented under Justin's reign that: 'Abbot Benedict shone forth in the glory of his miracles, which the blessed Pope Gregory wrote down in his book of *Dialogues*.' Benedict's Rule was endorsed by the Carolingians as the standard guide for monastic life.

224 *LP* (Davis 2000: 52–3).

225 *LHF* c. 20: 275–6. Regino summarises the bare essentials.

226 *LHF* c. 22: 277–8.

227 Actually 527–565.

228 Bede, *DTR* c. 66: 521 (Wallis 2004: 224).

Witigis. He also crushed the Moors, and their king Athala, who subsequently infested Africa, through the consul John, a man of remarkable courage. He also abbreviated the Roman laws, the prolixity of which was oppressive, and corrected harmful dissonances with admirable brevity. In Constantinople he built a church which is called Hagia Sophia in Greek. The quality of all the work on this building is so excellent that nothing similar can be found in all the regions of the world. In his time Cassiodorus was renowned in Rome for his divine and secular knowledge. He was first a consul, then a senator, and at the last he became a monk. In Rome, Dionysius the abbot wrote the paschal cycles. At Constantinople Priscian of Caesarea explored the depths of the grammatical art, as I might say, and then, no less, a subdeacon of the Roman Church called Arator, a wonderful poet, beautified the Acts of the Apostles in hexameter verses.[229]

In his [Justinian's] time, John, Agapitus, Silverius and Vigilius ruled the Roman Church. Silverius was sent into exile by Belisarius on the orders of the Empress Theodora, and he died there. Vigilius was also driven into exile by Justinian because he refused to recall Anthimus the bishop of Constantinople. After he had been recalled from exile, when he returned to Rome, he died in anguish of gallstones in the Sicilian city of Syracuse. Pelagius succeeded to the pontificate.[230]

At that same time Alboin, son of Audoin, was now the tenth to rule the Lombards, and had taken in marriage Chlothsuind, the daughter of Clothar king of the Franks.[231]

Childebert king of the Franks entered Spain with an army. He killed King Amalric, Alaric's son, in battle and carried off from there much

---

[229] Paul the Deacon, *Historia*, I.25: 72–3 (Foulke 2003: 45–7). Regino reproduces Paul's wording almost exactly, in contrast with his much more concise summaries of the *LHF* and *LP*. He omits 3 sections: on Justinian's titles of conquest; some more detail on his legal reforms; and a sentence praising the emperor as a great Catholic hero. The latter silence may indicate a reluctance to ascribe such qualities to emperors rather than popes: see above, introduction, pp. 23–5. Even in this long quote, Regino seems to have used Bede as his basic guide with extra detail gleaned from Paul: he inverts Paul's order to put Benedict before Justinian; and the sentence on Dionysius and his Easter tables is much closer to Bede's wording than Paul's: Bede, *DTR* c. 66: 521 (Wallis 2004: 225). Presumably Regino's borrowing from Paul begins at this point because Justinian provides a firm chronological bridge connecting him with Bede.

[230] A drastic abbreviation of the information in the *LP* (Davis 2000: 51–61); Regino also misses out a couple of popes. The theme of heroic popes standing up to unjust rulers helps explain the omission in the previous paragraph of Paul the Deacon's sentence on Justinian as a great Catholic.

[231] Paul the Deacon, *Historia* I.27: 79 (Foulke 2003: 49). Regino, as usual, takes Paul's information on Frankish history but leaves out a lot concerning internal Italian poltics.

BOOK I   89

gold and silver. Clothar stabbed the sons of his brother Clodomer with a knife. King Theoderic died. His son Theudebert reigned after him.[232]

[In his times the blessed Nicetius, archbishop of the see of Trier, shone with wonderful sanctity.][233]

498–509[234]

[Beginning] in the year of the Lord's incarnation 498, Justin the younger ruled for 11 years. The patrician Narses killed Totila king of the Goths in Italy.[235] The same man fought and killed Bucellinus and Emingus, the *duces* of King Theudebert of the Franks, who had been plundering Italy.[236] Narses was accused by the Romans before Justin and his wife Sophia of claiming as a reward the subjection of Italy.[237] The prefect Longinus was immediately sent into Italy to take the place of Narses. Among other things, Sophia sent a message that, because he was a eunuch, she would make him work in the women's quarters dividing up the portions of wool for the girls. To this he responded that he would weave her such a web that she would not be able to lie down as long as she lived; and immediately he ordered the Lombards to come and take over Italy.[238]

Pope John ruled the Roman Church.

Kings Childebert and Clothar entered Spain with an army and besieged Zaragoza. The inhabitants, after putting on hair-shirts, carried the tunic of St Vincent on top of the walls, and prayed to God with contrite hearts. By divine inspiration the kings turned to sympathy and lifted the siege. The bishop of the town gave King Childebert the tunic of the blessed Vincent as a reward. That king built a church in Paris in the blessed Vincent's honour.[239]

232 *LHF* cc. 23–5: 277–82. Regino cuts this material to the bare essentials but, aside from some material on the queen, the main omissions are detail rather than substance.
233 Only in Kurze's 'A' manuscripts, so this is a later addition to Regino's text, probably by his editor Adalbert: see above, Introduction, pp. 55–6.
234 Actually 565–578.
235 Bede, *DTR* c. 66: 521 (Wallis 2004: 225).
236 Paul the Deacon, *Historia*, II.2: 84–5 (Foulke 2003: 54–5). Here Regino summarises most of Paul's main points in the chapter. Presumably he included it after picking up on Bede's cue and looking for material on Narses.
237 Bede, *DTR* c. 66: 521 (Wallis 2004: 225).
238 Paul, *Historia*, II.5: 88 (Foulke 2003: 59) for this section except the last clause, which is Bede, *DTR* c. 66: 521 (Wallis 2004: 225). The wording is close to both sources and again Regino seems to be looking for material specifically connected to Narses, perhaps betraying a particular interest in invasions of Italy.
239 *LHF* c. 26: 283–4.

Albuin entered Italy with the Lombards and put his nephew Gisulf in charge of Friuli.[240]

King Theudebert entered Italy, started a battle with the Lombards and overcame them, and then died after returning to Francia. A little time later King Childebert died at Paris and was buried in the church of St Vincent. The kingdoms which his brothers and nephews had held came into the power of Clothar.[241]

In his [Justin's] time Bishop Medardus went to the Lord; King Clothar interred him at Soissons with due honour. After that Clothar died and was buried in the church of St Medardus. His four sons divided the kingdoms between them. Charibert received the kingdom of Childebert and had Paris as his seat; Guntram held Clodomer's kingdom and made Orléans his seat; Chilperic held the kingdom of his father Clothar and had the cathedral of Soissons; and Sigibert held Theoderic's realm and established its seat at Rheims or Metz.[242]

The Huns, who were also called Avars, learned of Clothar's death and attacked Sigibert. He came up to meet them in Thuringia and overcame them powerfully by the River Elbe.[243] This Sigibert sent an embassy to Spain requesting the hand of King Athanagild's daughter Brunhild, and he took her in marriage.[244] By her he had a son called Childebert.[245]

240 Paul, *Historia*, II.9: 91 (Foulke 2003: 65). In II.7, Paul says that this took place in 568. Regino ignores this date, which obviously did not fit the chronology he had calculated so far.

241 *LHF* cc. 26–8: 284–7. The comment on the sole rule of Clothar seems to be drawn from a marginal note found only in manuscript B1a of the *LHF*: see above, 421–449, n. 213. Regino misses out the *LHF*'s accounts of Clothar's conquests and some detail on internal dynastic politics. His inclusion of the St Vincent story reflects Regino's interest in the relationship between kings and the holy.

242 *LHF* c. 29: 288–9. Regino updates the spelling of Charibert's name to 'Herechbertus', and Chilperic's to 'Hilperic'. The *LHF* says that Sigibert's capital was Rheims while Paul the Deacon, *Historia*, II.10: 92 (Foulke 2003: 67) says it was Metz. Regino's inclusion of both underlines the seriousness of his attempt to integrate his sources.

243 Paul the Deacon, *Historia*, II.10: 92–3 (Foulke 2003: 67–8). Paul describes the four-way division of the kingdom in detail at this point, which must be the cue for Regino's insertion of the Avar story. The *LHF* also recounts a version of this story, but Regino evidently preferred Paul's simpler account. Regino omits, however, Paul's statement that the Franks were subsequently crushed by the Avars in the same place.

244 *LHF* c. 31: 291. Regino omits the *LHF*'s statement that Sigibert's marriage was in contrast to the unworthy unions with social inferiors secured by his brothers. In the ninth century kings exclusively married social inferiors rather than foreign princesses.

245 Paul the Deacon, *Historia*, II.10: 93 (Foulke 2003: 68).

Charibert abandoned his legitimate wife, who was called Ingoberga, and took in marriage the two sisters Marcovefa and Merofilda. On account of this abominable act he was excommunicated by St Germanus the bishop of Paris and, after he had been struck down by a just judgement of God, he died and was buried in the church of St Romanus.[246] Sigibert seized his kingdom.[247]

Chilperic took Brunhild's sister Galswinth as his wife, but after a short period of time he strangled her in bed on the prompting of Fredegund. Next he rejected Queen Audovera because on the urging of Fredegund he had stood as godparent to her own daughter, and he joined that same Fredegund to himself in marriage. He had three sons by the above-mentioned Audovera: Theudebert, Merovech and Clovis.[248] On the orders of his father Theudebert occupied the region across the Loire which his uncle Charibert had held, and at Poitiers he fought with Sigibert's *dux* Gundovald and overcame him. Sigibert came to Paris with an army and waged war against his brother Chilperic. In this battle the above-mentioned Theudebert met his death. Chilperic fled with his wife and children to Tours and prepared to defend himself there. When Sigibert pursued him there he was treacherously killed by two retainers of Queen Fredegund. His brother buried him in the church of St Medard. Albinus bishop of Angers was famous.[249] At that time Brunhild was staying in Paris with her young son. *Dux* Gundovald kidnapped the boy at night and fled secretly, taking him back to his paternal kingdom.[250] That same Brunhild was sent into exile in Rouen; Chilperic's son Merovech came there and took her to himself in marriage. On account of this he was

---

246 *LHF* c. 30–1: 290–1. The *LHF* has both the king and the second sister ('Marcovefa') being struck down by God. 'Legitimate wife [*legitima uxor*]' and 'abominable act [*scelus*]' are terms introduced by Regino to strengthen the *LHF*'s more neutral language; these words echo the language used later to discuss the divorce of Lothar II.

247 This sentence is not in any of Regino's sources, and apparently represents one of his rare direct authorial interventions. He presumably inferred Sigibert's acquisitions from the information in the following paragraph that he controlled the territories across the Loire. Nevertheless, Regino's emphatic intervention also suggests he wanted to stress the political consequences of Charibert's marital misdemeanours.

248 *LHF* c. 31: 292–3.

249 This sentence is not from the *LHF*. Albinus was venerated at Prüm: Haubrichs 1979: 159–60. Different manuscripts place this sentence in different places, suggesting that in Regino's original it was added between lines or in the margin.

250 *LHF* c. 32: 294–7. In a rare chronological statement, the *LHF* explicitly places these events in the imperial reign of Justin. This must have strengthened Regino's confidence in his reconstruction of the order of events. Regino omits the *LHF*'s strong condemnation of the raid as having had a worse effect than the Diocletianic persecutions.

afterward made a tonsured monk by his father and he was ordained as a priest. At that same time Germanus the bishop of Paris passed to the Lord and was interred in the church of St Vincent. Childebert [son of Sigibert] missed his mother Brunhild, and Chilperic ordered her to return.[251]

The patrician Narses came from Campania to Rome and he died there; his body was borne to Constantinople in a leaden casket with all his riches.[252]

Pope Benedict ruled the Roman Church.

The poet Fortunatus was held in great renown in Gaul. He was born in a certain place called Duplalis [Valdobbiadene], not far from the fortress of Ceneda and the city of Treviso. He was, however, brought up and trained in Ravenna and he was extremely distinguished in the grammatical, rhetorical and metrical arts. For the love of St Martin he crossed into Gaul and lived first at Tours and then at Poitiers, in which city he was ordained as bishop.[253]

King Alboin with the Lombards took Treviso, Vicenza, Verona and the other cities of the Veneto.[254] Then Alboin entered Liguria and seized Milan, and then all the cities of Liguria. The city of Pavia endured a siege over three years before surrendering to the Lombards; and they took all the cities by arms except for Rome and Ravenna and some other fortresses which were located on the shore of the sea. After Alboin had ruled in Italy for 3 years and 6 months, he was killed by the treachery of his wife. Elmigisus, who had murdered Alboin, fled with Queen Rosamond to Longinus the prefect of Ravenna, taking with them the king's daughter Albisinda and the entire treasury of the Lombards. They both perished there by poison. Longinus sent Alboin's daughter Albisinda to Constantinople together with the Lombard treasure.[255]

---

251 *LHF* c. 33: 297–9. Regino sticks fairly faithfully to the source's material, but drastically abbreviates it.

252 Paul the Deacon, *Historia*, II.11: 93 (Foulke 2003: 68).

253 Paul the Deacon, *Historia*, II.13: 93–5 (Foulke 2003: 68–70). Regino distils the essentials of Venantius Fortunatus's life from Paul's much more elaborate account. On Venantius' reputation at Prüm see Haubrichs 1979: 78, 95.

254 Regino here quotes Paul the Deacon, *Historia*, II.14: 95 (Foulke 2003: 71) but inserts information from II.12: 93 (Foulke 2003: 68), which relates Alboin's presence at Treviso.

255 Paul the Deacon, *Historia*, II.25–30: 102–7 (Foulke 2003: 79–85). Regino omits Paul's long geographical digression on the provinces of Italy (chapters 14–24 of book II). His narrative of the Lombard expansion and Alboin's murder is reduced to the essentials from Paul's much more anecdotal version.

The Lombards entered Gaul. Their arrival had long before been foreseen by Hospitius, a man of God who was a monk in Nice, after a revelation by the Holy Spirit. Amatus, King Guntram's *dux*, came to meet them and after battle was engaged he was killed by the Lombards. Nummulus was sent in his place: he killed many of the Lombards and forced them to retreat to Italy.[256]

510–516[257]

[Beginning] in the year of the Lord's incarnation 510, Tiberius Constantine ruled for 7 years.[258] He had ruled the palace when Justin was still emperor and had performed numerous daily acts of charity; God had furnished him with a great quantity of gold. For while strolling through the palace he saw on the pavement a marble slab on which the Lord's cross was carved. Ordering this to be lifted, he discovered underneath a great treasure of over a thousand centenaria of gold. The treasure of Narses was also revealed to him by a certain old man, to whom it had been entrusted along with some others; it was so great that the cistern in which it lay could hardly be emptied in several days by the porters. The empress Sophia tried to carry out a plot against him. When, according to imperial custom, he was proceeding to his villa to enjoy the vintage for 30 days, she summoned her husband Justin's nephew Justinian and wished to raise him to power. On learning this, Tiberius apprehended the empress and deprived her of all her treasures, leaving her only food. His army defeated the Persians and took away, along with 20 elephants, enough booty to satisfy human cupidity.[259]

When Chilperic king of the Franks sent messengers to him, he received from him many ornaments and gold pieces weighing a pound each with, on one side, a picture of the emperor and the words 'Tiberius-

256 Paul the Deacon, *Historia*, III.1, 3, 4: 112–14 (Foulke 2003: 94–7). Regino skips over the last chapters of Paul's second book, which discusses the ten-year interregnum after Alboin's death and the power of the *duces*. The present paragraph is a brief summary that plays down the successes of the Lombards much more than Paul did.

257 Actually 578–582.

258 Bede, *DTR* c. 66: 522 (Wallis 2004: 225). Regino omits Bede's statement that Alboin was still alive in this period.

259 Paul the Deacon, *Historia*, III.12: 119–21 (Foulke 2003: 108–11). Regino abridges slightly Paul's description of Tiberius' treasure-hunting and drops his account of the emperor's glorious enthronement. Prior to this section Regino misses out several chapters of Paul's work that describe Saxon invasions of Italy and Lombard invasions of Gaul as well as some of the Frankish dynastic politics already covered. He picks up the thread again at chapter 12 because here Paul refers explicitly to the death of Justin.

Constantinus, eternal Augustus' in a circle and, on the other, a chariot with a driver surrounded by the inscription 'Glory of the Romans'. In his days the deacon Gregory, while he was apocrisarius in the city of Constantinople, composed his book of Morals, and in the presence of the emperor he defeated Eutychius, bishop of that same city, who was in error concerning the resurrection.[260]

Pope Pelagius ruled the Roman Church. He had been installed without the ruler's approval because the Lombards were besieging Rome and nobody could leave.[261]

King Chilperic, acting on Fredegund's advice, instituted new taxes throughout his whole kingdom. Each landowner had to pay to the king one amphora of wine for every *arpenne* of his own land and a *modium* [of grain] for every *iugerum* [of land]. Because of this the greatly oppressed people loudly appealed to the Lord. The Lord sent a plague upon the house of the king; he himself began to be sick and two of his sons died. The terrified king burned the tax-lists and forgave the levy.[262] After this he recognised his wife, who bore him a son whom he called Clothar. He was later a great king who was the father of Dagobert.[263]

517–537[264]

[Beginning] in the year of the Lord's incarnation 517, Maurice reigned

---

260 Paul the Deacon, *Historia*, III.13: 122 (Foulke 2003: 111). Regino sticks closely to Paul here, though he misses out some material on internal Italian events and shortens the section on Gregory, perhaps through familiarity. Paul's discussion of Gregory is drawn from Bede, *DTR* c. 66: 522 (Wallis 2004: 225): such similarities would have confirmed to Regino that his chronology was sound. This is not the same Eutychius referred to above, 397–404 and 405–412.

261 Paul the Deacon, *Historia*, II.20: 126 (Foulke 2003: 121). The account in the *LP* is almost identical (it was also Paul's source). The *LP*'s statement that Benedict, Pelagius II's predecessor, lived at the time of the Lombard invasion may explain Regino's jump forward to this part of Paul's history.

262 *LHF* 34: 299–301. Regino's vocabulary here sharpens the point which is left implicit in the *LHF*, specifies the dynastic target of God's wrath, and creates an implicit moral comparison with the wealth of Tiberius. On textual clichés about oppressive taxes see Wickham 2005: 62–5.

263 *LHF* 35: 301. The *LHF* here states that these events took place in the reign of Tiberius. The comment that Clothar's auspicious birth came after Chilperic 'recognised' Fredegund is another editorial intervention by Regino, and may be a comment on the profitability of legitimate marriage, though it could also be translated more loosely as 'uncovered' or 'became aware of' [her adultery]. Forward glances like the reference to Dagobert, although taken on this occasion from the *LHF*, are characteristic of Regino's work: Airlie 2006a.

264 Actually 582–603.

for 21 years.²⁶⁵ Tiberius, feeling the day of his death drawing near, after taking counsel with the Empress Sophia, appointed him to the empire. He adorned his daughter with the royal decorations and gave her to him, and with her the whole empire.²⁶⁶ [In the time of Childebert, Avitus, Carileffus and Maximinus were abbots of Orléans.]²⁶⁷

The Lombards, who had been under the power of *duces* for 10 years, made Cleph's son Authari into their king. On account of this position they also called him Flavius, which was the forename used by the Lombard kings. Because of the restoration of the kingdom, those who were then *duces* handed over half of what they had for royal use so that it would be possible for the king himself to be sustained as well as those who assisted him in various offices.²⁶⁸

Emperor Maurice sent 50,000 *solidi* to King Childebert of the Franks through his legates, requesting that he should drive the Lombards out of Italy. When he entered Italy with the Franks, the Lombards handed over gifts and made peace with him. The emperor asked for his money back but Childebert, relying on his own strength, did not send a reply in this matter.²⁶⁹

The same Childebert waged war against the Spanish and overcame them in battle. The cause of this conflict was as follows. Childebert had given in marriage his sister Ingundis to Herminigild, son of King Leovigild of the Spanish. This Herminigild, on the recommendation of Leander bishop of Seville and on the urging of his wife, was converted to the Catholic faith. His impious father struck him down with an axe on the holy day of Easter itself. When, after the death of her husband, Ingundis wanted to return to Gaul, she was taken by pirates and led to Sicily, where she died. Her son was sent to the emperor.²⁷⁰

265 Bede, *DTR* c. 66: 522 (Wallis 2004: 226).
266 Paul the Deacon, *Historia*, III.15: 122 (Foulke 2003: 113). Regino cuts this passage back to the essentials, leaving out Paul's eulogising praise of Maurice's greatness.
267 This line was written in the margins of some manuscripts, though it is not clear whether the addition goes all the way back to Regino.
268 Paul the Deacon, *Historia*, III.16: 123 (Foulke 2003: 113–14). Regino sticks closely to Paul, omitting only his claim that this was a golden age of peace and harmony in the Lombard realm.
269 Paul the Deacon, *Historia*, III.17: 123–4 (Foulke 2003: 117–18). Regino abbreviates this chapter but omits nothing substantial.
270 Paul the Deacon, *Historia*, III.21: 126–7 (Foulke 2003: 125–6). Chapters 18–20 of Paul's third book were presumably skipped over by Regino as they are exclusively concerned with internal Lombard affairs. He edits three details from the present chapter: that Leovigild was an Arian; that Herminigild was a martyr; and that Ingundis was captured by soldiers manning the Gothic frontier, not by pirates.

At this time there was a deluge of water in the regions of Veneto and Liguria and in other parts of Italy such as is believed not to have happened since the time of Noah.[271] Straight after this the disease of inguinal devastated the people with such carnage that only a few survived out of a countless multitude. Pope Pelagius was killed by this pestilence. During this tribulation Gregory was chosen by everyone to be pope, and he was raised to the pontifical throne.[272]

At that same time the same Pope Gregory sent Augustine, Melitus and John with many other God-fearing monks to Britain, and by their preaching the English converted to Christ.[273]

Reccared king of the Goths, brother of the martyr Herminigild, was converted to the Catholic faith through the preaching of Bishop Leander. The English people were converted to Christ, and their king Aethelbert was baptised.[274]

Pope Gregory sent his books on pastoral care, which he wrote at the beginning of his episcopate, together with those concerning the exposition of the blessed Job which he had written a long time before in Constantinople, to the above-mentioned Bishop Leander. He also sent him the pallium with the blessing of St Peter.[275]

The Emperor Maurice sent an embassy to King Childebert telling him that since he had not previously removed the Lombards from Italy, he should now fulfil the task. He sent an army into Italy and after engaging in battle with the Lombards the Frankish forces were severely beaten.[276] Paternus, bishop of Avranches, was celebrated; he

---

Regino prefers Paul's account of these events to that of Bede, *DTR* c. 66: 522 (Wallis 2004: 226), which is briefer.

271 Paul the Deacon, *Historia*, III.23: 127 (Foulke 2003: 126). Chapter 22, missed out by Regino, contains an account of a failed Frankish invasion of Italy on Maurice's request. The rest of chapter 23 was Paul's account of the effects of the flood in Verona.

272 Paul the Deacon, *Historia*, III.24: 128 (Foulke 2003: 127–8). Regino leaves out Paul's description of Gregory's division of the Romans into seven groups; but adds the comment about the pontifical throne. The *LP* (Davis 2000: 63) also associates Pelagius' pontificate with the flood.

273 Paul the Deacon, *Historia*, III.25: 129 (Foulke 2003: 129–31). This short chapter is reproduced in its entirety and represents a rare exception to Regino's policy of omitting Bede's reports on the British Isles. His interest in conversion and the spread of Christianity is evident in this decision.

274 Bede, *DTR* c. 66: 522–3 (Wallis 2004: 226). Regino seems to use Bede here to gloss or confirm Paul's account, hence the repetition and the omission of much of Bede's detail.

275 *Collectio canonum Hispaniae* II: no. 98–9.

276 Paul the Deacon, *Historia*, III.29: 133 (Foulke 2003: 136–7). Regino skips three

BOOK I 97

was a man of Poitiers.[277] King Flavius Authari took in marriage Theodelinda, daughter of *dux* Gerbald of the Bavarians.[278]

Childebert again sent an army of Franks into Italy with 20 *duces* to subdue the Lombard people. For three months they overran Italy, demolishing many strongholds and taking away a countless multitude of captives. Nevertheless they could not harm King Authari, who had fortified himself in the city of Pavia. Because it was summer, the army was unused to the unhealthiness of the air and, greatly worn down with the sickness of dysentery, was forced to return home.[279]

Tassilo was made *dux* over the Bavarians by Childebert.[280]

King Authari sent legates to King Guntram, Childebert's uncle, so that with his approval peace might be confirmed between Childebert and that same Authari. Guntram was a peaceful king adorned with every good quality. When he was out hunting in the woods one day, as often happens his companions scattered all over the place and he was left alone with one faithful man. He was weighed down with a great slumber and went to sleep with his head resting on this man's knees. From his mouth a little animal emerged and tried to cross a shallow stream that flowed nearby. Then the man in whose lap the king rested drew his sword and made a bridge out of it for the animal. It used this to cross to the other side and went into a certain hole in a mountain. After a very short time it re-emerged and, crossing the stream on the same sword, went back into

---

intervening chapters of Paul, two on internal Lombard politics and the other on the marriage alliances of Childebert. He does not go into as much detail as Paul on the Frankish defeat. Regino also inverts Paul's statement that Childebert sent embassies to Maurice informing him he would finish what he had started with the Lombards; perhaps his aim is to shift the blame for the defeat away from the Frankish ruler.

277 This is not from Paul. Venantius, *Vita Paterni*, MGH AA 4.2, pp. 33–7, p. 34 has 'Pictavus civis'. Haubrichs 1979: 93.

278 Paul the Deacon, *Historia*, III.30: 133–4 (Foulke 2003: 137–8). Paul calls Gerbald a king, not a *dux*. Regino excises Paul's long digression on Theodelinda's providential arrival at the Lombard court.

279 Paul the Deacon, *Historia*, III.31: 136–8 (Foulke 2003: 141–5). Regino drastically edits and changes the emphasis of Paul's original: he removes the original's stress on the role of Maurice in instigating the attack and makes the campaign sound much more successful than had Paul.

280 Paul the Deacon, *Historia*, IV.7: 146 (Foulke 2003: 154), although Paul uses the title 'king' for Tassilo and the wording is different. It is not clear why Regino breaks the running order of his sources here. A possible explanation is that by establishing Frankish authority over the Bavarian *duces* he sought to undermine the significance of Authari's marriage to Theodelinda. The idea that the *duces* of Bavaria were appointed by the Frankish king was an exaggeration that reached canonical status in the *ARF*: see Becher 1993.

Guntram's mouth. Immediately after he was roused from sleep, he bore witness to a wonderful vision that he had seen. He described how he had crossed a certain river across an iron bridge and in a certain cave he had gazed upon a great mass of gold. When the man on whose lap he had slept related in order what had happened, the place was dug up and an inestimable treasure was discovered. From this gold the king made a solid canopy of amazing size and great weight and had it placed over the body of St Marcellus the martyr in the city of Châlons-sur-Sâone; nor is there any other work made out of gold which merits comparison with it.[281]

Not much later the same king, when he had bequeathed his treasures to churches and the poor, died and was buried in that same church. His kingdom was taken over by Childebert and his sons.[282]

At that same time the holy priest Goar came from Aquitaine and in the Trechergau in the territory of Trier, on the bank of the Rhine and the stream which is called Wochara, he constructed an oratory in honour of the holy mother of God. He applied himself to prayer, alms and preaching the word and, filled with virtues, he rested in that place.[283]

Round about this time King Chilperic was killed by the treachery of his wife Fredegund when he came back from the hunt, and he was buried in the church of St Vincent in Paris. Clothar, who was still a boy, was raised to the kingdom by his mother and Landric, who was then mayor of the palace.[284] Hearing that his uncle was dead, Childebert strove to take over his kingdom and came with a huge army of Franks and Burgundians up to the city of Soissons, where he encountered this Fredegund with *dux* Landric. When battle was joined, Childebert's army was seriously cut up and fled.[285]

Then Childebert died. He had had, however, two sons, one named Theudebert, who was the elder, by a concubine, and by the queen one

---

281 Paul the Deacon, *Historia*, III.34: 139–40 (Foulke 2003: 147–8). The story is largely left intact by Regino, although he avoids anachronism by leaving out a reference to Châlons as the kingdom's capital. Regino rarely includes Paul's digressionary stories: perhaps the purpose here is to stress a moral about the providential sources of wealth comparable to that of Tiberius, and perhaps as a contrast with Maurice's bribing of Childebert. *LHF* cc. 35 and 37 comment favourably on Guntram.

282 The death of Guntram and his burial in Châlons are mentioned in *LHF* c. 35: 302, and the sharing out of his kingdom is in *LHF* cc. 36, 37: 304, 306. However, the wording is apparently Regino's, as is the comment on Guntram's generosity.

283 *Vita S. Goaris, AASS* July II.

284 *LHF* c. 35: 302–4.

285 *LHF* c. 36: 304–6, omitting much detail.

BOOK I   99

named Theuderic. [This king's mayor of the palace was St Arnulf.][286] Theudebert received the realm of his father while Theuderic got Guntram's kingdom, that is Burgundy, with his grandmother Brunhild. After this war rose up on the River Orvanne between Clothar and Theuderic and such carnage was committed among people on both sides that the river, since it had been filled with human bodies, seemed to flow with gore rather than water. In this battle, so they say, an angel of the Lord was seen holding an unsheathed sword over the people.[287]

In these times the holy father Columbanus came from Ireland with the blessed Gallus and other very excellent disciples to Burgundy, and there with the permission of King Theuderic he built a monastery called Luxeuil. [After St Columbanus, Attalus was made abbot in Luxeuil.][288] Fleeing from Brunhild he [Columbanus] came to Alemannia, where he left his disciple Gallus. He himself passed into Italy and built a monastery called Bobbio, where he became the father [abbot] of many monks.[289]

At that same time King Authari died. Agilulf *dux* of Turin took Queen Theodelinda as his wife and was elevated to be king over the Lombards. Pope Gregory wrote many things to them concerning the maintenance of peace between the Lombards and Romans. He sent to the aforementioned queen four books that he had composed on the life of the saints. He called this the book the Dialogues, that is the conversation of two people, because he had written it talking with his deacon Peter. The Church obtained many useful things through this queen. Agilulf made a perpetual peace with Theuderic king of the Franks.[290]

The monastery of the saintly abbot Benedict was attacked by the Lombards at night. The monks made for Rome, taking with them the book of the holy Rule as well as a supply of bread and a measure of wine.[291]

Emperor Maurice was killed together with his sons Theodosius, Tiberius and Constantine by Phocas, who was master of horses for the patrician Priscus.[292]

286 Kurze proposed that this sentence came from *Vita Arnulfi* cc. 4 and 8, though the wording is not similar. Its position in the manuscript suggests the line originated as a marginal note.
287 *LHF* c. 37: 306–7. Regino neglects to mention that Clothar lost the battle.
288 Apparently added in the margin of the original manuscript.
289 This paragraph seems to derive from Regino's reading of Jonas, *Vita Columbani*.
290 This paragraph is compiled from Paul the Deacon, *Historia*, III.35, IV.5–6, 8, 13: 140–1, 146–7, 150 (Foulke 2003:148–50, 153–6, 160). Regino omits Paul's reference to Childebert still being alive at the time of Authari's death.
291 Paul the Deacon, *Historia*, IV.17: 152 (Foulke 2003: 162–3).
292 Paul the Deacon, *Historia*, IV.26: 156 (Foulke 2003: 168).

538–545[293]

[Beginning] in the year of the Lord's incarnation 538, Phocas reigned for 8 years.[294]

In his second year Pope Gregory went to the Lord, and he was succeeded in the pontificate by Sabinianus.[295] When he died, Boniface was made pope. He obtained from the ruler Phocas agreement that the apostolic seat should be the head of all the Churches, because the Church of Constantinople was describing itself as the leader of all the Churches. He went to the Lord after occupying the throne for 8 months and 20 days. In his place another Boniface was consecrated. He asked Phocas to allow a church to be consecrated for him in the ancient temple called the Pantheon, which had been built by the emperor Domitian, and the emperor agreed to this.[296] After him, Deusdedit was raised to the pontificate.[297]

Eleutherius, the emperor's patrician and chamberlain, killed the tyrant John in the city of Naples.[298]

The Persians waged a terrible war against the empire and entered Jerusalem, carrying off the banner of the Lord's cross.[299] The monk Anastasius suffered an illustrious martyrdom. He suffered many things for Christ at the hands of the Persians until he was finally beheaded by King Chosroes along with 70 others.[300]

In Francia a deadly war began between the brothers Theuderic and Theudebert at the instigation of their grandmother Brunhild, because Theudebert was said not to be the legitimate heir of the kingdom because he had been born to a concubine. They fought it out with a very great armed force at the fortress of Zülpich. Theudebert took flight and fled to Cologne. He was dragged away from there and was made a tonsured cleric by his brother. Not long afterward he was murdered by

---

293 Actually 603–610.

294 Bede, *DTR* c. 66: 523 (Wallis 2004: 227).

295 Paul the Deacon, *Historia*, IV.29: 158 (Foulke 2003: 172), which specifies that this happened during the reign of Phocas.

296 Most of this information is in Bede, *DTR* c. 66: 523 (Wallis 2004: 227); *LP* (Davis 2000: 64); and Paul the Deacon, *Historia*, IV.36: 160–1 (Foulke 2003: 177–9). Regino seems to have blended the detail he found in all three (though he omits Paul's material on Lombard affairs).

297 *LP* (Davis 2000: 64–5).

298 Paul the Deacon, *Historia*, IV.34: 160 (Foulke 2003: 176).

299 Bede, *DTR* c. 66: 524 (Wallis 2004: 227).

300 Bede, *DTR* c. 66: 524 (Wallis 2004: 228). Bede places this in the subsequent reign, but Regino splices the two sections together since they are part of the same story.

BOOK I   101

the same brother and his two sons were killed.[301]

After this the aforementioned Theuderic died of poison through the deceit of Brunhild, and his two sons were killed by her.[302] The kingdoms which these kings had held passed into the control of Clothar. Brunhild, on account of the many evil things which she had done, on Clothar's order was tied to the tails of wild horses and torn apart.[303]

Agilulf king of the Lombards died and his son Rodoald was established in the kingdom.[304]

546–571[305]

[Beginning] in the year of the Lord's incarnation 546, Heraclius reigned for 26 years.[306] He undertook a war against the Persians and after killing their king Chosroes he accepted their submission. With great veneration he also restored to Jerusalem, from where it had been taken, the wood of the Holy Cross.[307]

A third Boniface ruled the Roman Church, and also Honorius, Severinus and John.[308]

Edwin king of the English was converted to the faith of Christ together with all his people by the preaching of Bishop Paulinus. Pope Honorius sent a letter to the Irish refuting their error in the observation of Easter, as indeed did Severinus' successor John.[309]

At that same time Arnulf was mayor of King Clothar's palace. This man, as was afterward obvious, was beloved of God and after enjoying the glory of the secular world devoted himself to the service of Christ and was conspicuous as a wonderful bishop.[310] Clothar's son Dagobert

301 *LHF* c. 38: 307–9, whose account is much more sympathetic to Theudebert, characterising him as a victim of treachery. The line about tonsuring is Regino's; the *LHF* simply describes Theudebert being murdered at Cologne.
302 *LHF* c. 39: 309–10.
303 *LHF* c. 40: 310–11.
304 Paul the Deacon, *Historia*, IV.41: 168 (Foulke 2003: 190).
305 Actually 610–641.
306 Bede, *DTR* c. 66: 524 (Wallis 2004: 227).
307 Ado, *Martyrologium*: 313–14.
308 *LP* (Davis 2000: 65–8).
309 Bede, *DTR* c. 66: 525 (Wallis 2004: 228), though Regino omits Bede's further information on events in northern England.
310 Paul the Deacon, *Historia*, VI.16: 218–19 (Foulke 2003: 262–3). Regino seems to have searched out this report on Arnulf to fit with his subsequent excerpt from *GD*.

was entrusted to Arnulf during his childhood by his father, so that he might bring him up following his own wisdom and that he might show to him the path of the Christian religion.[311] After he had grown into a man he despised Sandragisil, who was the *dux* of Aquitaine and a beloved counsellor of his father, because of some act of contumacy; and he subjected him to the lash and disfigured him by shaving his beard.[312] When his father realised this he summoned him for punishment.[313] Fearing the wrath of his father, Dagobert took refuge in the church of St Denis and his holy associates and humbly implored their protection. Thanks to the support of their merits he could not be taken away from there by anyone, until his father forgave the crime he had committed. Because of this he loved that most powerful place above all others, and he later handed over to it great gifts and gave many estates.[314] After this Dagobert was sent by his father with *dux* Pippin to rule in Austrasia, and he was recommended to the counsels of St Arnulf, the bishop of Metz.[315]

After the death of Rodoald king of the Lombards, Rothari was set over that same kingdom.[316]

572–574[317]

[Beginning] in the year of the Lord's incarnation 572, Heracleonas the son of Heraclius reigned with his mother Martina for 2 years. Cyrus of Alexandria, with Sergius and Pyrrhus bishops of the royal city [Constantinople], taught that there was one operation of divinity and humanity in Christ, and one will, and because of this they were condemned by Pope Theodore and other bishops.[318]

311 *GD* c. 2: 401.
312 *GD* c. 6: 403.
313 *GD* c. 7: 403.
314 *GD* cc. 8–11: 403–4.
315 *GD* c. 14: 404. The detail on Arnulf is not in the *GD*, and may derive instead from *Vita Arnulfi*, cc. 16–17: 439. This paragraph drastically abbreviates the material provided by the *GD*, though the main thrust of the narrative is retained. Among those details omitted were: Dagobert's childhood hunting expedition; material on St-Denis and on Dagobert's mother; the appearance of Denis in Dagobert's dreams; Dagobert being made co-ruler by Clothar; and Dagobert's marriage. The latter omission may have been intended to help gloss over the fact that the king's son was, as Regino goes on to relate, born out of wedlock.
316 Paul the Deacon, *Historia*, IV.42: 169 (Foulke 2003: 193), who calls the king Arioald.
317 Actually 641–643.
318 Bede, *DTR* c. 66: 525 (Wallis 2004: 229).

Dagobert, the son of Clothar, while fighting violently with the Saxons, was wounded by them and called on his father for help via an envoy. He came quickly with an army and after he killed their *dux* Bertald he subjugated the Saxons by arms so completely that he killed every male inhabitant of that land who was longer than the sword which he then wielded courageously.[319]

Around that time Sisenand and after him Chintilla reigned in Spain. In their times a synod was twice held in the town of Toledo, where many things concerning the Catholic faith and the Christian religion were promulgated and affirmed in writing. Also under these kings, Isidore bishop of Seville flourished. He was second to none of the modern teachers, and he discussed many things to do with the rules of faith and ecclesiastical instruction.[320]

At that same time the wife of the king of the Persians, who name was Cesara, for the love of Christ travelled to Constantinople in civilian dress and after some days was baptised and raised from the holy font by the empress. Looking for her, her husband came peacefully with 60 soldiers to the emperor in Constantinople. After he had been received with fitting dignity by the emperor together with everyone he had brought with him, he was baptised and raised from the font by the emperor. Honoured with many gifts, he took his wife and went back home.[321]

575[322]

[Beginning] in the year of the Lord's incarnation 575, Constantine the son of Heraclius and brother of Heracleonas ruled for 6 months. Pyrrhus's successor Paul tormented the Catholics not only through his crazy doctrine, like his predecessors, but also with open persecution. For this he was condemned by the apostolic see, just like his predecessors.[323]

---

319 *GD* c. 14: 405–6, which in turn is drawn from *LHF* c. 41: 311–14. Regino abbreviates the story, even leaving out the detail that some of the action took place in the Ardennes.

320 Kurze speculated that this paragraph was based on the fourth and sixth councils of Toledo, whose texts mention the three figures named. However, the wording seems to be Regino's.

321 Paul the Deacon, *Historia*, IV.50: 173 (Foulke 2003: 203–5). Paul says 60,000 men and explicitly places the story in the reign of Heracleonas. The inclusion of the story illustrates Regino's interest in the spread of Christianity.

322 Actually 641.

323 Bede, *DTR* c. 66: 526 (Wallis 2004: 229).

576–604[324]

[Beginning] in the year of the Lord's incarnation 576, Constantine [Constans II] the son of Heraclius' son Constantine reigned for 28 years. Since he had been deceived by the above-mentioned Paul he was made into a heretic and he issued a *typos* against the Catholic faith, asserting that neither one nor two wills or operations must be identified in Christ, as if Christ must be believed to want or do nothing. Because of this the above-named bishops were condemned under anathema by Pope Martin and 105 bishops.[325] Because of this affair the same Pope Martin was exiled to Cherson and there he died; and there also the glory of his miracles shines. Eugenius was made pope, and after he died Vitalian succeeded in his place.[326]

After Rothari king of the Lombards died, Grimoald, an energetic man, acquired the kingdom.[327]

At that same time Clothar king of the Franks died and was buried in the church of St Vincent just outside Paris. Dagobert obtained leadership of the whole empire except what he conceded to his brother Herbert on this side of the Loire and the frontier which stretches through the lands of Gascony, that is the areas of Toulouse, Cahors, Agen, Périgueux and Saintes, as well as the area enclosed between these and the Pyrenees.[328]

King Grimoald pursued Perctarit, who was a powerful man. The king received him into his faith, but prodded by flattering and disparaging tongues he began to think about killing him. But by the diligence of his most faithful bodyguard Hunold he was lowered over the walls of Pavia on a rope and fled to Dagobert in Francia, thus evading death and danger.[329]

At that same time Archbishop Theodore and the very learned abbot Hadrian were sent by Pope Vitalian to Britain and they made many of

---

324 Actually 641–668.
325 Bede, *DTR* c. 66: 526 (Wallis 2004: 230).
326 Bede, *DTR* c. 66: 526 (Wallis 2004: 230); *LP* (Davis 2000: 72–4).
327 Paul the Deacon, *Historia*, IV.51: 174–6 (Foulke 2003: 205–8) describes Grimoald's succession. Regino omitted several intervening Lombard rulers in placing Grimoald directly after Rothari. He seems to have been less interested in these details than in fixing Grimoald's reign in his chronology.
328 *GD* cc. 15–16: 405–6. Regino leaves out Herbert's (*GD* Hairbert) attempt to claim the kingdom for himself.
329 Paul the Deacon, *Historia*, V.2: 180–3 (Foulke 2003: 209–13). Regino gives the bare essentials of one of Paul's longer anecdotes. Paul says that Perctarit fled to Francia, Regino specifies Dagobert.

BOOK I   105

the churches of England productive of the fruit of ecclesiastical doctrine. Of these men Archbishop Theodore described, with wonderful and discerning consideration, the sentences for sinners, in other words how many years' penance one should do for each sin.³³⁰

In these days the Emperor Constantine [Constans II] desired to seize Italy from the hands of the Lombards, so he left Constantinople and came to Athens, from where he crossed the sea and landed at Tarentum. From there he entered Beneventum and seized almost all of the Lombard cities that he came across. He razed Luceria to the ground. Then he encircled Beneventum with his whole army, where Romuald the son of King Grimoald had enclosed himself. The emperor, after receiving Romuald's sister as a hostage, raised the siege and set out for Naples. From there he went to Rome, and Pope Vitalian came to meet him at the sixth milestone from the city together with his priests and the Roman people. He gave to the blessed Peter a pallium made from golden textile; and remaining in Rome for 12 days he demolished everything that in ancient times had been made out of metal to decorate the city, to the extent that he even dismantled the basilica of the blessed Mary, which at one time was called the Pantheon, and carried away the bronze tiles from the roof. After this he went back to Naples and after travelling by land to the city of Reggio he entered Sicily and resided at Syracuse. For 6 years he remained in Sicily, where after many and unheard-of acts of pillage he was killed in the bath by his own men. After his death Mecetius seized control of Sicily without the consent of the eastern army. The soldiers of Italy – some from Istria, others from Campania, still others from the regions of Africa and Sardinia – came to Syracuse against him, and deprived him of life. The head of the false emperor was carried off to Constantinople.³³¹

When they heard about this, the people of the Saracens, who had already spread through Alexandria and Egypt, suddenly arrived with many ships and invaded Sicily. They entered Syracuse and made a great slaughter of the people, carrying off a lot of plunder as well as all the ornaments made of bronze and other metals which Constans had stolen from Rome. Then they returned to Alexandria.³³²

330 Paul the Deacon, *Historia*, V.30: 197 (Foulke 2003: 235). Paul here drew on Bede, *DTR* c. 66: 527 (Wallis 2004: 230), so Regino could fit the story into his chronology with confidence. As a compiler of a canon-law handbook, he had an interest in pentitentials.
331 Paul the Deacon, *Historia*, V.7–9, 11–12: 187–91 (Foulke 2003: 219–25). Although drastically abbreviated, Regino retains the essential thrust of Paul's narrative.
332 Paul the Deacon, *Historia*, V.13: 192 (Foulke 2003: 226).

605–611[333]

[Beginning] in the year of the Lord's incarnation 605, Constantine the son of the previous emperor Constantine [Constans] reigned for 17 years.[334] Pope Donus held the apostolic seat and after his death Pope Agatho was ordained.[335]

The emperor Constantine gathered 150 bishops in the royal city, among whom were the legates of the holy Church of Rome sent by Pope Agatho, John the deacon and Bishop John of Porto. They all condemned the heresy that asserted there was one will and mode of action in the Lord Jesus Christ. At that hour so many spider-webs fell among the people that they all marvelled; this was a sign that the filth of heretical depravity had been expelled. And George the patriarch of Constantinople was thus corrected, but those others who persisted with their defence were visited by the vengeance of anathema. The right and true faith is that just as there are two natures in our Lord Jesus Christ, those of God and man, so there are believed to be two wills or modes of action.[336]

In those times there was an eclipse of the sun on 2 May, and there soon followed a terrible pestilence lasting for the three months of July, August and September. And then it appeared to many people that a good and a bad angel proceeded through the town at night, and at the order of the good angel the bad one, who seemed to be carrying a hunting spear in his hand, knocked on the door of each house with his spear – as often as he did so, as many men from that house died the next day.[337]

At that same time King Dagobert ordered that Brunulf, the uncle of his own brother Herbert, be killed on account of his infidelity; he was killed

---

333 Actually 668–685.
334 Bede, *DTR* c. 66: 527 (Wallis 2004: 231). Evidently, Regino miscalculated the span again.
335 *LP* (Davis 2000: 75–6). Regino misses out Donus' predecessor Adeodatus.
336 Paul the Deacon, *Historia*, VI.4: 213 (Foulke 2003: 252–4). Regino ignores Paul's long account of Grimoald's career. He seems to be supplementing Paul from the longer account in Bede, who specified that George was patriarch of Constantinople and that the 150 bishops met in the royal city. However, he omits their statement that this was the sixth general council of the Church. In the introduction to his work on canon law, Regino asserted that the councils of Gaul and Germany were more relevant to his audience than others: Regino, *De synodalibus*, preface: 20. The heresy referred to is monotheletism.
337 Paul the Deacon, *Historia*, VI.5: 213–14 (Foulke 2003: 254–5). Regino misses out a line that makes clear the city in question is Pavia, and another that credits an offering to St Sebastian with a cure.

BOOK I   107

by the *duces* Amalgar and Arnebertus and the patrician Willibald.[338]

After the death of the blessed Arnulf, Dagobert still employed the counsel of the mayor of the palace Pippin and the bishop of Cologne Cunibert. With their strong advice he embraced the love of prosperity and justice and he was extolled with the goodwill of all the peoples who were subject to him. He had a son by a certain girl called Regintrude, to whom his brother Herbert stood godfather after coming from Orléans. While Bishop Amandus was blessing that same boy and making him a catechumen, and nobody answered 'Amen' at the end of the prayer, God opened the mouth of the boy, who was no more than 40 days old, and in the hearing of everyone he responded 'Amen'. That same boy was called Sigibert.[339]

Bishop Arnulf and Romaricus the abbot were famous.[340]

In this year King Dagobert's legates Servatus and Paternus returned from Constantinople. The emperor asked Dagobert that he should order all the Jews in his kingdom to be baptised according to the Catholic faith or else expel them from the realm, since he had recognised a sign in the stars that his empire must be destroyed with divine approval by circumcised peoples. And the king certainly carried this out with the greatest zeal, but what had been shown to the emperor was not about the Jews but rather circumcised Saracens.[341]

After this Herbert died leaving a very small boy called Chilperic, who also died a short time later. The kingdom which he had held passed to Dagobert.[342]

Grimoald king of the Lombards entered into a very strong treaty of peace with Dagobert. When the fugitive Perctarit learned about this, fearing Grimoald he arranged to leave Gaul and hurry to the island of Britain. Meanwhile Grimoald died. When Perctarit had sailed some way across the sea by ship, a voice was heard from the shore: 'Perctarit should turn back to his homeland because today is the third day since King

---

338 *GD* c. 21: 407–8. Regino uses nothing from *GD* cc. 17–20, which are concerned with Dagobert's gifts to St-Denis. *GD* c. 16: 406 says Brunulf had pushed Herbert to claim the kingdom.

339 *GD* c. 22, 24: 408–9. Regino smooths out the dynastic line by omitting a story about Dagobert divorcing his wife for sterility, and by not calling Herbert 'king', unlike his source. Chapter 23, ignored here by Regino, is a rumination on Dagobert's qualities.

340 This line seems to be a marginal addition, perhaps by Regino himself, although the exact place it was intended to occupy in the text is not certain: see Kurze's introduction, p. xvi.

341 *GD* c. 24: 409.

342 *GD* c. 25: 410. Regino irons out his source's implication that Dagobert had to struggle to gain this realm.

Grimoald died.' He immediately turned round and gained the kingdom of the Lombards and made his son Cunibert into his co-ruler.[343]

After the death of Pope Agatho, the younger Leo took his place; and after him Benedict was ordained.[344]

King Dagobert fought with the Slavs and overcame them. At that time a *dux* named Samo ruled over them.[345] He also restrained the rebellious Gascons with the sword.[346] The Huns and Bulgars joined in battle among themselves. The Huns defeated the Bulgars. Utterly defeated and driven from Pannonia, nine thousand with their wives and children appealed to King Dagobert for land they needed to live on. The king ordered that they be received in scattered houses in Bavaria for the winter, and one night he ordered them all to be killed together with their wives and children.[347]

Around this time, after the death of Sisebod king of Spain, Sisenand, one of the leading men, asked King Dagobert to bring him help so that he could obtain the kingdom of Spain. In return for this favour he promised to give the king a gold dish weighing 50 pounds. The king sent an army under the *duces* Abundatio and Venerando, and Sisenand obtained the kingdom of Spain through the might of the Franks. However, breaking his promises, he did not send the Goths' dish, but paid King Dagobert 200,000 solidi instead. The king gave this silver to St Denis.[348]

Hediltrudis [Aethelthryth], queen and virgin, had great renown among the English.[349]

The Saracen people proceeded from Egypt to Africa with a great multitude, took Carthage by siege, cruelly sacked it and razed it to the ground.[350]

---

343 Paul the Deacon, *Historia*, V.32: 197–200 (Foulke 2003: 235–9); the last clause is from V.35. Regino leaves out Perctarit's ejection of Grimoald's son.

344 *LP* (Davis 2000: 80–1).

345 *GD* c. 27: 410.

346 *GD* c. 36: 414.

347 *GD* c. 28: 411. Regino consolidates Dagobert's conquests in this paragraph, though not exhaustively (*GD* c. 30 concerns triumphs over the Saxons).

348 *GD* c. 29: 411, missing out some details (for example that the Goths stopped Sisenand from sending the dish).

349 Bede, *DTR* c. 66: 528–9 (Wallis 2004: 232). It is rare for Regino to include Bede's reports on British affairs other than those linked to the spread of Christianity. Bede adds that she was preserved incorrupt in bed for 12 years, then took the veil.

350 Paul the Deacon, *Historia*, VI.10: 216 (Foulke 2003: 258). Regino seemingly preferred Paul's chronology to that of Bede, who placed this story in the reign of Justinian II.

612–631[351]

[Beginning] in the year of the Lord's incarnation 612, the younger Justinian, son of Constantine, reigned for 10 years.[352] John, Conon and Sergius ruled the Roman Church.[353] Justinian took Africa away from the Saracens and made peace with them on sea and on land. He ordered his *protospatarius* Zacharias to bring Pope Sergius to Constantinople because he was unwilling to approve and subscribe to the error of the synod that the emperor had held at Constantinople. However, he was repelled by soldiers and could not carry out the emperor's orders.[354]

The tyrant Adalgis, *dux* of the city of Trent, supported by Aldo and Grauso, citizens of Brescia, and many other Lombards, rebelled against King Cunibert and expelled him from the kingdom.[355] But Cunibert gathered his men again and killed the tyrant in battle.[356]

King Dagobert came to Metz and with the counsel of the bishops and leading men he raised his son Sigibert to the kingdom of Austrasia, and commended him to Bishop Cunibert of the church of Cologne and the *dux* Pippin.[357]

In the following year a son whom he called Louis was born to him by Queen Nanthild.[358] Dagobert specified that the kingdoms of Neustria and Burgundy should be given to him after his own death.[359]

After this that same Dagobert died and was buried in the church of

351 Actually 685–695.
352 Bede, *DTR* c. 66: 529 (Wallis 2004: 232). Regino gives a span of 20 years instead of 10.
353 *LP* (Davis 2000: 82–9).
354 Paul the Deacon, *Historia*, VI.11: 216 (Foulke 2003: 258–9). The protospatarius was leader of the imperial bodyguard.
355 Paul the Deacon, *Historia*, V.38: 201–2 (Foulke 2003: 241–2), and V.36: 200 (Foulke 2003: 239) for the detail that Adalgis was *dux* of Trent.
356 Paul the Deacon, *Historia*, V.41: 206–7 (Foulke 2003: 248–9). Regino cuts Paul's anecdote to the bare essentials. He presumably placed this story here because in Paul's work it followed the death of Perctarit.
357 *GD* c. 31: 412, which however says the *dux palatii* was Adalgis. Regino may have inferred the need for this amendment from c. 46, which pairs Cunibert with Pippin (see also above, 605–611). In any case, as with the earlier pairing of Arnulf with Dagobert, the change is presumably meant to emphasise the Pippinid/Carolingian influence at the late Merovingian court and thus provide a sense of dynastic continuity that papered over the coup of the 750s. Kurze's B manuscripts add at this point: 'Nuvellae Gerdrudis filia Pippini et Treveris Modesta clarescunt', an addition that probably belongs to the tenth century, but not to Regino or Adalbert.
358 Louis = Clovis; the updating of the name was already present in *GD*.
359 *GD* c. 32: 412.

St-Denis. He was far-sighted in counsel, circumspect in judgement, vigorous in the art of warfare, generous in alms-giving, zealous in maintaining the peace of the Churches and especially devoted to the enrichment of the monasteries of the saints. Although he honoured all the holy places, nonetheless he favoured the monasteries of St-Denis, St-Martin and St-Maurice above the rest, and ennobled them with every ecclesiastical dignity. His sons held his kingdom, just as he had divided it while he was alive. Louis's kingdom was administered by the mayor of the palace Ega along with Queen Nanthild.[360]

Around this time, when a great solitude existed in the fortress of Monte Cassino, Franks coming from the regions of Le Mans and Orléans removed the bodies of the venerable father Benedict and his sister Scholastica, and took them off to their own homelands.[361] The body of St Benedict was interred in the monastery called Fleury in the territory of Orléans. That of St Scholastica was buried with the devotion of the pious in the region of Le Mans.[362]

After the death of King Cunibert there was a great dispute among the leading men over the kingdom of the Lombards. Very many of them were killed and some were blinded. Even the women who had boasted that they would be queens were disfigured by having their noses and ears cut off. In the end, Herbert *dux* of Turin obtained the kingdom.[363]

632–634[364]

[Beginning] in the year of the Lord's incarnation 632, Leo seized the imperial dignity. He deprived Justinian of power, keeping him in exile in

---

360 GD cc. 42–6: 419–22. Regino excises all material not related to Dagobert's qualities and the succession, which he makes much smoother than his source. Chapters 33–41, untouched by Regino, cover a variety of incidents including the death of Sadregisel, acts of generosity to St-Denis, and the subjection of the Bretons. The omission of the latter may reflect the author's sympathy to the Bretons, or at least his lack of interest in using stories about them to endorse Frankish claims to hegemony: see also below, 862, 866, 873, 874, 889, 890. By mentioning three saints to which the king was generous, Regino dilutes the *GD*'s emphasis on St-Denis. Regino also omits the *GD*'s long account of the division of Dagobert's treasure (c. 46).

361 Paul the Deacon, *Historia*, VI.2: 211–12 (Foulke 2003: 250–1), which placed these events in the age of Perctarit and Cunibert. Regino leaves out Paul's allegations of subterfuge, and states the whole bodies were taken, not just the bones as in Paul's account, which also claims bits were left behind.

362 Ado, *Martyrologium*: 222–3.

363 Paul the Deacon, *Historia*, VI.17–22: 219–21 (Foulke 2003: 263–6). Regino provides only a brief summary, and updates the name Aripert to Herbert.

364 Actually 695–698.

Pontus, and ruled the kingdom of the Romans for three years.[365]

Pope Sergius discovered a large portion of the wood of the Lord's cross in the sanctuary of St Peter. Since that time, on the feast of its exaltation it is kissed and adored by all the people in the Constantinian basilica. In Britain, Cuthbert bishop of the church of Lindisfarne was renowned. In Gaul, Bishops Audoenus of Rouen, Eligius of Noyon and Sulpicius of Berry were celebrated. In these times the venerable man Willibrord, also called Clemens, who was one of the people of the English from Britain, for the sake of the Gospels crossed to Gaul, was consecrated bishop of the Frisians by Pope Sergius, and was sent among that people to preach.[366]

635–641[367]

[Beginning] in the year of the Lord's incarnation 635, Tiberius reigned for 7 years.[368] He rebelled against Leo, invaded his kingdom and imprisoned him in the same city for all the time he ruled.[369]

Dux Gisulf of the Beneventans ravaged Campania by fire, the sword and the taking of captives. John ruled the Roman Church. He redeemed all the captives which Gisulf had taken, and made the Lombards return home. To him succeeded another John.[370]

King Louis dug up the body of the blessed Denis. Acting less from religious feeling than from greed, he broke off and stole the bone of his arm. Immediately struck dumb, he fell into madness and after two years his life and his reign ended.[371]

---

365 Paul the Deacon, *Historia*, VI.12: 217 (Foulke 2003: 259); Bede, *DTR* c. 66: 529 (Wallis 2004: 233). Regino's wording is closer to Paul's than to Bede's. However, Paul places the material in the preceding entry later in his narrative; Regino's re-ordering may suggest he is using the *GD* as his main chronological control at this point.

366 Bede, *DTR* c. 66: 529–30 (Wallis 2004: 233). Here Regino is combining entries that Bede clearly divides between Justinian and Leo. Perhaps he was becoming aware of the increasing difficulties for his chronology caused by Bede's lack of interest in Frankish history, and tried to solve it by structuring his narrative around papal rather than imperial reigns – at least that is what he seems to do here, by focusing on events during the pontificate of Sergius. The list of famous bishops seems to come from *GD* c. 51: 425.

367 Actually 698–705.

368 Bede, *DTR* c. 66: 530 (Wallis 2004: 233).

369 Paul the Deacon, *Historia*, VI.13: 217 (Foulke 2003: 259–60).

370 Bede, *DTR* c. 66: 530 (Wallis 2004: 234); Paul the Deacon, *Historia*, VI.27: 224 (Foulke 2003: 271–2), which is itself based on Bede.

371 *GD* c. 52: 425. Regino leaves out the *GD*'s closing lines about Louis's semi-

At this time the synod held at Aquileia, because of the ignorance of the faith, hesitated to adopt the Fifth Universal Council. That synod was held in the times of Pope Vigilius against the heretics who asserted that the blessed Mary had given birth to just a man, and not to both God and a man. In this synod it was instituted as Catholic doctrine that the ever-virgin Mary should be called Mother of God since she gave birth not just to a man, but truly to God and man.[372]

At that time Lambert the bishop of the church of Tongres [Liège] was famous. While, inflamed with the zeal of religion, he was rebuking the royal house, he was taken by surprise, trapped and killed in the building of the church in the settlement of Liège by the most evil Dodo and other men sent from the palace.[373]

642–647[374]

[Beginning] in the year of the Lord's incarnation 642, Justinian reigned again for 6 years with his son Tiberius.[375] He retook the kingdom and killed those patricians who had expelled him. He also seized Leo and Tiberius, who had usurped his place, and ordered that they should be butchered in the middle of the circus in front of all the people. He ripped out the eyes of Gallicinus the patriarch of Constantinople and sent him to Rome, replacing him as bishop with Abbot Cyrus, who had supported him while he was exiled in Pontus.[376]

Sisinnius and Constantine ruled the Roman Church.[377] Justinian ordered this Constantine to come to him and he received him honourably and sent him home. Prostrating himself on the ground he asked the pope to intercede for his sins and he renewed all the privileges of his Church. When he sent an army to Pontus to apprehend Philippicus, whom he

---

redemption, though he does not go back to the much more condemnatory account in *LHF* c. 44: 316–17. This is the end of *GD*.

372 Paul the Deacon, *Historia*, VI.14: 217 (Foulke 2003: 260). Regino leaves out Paul's reference to this fault being corrected, perhaps to hint at the Lombards' falling from divine favour.

373 *Vita Landeberti*, *AASS* Sept V: 474; Ado, *Martyrologium*: 319 (which does not contain a reference to Dodo or Liège). Regino's emphasis here again implies that the royal house was losing divine favour. The development of writings on Lambert's cult is discussed by Kupper 1984.

374 Actually 705–711.

375 Bede, *DTR* c. 66: 531 (Wallis 2004: 234).

376 Paul the Deacon, *Historia*, VI.31: 225–6 (Foulke 2003: 273–4); or Bede, *DTR* c. 66: 531 (Wallis 2004: 234). Paul used Bede at this point.

377 *LP* (Davis 2000: 91–5).

BOOK I   113

had banished there, that same pope restrained him but still could not prevent it.[378]

The army which had been sent against Philippicus defected to his side and made him emperor. Coming against Justinian at Constantinople, he fought him at the twelfth milestone from the city, killed him and took over his kingdom. Justinian had reigned, as we set out, 6 years in this second turn. Leo in banishing him had cut off his nostrils so that, after he had assumed the empire, almost every time he wiped away a drip of rheum with his hand he ordered the butchering of someone who had acted against him.[379]

While this was going on in the east Ansprand, who had been exiled in Bavaria for 9 years, came to Italy with the Bavarians and fought and defeated King Aripert. Wishing to flee to Francia, Aripert entered the River Ticino and tried to swim across with his horse, but because he was weighed down with gold he was suffocated by the water and died. Ansprand obtained the kingdom but only for three months. After his death his son Liutprand was installed on the royal throne.[380]

Among the Frankish people Pippin was released from life and his son Charles succeeded him in his princely power [*principatus*], although only after many wars and battles to seize it from the grasp of Raginfrid. For while he was being held in custody he was rescued by divine favour and escaped. At first he began two or three fights against Raginfrid with a few men, and finally conquered him in a great battle at Vinchy. Nevertheless it is said that he gave him one city to live in, namely Angers, while he himself undertook to rule the entire Frankish people.[381]

378 Paul the Deacon, *Historia*, VI.31: 226 (Foulke 2003: 274); or Bede, *DTR* c. 66: 531 (Wallis 2004: 234). Paul used Bede at this point.
379 Paul the Deacon, *Historia*, VI.32: 226 (Foulke 2003: 275). 'As we set out' is Regino's addition, showing that he was constantly appropriating the material he was compiling and adopting an independent authorial voice. The opening three sentences are also in Bede, which is where Paul found them.
380 Paul the Deacon, *Historia*, VI.35: 227–8 (Foulke 2003: 277–9). 'While this was going on in the east' seems to be Regino's own comment, again making his editorial voice clear. He leaves out a list of Aripert's virtues; glowing obituaries are apparently reserved for Frankish rulers.
381 Paul the Deacon, *Historia*, VI.42: 231–2 (Foulke 2003: 284). Now that Regino can no longer rely on *GD*, and since the more equivocal *LHF* ends with Vinchy, he has to depend on Paul for information about the Franks. Surprisingly, he leaves out VI.37: 229 (Foulke 2003: 280) which contains a passage on the greatness of Pippin. However, he does have Charles 'succeeding' Pippin rather than 'seizing' power from Raginfrid. 'It is said' is also an intervention by Regino; and wearing his editorial hat he excises Paul's cross-reference to an earlier mention of Charles.

648–649[382]

[Beginning] in the year of the Lord's incarnation 648, Philippicus reigned for 1 year and 6 months.[383] After he had been confirmed in the imperial dignity, he ordered that Cyrus should be ejected from his bishopric and return to rule his monastery in Pontus. He sent letters of depraved dogma to Pope Constantine, which he rejected. The Roman people decided that they would not take the name of this heretical emperor on their documents or his image on their coins. Anastasius, who is also called Artemius, rose against him and deprived him of his kingdom and his eyes.[384]

650–653[385]

[Beginning] in the year of the Lord's incarnation 650, Anastasius ruled for 3 years.[386] He sent letters to Pope Constantine through Scholasticus, the patrician and exarch of Italy, declaring himself to be a promoter of the Catholic faith and a proclaimer of the sixth council.[387] After the death of *dux* Gisulf of the Beneventans, his son Romuald took his place.[388]

Around this time Petronax, a citizen of the town of Brescia, inspired by divine love, proceeded to the fortress of Monte Cassino and he rebuilt the monastery of St Benedict, which at that time had been ruined for 110 years, and he became the father [abbot] of many monks there.[389]

Gregory was made pope. He appointed Boniface, who came from Britain, as a bishop and through him he preached the word of salvation in *Germania*, and he enlightened that people who remained in darkness with the light of the Gospels.[390]

---

382 Actually 711–713.
383 Bede, *DTR* c. 66: 531 (Wallis 2004: 235). Here Regino counts the 6 months as if it were a full year.
384 Paul the Deacon, *Historia*, VI.34: 226–7 (Foulke 2003: 276–7); or Bede, *DTR* c. 66: 532 (Wallis 2004: 235).
385 Actually 713–716.
386 Bede, *DTR* c. 66: 532 (Wallis 2004: 235).
387 Paul the Deacon, *Historia*, VI.34: 227 (Foulke 2003: 277).
388 Paul the Deacon, *Historia*, VI.39: 230 (Foulke 2003: 282).
389 Paul the Deacon, *Historia*, VI.40: 230 (Foulke 2003: 282). Regino drops Paul's reference to the body of Benedict being there (since he had already described its removal to Francia). Regino has the sack of Monte Cassino near the end of his entry for 517–37, so the span of 110 years seemed to approximately fit his relative chronology.
390 *LP* (Davis 1992: 4), reworded by Regino.

BOOK I   115

The ruler [*princeps*] Charles engaged in many battles against Radbod king of the Frisians. By divine will the tyrant was struck down in the fourth year of the said ruler.[391] In the fifth year of his reign the same Charles fought against the Saxons and defeated them.[392] Emperor Anastasius sent a fleet to Alexandria against the Saracens. The army turned round in the middle of its journey and chose Theodosius as emperor, confirming him on the imperial throne with force. This Theodosius defeated Anastasius at the city of Nicaea in a terrible battle in which 7,000 of the army were killed. After giving oaths he had him made a cleric and ordained as a priest.[393]

654[394]

[Beginning] in the year of the Lord's incarnation 654, Theodosius reigned for one year.[395] After he had taken up the kingdom he soon put up in its original place in the imperial city the picture of the holy synods that had been torn down by Philippicus. In these days the River Tiber flooded so much that having overflown its channel it did damage to many things in Rome; in the Via Lata it rose to one and a half times the height of a man and from St Peter's gate to the Milvian Bridge the waters flowed together as they descended.[396]

---

391 *ASA* 716. Regino (or his source manuscript) adds details: 'king of Frisians'; 'fourth year...'; and also misses out a reference to Radbod coming to Cologne in March.

392 *ASA* say that Radbod died in 719 and Charles beat the Saxons in 720, which fits with Regino slotting these events in consecutive years. From this it seems that Regino thought Charles's reign began in 716, which was presumably where his copy of the annals began. Bede mentions that the year 716 fell in Anastasius' reign, which is probably why Regino anchors Charles here even though his absolute chronology was evidently off: Boschen 1972: 191–3; Sonntag 1987: 114–16. Other Frankish sources (for example *AF* 714: 1) state that Charles's reign began in 714, the second year of Anastasius, though Regino seems not to have been aware of this.

393 Paul the Deacon, *Historia*, VI.36: 228 (Foulke 2003: 279–80). There is a similar version in Bede, *DTR* c. 66: 533 (Wallis 2004: 236). The line about 7,000 deaths is not from either account, so presumably derives from an interpolation in Regino's copy of the *Historia*, or an oral tradition: see Sonntag 1987: 91. Kings who became churchmen are a recurring interest of Regino and of his community, and it is conceivable that versions of stories like this one circulated in Prüm in his own time.

394 Actually 716–718.

395 Bede, *DTR* c. 66: 533 (Wallis 2004: 236).

396 Paul the Deacon, *Historia*, VI.36: 228–9 (Foulke 2003: 280). Regino splits Paul's chapter in half at the point where Theodosius deposes Anastasius, which is closer to Bede's structure.

655–718[397]

[Beginning] in the year of the Lord's incarnation 655, Leo reigned for 9 years.[398] In his times the people of the Saracens came to Constantinople with a huge army and surrounded it. They besieged the city for three continuous years while the citizens appealed to God with great urgency. Many of the invaders died from hunger, cold, disease and fighting, and as if wearied by the siege they departed. Most of them died in a storm on the sea; within Constantinople, indeed, 300,000 people perished through disease during the siege.[399]

King Liutprand translated the bones of the saintly bishop Augustine from Sardinia and interred them in Pavia with due honour.[400] That same king besieged Ravenna and invaded and destroyed Classe.[401]

In the 10th year of his reign, the ruler [*princeps*] Charles fought and defeated the Bavarians.[402]

In the 15th year of his reign the same king entered Alemannia, fought against Lantfrid and subjected that whole people to him.[403]

In the 16th year of his reign he entered Gascony and terrified Eudo *dux* of Aquitaine with war.[404]

---

397 Actually 718–741.

398 Bede, *DTR* c. 66: 534 (Wallis 2004: 236). This is Bede's last entry, which explains why Regino here jumps to dating by the reign of Charles Martel. The incredible length of the regnal span in this annal seems to result from Regino's attempt to reconcile two conflicting pieces of information: that 716 fell in Anastasius' reign and was the first year of Charles Martel; and that Charles's reign began in the reign of Leo. The former fact was derived from Bede (see 650–653, n. 392); the latter from Paul the Deacon, *Historia*, V.42, VI.37: 231–2, 229 (Foulke 2003: 280–1, 284), who associates Anastasius with Pippin and Leo with Charles. The lack of chronological clarity produced by Regino's solution to this problem may also explain why he omitted Paul's account of Charles's succession, and why he describes Charles's activities using a relative chronology rather than the absolute dates supplied by his copy of the *ASA*.

399 Paul the Deacon, *Historia*, VI.47: 233–4 (Foulke 2003: 288); Bede, *DTR* c. 66: 534–5 (Wallis 2004: 236–7). Regino leaves out a section of the story relating how the Saracens were defeated by the Bulgars before the sea journey.

400 Bede, *DTR* c. 66: 535 (Wallis 2004: 237) – Bede's last line, also used by Paul the Deacon, *Historia*, VI.48: 234 (Foulke 2003: 288–9).

401 Paul the Deacon, *Historia*, VI.49: 234 (Foulke 2003: 289).

402 Regino, following his source (a version of the *ASA*), removed the complex political context in reducing the Frankish conquests to terse stories of triumph. Although Regino's text of the *ASA* was evidently different from surviving manuscripts, its account of the reign of Charles Martel contained gaps very similar to those of known versions.

403 *ASA* 730: 8, surviving versions of which do not call Charles king.

404 *ASA* 731: 8.

In the 17th year [of his reign] the Saracens came out of Spain with their wives and children and entered the province of Aquitaine in Gaul with the intention of living there. Charles, indeed, as mentioned, was then quarrelling with Eudo the ruler [*princeps*] of Aquitaine, but they nevertheless joined as one with common agreement in order to fight those same Saracens. The Franks attacked them and killed 375,000 of them. Eudo also attacked their camp and in the same manner killed many and destroyed everything.[405] They [the Saracens] killed 1,500 of the Franks, as is stated in the letter sent by Eudo to Pope Gregory about that same victory.[406]

At that same time Emperor Leo tore down and burned the images of the saints and told Pope Gregory to do the same in Rome if he wanted to retain his favour. But the pope disdained to comply. The whole of the army of Ravenna and the Venetians also resisted such orders with one spirit, and if the pope had not stopped them they would have set up an emperor over themselves.[407]

At that same time King Liutprand attacked the strongholds of Emilia, namely Fregnano, Monteveglio, Busseto, Persiceto, Bologna, the Pentapolis and Osimo, but after some days they were returned to the Romans thanks to the efforts of the Roman pope.[408]

Emperor Leo moved on to worse evil so that by force and coaxing he compelled all the inhabitants of Constantinople to pull down the images of the saints, and whatever he could get hold of he had burned on a fire in the middle of the city. And because many of the people hindered such wickedness from being carried out, some of them were beheaded and others forfeited parts of their bodies. Since the Patriarch Germanus had not consented to this error he was driven from his seat and the priest Anastasius was appointed in his place.[409]

Around this time the ruler [*princeps*] Charles sent his son Pippin to

---

405 Paul the Deacon, *Historia*, VI.46: 233 (Foulke 2003: 287). The regnal year and 'as mentioned' are introduced by Regino. He presumably entered this story here because Paul placed it at the time of Charles's struggle with Eudo.
406 *LP* (Davis 1992: 8). The number of deaths is also mentioned by Paul, though not the letter, so Regino's version must be a compilation of both sources.
407 Paul the Deacon, *Historia*, VI.49: 234 (Foulke 2003: 289); *LP* (Davis 1992: 11–12).
408 Paul the Deacon, *Historia*, VI.49: 234–5 (Foulke 2003: 290–3); *LP* (Davis 1992: 12–13). The reference to the efforts of the pope is apparently Regino's own. He may have been working back from later (papal) claims that the pope had rightful possession of these territories.
409 Paul the Deacon, *Historia*, VI.49: 235 (Foulke 2003: 293).

King Liutprand so that according to his custom he could have his hair cut. And he, in cutting Pippin's hair, became a father to him and sent him back to his natural father enriched with many royal gifts.[410]

In the 18th year of his reign Charles came to the Wistragau with an army and subjected it to his domination.[411]

In the 20th year of his reign he once more entered Gascony with a strong force and deprived Eudo of his realm and his life.[412]

In the following year he fought against the sons of that same Eudo.[413]

In the 22nd year of his reign the army of the Saracens returned to Gaul and made much devastation. Charles came against them near Narbonne and engaging them in the same way as before he laid them low with the greatest slaughter.[414]

In the 24th year of his reign the Saracens once more crossed the frontiers of Gaul and, entering Provence, they captured Arles and destroyed everything around it. Then Charles sent a message to King Liutprand asking for help against the Saracens. He, without delay, hurried to Charles's aid with the whole army of the Lombards. When the Saracens heard about this they immediately fled from those regions.[415]

In the 26th year of his reign Charles, the most warlike and victorious ruler [*princeps*] of the Franks, died.[416]

Unless I am mistaken there are therefore 718 years, 3 months and 2 days from the incarnation of the Lord, calculated from the 42nd year of Octavian's reign to the last of Emperor Leo, who is known to have reigned in the times of the ruler [*princeps*] Charles.[417]

---

410 Paul the Deacon, *Historia*, VI.53: 237 (Foulke 2003: 296). This story helps Regino set up Carolingian dynastic progression and establishes their claim to influence in Italy.

411 Elaborating on *ASA* 733: 8.

412 *ASA* 735: 8.

413 *ASA* 736: 8.

414 *ASA* 737: 8 for the ordinal date; Paul the Deacon, *Historia*, VI.54: 237 (Foulke 2003: 296–7) for the detail.

415 Paul the Deacon, *Historia*, VI.54: 237 (Foulke 2003: 296–7). Several minor Frankish annals mention the Provence campaign of 739, one of which Regino presumably followed. This is Regino's last excerpt from Paul – significantly, this concerns Liutprand helping out the Franks rather than his virtues and victories, which Paul finishes by describing.

416 Based on *ASA* 741: 10.

417 The last comment makes explicit the design of book I: Regino had always intended to end with Leo and Charles Martel. Regino was, as he feared, mistaken – he should

BOOK I   119

Let us see, furthermore, if we can reconcile the same years of the Lord with the eras of the Roman popes, and consider how the spans of the secular rulers and the prelates correspond.

[At this point Regino enters a list of the popes from Peter to Zacharias, with the lengths of their pontificates in years, months and days, from the *Liber Pontificalis*.]

We therefore consider that the total number of years from the times of the blessed apostle Peter up to Pope Zacharias, who governed the Roman Church at the start of Pippin's reign, is 703, plus 8 months and 26 days.[418] Adding to these the 15 years of Octavian, 23 of Tiberius, 3 of Gaius and 3 of Claudius (because the apostle Peter came to Rome in the 4th year of Claudius and so this year should be included in his pontificate) produces a total of 747 years. The years of the popes thus exceed those of the rulers of the Romans by 29 years. Let the prudent reader see which of these calculations should be followed. Nonetheless, we know for certain that neither the number of years of the emperors nor that of the prelates agrees with the Dionysian cycle, since one is found to be higher and the other lower; for according to Dionysius the ruler Charles died and Pippin took power in the year of the Lord's incarnation 741.[419] It could also be the case that the number of years has been corrupted by the scribes' errors.

We have therefore brought this [narrative], beginning with the very year of the Lord's incarnation, up to this point so that, because the following little book set out by our humble self reveals the times and deeds of rulers according to the same incarnation years, likewise it may show the main points of what was done under each ruler, and when and where; and also make known specifically the triumph of the saints, martyrs and confessors, and where and under which kings they secured

---

      have added up his spans to 715 years and 5 months. 'Calculated' = 'computati', a technical term relating to the calculation of time: Borst 1993: 19–20. The association of Leo and Charles came from Paul the Deacon: see 655–718, n. 398.

418 Again Regino is mistaken – it should be 725 years, 5 months and 16 days. As well as his inaccurate calculation, he copied some of the information from the *Liber Pontificalis* wrongly, and did not allow for periods between papal reigns. The Pippin mentioned here is Pippin III, Charles Martel's son.

419 The Dionysian cycle refers to the calculation of Easter dates according to AD dates pioneered by Dionysius Exiguus in the sixth century: Borst 1993: 24–6, 74–5. Regino is here referring to his copy of the *ARF*, which began with the death of Charles Martel in 741 and was evidently appended to a computistical text. For the relationship between histories and Easter tables see McKitterick 2004: 97–100; Story 2005. On the computistical sources available to Regino see Boschen 1972.

the crown of glory. Therefore where the first [book] finishes let the second consequently begin, and where the second starts let the first be assigned its conclusion.[420]

THE FIRST BOOK ENDS

---

[420] This paragraph confirms that Regino saw his work as a unified whole; and that his use of AD dating was driven by his intention to make the distant past fit the pattern of the *ARF*.

REGINO OF PRÜM'S *CHRONICLE*

BOOK II

HERE BEGINS THE BOOK CONCERNING THE DEEDS OF THE KINGS OF THE FRANKS

741

In the year of the Lord's incarnation 741, Pippin's son Charles, mayor of the palace and most warlike *dux* of the Franks, died.[1]

742

In the year of the Lord's incarnation 742, his sons Carloman and Pippin led an army against Hunald the *dux* of Aquitaine and seized the stronghold called Loches. On the same journey they divided the kingdom of the Franks between them in a place called Vieux-Poitiers. Afterward, in the same year, Carloman destroyed Alemannia with an army.[2]

743

In the year of the Lord's incarnation 743, Carloman and Pippin led an army against Odilo the *dux* of Bavaria, engaged him in battle and were the victors. Carloman went to Saxony without his brother and seized the fortress called Seeburg. At an assembly as a condition of peace he took Theoderic the Saxon as a hostage. After he had given oaths he was released to return to his homeland, but he deceived them by putting off his oaths.[3]

744

In the year of the Lord's incarnation 744, Carloman and Pippin again entered Saxony with an army and the above-mentioned Theoderic was captured again.[4]

---

1 *ARF* 741: 2.

2 *ARF* 742: 2–4.

3 *ARF* 743: 4; the last sentence is not in the original, and seems to represent Regino's inference based on what he read in the following annal – why would the Franks have taken him again if he hadn't defaulted on oaths?

4 *ARF* 744: 4.

745

In the year of the Lord's incarnation 745, Carloman confessed to his brother Pippin that he was minded to give up the secular world, and for the love of God to quit the earthly kingdom in order that in the future life he might receive possessions multiplied a hundredfold.[5] And in this year they undertook no campaign but each of them prepared himself, Carloman for the journey that he had decided on, and Pippin so that he might escort his brother to his destination honourably with offerings and due munificence.[6]

746

In the year of the Lord's incarnation 746, Carloman set out to Rome, and there he sheared his hair and built a monastery at Monte Soracte in honour of St Sylvester. After spending some time there he left and came to the monastery of St-Benedict at Monte Cassino, and there he was made a monk.[7] There is a memorable exemplary story told about this holy man. When he was still stationed at the monastery in Rome which he had built, he was venerated and lavished with praise by everyone because of his royal nobility and, more importantly, because of his contempt for the earthly kingdom and the glories of the present world. This man, filled with God and fearful of the applause of human praise, and who had given up so much for Christ, arranged to take flight rather than be exposed to vainglory. He told this only to a faithful friend whose fidelity he had tested in every way since childhood, and together with him he fled at night unknown to everyone and reached Monte Cassino. He carried nothing with him of all his possessions which were materially necessary; naked, he emulated Christ. And following custom he knocked on the door of the monastery and asked if he might speak to the abbot. When he came into his presence he immediately fell to the ground declaring that he was a murderer and guilty of all sorts of crimes, and he begged for mercy and asked for a place of penance. The father [abbot], realising he was a foreigner, asked him which land and people he came from. He confessed that he was a Frank and that he had left Francia for such crimes that he was ready to bear exile volun-

---

5 This clause is not from the source, and seems to represent Regino's gloss.
6 *ARF* 745: 4.
7 *ARF* 746: 6. The rest of this entry is an authorial intervention by Regino. Stories such as this may therefore have circulated in his monastery. Traditions about Carloman could also have come back from Rome with Abbot Marcward in the 840s. See above, Introduction, pp. 32–3.

tarily, provided he might not be deprived of the heavenly homeland. The spiritual father nodded assent to his pleadings and ordered that together with his companion he should be received in the cell of the novices, and there he should be tested as the Rule orders, all the more rigorously since he was from a barbaric and unknown people, thus fulfilling the apostolic saying: 'Test the spirits to see if they are from God.'[8] Thus tested in every suffering, together with his companion he was joined to the brotherhood after the lapse of a full year, professing stability, a change of disposition and obedience, according to the Rule of St Benedict.[9] He began to live a blame-free life among the brothers, strong with all the virtues. It came to pass, moreover, that in accordance with custom he was appointed to assist the cook for the week. Although he did this willingly he unwittingly gave offence in many ways. The cook, seething with wine, gave him a slap and said: 'Do you have to serve the brothers food like this?' Not at all upset, and with a placid expression, he responded: 'May God and Carloman forgive you, brother.' For he had not revealed his name to anyone in case he was recognised by it. When he made a mistake again in preparing certain foodstuffs he was once more struck by the cook, to whom he made the same appeal as before. And when he was cruelly knocked down by the cook for a third time, his inseparable companion in his wandering took offence that such a great man should be treated in so insulting a fashion by such a vile person, and unable to bear it any longer he grabbed the pestle which was used to knead the bread served with the brothers' vegetables and struck him with all his might, saying: 'May God show you no mercy, worthless servant, nor Carloman forgive you.' When they heard this, the brothers' bile rose that a foreigner received because of their mercy should have presumed to do such things. Immediately, therefore, he was placed in custody so that his presumptiousness could be severely punished the next day. The following day he was taken from custody and placed standing in the middle of the community. Asked why he had dared raise his hand against a servant of the brothers, he responded: 'Because', he said, 'I saw a man who is better and more noble than all those of my acquaintance in the world insulted by a servant more vile, not only with words, but also with blows.' Roused to great anger that he should regard someone who had come as a pilgrim more highly than the others, they asked who this man was that preceded everyone in goodness and nobility, and why he had not made an excep-

---

8 John 4:1, cited also by c. 58 of the Benedictine Rule (on the admission of new brothers).

9 This passage closely resembles parts of c. 58 of the Rule.

tion for the abbot of the monastery. Forced by necessity he was not able to conceal what God wished to be revealed, and said: 'He is Carloman, former king of the Franks, who for the love of Christ gave up his claim to his realm and the glory of the world, and who so humbled himself from such a lofty position that he is now made to suffer not only the insults of the most worthless persons, but is also afflicted by their beatings.'[10] When they heard this, the audience rose trembling from their seats and prostrated themselves at his feet. They asked forgiveness for their contempt, protesting their ignorance. He, on the other hand, threw himself on the ground and in tears began to deny that it was true, saying that he was not Carloman but a sinner and a murderer, and that his companion had made this up out of fear at the offence he had committed. What more? He was recognised by all and treated with great reverence. We could not allow this story to be passed over.[11] Now let us return to the chronicle.

747

In the year of the Lord's incarnation 747, Grifo fled to Saxony. Pippin made a journey through Thuringia and invaded Saxony as far as the River Meissau in the place called Schöningen. And Grifo joined forces with the Saxons and encamped on the River Ocker at the place called Ohrum.[12]

748

In the year of the Lord's incarnation 748, Grifo left Saxony and came to Bavaria and subjugated that same command [*ducatus*] to him, seized

---

10 Carloman was not a king.

11 This story's broad message about royal humility would have had particular resonance in Prüm, which had been home to various Carolingians: see above, Introduction, pp. 32–3. The story turns on how Carloman's inherent nobility was made apparent only through his acceptance of humility, utter debasement and self-denial. In this sense it works almost as a mirror for imprisoned princes like Hugh of Lotharingia (who was, however, dead by the time Regino wrote: see below, 885). The story echoes the Benedictine Rule thematically and verbally: cc. 3 (decisions to be made by the abbot and the brothers); 35 (weekly cook service); 40 (against drunkenness); 46 (wrongdoers should confess to the abbot and community); 58 (new arrivals to spend time as novices); 66 (new arrivals to be greeted and brought to the abbot); 67 (brothers not to speak of matters outside the monastery); 69 (monks not to defend each other); 70 (brothers not to strike each other). See Borst 1973: 528–31. Carloman is portrayed as a paragon of Benedictine virtues, shaming the monks in the very home of the Rule itself.

12 *ARF* 747: 6.

Hiltrude with Tassilo and made them subject to his power. Swidger came to help the aforementioned Grifo. Hearing this, Pippin came with an army and subdued all the above-named. He took Grifo and Lantfrid with him back to Francia and made Tassilo *dux* of Bavaria. Grifo, on the other hand, he sent to the region of Neustria and gave him 12 counties. From there Grifo again fled to Gascony, and came to Waifar *dux* of the Aquitanians.[13]

749

In the year of the Lord's incarnation 749, Burchard bishop of the church of Würzburg and the chaplain Fulrad were sent to Pope Zacharias in Rome, to ask about the kings in Francia whether or not it was good that in those times there were people called kings who did not have royal power. And the aforementioned pope told Pippin that it seemed to him better to call someone king who had power than someone who remained without royal power. And so the Christian order might not be disturbed, he ordered by apostolic authority that Pippin should be made king and anointed with the oil of holy unction.[14]

750

In the year of the Lord's incarnation 750, Pippin was chosen as king according to Frankish custom and anointed by the hand of Boniface of holy memory, archbishop of the town of Mainz, and he was elevated to the kingdom by the Franks in the town of Soissons. Childeric, however, who had falsely been called king, was tonsured and sent into a monastery.[15]

751

In the year of the Lord's incarnation 751, King Pippin made another journey into Saxony, and Bishop Hildegar was killed by the Saxons in the fortress called Iburg. Nonetheless King Pippin proved to be the

---

13 *ARF* 748: 6–8. Regino makes grammatical changes and adds the last seven words of the first sentence as well as the gloss 'to Francia'.

14 *ARF* 749: 8. The word 'Rome' is added, as well as the reference to anointing. The anointing may not have taken place as the annalist suggested, but by Regino's day it was assumed that it had: McKitterick 2004: 133–55. Regino may have been extrapolating backward from the anointing mentioned in 752 in order to stress that this was done in accordance with papal orders rather than autonomously.

15 *ARF* 750: 8–10. 'Of the town of Mainz' is an addition by Regino.

victor and came as far as the place called Rehme before returning to Francia. There it was announced that his brother Grifo, who had fled to Gascony, had been killed. In that same year Pope Stephen came to Francia seeking solace and help for the rights of St Peter. Carloman the monk, brother of the above-mentioned king, also came to Francia on the orders of his abbot in the hope of disrupting the pope's request. In this year the lord king celebrated Christmas at the villa of Thionville and Easter at Quierzy.[16]

752

In the year of the Lord's incarnation 752, the abovementioned Pope Stephen confirmed Pippin as king with holy unction and anointed his two sons Charles and Carloman to the royal dignity. In that same year the holy archbishop Boniface, while preaching the word of God in Frisia, was killed by pagans and lay as a martyr of Christ.[17]

Abbot Waltfred was famous in Italy.[18]

753

In the year of the Lord's incarnation 753, King Pippin went to Italy by apostolic invitation, seeking to do justice for the apostle Peter. King Aistulf of the Lombards, who had refused this justice, made for the Thermopiles, or the barriers, of the Lombards and came against King Pippin and the Franks. And after battle commenced, with the help of God and the intercession of the blessed Peter, Pippin and the Franks were victorious. In the same year Pope Stephen was escorted back to his see by the legates of King Pippin, namely Fulrad and many others; and when King Aistulf was surrounded in the city of Pavia, by necessity he was forced to promise that justice would be done to St Peter. On account of this promise King Pippin received 40 hostages and went back to Francia after confirming it with oaths.[19]

16 *ARF* 753: 10. There are no *ARF* entries under 751 or 752 and Regino, or the scribe of the manuscript he was copying from, carried on with the entries as if there were no gap in years – he only brings his chronology back into line in 760. The last line of this entry only appears in Kurze's MS D1 of the *ARF* – on this manuscript (Vienna 473) see Reimitz 1999; McKitterick 2004: 121–3, 215–16. Regino was presumably using a manuscript related to this one, which also contains some of the other texts he knew, though he didn't reproduce the similar addition that D1 included in *ARF* 757.

17 *ARF* 754: 12.

18 *Vita Waltfredi*, *AASS* Feb II. He was abbot of Palazzuolo: Haubrichs 1979: 93.

19 *ARF* 755: 12. The word Thermopiles is not in the *ARF*.

We judge that it will not be superfluous if we insert into this work the letter written about this matter by the same Pope Stephen. It runs like this:[20]

'"Bishop Stephen, servant of the servants of God. Just as nobody ought to boast about his own merits, so he should not remain silent about the works of God, which are done in him through his saints without their merits, but should proclaim them, because this is what the angel advised Tobias.[21] Consequently, on account of the oppression of the Holy Church perpetrated by the most savage, blasphemous and unspeakable King Aistulf, I came to lord Pippin, a most Christian king and faithful subject of St Peter, in Francia. There I fell ill almost to the point of death and stayed for some time in the Paris area in the venerable monastery of the holy martyr Denis. There, when the doctors were beginning to give up hope for me and I was in the church of that same blessed martyr in prayer beneath the bells, I saw before the altar St Peter and St Paul, teacher of the peoples. From personal knowledge I recognised them from shields which were adorned with their pictures, and a third man who was thinner and taller, the blessed St Denis, was on St Peter's right. And the good shepherd St Peter said: 'This brother of ours prays for health.' And the blessed Paul said: 'Presently he will be healed.' And, approaching, he put his hand on the chest of St Denis in a friendly manner and looked back at St Peter; and St Peter cheerfully said to St Denis: 'His health is in your gift.' And immediately the blessed Denis, holding a censer of incense and a palm in his hand, came toward me with a priest and a deacon who were standing at his side, and said to me: 'Peace be with you brother, and do not be afraid: you will not die before you successfully return to your see. Rise in health and dedicate this altar in honour of God and his apostles Peter and Paul, whom you

20 This is Regino speaking and not the original annalist. The following text (inserted and slightly abbreviated by Regino) is edited as *Ex Hilduini abbatis libro de Sancto Dionysio*, MGH SS 15: 2–3, though is better known as the *Revelatio* (or *Gesta*) *Stephani papae*. It was written at St-Denis not long before 835 by abbot Hilduin or Hincmar of Rheims, who was then at the monastery, though the possibility that the text preserves genuine traditions about the events of 754 should not be ruled out: Stoclet 2000. Its presence at Prüm is most likely attributable to Hilduin, who had close links with the monastery and possibly ended his life there, but Regino's interest was presumably fired by the text's illumination of dynastic history, one of his great themes. The text itself is dated to 754, which Regino changed to 753 to agree with the version of the *ARF* he was using: see 751 n. 16; but also perhaps because it glosses this annal's material on Pippin going to help the pope. Regino drops the final section of the text, which elaborates on Stephen's devotion to St-Denis. It is also interesting that he allows Bertrada's associations with Prüm (her grandmother was the monastery's founder) to pass unmentioned.

21 Tobit 12:6.

see, and perform masses of gratitude.' Not long after I became well and I wanted to carry out what I had been told to do; and those who were present said that I had been out of my mind. Therefore I reported to them and to the king and all his men in turn what I had seen, and how I had been cured, and I carried out everything I had been told to do."[22] These things happened in the 753rd year from the incarnation of the Lord, on 28 July, when strengthened by the virtue of Christ, after celebrating the consecration of the said altar and before the offering of the sacrifice, he [Stephen] anointed as kings of the Franks King Pippin and his two sons Charles and Carloman. But he also blessed the king's wife Bertrada, dressed in her royal robes, with the grace of the sevenfold Holy Spirit in the name of God. He also consecrated through an apostolic blessing the leading men of the Franks and bound them on the authority of St Peter given to him by Christ, imploring them that neither they nor any of their descendants should in future ever presume in any way to make a king over them from any family other than the descendants of that one which divine providence had seen fit to choose to protect the apostolic see and through him, that is the representative of St Peter, and indeed of the Lord Jesus Christ, to raise to royal power and to consecrate with the most sacred unction.'

After inserting this account, let us return to the chronicle.

When King Pippin, as was mentioned above, entered Italy, the monk Carloman stayed with Queen Bertrada at the city of Vienne, where he was seized by illness and ended his final day.[23]

[From this point until Charlemagne's death in January 814, Regino returns to the *Annales Regni Francorum* and reproduces it without further notable interventions or alterations, other than in his description of the death of Gerold of Bavaria in 799: 'one can read about him in the Vision of Wetti, which lists him among the martyrs' (a reference to Heito of Reichenau, *Visio Wettini*, c. 27). For a full translation of the *ARF* see Scholz and Rogers 1972; a substantial part is translated in King 1987. The *ARF* section concludes in the 813 annal with Charlemagne fighting the Danes.][24]

---

22 This is the end of Stephen's letter; the following commentary is also part of the *Revelatio* text from St-Denis.
23 *ARF* 755: 12.
24 One group of *ARF* manuscripts stopped in 813: see McKitterick 2004: 20, 111–13. On Regino's use of the *ARF* see also above, Introduction, pp. 29–30.

BOOK II   129

813

...

In that same year [January 814] the emperor Charles died and was buried with honour at Aachen in the church of the Holy Saviour and Holy Mary Mother of God, which church he had had built from the foundations with magnificent works. His son Louis took up the imperial sceptre.[25]

I discovered the things which have been laid out above in a certain booklet composed in the language of plebeians and rustics. I have corrected them in places to regular Latin, and I have also added certain things which I heard from the stories of the elders [*seniores*].[26] The other things that follow have been recorded by the efforts of my humble self according to what I found written in books of chronicles [*libri chronicarum*],[27] or what I have been able to learn from the accounts of the elders [*patres*] by listening. What is more, concerning the times of the emperor Louis [the Pious] I have included very little because I have not found written texts, nor heard from the elders [*seniores*] anything that was worth committing to memory. However, I have more to say about the deeds of the emperor Lothar and his brothers, the kings of the Franks. And where it comes up to our own times, I have made my narrative broader: 'for things we have seen', as Jerome says, 'are told in one way, and those we have heard in another: those things we know better, we also explain better.'[28]

818

In the year of the Lord's incarnation 818, Bernard, king of Italy and son of Pippin, after being summoned to the emperor at Aachen, was captured by trickery and deprived of first his eyes and then his life.[29]

---

25 Derived from *AP*, and obviously part of the little book that Regino mentions in the next passage. The *AP* were, therefore, a continuation of the *ARF*. See Boschen 1972.

26 Presumably referring to the Carloman and Stephen stories. Regino's correction of his sources and Adalbert's subsequent correction of Regino are analysed by Prinz 1973.

27 Presumably a reference to *AP*.

28 Jerome, *Contra Rufinum*, II.25: 'Aliter enim audita, aliter visa narrantur. Quod melius intelligimus, melius et proferimus.' The quote is approximate to the original but not exact, suggesting that Regino was quoting from memory.

29 Bernard was not killed but rather died of his wounds: see Noble 1974; Depreux 1992. The date is correct and may have come from the *AP*. Bernard's memory would

This Bernard, moreover, had a son called Pippin who fathered three children, Bernard, Pippin and Herbert. In our times, this Herbert killed Count Rudolf the son of Baldwin. Soon afterward he was killed by Baldwin, a follower of Rudolf's brother Baldwin. This Baldwin holds the command [*ducatus*] in Flanders to this day.[30]

829

In the year of the Lord's incarnation 829, Tancrad, the second abbot of the monastery of Prüm, died. He was succeeded in command by Marcward, a sensible man and one given over to holy religion.[31]

836

In the year of the Lord's incarnation 836, the Bretons broke treaties and began to rebel with their *dux* Morman. The emperor led an army against them, but he did not prevail.[32]

837

In the year of the Lord's incarnation 837 Morman king of the Bretons died, and the leadership [*ducatus*] of that people was granted to Nominoë by the emperor at Ingelheim.[33]

---

have been kept alive due to the later significance of his descendants in Lotharingian politics, described in the following sentences.

30 Herbert was count of Vermandois. The elder Baldwin was count of Flanders (d. 879); his sons were Baldwin II, count of Flanders (879–918), and Rudolf (probably) count of Cambrai. The killing of Rudolf in 896 was part of a struggle for control of St-Quentin, St-Vaast and other fortified centres, which was in turn part of a larger dispute over the kingdom between King Odo of west Francia, King Zwentibald of Lotharingia and Charles 'the Straightforward' (or 'Simple'), would-be ruler of the western kingdom: *AV* 896: 78; and see also below, 903. Herbert was killed at some point in the period 900–908. For discussion see Werner 1959c; Schneider 1973: 172–82; Nonn 1983: 119–20; Nicholas 1992: 19. Airlie 2006a analyses this flashforward in the context of Regino's narrative.

31 *AP*: see Boschen 1972: 220. Tancrad had been abbot since 804. Marcward came from the monastery of Ferrières and was abbot 829–53, presumably having been appointed by Louis the Pious.

32 Louis the Pious's only engagement with Morman was a battle following a raid in 818. The Franks won and Morman was killed: Chédeville and Guillotel 1984: 227–8; Smith 1992: 65–6; Pettiau 2004: 178.

33 Morman actually died in 818: see previous note. Contemporary Frankish sources did not call the Breton leaders kings – in fact, according to earlier sources on this incident, one reason that Louis attacked the Bretons was that they had presumed to call their ruler king. Nominoë's authority was confirmed by Louis in 831: Smith 1992: 65, 80.

838

In the year of the Lord's incarnation 838, Louis was deprived of command [*imperium*] by his own men and placed in custody, and control of the kingdom [*regni monarchia*] was given to his son Lothar by the election of the Franks. Then Louis was rescued in turn from imprisonment by his son Louis [the German] and by the Franks, and was restored to the imperial throne. This deposition occurred principally due to the various fornications of his wife Judith.[34]

839

In the year of the Lord's incarnation 839, Lothar forsook Francia and went to Italy. Ebo the [arch]bishop of Rheims was deposed in a general synod, and many others who had conspired in the deposition of the emperor were condemned to exile.[35]

840

In the year of the Lord's incarnation 840, the emperor Louis fell ill while pursuing his son Louis across the Rhine. After he was sent in a boat along the river Main, he was brought into the Rhine and he left his life there on an island next to Ingelheim. From there he was carried to Metz and honourably interred in the church of St Arnulf. Immediately, Lothar left Italy and seized power [*imperium*].[36]

841

In the year of the Lord's incarnation 841, Louis and Charles, feeling indignant that they might be robbed of the paternal kingdom entirely, gathered an army from all sides and soon engaged their brother in battle at Fontenoy. In this battle the power of the Franks was so diminished, and

---

34 Here Regino describes the events of 833–4. By nailing the blame exclusively on Judith's sexual behaviour, Regino reflected a ninth-century political critique of queens' morality that came to a head in the divorce case of Lothar II. See Stafford 1983; Airlie 1998.

35 Here Regino was describing the events of 834–5. The deposition of Ebo was big news in 830s Trier, where Thegan wrote a biography of Louis that dwelled on the archbishop's supposed culpability. Despite being in Trier, Regino seems not to have known this source.

36 Regino knew the date of Louis's death from *AP*. In the absence of other fixed dates, it is possible that he decided to line up the other events he knew about in the preceding years. On Lothar's activities in this period see Screen 2003.

their famous manhood [*virtus*] so weakened, that thereafter they were incapable not only of expanding the kingdom, but also of defending its frontiers.³⁷ In the end Charles and Louis won, but not without serious losses among their own men.

842

In the year of the Lord's incarnation 842 the three above-mentioned brothers divided the empire of the Franks between them.³⁸ They ceded the western kingdom to Charles, from the Breton ocean to the River Meuse; meanwhile Louis received the eastern kingdom, namely all of Germany up to the River Rhine and several towns beyond it with their surrounding territories, on account of an abundance of vines.³⁹ Lothar, on the other hand, who was both eldest by birth and called emperor, was allotted the middle kingdom in between the others, which has until the present day been called 'Lothar's kingdom' [*regnum Lotharii*] after him.⁴⁰ He also received the whole of Provence and the entire kingdom of Italy including the town of Rome itself, which even now is venerated by all the Holy Church with a certain special status because of the presence of the apostles Peter and Paul, and which formerly was called the mistress [*domina*] of the lands of the earth because of the undefeated power of the name of Rome.⁴¹

847

In the year of the Lord's incarnation 847 Hetti the [arch]bishop of Trier left this world, and Theutgaud obtained his see.⁴²

---

37 Regino dated Fontenoy from *AP*. The battle was much discussed in the later ninth century: Nelson 1998. The phrase 'power of the Franks' (*vires Francorum*) is one of Regino's favourites.

38 The Treaty of Verdun was concluded in 843; its significance for the empire's central regions is explored by Innes 2000: 208–13; Hummer 2006: 165–90.

39 Mainz, Speyer and Worms all ended up in the eastern kingdom, though they are west of the Rhine. Their political and strategic significance was probably more important than the local viticulture.

40 In fact the kingdom was named after Lothar II – Regino's shifting of the story reflects his negative view of Lothar II: Airlie forthcoming. On the origins of Lotharingian regnal identity see Anton 1993; Parisse 1995; Bauer 1997.

41 Regino's comment on Rome as a religious centre may have helped undercut the basis of Lothar's imperial status. More generally it illuminates his perception of the present age as distinct from the imperial past of book I: see above, Introduction, pp. 23–5.

42 This came from *AP*.

851

In the year of the Lord's incarnation 851 Queen Ermengard, the wife of Emperor Lothar, died. She was a venerable matron and pleasing to God, and bore three sons to Lothar, namely Louis, Lothar and Charles.[43]

853

In the year of the Lord's incarnation 853 the Northmen went round Brittany by sea and occupied the mouth of the River Loire. By means of a sudden assault they attacked the city of Nantes and destroyed everything with murder, pillage and fire. They killed the bishop of that town on the Sabbath of Holy Easter in the church while he was celebrating baptism in the usual way, and also slaughtered the clerics. Devastating the entire surrounding region, they occupied first Angers and then the town of Tours, and just as a monstrous storm destroys everything, so they consumed all.[44] They also burned the temple of the most excellent bishop Martin with fire. This was the first time, so they say, that the Northmen's fleet landed on the banks of the Loire.[45]

In that same year Eigil was made abbot of the monastery of Prüm.[46]

About this time Charles seized his nephew Pippin [II] king of Aquitaine, who was betrayed to him by the Aquitanians themselves because with the dissolution of peace that province was devastated by its own people, and many evil things were done there that went unpunished. On the advice of the bishops and leading men, he tonsured the captive and sent him dressed in monastic habit into the monastery of St-Médard at Soissons. He took flight from there with the agreement and help of two monks, escaped, but was captured again and placed in custody

---

43 Louis II of Italy, Lothar II, and Charles of Provence. Ermengard died 20 March 851, dated accurately from *AP*. Her epitaph survives: Dutton 2004: 371–2. Note that the titles of queen and empress were often used interchangeably in this period.

44 '... velut inmanis tempestas cuncta prosternit.' Cf. Justin, *Epitome*, VI.2.16: 53 (Yardley 1994: 69): 'urbes expugnat et quasi tempestas quaedam cuncta prosternit' (on Conon the Athenian). The similarity suggests that Regino had internalised some of Justin's imagery. See also Boschen 1972: 221.

45 Or, alternatively, 'the Loire coast.' Here Regino seemingly runs together two separate attacks, one from 843 and the other from 853: his cue was the *AP*, which recorded the assault on Tours in 853. On this incident see *AB* 853: 76–7; *AX* 854: 18; *AF* 853: 34–5; and cf. *GSR* III.9: 212–18. Other sources place the 843 attack on Nantes on the feast of John the Baptist rather than Easter. The raid was mired in Franko-Breton politics: *AB* 843: 55–6; Smith 1992: 94–5; Nelson 1992: 136–7.

46 This came from the *AP*. Egil, like his predecessor Marcward a product of the monastery of Ferrières, was abbot 853–60.

in the very well fortified castle of Senlis.[47] This Pippin was the son of Pippin [I, of Aquitaine], son of the Emperor Louis [the Pious]. They say that his father[, namely the emperor Louis,][48] wanted to promote him to clerical office when he was still a child, and to commend him to Drogo, the bishop of Metz, his own uncle of course, for education in the liberal arts and the teachings of the Church. But the boy's brother Lothar obstructed his father's will and in no way allowed him to be tonsured but seized him by force from his father's hand: for the same boy was, so they say, extremely handsome.[49] Later, his father [the emperor Louis, when he was dividing the empire between his sons] only gave him the province of Aquitaine.[50] However, it brought him little prosperity that he was called back from his [priestly] training and the praise of God. For by day and by night he gave himself over to drunkenness and carousing, and in the end his mind was overcome and he fell into a manic passion. He ended the present life in disgrace, leaving behind as successor his son Pippin [II], whom we recently mentioned above.[51]

855

In the year of the Lord's incarnation 855, Lothar assembled the leading men and divided the control of the kingdom among his sons. He handed over Italy to Louis and ordered that he be called emperor.[52] To his namesake Lothar he gave the kingdom which is named after him;[53] and

47 Pippin II of Aquitaine, son of Louis the Pious's second son Pippin, had been airbrushed out of the family picture at the Treaty of Verdun though he continued to wield significant influence in Aquitaine at the expense of his uncle Charles the Bald. He was sent to St-Médard in 852: *AB* 852: 74–5. *AB* 853: 76 says the two monks planned to help him escape but were foiled. By 854 he was free and back in Aquitaine, possibly with Charles's approval in a bid to undermine the invasion of Louis the Younger: *AB* 854: 79 and n. 8. He ended up at Senlis in 864: *AB* 864: 119.

48 This comment appears in Kurze's A manuscripts, and so may be taken as a gloss inserted by Adalbert: see above, Introduction, pp. 55–6. Regino is here talking about Pippin I.

49 Ermold, *Ad eundem Pippinum*: 218–20 and Jonas, *De institutione regia*: 148 also comment on Pippin's beauty.

50 In the *Ordinatio Imperii* of 817. The square brackets indicate an insertion by Adalbert.

51 Pippin I died on 13 December 838. Although Pippin II was initially seen as his father's successor he was later removed from the dynastic top table with exclusion from the 843 treaty.

52 Louis was designated king in 839, and crowned in Rome in 844.

53 Lotharingia was named after Lothar II; here, Regino seems to suggest that it was Lothar I: cf. above, 842.

to Charles, who was younger, he gave the kingdom of Provence. Having therefore ordered and disposed of the affairs of the kingdom, saying goodbye to his men, he renounced the world. Entering the monastery of Prüm, he set aside the hair of his head and took up the dress of the holy way of life. He ended his last day in the profession of religion on 29 September.[54]

856

In the year of the Lord's incarnation 856, King Lothar joined Queen Theutberga to himself in matrimony.[55] The greatest ruin resulted from this union, not only for him, but also for his whole kingdom, as what follows will show in a clearer light.

858

In the year of the Lord's incarnation 858, King Charles, who ruled Provence and was the son of the emperor Lothar, died.[56] There was no little controversy between King Lothar and his uncle Charles [the Bald] over his kingdom.[57]

859

In the year of the Lord's incarnation 859, Lothar committed the command [*ducatus*] between the Jura and the Mons Iovis to abbot Hubert, because he was then considered to be very faithful since they were related through his sister Theutberga.[58]

---

54 Lothar's death is from *AP*. See also *AF* 855: 37; *AB* 855: 81. The latter states that Lothar had been planning Prüm as his burial site. Lothar was a prominent benefactor of the monastery: DD L 56, 57, 68, 85, 87, 99, 122, 130, 131, 132, 137, 139.

55 Actually 855.

56 25 January 863.

57 In fact, the conflict was between Lothar and his brother Louis II, who won concessions of territory north of the Alps: *AB* 863: 104; Ado, *Chronicon*: 322–3. Regino seemingly back-projected later tensions between Lothar and Charles.

58 In fact Hubert already held this region, Transjurane Burgundy, which was a discrete unit (though Regino's labelling of it as a *ducatus* is anachronistic): see Castelnuovo 1998. He also controlled the key abbey of St-Maurice-d'Agaune. In 859 Lothar II conceded Transjurane Burgundy to Louis II: *AB* 859: 91. This is probably why Hubert is subsequently found holding offices at Tours and Lobbes in Charles the Bald's kingdom before his murder in 864: *AB* 860, 862, 864: 93, 98, 121; *AX* 864: 23.

860

In the year of the Lord's incarnation 860, Eigil voluntarily renounced the abbacy of Prüm, and Ansbald, a man notable in all sanctity and goodness, succeeded him in command.[59] In these times the elder Louis [the German], brother of Emperor Lothar [I], very strenuously prosecuted many wars against the Slavic peoples.[60] Accordingly, he invaded the lands of the Moravians and completely tamed everything by force of arms, capturing their leader Rastiz and ordering his eyes to be gouged out for violating treaties.[61]

At this time a great fire of discords and disputes seethed among Charles [the Bald]'s leading men. In short, Lambert, who held the command [*ducatus*] between the Loire and Seine, treacherously killed Vivian, who was a powerful man.[62] In turn Count Gauzbert with some other men butchered the same Lambert equally treacherously. This Gauzbert was beheaded on Charles's orders.[63] Seeing the destitute land devoid of leaders and counsel, the Bretons took up arms and invaded the borders of the kingdom of the Franks. They crossed the Loire and advanced as far as Poitiers, ravaging everything with murder, pillage and fire,

---

59 *AP*. Egil became Archbishop of Sens (860–70). His withdrawal may have been tied up with the politics of Lothar II's divorce: Wisplinghoff 1999: 442. Ansbald was abbot from 860–86.

60 For Louis's campaigns against the Slavs see *AF* 844, 848, 849, 851, 855, 858, 862, 864, 869: 22, 27–9, 32, 37, 41, 43, 48–9, 51–2, 58–60; Goldberg 2006a: 119–46.

61 The Moravian Empire rose from the 830s to a position of pre-eminence in central Europe: Barford 2001; Goldberg 2004. Rastiz was not caught and blinded until 870: *AF* 870: 64, which presents the blinding as a merciful sentence on Louis's part.

62 Regino's characterisation of this region as a *ducatus* is anachronistic, although a series of adjacent counties and abbeys focused on St-Martin at Tours were from the mid-ninth century regarded as a single command against the Vikings and Bretons: Werner 1997; Koziol 2006b: 361, 374.

63 Regino simplifies some very complicated political events. Lambert was a powerful figure on the Breton march who drifted in and out of Charles the Bald's fidelity and by 849 was count of Nantes. Vivian, who belonged to a family with a history of conflict with Lambert's, was count of Tours, abbot of St-Martin and probably chamberlain. The memory of their families' rivalry seemingly coloured Regino's account: in fact Vivian was killed by the Bretons at the battle of Jengland (851), which Regino goes on to describe in this annal. Lambert was captured and killed along with his brother in 852: *AB* 852: 74. *AFont* 851 says that he was killed by Gauzbert, implicitly on the king's orders. Gauzbert's death is placed in 853 by *AAng*. *AF* 854: 35 says that this was done on Charles's orders, and that this caused his kin to invite Louis the German to invade. Gauzbert's power-base and family connections are not clear, though his execution evidently created significant problems for Charles in Aquitaine. For discussion of these three figures see Nelson 1992: 135–9, 142–3, 165–6, 171–2; Smith 1992: 94–101.

and returned home loaded with prodigious plunder.⁶⁴ To check the insolence of this presumption, Charles entered Brittany with a great army. Battle was joined.⁶⁵ The Saxons, who were mercenaries, were put in the front line to receive the wheeling charges of the swift horses, but on the first attack they hid themselves in the [Frankish] battle-line in fear of the Bretons' javelins. According to their custom the Bretons, running hither and thither with horses trained for this kind of fighting, first attacked the Franks' closely packed battle-line and with all their might hurled their spears into its midst; and then while feigning flight they nevertheless drove javelins into the breasts of their pursuers. The Franks, who were accustomed to close hand-to-hand sword fighting, stood thunderstruck. Shocked at the unexpected strangeness of the crisis, they were neither able to counter-attack properly nor to protect themselves by gathering into a group.⁶⁶ Night fell, breaking off the battle. Many of the Franks had been killed, more were wounded, and countless horses died. On the following day the fighting began again, but ended in even graver misfortune. Upon seeing this, Charles was torn apart by a very great fear and secretly fled at night without the army's knowledge, leaving behind his pavilion, tents and all the royal gear.⁶⁷ When morning came, and the army found out that the king had slipped away in flight, it was filled with very great dread and could think of nothing except fleeing. The Bretons rushed in with a shout and breached the Frankish camp, which was stuffed with all sorts of booty, and seized all their war supplies. They pursued the fleeing Frankish line, and either put the stragglers to the sword or captured them alive. Flight saved the rest. Thus the Bretons, enriched with the

64 The Bretons, joined by Lambert, stepped up their raiding in 850–1 and took Rennes and Nantes: Nelson 1992: 165. They were led by Nominoë, who died in March 851: Pettiau 2004: 179–80.
65 The Battle of Jengland (near Redon), 22 August 851, was a major defeat for the Franks inflicted by Nominoë's son Erispoë: *AAng* 851: 486; Lupus of Ferrières, *Letters*, no. 83: 69 (Regenos 1966: 102–3) (which sarcastically refers to the engagement as 'the most magnificent festivities'); Nelson 1992: 165–6; Smith 1992: 99–100. The *AB*'s silence on the defeat is conspicuous. *GSR* I.7: 128–31 describes part of the campaign in which the Franks killed some Breton enemies of the monastery of Redon.
66 The Bretons' mode of fighting is discussed by Leyser 1982a: 26–8; their feigned retreats may have been a manoeuvre designed to replenish their supply of spears. The Franks found it difficult to deal with the fast mounted attacks of the Bretons: for general discussion see Halsall 2003: 177–214; and 114 on the use of Saxons as mercenaries.
67 Although it is plausible that Charles organised a retreat from the difficult terrain, it is unlikely that he abandoned his army: Nelson 1992: 165.

resources of the Franks and equipped with their arms, regrouped in their own land.[68]

861

In the year of the Lord's incarnation 861, Charles held an assembly at Compiègne where, on the advice of his leading men, he entrusted the command [*ducatus*] against the Bretons between the Loire and the Seine to Count Robert, who ruled it for some time with enormous vigour.[69]

862

In the year of the Lord's incarnation 862, Nominoë king of the Bretons died, struck down by God's command.[70] For while he was devastating the churches of God and brutally ravaging the frontiers because they kept due fidelity to Charles, one day, when he wanted to mount his horse so as to finish the evil that he had started, suddenly he saw that the holy bishop Maurilio stood before him with a pitiless expression and terrible eyes, repeating: 'Desist immediately, cruel bandit, from devastating the churches of God.' As he was saying these things he raised the staff he was carrying in his hand and struck Nominoë on the head; he was taken back home by his men and ended his life and his reign. This Maurilio was bishop of the town of Angers, the edges of which city bordered on the frontiers of Brittany and had therefore been seriously plundered by the Bretons.[71] Nominoë's son Erispoë obtained the paternal kingdom.[72]

68 Regino's version of the story could suggest a Breton source, but the narrative focuses more on Charles's cowardice than the Bretons' triumph. Such an anti-Charles tradition was more likely a product of Lothar's Prüm, especially as Lothar may have been backing the Bretons in this period. Charles had also failed to confirm Prüm's exemption from military service: Halsall 2003: 99

69 Robert 'the Strong' was an aristocrat from the Rhineland who rose to prominence in west Francia: Werner 1960. His sons Odo (888–98) and Robert (922–3) were later kings of west Francia, and the Capetian dynasty descended from them. After Jengland he was made count of Angers and lay abbot of Marmoutier to fill the gap left by Lambert and Vivian. However, there was no assembly at Compiègne between 847 and 860; by designating his position as a coherent *ducatus*, Regino probably back-projected the position later held by his son Robert: Nelson 1992: 166–7.

70 Nominoë died in March 851, prior to the Battle of Jengland: Pettiau 2004: 179–80.

71 Maurilio died *c.*427. See Haubrichs 1979: 73, 99.

72 Erispoë was the victor at Jengland. He was recognised by Charles the Bald and acknowledged in control of various territories: *AB* 851: 73; Smith 1992: 111–12; Pettiau 2004: 176–7.

863

In the year of the Lord's incarnation 863, Charles again crossed the Bretons' frontier with a huge army, but achieved little of what he had wished. Finally, he made peace with them. Therefore, with both sides exchanging hostages and oaths, King Erispoë came to him and placed himself under Charles's lordship. Charles, moreover, honoured Erispoë with great gifts and allowed him to return to his kingdom [*regnum*].[73] He himself returned to Francia.

864

In the year of the Lord's incarnation 864, King Lothar began to look for pretexts by which he could separate himself from marriage to Queen Theutberga.[74] He hated her because of Waldrada, who had been his concubine since he was still a young man in his father's house. Accordingly, he desired her with a great love inflamed by the devil. Therefore, the king pressured with every kind of tactic Gunther [arch]bishop of Cologne, who at that time was archchaplain, concerning a divorce of this kind, first through legates sent in secret, and then in person.[75] And so that he might be more inclined to agree, Lothar promised that he would marry the bishop's niece as long as he could repudiate the said Theutberga, on whatever grounds, with the authority and licence of Gunther and the other bishops. Fickle of character and hasty of action as he was, he immediately set about the matter with all zeal, seduced, as later became clear, by vain hope. In turn Gunther discussed the case with Theutgaud archbishop of Trier and, knowing him to be a simple man who was not particularly learned in divine scripture or trained in canon law, showed him some passages from the Old and New Testaments which he elucidated contrary to what is taught by ecclesiastical

---

73 This presumably refers again to the Franko-Breton conflicts of 850–851, and the grants to Erispoë that followed Jengland: see previous note. 'Regnum' was a flexible word that could mean kingdom, but had a range of other less precise meanings like 'territory': Goetz 1987. Nevertheless, Regino's explicit designation of Erispoë as king is unusual, and perhaps reflects his own age of multiple 'kinglets' (on which see below, 888).

74 Lothar initiated divorce proceedings in 857: *AB* 857: 84. It is often claimed that Waldrada was a common-law wife under a form of less-formal marriage known as *Friedelehe* (eg. Bishop 1985: 57), but this concept is largely an invention of modern historians: Airlie 1998: 14–15; Mazo Karras 2006.

75 Regino got some of his information here from Pope Nicholas's long letter to the East Frankish bishops in October 867: Nicholas, *Epistolae*, no. 53.

law. He dragged this unwary man with him into the pit, a blind man leading the blind.[76]

What else? Everything was done which seemed to be necessary to carry through this scheme. They called a council at Metz, stood the queen in the middle as if she had been summoned according to the canons, and produced witnesses and texts which accused her of very serious crimes. Among other things they testified that Theutberga had confessed to having been polluted by lying together incestuously with her own natural brother. Without delay the rulings of the fathers concerning incest were read out and she was not only separated from her legitimate husband, but also forbidden to make any marital union. A penance was pronounced according to the degree of guilt, and by such nefarious scheming the king's long-nurtured wish was fulfilled.[77]

Not long afterward they called another synodal assembly at Aachen, where the king presented a document of his claims.[78] This set out how he had been conned by the seditious arguments of deceitful men about a certain woman called Theutberga; indeed, he emphatically repeated, he had had to endure the sentence of divorce by the judgement of the bishops. If she had been fitting for the marital bed and not soiled by the pestilential pollution of incest, nor publicly condemned by her own confession, he would have kept her willingly. Now he declared himself unable to abstain, and that without union he would not be able to bear the ardour of his youthful state. Therefore the acts of various councils were brought out and many things about people who commit incest were repeated. After these had been read out they pronounced this definitive ruling:[79] 'We believe she was not a suitable and legitimate spouse, nor had she been prepared by God as a wife, having been shown by her public confession to be marked with the crime of incestuous fornication. Wherefore to our glorious leader, for his most devoted dedication to divine worship and most victorious protection of the kingdom, we do not deny the legitimate marriage conceded to him by God – and not only us, for indeed the authority of the canons has forbidden incestuous relations. This accords with the indulgence of the Apostole who said:

---

76 Matthew 14:14.

77 Theutberga's 'confession' to sodomy, incest and abortion was extracted at two synods at Aachen (not Metz) in January and February 860: *AB* 860: 92; Hartmann 1998, nos. 1–2.

78 29 April 862. Regino must have had a copy of the proceedings as the next few sentences are taken directly from them: Hartmann 1998, no. 9, cc. 4, 7, 10: 72–4.

79 The preceding two sentences are Regino's intervention.

"It is better to be married than to burn."'[80]

After these things had been done Waldrada appeared in public surrounded by a large entourage, and the whole royal court hailed her as queen.[81] Bishop Gunther's niece was summoned to the king and, so they say, he raped her once and sent her back to her uncle amidst the jeers and derision of everyone. Consequently, all these things were brought to the attention of Pope Nicholas, who at that time presided over the Roman Church, by the efforts of Queen Theutberga's brothers.[82]

865

In the year of Lord's incarnation 865, the legates of the apostolic see Hagano and Rodoald were sent to Gaul to find out whether the affair had taken place in the way that it had been explained to the great pontiff. When they entered Francia they were corrupted by bribes and favoured iniquity over fairness.[83] Nevertheless, when they came to the king and told him the reasons for their embassy, they got the answer that he had done nothing other than what the bishops of his kingdom had told him to do in a general synod.[84] Those legates therefore counselled the king that he should send the bishops who had been in charge of that synod to the apostolic seat, so that they might satisfy the universal pope with their words and written evidence. Enriched with great wealth, the legates returned to Rome and announced to the pope what they had seen and heard in Gaul, adding that they had not found one learned

---

80 1 Corinthians 7:9, a classic text in early medieval discussions of divorce. This is where Regino stops quoting his source directly.

81 Apparently based on Nicholas, *Epistolae*, no. 53.

82 Theutberga's brothers included Hubert, with whom she was accused of having incestuous sexual relations, and Boso, whose own marriage to Engiltrude was a matter of controversy: see below, 866. On Hubert, see above, 859. He went to Rome in 862.

83 The legates were Bishops Rodoald of Porto and John of Ficocle (or Cervia) – Hagano of Bergamo was rather the emperor's legate at the council of Metz in June 863 (Hartmann 1998, no. 14). The corruption of the legates is reported in Nicholas, *Epistolae*, no. 53: 343. At least one of the pope's letters from 863 (Nicholas, *Epistolae*, no. 18) containing his condemnation of Lothar circulated widely in a dossier of texts, which also included Gunther and Theutgaud's defence: *AB* 863, 864: 106–10, 113–16; and *AF* 863: 50–1 (which says that 'writings of both sides' can be found 'in several places in Germany').

84 This refers to the synod of Aachen in 862, whose rulings were confirmed by another at Metz in 863: *AB* 862: 102; Hartmann 1998, nos. 9 and 14. These councils confirmed the validity of the divorce.

bishop in Lothar's realm who had a clear grounding in the study of the canons. Meanwhile, Archbishops Theutgaud and Gunther set out for Rome with the thought in their minds that they would demonstrate that the king was innocent in the matter described above, and that they and the rest of their fellow bishops had followed ecclesiastical and apostolic decrees. It is an indication of their stupidity that they thought they could deceive with some perverse doctrine the see of Peter, which has never been mistaken nor could ever be deceived by any heresy. Therefore when they came into the presence of Pope Nicholas they presented a document containing the acts of the synods that they had organised at Metz and Aachen.[85] When this had been read out by a notary in front of everyone, the pontiff asked if they could confirm orally what was written. They responded that it seemed illogical that they would prefer to annul with words what they had already confirmed with their own hands. And so with their statements neither accepted nor rejected they were ordered to go to their lodgings until they were called back. After a few days had passed they were summoned to a synod that the pope had gathered, at which their writings were condemned and anathematized and by the judgement of all the bishops, priests and deacons they themselves were deposed and deprived of all ecclesiastical office.[86] Having thus been disgracefully dishonoured they went to the Emperor Louis, the brother of King Lothar, who at that time was staying in the region of Benevento, complaining loudly with words and writings that they had been deposed unjustly, and that an insult had been done to the emperor himself and to the whole Holy Church since it was unheard of, and could not be read about anywhere, that any metropolitan could be demoted without the knowledge of the ruler or without other metropolitans being present.[87] On top of that, these blasphemers added many other things against that same pope, which we think would be superfluous to list here; they supposed that with the support of the emperor together with the influence of his intercession they might both efface the blemish of criminal accusation and regain the status of their previous dignity. But they were frustrated in this hope, although the emperor had been willing to help in response to their pleadings.[88] Theutgaud

---

85 This booklet is no longer extant. Regino could have taken this information from Nicholas, *Epistolae*, no. 53: 343–4.
86 This synod was held in Rome in October 863: Hartmann 1998, no. 16.
87 Regino in this annal seems to be using the two archbishops' letter to the emperor which has not survived.
88 *AB* 864: 112–13 describes how Louis and the Empress Egelberga travelled to Rome in person to argue the archbishops' case, but implies that the pope persuaded them

bore the sentence of deposition handed down from the apostolic seat with patience, and did not presume to lay hands on anything at all that pertained to the holy ministry of his previous status. Gunther, on the other hand, his soul puffed up with pride, was not afraid to usurp with reckless daring the office that had been forbidden to him, heedless of the apostolic excommunication. Thus they returned to Francia rightly spattered with embarrassment. And while they went for a second and third time to the apostolic see to obtain the grace of restoration and reinstatement, in the end they were overcome by illness in Italy and died as exiles and foreigners, and only lay communion was permitted to them.[89]

866

In the year of the Lord's incarnation 866, Bishop Arsenius, the *apocrisarius* and counsellor of Pope Nicholas, was sent to Francia as his representative.[90] Such was the power and authority with which he was invested, it was as if the supreme pontiff himself had come. In the end, having called an assembly of the bishops, he gave King Lothar a choice: he could either set aside relations with the concubine Waldrada and be reunited with his own wife, or he himself and everyone who supported him in this wickedness would be immediately struck with the sword of anathema. Stuck in this predicament, he took Queen Theutberga back as his wife like it or not, on the condition, confirmed by an oath, that he would keep her with him from now on according to the way the laws of propriety dictate a legitimate wife ought to be held, and that he would neither separate her from him nor take another in her place while she still lived.[91] After this, on the command of the apostolic lord and by the authority of God and St Peter, he ordered Waldrada to go to Rome so that she might seek to explain herself.

He [Arsenius] declared to everyone that Engiltrude, wife of the former Count Boso, had also been excommunicated by the apostolic see because

---

that he was in the right. Louis took up the archbishops' case again at a synod held in February 865 in Pavia: Hartmann 1998, no. 21.

89 Theutgaud died in 868 of fever after receiving absolution from Nicholas's successor Hadrian II; Gunther submitted to Hadrian in 869 and accepted lay communion, then died in 871. Regino's arrangement of material here makes clear the implication that this was divine retribution for Lothar's divorce.

90 Actually 865. Arsenius was bishop of Orte; the *apocrisarius* was a high papal official. His mission is also described by *AB* 865: 123–7; *AF* 865: 53–4.

91 3 August 865, at Douzy. Details are given by *AB* 865: 124–5; *AX* 866: 23; BM no. 1307a.

she had abandoned her own husband and gone off to Gaul with his vassal Wanger.[92] He renewed this excommunication with all the bishops who were present. After that the same Engiltrude presented herself to Arsenius in the city of Worms, where he had gone to meet King Louis [the German]. She swore an oath in the presence of the legate which went like this:[93] "'I Engiltrude, daughter of the late Count Matfrid and who used to be the wife of Count Boso, swear to you the lord bishop Arsenius, legate and *apocrisarius* of the most high Holy Catholic and apostolic see, and through you to my lord the supreme pontiff and universal pope Nicholas, by the Father, Son and Holy Spirit and the four gospels of the divine Christ, which I kiss with my mouth and touch with my own hands, that henceforth having forsaken the malice which I held toward my husband Boso so that like a lost sheep I may return to the holy Catholic and apostolic Church under the conditions that the supreme pontiff and universal pope the lord Nicholas imposed on me, in whatever form you may ordain, I will go to the Italian kingdom either with you or before you, and I will fulfil and not refuse to carry out whatever the apostolic lord decides and commands." But she did not carry out this fearsome oath.[94] In fact she travelled as far as the River Danube with that same Arsenius, and there said that she was going to visit some relative to obtain horses from him, and promised to join up again with the legate at Augsburg. On this pretext, she turned her path out of Alemannia and returned to Francia. When the oft-mentioned Arsenius heard about this, he sent a letter to all the archbishops and bishops and faithful adherents of God's Holy Church who dwelt in Gaul, Germany and Neustria, imploring everyone on the authority of almighty God and of the blessed lords Peter and Paul and of the lord pontiff and universal pope that nobody receive her in his parish.[95] Instead, without exception they should preach in all their churches that

---

92 Regino's source was probably Nicholas, *Epistolae*, no. 53: 341, although that text does not name Wanger. On the Engiltrude case see Reynolds 1999. Regino's description of Engiltrude as 'uxor quondam Bosonis comitis' creates problems in identifying this Boso – was he (*quondam*) the 'former' or 'late' count, and if the latter, 'late' from whose perspective, Regino's or Arsenius'? Staab 1998 argues that Boso was the count of Vienne who was consecrated king in 879 but Bougard 2000 raises decisive objections to this theory. There is a convenient account of Boso's career, including the evidence that he was a brother of Theutberga and Hubert, in Hlawitschka 1960a: 158–62.

93 The rest of this paragraph, except where noted, is quoted directly from Arsenius' letter to the bishops of Gaul and Germany: *Epistolae ad divortium Lotharii II regis pertinentes*, no. 11.

94 This line is not in the source letter.

95 This and the preceding sentence are paraphrases rather than quotes.

BOOK II

she was excommunicate and removed from all Christian communion, and in addition bound by the chain of anathema and condemned to be among the impious and wicked, until she accepted a suitable penance before the apostolic lord for her pernicious deeds and the perjury she had perpetrated.'

Having briefly recorded these things, let us return to the lamentable case of King Lothar.

So, having settled matters in Gaul, the legate of the holy see returned to Rome, whence he had come; and once again Waldrada and her accomplices took up their fight, and the king's feelings were stirred against Theutberga.[96] His anger was aroused, and the smouldering embers of discord and hatred once more burst into great flame. Theutberga was despised, loathed, scorned and accused of the crime of adultery, and every sneaky trick was used to work out how she could be punished, as if she were the guilty party. Foreseeing that her life was in danger, she fled secretly and went to Charles [the Bald], entrusting herself to his protection.[97] When rumour of this spread and Pope Nicholas found out, he sent a letter of praise to King Charles containing the following:[98]

'Among the other devout champions of the Holy Church and strenuous defenders of truth, we recall that none has been more concerned about the humiliation of the glorious Queen Theutberga, and none has lamented more her misfortunes, than someone of your religious temperament.' And after a similar exhortation he added:[99] 'We do not wish your excellency to be ignorant of precisely how King Lothar, against sworn oaths, imposed countless torments on his wife Theutberga and subjected her to many oppressions, so that she has now been

---

96 Waldrada accompanied Arsenius as he set off for Rome: *AB* 865: 126–7. However, she did not complete the journey and by the end of the year was back with Lothar.

97 Regino may only have known of Theutberga's flight west by inference from the letter he subsequently quotes. She fled there for the first time in 860, seeking the protection of her brother Hubert; and again in 864 after Hubert's death, when Charles gave her Avenay, a nunnery often held by women of the Carolingian family: *AB* 860, 864: 93, 121. Between these two dates, her movements are obscure.

98 The following is quoted from the letter (Nicholas, *Epistolae*, no. 48, dated 25 January 867), with Regino's omissions and interventions noted. Despite what Regino says, the letter is by no means laudatory: it laments Charles's decision to make common cause with Lothar and urges him to help Theutberga. Regino, *De synodalibus*, II.76: 288 also quotes from the letter.

99 The omitted exhortation is not at all similar. Nicholas complains that Charles, having been bought off by the gift of a monastery, is helping Lothar slip back into his old ways, and deplores their 'nefarious pact to ruin Theutberga'. See also *AB* 866: 132, which identifies the abbey in question as St-Vaast in Arras, an island of Lotharingian influence in west Francia since the Treaty of Verdun.

compelled to write to us that she wishes to be stripped of her royal dignity and marriage, and will be content to live a life of solitude and deprivation. We wrote to her that this could not happen unless her husband Lothar chose the same life.[100] Truly, as we learned from the reports of many people, Lothar for his part ordered an assembly to attend him and planned to subject Theutberga to a personal examination and judgement. And if he succeeded in showing, by means of deceitful conjuring-tricks and circuitous proofs, that she was not his legitimate wife, he wanted to remove her from him completely. If, on the other hand, he was willing accept her as his rightful wife, his next step would have been to accuse her of being an adulteress, and on this account to arrange a duel between one of his men and one of Theutberga's. And if the queen's man were to fall, he ordained that she should be killed immediately.[101] We believe that given the magnitude of your understanding of how things work you will already have worked out the extent to which these things are contrary to all divine law. But we want to give a brief explanation of this anyway, in the first place to show that Theutberga ought not to be challenged further to make another response to the foregoing dispute, since a matter which has been well judged once and settled by the taking of oaths should not be brought up again, except perhaps where a higher authority exists; and in the second place that because she sought the sanctuary of the Church and always wanted an ecclesiastical judgement, she should not have been subjected to a secular judgement. After this, however, because we were called upon to adjudicate by both sides, that is by both Lothar and Theutberga, and we evaluated the arguments of each of them, it is not appropriate that this matter pass to any other judge, since according to the sacred canons it is not permitted to appeal from judges appointed by common agreement, and where a challenge is made, an appeal is not allowed unless there is a higher authority. Therefore, because nowhere is there a higher authority than that of the apostolic see, which has followed their respective arguments, we do not know of anyone who would be allowed to judge its judgements, or to overturn its verdict.' And after a few words he continued:[102] 'Who, then, does not see that Lothar's accusations of adultery against Theutberga are full of deceit?

100 Prevailing interpretations of canon law dictated that one spouse could not withdraw from the marriage to take a monastic vow unless the other did likewise, a position advocated by Regino, *De synodalibus* II.109: 302. For discussion see Bishop 1985. The letter Nicholas here refers to is Nicholas, *Epistolae*, no. 45.

101 On ordeals see Bartlett 1986.

102 Regino omits a sentence giving further reasons dismissing the grounds for a challenge.

BOOK II   147

When it comes down to it, if, as he boasts, she is not his wife, then what business is it of his to construct an accusation of adultery against her, since she could not have commited adultery if she is not anyone's wife? Furthermore, if she were accused of adultery by Lothar and was then found guilty and a punishment prepared, he would thereby unavoidably acknowledge that she was his wife.' And after he had mentioned certain things in connection with this:[103] 'In addition, whether the judgement about the marriage bond or the charge of adultery is challenged, it is clear that on no account can Theutberga enter legal dispute with Lothar, nor be subjected to a legitimate dispute, unless she is first restored to her power at once and also allowed to associate freely with her relatives. A place should be provided among them where she has nothing to fear from the power of the multitude and where it will not be difficult to produce witnesses and the other people required for this sort of dispute both by the sacred canons and the venerable laws of the Romans. But at the same time we do not say all this in order that things may be done which, as we showed above, cannot be done without our decree and decision.'[104]

The most holy pontiff was thus filled with the same zeal for God which had once inflamed the priest Phineas, and in the basilica on the very day of the Purification of Mary the holy Mother of God he excommunicated Waldrada and separated her from all association with Christians.[105] He sent a letter to all the bishops of Gaul and Germany setting out the reasons for and manner of the excommunication. For the sake of brevity I will include here the sense of this letter rather than every one of its words:[106]

'Concerning Waldrada, the persistently unrepentant adulteress, we had decided to make the manner of punishment less severe, and not

---

103 The missing section contests the validity of the ordeal by battle and urges Charles to protect Theutberga.

104 Regino cuts this final sentence short: it goes on to clarify the point that Nicholas was raising hypothetical arguments to demonstrate the illegality of Lothar's actions from various perspectives, not prescribing a coherent course of action.

105 2 February 866. The Virgin Mary and her feast-days featured prominently in the symbolic warfare of Lothar's divorce: Airlie 1998: 21–3, 34–5. Phineas saved the Israelites from God's wrath by killing a couple engaged in immoral intercourse: Numbers 25. He was referred to in two letters used by Regino: Nicholas, *Epistolae*, nos. 42, 53: 316, 340.

106 This letter, dated 13 June 866 (thus before the letter to Charles the Bald) and addressed to the bishops of Italy, Germany, Neustria and Gaul, is Nicholas, *Epistolae*, no. 42. Regino is as good as his word this time, retaining the thrust of the letter without altering the meaning.

to pronounce against her the sentence of the just punishment which she deserved for such an evil crime, unless she was resolved to remain permanently with an obstinate spirit in the pigsty of adultery. Therefore, because she paid no heed to our warnings and frequent admonitions; because she has neither acknowledged nor as yet confessed her guilt, nor has she asked our pardon through an embassy to us – us, who have undertaken to prosecute her case; and finally because when she had taken the right path to us and sought the help of the blessed apostle Peter she then turned back to Satan and did not give up her plans for the destruction of Queen Theutberga, we declare with the distinguished apostle what must be repeated against her and her like time and again, that because of her stubbornness and her impenitent heart she is storing up trouble for herself on the Day of Wrath.[107] Therefore we have excommunicated her for the things she has done, and until she gives satisfaction to the Holy Church and especially to us, who have more care for her than anyone and who have followed and investigated her case from the start, and until she removes all sinister suspicions by following our advice, we have decreed by the power of the Holy Spirit and the blessed apostles Peter and Paul, and by the authority of our humble station, that she and all her accomplices, associates and supporters be deprived in every respect of receiving the precious blood and body of the Lord and of any kind of association with the Holy Church. We recall that this sentence was published by us on 2 February, and we sent it to you in writing. And so that our effort may not have been in vain, may you, my brothers, join us in taking up spiritual arms against the aforementioned adulteress and her allies. Each in his own parish should make known orally that she and her backers have been excommunicated until she submits herself to a fitting penance by our special decision.'

That same most revered pontiff also sent a letter to King Lothar containing the following things:[108]

'When our legate came back and we heard about, if you will allow us to say so, the beginnings of your correction, we gave appropriate thanks to God and prepared our heart to render the thanks due to you as well. But, alas, the arrival of some adverse news quickly prevented the carrying out of our intention.[109] Thus we are forced to alter our tone

---

107 Romans 2:5.

108 Nicholas, *Epistolae*, no. 46, dated 24/5 January 867, so sent simultaneously with the letter to Charles the Bald quoted by Regino above.

109 Lothar had accepted Theutberga back under pressure from Arsenius in 865,

and we, who had been inclined to open our mouth in thanks, are now forced to direct the duty of our tongue to lamentations and chiding.[110] For we have learned that you, having for some length of time been doing the Church of God considerable harm through your ongoing wickedness, are still inflicting harm; and that, having been living in filth, you are defiling yourself further.[111] Indeed, we suppose that you are not satisfied simply with committing adultery unless you also trap the souls of men in the snares of perjury and plunge them into ultimate ruin. But how amazing is it that you have obtained the destruction of only a few souls through perjury, considering that your position is so exalted that by your adulterous example you might have cast so many thousands of men into the chaos of perdition?[112] Moreover, that which Theutberga tried to allege as if speaking Waldrada's testimony, namely that the latter was your legitimate wife, was futile since nobody needed any testimony of hers on this point, whether she made it voluntarily or against her will. Rather, it is our opinion and understanding that it is fair and just that even after Theutberga is dead there are no laws or rules according to which you will ever be able or permitted to take Waldrada as your wife. Therefore, whether or not Waldrada was your legitimate wife at some point, the Church of God requires no satisfaction from Theutberga. One thing, nevertheless, we know, namely that by the decision of God, who will sit in judgement over adulterers, neither we nor the Church of God will let you off completely unpunished if at any point you take up with Waldrada again even if Theutberga dies.' And after a few other things he carried on:[113] 'Therefore with the greatest devotion give your full attention to nurturing and cherishing your foresaid wife Theutberga as if she were your own flesh, and take care not to concoct any plots to separate her from you.[114] If she wants to leave you, rebuke and indeed correct her, and busy yourself in every way with dissuading her from any such intention. But if she seeks a divorce

---

but repudiated her again shortly afterward. This led to the excommunication of Waldrada in 866 and the ultimatum that Lothar had a year to renounce her before suffering a similar fate: Airlie 1998: 34.

110 Regino here omits a section in which Nicholas reviewed the case and lamented that Lothar had broken his word again.

111 Two sentences reinforcing the sentiment are left out.

112 One line is omitted: 'Nam maiora facit crimine sublimitas dignitatum.' Carolingian political theology nurtured the idea that the king's moral conduct had a direct impact on the fortunes of his people and kingdom: see for example Meens 1998.

113 The missing lines insist that Waldrada be sent to Rome.

114 Contemporary writers often conceptualised marriage as if the partners metaphorically became one person: Bishop 1985.

for the love of chastity and keeps on demanding a dissolution of the marital bond, then it is certain, as the apostle said: "The wife does not have power over her own body, but the husband."[115] But if you yourself wish to dissolve the marriage on the pretext of seeking the chastity of religion, we will allow that as long as it is not done insincerely. For as it is written: "That which God has joined, let man not separate."[116] God and not man separates, when in the gaze of divine love marriages are dissolved with the consent of both spouses. If then you want it this way, we allow it with a willing disposition and offer our rapid consent; but we forbid your mutual separation to take place in any other way.[117] Further, if she is accused of sterility, then think about the 90-year-old Sarah, and also about Anna and Elizabeth; yet perhaps this sterility is not caused by infertility but by unrighteousness.[118] Therefore, most glorious king, be content with your own wife and do not seek any other consort but her.[119] So, heed our counsel and embrace our warnings as you would those of an affectionate father, and restrain your mind, your tongue and your body from all depravity. In particular, avoid association with your concubine Waldrada, whom you previously repudiated, and surrender her company to perpetual oblivion. For she is excommunicate and is banned from the companionship of all Christians until she comes into our presence; the whole west already knows this, and through our messengers it will be made known any time now in the east with its other territories. Therefore beware that you be not struck down by a sentence as harsh as hers, and that for the sake of a passion for one little woman and the pleasure of a fleeting moment you be not bound and chained and dragged into sulphurous foulness and eternal ruin.'[120] And after mentioning a few more relevant things he concludes the letter like this:[121] 'Let it be enough that we have now written this to you and as if our words of censure have run the gamut of your excesses

---

115 1 Corinthians 7:4. The pope omitted the rest of the passage: 'likewise the husband does not have the power of his own body, but the wife'. The key discussion of the case's gendered discourse is Airlie 1998.

116 Matthew 19:6.

117 Regino misses out some supporting quotations. Nicholas's implication is that Lothar would also have to take up the religious life (cf. above, n. 100).

118 Regino drops Nicholas's further elaborations on this point. The pope made the same point in a letter sent to Theutberga at the same time: Nicholas, *Epistolae*, no. 45: 320.

119 Again, Regino leaves out Nicholas's further musings here.

120 Lothar had been given a deadline of 2 February 867 to avoid excommunication: see above, n. 109.

121 Regino only leaves out a supporting quotation.

between us. In future, as the precept of the Lord has it, take care that we do not ever summon to us two or three witnesses; or indeed that we do not tell this to the Holy Church; and, which we do not wish to happen, that in future you do not become like a heathen and tax-collector.'[122]

Well now, we have undertaken to record a few things of the many that took place so that they might thus become known in part to those who do not know about them, and so as not to be tiresome to those who are in the know. The nature of the outcome produced by the calamity of this pestilential sickness, which resisted the remedy of an apostolic antidote, and the scale of the cost to the kingdom from this deadly infection, as predicted by the oft-mentioned most holy pope inspired by the Holy Spirit, will be revealed below in its proper place.[123]

Around this time[124] King Louis [the German] invaded the kingdom of his brother Charles [the Bald] with an army, wishing to subjugate the western kingdoms to his rule and to seize his brother's rightful portion, which had properly fallen to him by the line of inheritance.[125] He forgot bonds of brotherhood and blood and ignored the treaty which they had formerly concluded by mutual agreement, heedless too of the oaths with which he had bound himself before God with great imprecations. The incentives which had kindled him into committing this outrage were as follows. Charles, as we noted before, had put some of the realm's more noble men to the sword either after they had been subject to public judgements or after they had fallen for a trick.[126] Afraid lest they suffer a similar fate, the rest of them stirred up King Louis, who ruled across the Rhine, and seduced his mind into gaining the kingdom of his brother by promising that along with the kingdom they would give themselves over to his command. Because the hearts of kings are greedy and never satisfied,[127] he was easily led into expectation by this persuasion and as

---

122 Matthew 18:15–17. The allusion is rather obscure. The full biblical text reads: 'If your brother sins against you, go and show him his fault, just between the two of you. If he listens to you, you have won your brother over. But if he will not listen, take one or two others along, so that every matter may be established by the testimony of two or three witnesses. If he refuses to listen to them, tell it to the church; and if he refuses to listen even to the church, treat him as you would a pagan or a tax-collector.'

123 See below, 883.

124 858.

125 The language here is derived from Deuteronomy 32:9: 'For the Lord's portion is his people, Jacob his allotted inheritance.' Cf. below, 876.

126 See above, 860.

127 This is from Justin, *Epitome*, 38.6.8: 217 (Yardley 1994: 242), describing the Roman people's antipathy toward kings.

we said he invaded the frontiers of the kingdom with a strong force. Charles, feeling the power of the kingdom had slipped away from him, sought a hiding place for his flight in the furthest reaches of Aquitaine.[128] Louis, as he had set out to do, took the kingdom and came to the city of Sens. After he had sent his army back home to *Germania*, he began to arrange the affairs of the realm together with the leading men. But suddenly fortune changed: for the leading men who had invited him into the kingdom realised that he was behaving very differently toward them from what they had supposed and, touched by remorse, went back to Charles. Charles rejoiced that he had regained power from such a desperate situation, and after gathering forces from all sides he attempted to engage his brother in war. Because Louis realised that he had been deserted by his own men whom he had brought with him as well as by those whom he appeared to have won over there, he quickly took flight and left the kingdom in fitting shame.[129]

At this time Abbot Hubert, the brother of Queen Theutberga, began to rebel against King Lothar.[130] He gathered a strong force of bandits and began pillaging and, after killing or putting to flight Lothar's followers who held lands in nearby areas, handed out their fields and estates to members of his own faction. In order to stifle this temerity King Lothar led forth an army not just once, but also a second and third time, and repeatedly sent a multitude of armed men, with war-leaders, against him. But he was not at all successful in quenching Hubert's presumptiousness, because the inaccessible places among the Jura and the Pennine Alps provided the rebels with a very well defended refuge, and the deep curves of the valleys and steepness of the mountains presented the king and his army with very narrow passages and a difficult access.[131] Nonetheless, that same rebel Hubert was finally killed by Count Conrad

---

128 'Power of the kingdom' (*vires regni*) is one of Regino's stock phrases.

129 The causes of Louis's invasion lay in a rebellion in Neustria led by Robert the Strong. Charles was almost defeated, and his survival was only assured by the bishops' refusal to submit to his brother. Regino's account is broadly accurate. Louis did come to Sens, whose archbishop (Wenilo) was the only prelate to defect. Charles fled to Burgundy, not Aquitaine, after choosing not to face his brother in battle in September. After the tide turned, Charles was restored in January 859. For details see *AB* 858–9: 88–9; *AF* 858–9: 41–5; Nelson 1992: 185–91; Goldberg 2006a: 248–58.

130 Presumably a reference either to the late 850s, when Lothar first repudiated Theutberga and set his brother against Hubert by granting him Transjurane Burgundy (see above, 859), or to 863–4 when Hubert is reported to have been resisting Louis II there: *AB* 864: 121.

131 Cf. below, 888.

BOOK II 153

near the fortress called Orbe.[132]

In the year of the Lord's incarnation 866, Erispoë king of the Bretons was killed by his own men, and the *dux* Salomon was chosen in his place.[133] For this man was vigorous and warlike, and in both appearance and mind well suited to the government of the kingdom. For the third time, Charles decided to attack the Bretons with an army, but when he neared their borders and heard that they were prepared to resist him with all their forces, he had a sudden change of heart and decided it was better to accept peace than to wage war. He therefore renewed the pact with Salomon that he had previously made with Erispoë, and left.[134]

867

In the year of the Lord's incarnation 867, the Northmen took over the mouth of the River Loire and began once more to plunder with great cruelty the areas of Nantes, Angers, Poitiers and Tours.[135] Robert, who held the march, and Ranulf *dux* of Aquitaine gathered together many men and led a force against them.[136] Realising that they were being pursued by an army, the Northmen retreated to their fleet in great haste. But when they saw the multitude of those chasing them was getting close, they realised that they could not get away and entered a certain village [*villa*] where they barricaded themselves in as well as

---

132 *AB* 864: 121 says he was killed by his own men; *AX* 864: 23 attributes the killing to the 'sons of Conrad', that is Conrad the Younger and Hugh the Abbot. Louis II gave Hubert's county to Conrad in 864. On these men see Borgolte 1986: 258–9, 290–1.

133 Actually November 857. The murder of Erispoë by his cousin Salomon was one of the events that triggered the revolt and invasion of 858: see *AB* 857: 85; Smith 1992: 103. It is odd that Regino here restates the date of his annal. This inconsistency may reflect the process of revision; or it may have been a deliberate attempt to restore the (erroneous) absolute chronology of the text after the wide-ranging account of Lothar's divorce.

134 Salomon was generally loyal to Charles the Bald, who had granted him *honores* in 852: *AB* 852: 74. The pact with Salomon was sealed in 863 (*AB* 863: 105, after the Breton had participated in uprisings against the king) and confirmed and reinforced several times: *AB* 864, 867, 868: 118, 139, 151. On Salomon see Pettiau 2004: 183–4. Most of the conflict in this period was between Salomon and Robert, his erstwhile ally, rather than Salomon and Charles.

135 The Loire was a regular focus of Viking activity from the 840s. *AB* 866: 135 describes a particular incident involving a Viking raiding band returning to the river from Le Mans.

136 Actually 866. Robert the Strong, count of Angers, was Charles's main supporter in the region. He had been given responsibilities in Burgundy in the previous year: *AB* 865: 128. Ranulf was count of Poitiers.

they could in the time available.[137] In that village there was a very large stone church into which most of the Northmen went along with their leader Hasting.[138] Robert and Ranulf, along with their men, rushed in on them and without delay slaughtered any of them they found outside the church. When they reached the church they saw that it was a well-fortified place and observed that there was a considerable crowd of pagans hiding inside. After a short deliberation, since the sun was already setting, they set up an encircling camp and pitched tents so that the next day they might put up ramparts and use their siege engines to assault the enemy with all their might. Boiling in the great heat, Robert set aside his helmet and armour for a moment to cool down in the breeze; and while everyone was preoccupied with setting up the camp, the Northmen suddenly burst out of their fortification and with a great cry charged at Robert and his men. But although sudden and unexpected emergencies can upset even the bravest men in battle, they nevertheless grabbed their weapons as quickly as they could, manfully fought off the enemy and forced them, retreating, to withdraw to the church. Rushing into the attack without his helmet and armour, Robert was killed in the entrance of the church because he fought without enough care and pursued the enemy without restraint. His now lifeless body was dragged inside by the Northmen. Also Ranulf, who was standing some distance away and observing the outcome of the battle, was seriously wounded by an arrow fired by one of the Northmen from a window in the church. He was carried away from the battle by his men and survived for barely three days. With such unhappy misfortune was this battle begun and ended. After the loss of its leader, the army was filled with sorrow and doubt in equal measure and at that very hour they lifted the siege and went home. The Northmen jubilantly made for their fleet.

Not much later Hugh the Abbot was substituted in Robert's place. He was vigorous, humble, just, peaceful and fundamentally honest in all his ways. Since Odo and Robert, Robert's sons, were still very young at the

137 This was the battle of Brissarthe: see Halsall 2003: 203, 207. Regino's account, much the most detailed, broadly agrees with *AB* 866: 135, which also reports Robert's death and Ranulf's fatal injury, adding that counts Gauzfrid and Harvey were also present. Archbishop Hincmar of Rheims (author of the *AB* at this point) regarded the deaths as just reward for the dead magnates' possession of lay abbacies. *AF* 867: 57 describes Robert as a 'second Maccabeus', and suggests that stories of his deeds were circulating in the eastern kingdom, presumably encouraged by the count's relatives. Regino, who also places Robert's death in 867, may have been relating one of these stories.

138 On Hasting see below, 874, and Abels 2003.

BOOK II

time of their father's death, his command [*ducatus*] was not committed to them.[139]

At that time the people of the Saracens came from Africa to Benevento and penetrated almost all of that area, ravaging everything with murder, pillage and fire.[140] The emperor Louis [II] gathered an army against them and, fearing that the forces of his kingdom might not be enough in the face of the enemy's countless multitude, sent legates to his brother Lothar in Gaul requesting urgently that he might come to his aid with the help of God and the power of the Franks, in order to curb the effectiveness and rein in the audacity of that foresaid most shameful people. Without any delay at all and with enormous industry, Lothar gathered an army from all sides and came to help his brother as fast as he could.[141] Then many battles were fought and won with God's aid, not only by force, but also by luck.[142] In the midst of this, Lothar's army was exhausted by a serious pestilence. Weakened by the unaccustomed heat and the intemperance of the climate, it was gripped by the sickness of dysentery, or diarrhoea, which caused the deaths of a countless multitude. Very many also died from spider-bites; so that even then it was becoming clear that God was opposed not only to Lothar, because of his hard and impenitent heart, but also to his entire kingdom.[143] This is why he did not return to Francia without, as has been said, serious losses among his men.

868

In the year of the Lord's incarnation 868, Nicholas, the most holy and most blessed pope, departed for the celestial kingdom after many labours for Christ and many battles for the inviolable state of the Holy Church,

---

139 On the transfer of Robert's offices to Hugh and others see *AB* 866, 868: 136, 143–4. Hugh was lay abbot of St-Germain, Auxerre and then St-Martin, Tours. On his career see Werner 1979; Nelson 1992: 177–9, 190–1, 201, 210, 251–2; MacLean 2003a: 65–7, 103–5, 116–17.

140 The Muslims arrived in Benevento in the early 840s: Kreutz 1996: 24–6. Louis arrived there at the end of 866. His campaign was a central part of his attempt to gain influence in the south of the peninsula: *AB* 866: 130–1; Wickham 1981: 62; Kreutz 1996: 37–47.

141 Lothar did not travel to Italy, though it is possible that he sent troops to help his brother, who had supported him during his dispute with the pope: BM 1239a for discussion. D L2 29 records Lothar's gift to Louis and Engelberga of lands in Italy in May 866, which may not be unrelated.

142 'Feliciter'. On Regino and the concept of luck see above, Introduction, pp. 14–15.

143 On the scriptural significance of spiders see Lošek 1994.

to receive the unwithered crown of glory from most bountiful God for the faithful administration of the office entrusted to him.[144] More things worthy of record could be said about the things he did that were pleasing to God, if in the name of brevity we had not undertaken to summarise the causes of events rather than to explain them in detail. In fact from the blessed Gregory up to the present day, no prelate raised to the pontifical office in the city of Rome seems his equal.[145] He commanded kings and tyrants, and exercised authority over them as if he was the lord of the lands of the earth.[146] To bishops and priests who were pious and obedient to God's commands he appeared humble, gentle, pious and mild, and to the irreligious and those who had strayed from the right path he appeared terrible and full of severity, so that he might deservedly be thought of as another Elias resurrected and awakened for our times by God, if not in body then in spirit and virtue.[147]

This man of most sacred memory was succeeded in the pontificate by Hadrian [II].[148] When King Lothar had learned about this from a reliable source, he wrote him a letter that went like this:[149] 'An unfortunate but still unconfirmed story has forcefully transfixed, so to speak, the ears of our serenity, intimating that Lord Nicholas of blessed memory has been called by Christ to withdraw from this vale of tears to be inestimably crowned, as we believe, with the saints. It is not a matter for bewilderment that the whole Christian religion mourns such a pontiff and that the whole ecclesiastical order laments this wisest of popes. In truth, though, we mourn him even more – we who entrusted to him at the appropriate time and in part the weighing up of the causes of our defamation and the fraudulent complaints of our opponents on the scales of justice and equity like a benevolent father. But, and we repeat this with sadness, the plots and lying deceits of our enemies counted more with his saintliness than did our plain and honest defence. For

---

144 Nicholas died on 13 November 867.
145 Pope Gregory I the Great, 590–604.
146 'Domnus orbis terrarum'; cf. above, 842, where imperial Rome is described as having been formerly 'domna orbis terrarum'.
147 Elias is another name for the prophet Elijah discussed in 1 and 2 Kings, and who was mentioned in the New Testament as a forerunner of Christ. In 1 Kings 17:1 he delivers a message from God to Ahab, king of Israel, about impending doom; and in 1 Kings 21:17–24, 22:38 he warns Ahab and Jezebel that they will die violent deaths. Jezebel was used in Carolingian texts as an archetype of the bad queen who corrupted her husband.
148 He was consecrated 14 December 867. For his biography see Davis 1995.
149 *Epistolae ad divortium Lotharii II regis pertinentes*, no. 18 (around February 868). Regino quotes the letter faithfully and accurately; none of his omissions is significant.

we incessantly appealed to him with letters and words, and through various embassies repeated the same humble request, that according to divine and human laws we and our accusers might earn a papal hearing, offering to attend in person as reason dictates: but we were always rebuffed.' And after a few words he continued: 'But because omnipotent God, the master of shepherds, has raised your highness to that holy seat, if the time seems propitious we desire very much to see you, so that by your words, which are fitting to God, we may be revived and may receive your honeyed blessing.' And at the end of the letter he says: 'Meanwhile we beseech you in every way to send us letters reassuring our highness of your desired approval, and that you deign to bestow upon us the title of a beloved son.'

The said pope wrote back[150] that the see of St Peter was always ready to receive due satisfaction, and had never refused anything that the laws of God and man decree to be just. Therefore, if he knew that he was free from reproach, then it would be proper for him to approach the apostolic seat with complete trust that he would secure the blessing he wanted. If, on the other hand, he recognised that he was guilty then he should likewise hasten to come without delay so that he could undertake an appropriate penance as remedy.

In these times the majority of the most ferocious and bellicose people of the Bulgars, after casting aside their idols and renouncing their pagan superstitions, put their faith in Christ; and, cleansed by the salvation-bringing water of baptism, they went over to the Christian religion.[151] Priests and men of religion were sent to that people by the apostolic see to educate the still-uninstructed people in the divine precepts and, polishing their raw barbarism with the sacred doctrines, they prepared a pleasing dwelling place for Christ. So that this work of sincere and holy devotion would have a happy outcome, the most Christian king Louis, who ruled the Germans, offered no little support.[152] It is said that after he had received and understood the grace of baptism, the king of the Bulgars began to live with such perfection that, although by day he went among his people clothed in the trappings of royalty, by night he dressed in a sack and secretly entered the church and lay down prostrate in prayer on the stone floor, spreading only a blanket beneath

150 Hadrian's letter does not survive.
151 The Bulgars accepted baptism under Byzantine influence in 864, though they were also allied with Louis the German: *AF* 863: 49; *AB* 864: 118; Nicholas, *Epistolae*, no. 25. For discussion see Shepard 1995: 239–47; Barford 2001: 221–2.
152 Louis sent missionaries in 867: *AF* 867: 56. However, the Bulgars' ecclesiastical allegiance ultimately lay with Byzantium.

him.¹⁵³ Not much later he was moved by divine inspiration to give up his earthly realm so that he might reign with Christ in heaven for eternity. After appointing his elder son in his place he had his hair cut, took up the dress of the holy way of life and became a monk, dedicated to alms, vigils and prayers by day and night.¹⁵⁴ Meanwhile his son, whom he had made king, retreated far from his father's intentions and deeds and began to act like a despoiler, giving himself over to drunkenness, carousing and lust, and making every effort to recall the recently baptised people to the pagan way of worship. When his father heard about this he was incensed with a great anger. He removed his holy habit, took up his sword-belt, put on his regal clothing and, gathering the God-fearing to his side, pursued his son. He soon captured him without difficulty, gouged out his eyes and imprisoned him. Then he summoned an assembly of the whole kingdom and established his younger son as king, threatening him in front of everyone that he would suffer a similar fate if in any way he deviated from correct Christianity.¹⁵⁵ Having accomplished these things he put down his sword-belt and, resuming the dress of holy religion, he entered the monastery and spent the rest of his earthly life in holy monastic conduct.¹⁵⁶

869

In the year of the Lord's incarnation 869, Lothar set out for Rome and when he arrived he was honourably received by Pope Hadrian.¹⁵⁷ When the pope asked him if he had been observing the admonitions of the pious father Lord Nicholas with every vigilance and if he had kept the oath he had made free of corruption, he responded – misled by him who did not remain true, and who is not only a liar but indeed the father of all liars¹⁵⁸ – that he had observed everything as if he had been ordered to do so by God himself. And because the leading men and magnates who had come with him gave the same testimony, and no opposing person

---

153 The Bulgar king was Boris (852–889), and his Byzantine baptismal name was Michael.
154 Boris-Michael abdicated to become a monk in 889; his eldest son was Vladimir (889–893).
155 The new ruler was Simeon (893–927).
156 *AB* 866: 136–8 tells a different exemplary story about the Bulgar king Boris-Michael.
157 They met on 1 July 869 at Monte Cassino, then went on to Rome. *AB* 869: 154 gives details of Lothar's journey.
158 John 8:44.

could be found who would dare to enter into a proper legal process against royal authority, the universal pope continued:[159] 'If the truth supports the words of your testimony, then with every joy in our heart we offer many thanks to omnipotent God. It remains, dearly beloved son, for you to go to the altar of St Peter, where by God's favour we will offer up the salvation-bringing host not so much for your person as for the safety of your soul. It is fitting that you join us in this, so that by your participation you may deserve to rejoin the body of Christ, from which you seemed to have become separated.' So, after the solemnities of the mass were finished, the supreme pontiff invited that king to Christ's table and, after he had taken in his hands the body and the blood of the Lord, he spoke these words to him: 'If you know yourself to be free of the crime of adultery that was prohibited and forbidden to you by Lord Nicholas, and you are resolved in your mind that for the rest of your life you will never again engage in wicked sexual relations with your long-repudiated concubine Waldrada, then approach faithfully and receive the sacrament of eternal salvation that will be helpful to you in the remission of your sins. If, however, your conscience accuses you and proclaims that you are cut with a deadly wound, or if you are minded to return to the pigsty of adultery, then do not dare accept it, lest the thing which divine providence has prepared for the salvation of the faithful brings you to judgement and damnation.'

Without a second thought Lothar, mad and stubborn as well as blind, took the communion of the body and blood of the Lord from the pontiff's hand, without fear of the saying: 'It is a terrible thing to fall into the hands of the living God;'[160] 'For anyone who eats and drinks unworthily, eats and drinks judgement on himself.'[161] Then the pope turned to the king's followers and supporters and offered communion to each of them with these words: 'If you neither showed favour nor offered consent to your lord and king Lothar in the crime of adultery of which he is accused, and if you did not communicate with Waldrada and others who were excommunicated by the apostolic see, then may the body and blood of our Lord Jesus Christ be helpful to you to eternal life!' Therefore, whoever knew that these words applied to him, and still presumed with daring recklessness to accept the communion proffered with such a warning, was struck down by divine judgement and removed from

159 Although reported in direct speech, Regino apparently had no written sources for the details of this entry.
160 Hebrews 10:31.
161 1 Corinthians 11:29.

this life before the beginning of the next year. A very few who declined to take the communion barely avoided the danger of death.[162]

When Lothar left Rome he was gripped by an illness and after arriving in the city of Piacenza he ended his final day on 8 August.[163] There were so many casualties among the king's followers that it seemed as if an enemy sword rather than a plague had cut down the nobility and manliness of the whole realm, which at that time was so rich that it filled the lands of the empire like a packed and sprouting crop-field or a swarm.[164]

On learning from a reliable source that King Lothar was dead, Charles soon moved to occupy his kingdom. Coming to Metz, he was favourably received by Adventius, bishop of that town, and several other bishops, and he was elevated to the kingdom.[165] From there he went on to Aachen and entered the palace, because it was seen as the seat of the kingdom, and many more people flooded to him there.[166]

At that time, however, the towns of Trier and Cologne were without bishops since, as we set out before, their pontiffs had both been taken from this light in Italy.[167] After taking counsel with the leading men, Charles put Bertulf, the foresaid Bishop Adventius's nephew, in charge of the church of Trier.[168] This man obtained the episcopal dignity thanks to the intervention and influence of the said Adventius, who at that time had a lot of sway over the king because he had ingratiatingly cooperated in his acquisition of the kingdom. In addition, the king tried to put Abbot Hilduin on the episcopal throne of Cologne, and in the palace of Aachen got Bishop Franco of Tongres [- Liège] to ordain him as priest

---

162 For a rather different account of Lothar and Hadrian's meeting see *AB* 869: 155–6. *AF* 869: 59, even more disapprovingly, goes so far as to imply that Lothar left Rome without having his request granted. Regino describes the communion as a kind of ordeal.

163 Regino probably got the date of Lothar's death from *AP*. Details of his death are also given by *AB* 869: 156; *AF* 869: 59; *AX* 870: 28. He was buried at St-Antoninus in Piacenza.

164 Cf. Regino's comment on aristocratic casualties at Fontenoy: above, 841. Regino's imagery here echoes Justin, *Epitome*, 25.2.7–9: 168 (Yardley 1994: 192).

165 9 September 869. Charles only received news of Lothar's death on 23 August. Details of his movements and the king-making ceremony at Metz are given by *AB* 869: 156–62.

166 Charles was very active in the final months of the year, taking a new wife and courting the Lotharingian magnates: *AB* 869: 162–5.

167 Above, 865.

168 January 870.

of the church of St-Peter in the said metropolis.[169]

While all this was going on in Lothar's kingdom, King Louis [the German], since he had been held up by illness, was lying in bed in the lands of the Bavarians. When he heard that the oft-mentioned kingdom had been invaded by his brother in such a way, he took it badly. Without delay he despatched legates to earnestly press Charles to desist from his reckless invasion and not to usurp for himself with undue presumption that which belonged equally to both of them by hereditary right. He ought to leave the kingdom until God had returned Louis to his former health and he was able to come so that they could negotiate face-to-face and decide by mutual consent what the laws of justice and fairness had to say about the status of that realm. At the same time as he was sending the legates ahead with these orders, he secretly despatched Archbishop Liutbert of Mainz to Cologne and exhorted him that he should endeavour in every way to pre-empt the ordination of Hilduin and seek to consecrate as bishop a cleric from the city itself through an election of the citizens.[170] Taking some other bishops with him, he arrived at the fortress of Deutz by a direct route. Fearing that Charles's supporters were perhaps laying a trap for him, he absolutely did not cross the Rhine but instead decided to send messengers ordering the more respected of the clergy and the more noble among the people to come and meet him at that same stronghold. When they had complied with his orders, the bishop told them on behalf of the king that they should confer among themselves and as fast as possible choose a leader from within their own flock. He had been sent to consecrate immediately whoever they decided by common counsel to put in charge. They responded that since Hilduin had already been given the bishopric and had been ordained as priest of that see, and almost everyone had accepted his leadership by offering their hands, there was no reasoning that would allow them to elect someone else. He replied to them: 'If you disdain the election granted to you by the king, it is in the king's power and authority to give to you whom he wants to give to you as bishop. But know this for certain, that before three days are out you will have someone other than Hilduin as your bishop.' After hearing this they unanimously elected Willibert, a venerable man, whom the said bishop ordained with his co-priests despite his great protestations

---

169 Hilduin was a relative of Gunther and a member of Charles the Bald's palace chapel. He was also abbot of St-Bertin: Nelson 1992: 214, 224. Franco was bishop for nearly half a century (855–901) and also a member of the Carolingian family.

170 Liutbert (archbishop 863–889) was the foremost prelate in the eastern realm, and Louis's archchancellor (one of the highest offices at court).

and refusals. With all the clergy and people Liutbert crossed the River Rhine and established him with honour on the episcopal throne, and after everything had been carried out according to the correct procedures he withdrew in all haste.[171]

When he learned of the ordination Charles was incensed by a great anger and soon set out for Cologne; for while these things were being carried out by Louis's legates, Hilduin remained at the royal court in the palace of Aachen. Bishop Willibert and all those who had consented to his ordination crossed the Rhine to evade the king's fury. Finding nobody on whom he could inflict revenge for the insults done to him, the king went back by the road on which he had come. Meanwhile legates were again sent by Louis beseeching him to leave the kingdom. When he did not comply Louis finally sent Archbishop Liutbert and Altfrid, a bishop from Saxony, a most prudent man, as ambassadors, commanding Charles to choose one of two courses: either get out of the realm fast, or do battle with his brother.[172] They approached him with such skill and resolution that without delay he withdrew and went back to his own kingdom. After this the two kings arranged to hold a meeting in the place called Meersen by the Meuse.

870

In the year of the Lord's incarnation 870, Louis and Charles together with their leading men came to Meersen and divided the late Lothar's kingdom between them equally. We think it would be superfluous, however, to record how this division was made, because almost everyone knows already.[173]

After the meeting was over, Charles went to Herstal because that palace had fallen in his share; Louis on the other hand went back to the palace at Aachen where, having been overcome by bad health, he rested in bed

---

171 *AF* 870: 61–2 approvingly describes the incident in similar, albeit briefer, terms. Willibert was consecrated on 7 January. See also *AX* 871: 29. Neither *AF* nor *AB* mentions the appointment. For the political context see Goldberg 2006a: 296.

172 Altfrid was bishop of Hildesheim (847–874), and had acted as Louis's envoy in Lotharingia before: *AB* 865: 121–2. The legates arrived as Charles was (re-)celebrating his marriage to Richildis: *AB* 870: 165–6. Regino's account of the ultimatum agrees with that of the *AB*.

173 8 August 870. The Treaty of Meersen, which split Lotharingia into eastern and western halves, is described in detail by *AB* 870: 168–70. See also *AF* 870: 62–3; MGH Capit. 2, no. 251. Regino's reference to his audience's familiarity with the treaty may reflect the fact that copies of other such divisions are known to have been distributed around the realm: *AF* 876: 82.

BOOK II   163

for nearly two months.[174] For after he had arrived from the east and entered the lands of the Ripuarians, he had stopped off for lodgings at a certain royal residence called Flamersheim.[175] When he climbed up to the solarium of the house together with a large entourage, the solarium itself collapsed when the timbers, which were very old and weakened by rot, broke. The king was so badly injured amid the rubble that he dislocated two ribs. And when everyone ran across, believing him to have been killed, he picked himself up from where he had fallen and showed himself to his men to reassure them that nothing bad had happened to him. Although it is scarcely believable, he hid his frailty and set out the next day to meet his brother at Meersen.[176] This ruler was so hard and had such courage that, even though several people heard the crack of the broken ribs rubbing against each other, nobody heard him gasp or let out a groan.[177]

At that time Charles deprived his son Carloman of his eyes.[178] The said king had three sons by Queen Ermentrude, namely Charles, Carloman and Louis; but two of these unfortunately died. Led by the flippancy of youth, [the younger] Charles of course wanted to test the daring and much-praised courage of Albuin, who was the brother of Bivin and Betto. One evening when Albuin was returning from the hunt, Charles pretended to be someone else and launched a solo attack on him, making as if he wanted to steal by force the horse he was riding. Albuin, who was expecting just about anybody except the king's son, drew his sword and struck him on the front of the head, quickly knocking him to the ground. He left him half-dead and pierced with many wounds, and took away his weapons as well as his horse. His limbs incapacitated and his face deformed, Charles survived only for a short time. Realising that the man to whom he had done such things was the king's son, Albuin fled in a hurry and avoided the risk of death.[179]

174 He issued charters there in September and October: DD LG 132–3.
175 'Land of the Ripuarians' is an antiquarian name for the middle Rhine.
176 AF 870: 62–3 and AB 870: 168 offer congruent versions of this story. On the significance of the sun-terrace ('solarium') in Carolingian architecture see de Jong forthcoming.
177 Physical self-control was a highly prized attribute for kings and male aristocrats.
178 873: for details, see below.
179 Charles died 29 September 866. AB 864: 111–12 tells a similar version of the story, and describes Charles's wound as 'reaching from his left temple to his right cheekbone and jaw.' Ado, Chronicon: 323 says he was 'dishonoured' by this injury. Violent horseplay was a habitual bonding and training pastime of young male aristocrats: Innes 2003; Halsall 2003: 118.

When Carloman was still a young boy, he had been tonsured as a cleric on his father's orders.[180] In the course of time, against his will and under pressure, he was ordained to the office of deacon in his father's presence, and he read out the Gospel in public and helped the bishop celebrate mass, as is the custom.[181] After this, through apostasy, withdrawing from his ecclesiastical obligations, he heedlessly rejected and spurned the grace that had been given to him by the laying-on of hands, so becoming a new Julian.[182] So, gathering together a considerable gang of bandits, he began to lay waste the churches of God, attack the peaceful, plunder everything and commit unheard-of evils.[183] For these things he was frequently punished by his father but despite this he did not cease at all from the depravity he had begun. Finally his father ordered his eyes to be gouged out, as we mentioned above. By a just judgement of God, he who had driven from his heart the interior light, which is Christ, also lost the light of the outside world. He who had willingly given himself over to inner darkness was cast into the outer. The blind man made his way to his uncle Louis and complained mournfully to him about the distress of his hardships and misfortunes.[184] Moved by pity, Louis gave him the monastery of St Willibrord at Echternach to sustain him in the present life, and soon afterward he died and was buried there.[185]

871

In the year of the Lord's incarnation 871, Pope Hadrian migrated to the Lord, and John took up the dignity of the supreme pontiff.[186]

---

180 Cf. *AB* 854: 79.
181 Carloman was tonsured and ordained in 860 and subsequently given control of several abbeys, including St-Médard in Soissons, St-Amand, St-Riquier, Lobbes and St-Arnulf in Metz. Charles the Bald clearly intended to exclude him from the succession, but he retained a very high status and a military entourage: *AB* 868: 152.
182 Julian 'the Apostate' was the fourth-century emperor who returned to paganism; he is mentioned above by Regino, 310–313.
183 Carloman's rebellions began in 870, seemingly triggered by the potential availability of Lotharingia. Despite Regino's dismissal of them as 'bandits', he had some very high-level backers: Nelson 1988; Nelson 1992: 226–31.
184 Blinding was a punishment reserved for usurpers (Bührer-Thierry 1998), but Charles's use of it on his son was exceptional. See *AB* 873: 181; *AF* 873: 70; Nelson 1988.
185 Carloman was initially sent to Corbie, and Louis the German may have connived in his escape from there: *AB* 873: 183–4. According to this source, Louis handed him over to Liutbert of Mainz for incarceration in St-Alban's, Mainz, rather than Echternach.
186 John VIII actually took over on 14 December 872. He was pope until his murder in

In these days Adalgis, the Beneventan *dux*, corrupted by the persuasions of the Greeks, raised his hand against the Emperor Louis. What is more, at his urgings many cities in the provinces of Samnium, Campania and Lucania withdrew from Louis and submitted themselves to Greek domination. When he found out about these things the emperor moved his army to the province of Samnium in order to attack its main town, the very rich and opulent Benevento. When he realised that the army was approaching, Adalgis was filled with dread and resorted to sneaky tricks. He left Benevento and presented himself willingly to the emperor, declaring that he was and always had been ready to serve him, and assuring him with an oath that he had never offered cooperation to the rebels. Then he won the king over with gifts and soon returned to his former favour.

The emperor moved his forces into Campania and Lucania against the cities which had defected from him. He regained their submission without difficulty except for Capua which, because it was built from squared stones, supplied its inhabitants with the daring to resist. Therefore, encircling it with a siege that prevented anyone from getting in or out, he devastated the surrounding area and pillaged everything with the rapacity of an enemy. In the end, the vines, olive-yards and other fruitbearing trees were torn up by the roots. In desperation the Capuans went to the town's bishop, they raised on a bier the body of the holy bishop Germanus, whose soul the venerable father Benedict had seen being carried to heaven by angels in a burning orb, and like supplicants carried it through the open doors to the emperor's camp, praying that by the intervention of that same saint he might show them forgiveness. The emperor, since his whole person flooded with piety, was moved by mercy; he benevolently forgave their errors and aberrations, and commanded his army to stay its hand from destruction. Having thus kicked out the Greeks, he stationed garrisons drawn from the ranks of his followers in the cities he had retaken and set out for Benevento, where he had decided to stay for a while. Tired from the long siege of the city, the army began to pine for its homeland, to long for peace after the hardships they had endured, and in their minds' eyes to recall the sweet embraces of their wives and children; because of this they began to disperse daily, little by little.[187]

Meanwhile Adalgis, who was naturally cunning, asked the emperor

---

882. His biography has not survived. The most recent modern study of his pontificate is Arnold 2005.

187 The imagery recalls Justin, *Epitome*, 12.3.2: 90–1 (Yardley 1994: 110).

why he was ruining the resources of his own people for no apparent reason, and why he was allowing the fields and villages under his command to be destroyed as if by an enemy; it was fitting that he should give to the weary their desired rest, and that the region which had now been almost destroyed should be saved by princely mercy. Since he had been persuaded by these suggestions, the emperor disbanded most of his army and gave it permission to return home. He himself stayed where he was with a few men, suspecting nothing untoward. When he saw that the king had been left without his forces, Adalgis set in motion the evil scheme that he had been planning for a long time. Together with the accomplices in his conspiracy, he moved to capture the palace in which the emperor was taking a midday rest.[188] The king was roused by the racket and commotion caused by the attackers and jumped out of bed, grabbed his weapons, and, confused by the sudden assault, advanced to the door of the house with a few of his bodyguards. He defended the entrance with his sword and kept the enemy from the threshold. When Adalgis realised that the doors of the house could not be entered without danger, he withdrew from the entrance on foot and ordered that the palace be destroyed by fire. In the meantime the king tried to offer him his hand and urgently requested peace. He got the response that he would not get what he asked for unless he first swore an oath that for the rest of his life he would never enter the territory of Benevento, nor exact any revenge for the shame which he was currently suffering. After the relics of the saints had been brought out, he was forced by the circumstances to swear the oath that had been demanded from him, and the next day he immediately left Benevento.[189]

872

In the year of the Lord's incarnation 872, Emperor Louis came to Rome and there, celebrating an assembly in the presence of the supreme pontiff, he made many complaints about the tyranny of Adalgis. The Roman senate declared that same Adalgis to be a tyrant and an enemy of the state, and decreed a war against him.[190] By the authority of God and St Peter, Pope John absolved the emperor from the oath by which

---

188 13 August.
189 Shorter but broadly consistent accounts are offered by Erchempert of Monte Cassino, *Historia*, c. 34: 247; Andrew of Bergamo, *Historia*, c. 16: 228–9; *AB* 871: 175–6 (which says that the assault started at night and lasted three days). The descriptions of Louis's terms of surrender in Regino and the *AB* are very similar.
190 Regino's reference to the senate is a conscious anachronism.

BOOK II

he had bound himself, emphasising that it counted for nothing against him because he had been forced to make it to escape the danger of death; and that that which was spoken against the well-being of the state was no oath, however many imprecations it was made with.[191] By these exhortations he incited the king's spirit to take up the fight again. However, so that his men would not call him a perjurer, he did not go forth against the tyrant in person, but sent the queen with an army. When Adalgis received definite indications that war was being raised against him with great force and that he had been denounced as an enemy and a tyrant, he was overcome by dread at the knowledge of his wickedness and placed his hopes for life in flight. He withdrew to the island of Corsica and hid there for some time.[192]

873

In the year of the Lord's incarnation 873, an inestimable multitude of locusts came from the east in the month of August and devastated almost all of Gaul.[193] They were bigger than other locusts and had six pairs of wings; and, amazing to say, they flew through the air in distinct units and after landing on the ground made their camp like divisions of an army.[194] With a few others, the leaders travelled one day ahead

---

191 The pope was in fact Hadrian. *AB* 871: 176 says Louis summoned Hadrian to absolve him immediately after his departure from the south. However, he was probably formally released from his oath in May the following year when he was in Rome for a public crown-wearing before setting out against Adalgis: *AB* 872: 179. Louis needed to reassert his status after rumours circulated that he had been killed in Benevento: *AB* 871: 176; *AF* 871: 66.

192 Louis sent a further army in 872 (*AB* 872: 179), but his final attempt to defeat the Beneventans took place in 873, and failed: Erchempert of Monte Cassino, *Historia*, c. 36: 248. He stayed at Capua and came to terms with Adalgis after he acquired Greek support: *AB* 873: 183. Adalgis is not known to have fled, despite Regino's claim. The claim that Engelberga led the army is plausible given her great power: Odegaard 1951; MacLean 2003b: 26–32.

193 The locusts were probably recorded in *AP* 873. Many contemporary sources record details of this evidently remarkable plague, for example *AF* 873: 71; *AB* 873: 184; *AX* 873: 33; *AV* 873: 40. The sources and the locusts themselves are analysed by Thornton 1996; see also Nelson 1988: 122–3.

194 The phrases 'bigger than other locusts' and 'amazing to say' are also found in a description of locust activity in Paul the Deacon, *Historia*, IV.2: 145 (Foulke 2003: 151–2), though Paul's description of their behaviour (they were remarkable in that they didn't eat the crops) is otherwise completely different from Regino's. Perhaps more significant are the similarities between Regino's account and Proverbs 30:27: 'Locusts have no king, yet they advance together in ranks.' This text was cited by Andrew of Bergamo, *Historia*, c. 17: 229 in his description of the locusts' appearance in Italy. See Boschen 1972: 220–1.

of the army as if to scout out suitable places for the multitude. Around the ninth hour they settled in the place where the leaders had been the day before, and they did not move from there until sunrise. Then they set out in their squadrons, so that one would think these small creatures had military discipline. They fed on the crop-fields, which were so completely devoured by them that they seemed to have been destroyed by an immense storm.[195] A day's travelling for them consisted of four or five miles. Covering the surface of the earth, they came as far as the British sea, into which by God's will they were blown by the violent gusts of the winds and, carried away into its vast expanse, they were immersed. The seething and flooding of the ocean cast them back up and filled the beaches. Such piles of them were made that they were heaped up like mountain peaks. The air was corrupted by their stench and foulness, causing a dire plague from which many who lived nearby perished.[196]

Around that same time Charles besieged the town of Angers.[197] After they had killed Robert and Ranulf and several other well-born men who were defending with arms the frontiers of their homeland, because God was angry with the inhabitants of the land and since nobody could be found to resist their violence, the Northmen became excited by the pillaging of a few cities and territories and realised from the plunder available in each how much wealth they could get from all of them. They entered the city of Angers and found it empty because its inhabitants had scattered in flight. When they saw that it was impregnable because of its very strong fortifications and due to where it was sited, they were filled with joy and decided that it would provide a secure refuge for their people and their troops against those peoples who might be provoked to war. Immediately they brought their ships up the River Mayenne and moored at the walls, went inside with their wives and children as if they were going to live there, repaired the damage and rebuilt the ditches and palisades.[198] From there they launched surprise raids and devastated the surrounding regions. When Charles had been told that such a pernicious plague had implanted itself in the heart of the kingdom, he immediately gathered there an army from all the kingdoms under his

---

195 Regino's imagery here echoes Justin's: see above, 853, n. 44.
196 The image of locusts being blown into the sea is found in several classical and patristic texts, discussed by Boschen 1972: 222.
197 Viking raiders seem to have established a lengthy occupation of the city in that year or earlier: *AB* 873: 183.
198 This is a rare reference to the Vikings having families with them.

control as if to put out a fire that threatened them all,[199] and pitching his camp in a circle he laid siege to the city. And because the Mayenne flows past the walls of the city on the Breton side, he ordered Salomon king of the Bretons to summon his forces and come quickly, so that they could defeat their common enemy with a united force.[200] Bringing with him many thousands of Bretons, Salomon pitched his tents on the bank of the Mayenne. The city was thus surrounded by besiegers from all parts. For many days it was beleaguered from all sides with the greatest effort, and new high-quality kinds of siege-machines were brought to bear. But the king's efforts did not produce a happy outcome, because the layout of the place did not permit easy access and the strong force of pagans resisted with the greatest spirit, because they were fighting for their lives. The immense army was worn down by the long tedium of the siege, by hunger and by a grave pestilence. When the Bretons saw that the town was unconquerable they tried to divert the river from its course so that, when its natural channel was dried out, they could attack the Northmen's ships. They therefore started to dig a trench of amazing depth and width. This filled the Northmen with such dread and fear that without delay they promised Charles a huge amount of money if he would raise the siege and allow them free passage out of his own kingdom. The king, overcome by base lust, took the money, withdrew from the siege and showed the enemy a clear road. Boarding their ships, the Northmen returned to the Loire and by no means left his kingdom as they had promised. Instead, they remained in that same place and committed acts that were far more evil and monstrous than before.[201]

---

199 An image that echoes Justin, *Epitome*, 1.7.9: 9 (Yardley 1994: 20).

200 Salomon had been loyal to Charles for some time, and had helped him militarily before: *AB* 868: 151–2; Smith 1992: 107. The Mayenne was a frontier between the Breton and Frankish realms: Smith 1992: 144.

201 Werner 1959a argued that Regino was an eyewitness to this siege; but Schleidgen 1977: 14–16 showed that the detailed arguments on which his supposition depended do not fit the manuscript evidence. *AB* 873: 183–5 offers a different account which plays down Salomon's role, does not mention the plan to divert the river, and presents Charles as forcing the besieged city to submit. This source, whose detail suggests eyewitness authority (argued by Nelson in *AB* 873: 185, n. 17) says that the terms of surrender involved the Vikings retreating to an island in the Loire (possibly Noirmoutier) in order to hold a market, after which they would either accept baptism or leave. *AV* 873: 40, like Regino, interprets this agreement in a negative light, though adds that Charles received hostages.

874

In the year of the Lord's incarnation 874, the Emperor Louis, who ruled the kingdom of Italy, died.[202] In truth he was a pious and merciful ruler, devoted to justice, pure in his simplicity,[203] a defender of the churches of God, a father to orphans and urchins, and a liberal giver of lavish alms who submitted himself humbly to God's servants, so that his justice may live on forever and his horn is exalted in glory.[204]

In the same year Salomon king of the Bretons was treacherously killed by his generals [*duces*] Pacsweten and Wrhwant.[205] After his death these two wanted to divide his realm between them but they disagreed on the shares because most of the people favoured Pacsweten's faction; and both sides began to wage war with the greatest force. Although Pacsweten had the greater following, he nevertheless engaged the help of the Northmen for money.[206] He mingled them with his army to enhance its strength and then set out to wage war against his rival. Realising that the strength of the kingdom had fallen to Pacsweten, Wrhwant's followers began to drift away from him so that barely a thousand remained in the battle-line with him, and even these began to urge him to withdraw and avoid the danger of death – he could not hold back a countless multitude on his own with just a few men. To them he responded: 'God forbid, brave comrades,' he said, 'that I do today

---

202 Actually 12 August 875. Louis's death was possibly recorded in *AP*. Regino's wording illustrates how the imperial title had become an honour generally held by the king of Italy rather than a position carrying more wideranging authority: Zimmermann 1974.

203 *Simplicitas* is deployed here and elsewhere in the text as a positive attribute with connotations of candour and honesty. Charles the Straightforward (traditionally 'the Simple') (898–929) may have been given his nickname with similar qualities in mind: Schneidmüller 1978. Regino evidently considered it an appropriate epithet for a king; for arguments to the contrary see Koziol 2006a: 238, n. 14.

204 Psalms 92:10: 'My horn shalt thou exalt like the horn of a unicorn.'

205 Salomon was killed 28 June 874 as a result of court intrigue. Pacsweten, count of Vannes, was a wealthy landowner and Salomon's son-in-law; Wrhwant (various spellings are used – Vurfandus, Uuruuant, Guorhwant – I have followed that of Smith 1992) seems to have been a lesser figure, though he may have been Erispoë's son-in-law: Davies 1988: 21. Chédeville and Guillotel 1984: 355–6 argue that his power-base was in northern Brittany. Hincmar (*AB* 874: 186) names a third conspirator, Wigo son of Riwallon, who was Salomon's nephew and count of Cornouaille, and adds more detail of the (in his view richly-deserved) murder. For discussion see Smith 1992: 120–1; Pettiau 2004: 181, 186.

206 Hiring bands of Vikings as mercenaries was a common practice in the Frankish world, though ecclesiastical authors often condemned it: see Coupland 1995; Halsall 2003: 113.

what I have never done before, namely turn my back on my enemies and bring infamy on our glorious name. It is better to die nobly than to rescue one's life dishonourably. Do not despair of victory. Let us test the forces of fortune with the enemy, for our salvation does not rest in numbers, but rather in God.' When he had roused his men's spirits with such exhortations, he charged against the enemy who numbered, so they say, over 30,000. A shout was raised to the sky and battle was joined with the greatest courage. Wrhwant and his men penetrated the enemy's very tightly packed battle-formation and, just as the grass of the meadows falls before the cut of the scythe and abundant crops are knocked down by the raging tumult of a storm, so he cut down and scattered everything with his sword. Seldom was so much blood poured out in any battle in that kingdom.[207] Pacsweten, seeing his men butchered like animals, fled with the few who had not yet been extinguished by the sword. Then the Northmen whom he had summoned to help him entered the monastery of the saintly Bishop Melanius and there, as they were accustomed to do, they barricaded themselves in until the following night when they scattered in flight and returned to their ships. This battle took place in a field near the city of Rennes.[208]

This Wrhwant was illustrious in descent among his people, but because of his proven courage he was even more famous for his nobility, which was so great in him that in the greatness of his spirit and the renown of his vigour he seemed, as we said, to be second to none among his people.[209] In order to illustrate the boldness and steadfastness of his character it pleases me to record only one story of the many about him. One winter, Salomon pitched camp against the Northmen in order to protect the frontiers of his kingdom from their incursions.[210] One day, when he had been there for some time and was holding a discussion among his men about the daring and hardness of the Northmen, the aforementioned Wrhwant, overestimating his own strength, arrogantly boasted that if the king withdrew with the army then he would dare to stay behind at that same place with only his own men, and remain there

---

207 This phrase recalls one of Justin's: *Epitome*, 11.14.2: 87 (Yardley 1994: 105).
208 This battle is not extensively described in other sources, but it is known that Wrhwant and Pacsweten were both dead by 876: Smith 1992: 121. Pettiau 2004: 186 suggests the battle may have been fought in early 876.
209 This is not dissimilar to the description of Lysimachus in Justin, *Epitome*, 15.3.1: 118 (Yardley 1994: 140).
210 What follows may relate to the incident mentioned in *AB* 869: 163, when Salomon is said to have made a peace with the Vikings on the Loire.

for three days after the king's departure.[211] The distance between the Breton camp and the fleet of the Northmen was only eight miles. These words, which Wrhwant had spoken in jest, were reported to the leader of the pagans, Hasting, though I do not know by whom. Not much later Salomon made peace with the Northmen after giving them 500 cows.[212] After hostages had been received and he was arranging to return to his own realm, Hasting's ambassador said this to him: 'My lord has been told that you have a man who boasted that he would dare to stay behind in this place alone with his own followers after you had withdrawn. If he is as brave as he thinks he is, then let him remain without hesitation because my lord wants to see him and desires to make the acquaintance of this bold man.' When the king asked Wrhwant whether he had said such a thing, he responded that he had and that he wanted to prove these things in deed; and immediately, he begged permission to stay there. When the ruler berated him, asking why, after he had been taken hold of by foolish stubbornness, he so wanted to die and to deliver his men to death for words cast vainly into the wind, he did not back down at all and claimed that if he were not given permission to stay then he would in no way be faithful to him in future. When Salomon saw that his mind was made up, he wanted to give him help from among his own bodyguard; but he refused to take it, asserting that if he had anyone with him other than his own men then what he had sworn would no longer be true. The king and all his forces returned to their realm and Wrhwant stayed behind in the same place with about 200 men and waited for five days.[213] On the sixth night Hasting released a certain prisoner from his chains and sent him to Wrhwant with orders that he should come to meet him between the second and third hours of the coming day at the ford of a certain stream, so that they might enjoy a face-to-face talk.[214] Without hesitation Wrhwant told his men to take up their arms and went to the appointed place immediately. When he saw that the ford of the stream would act like a barrier between his men and the enemy he did not want to take up a position there at all, so he

211 Aristocrats' military entourages were key components of armies in this period: Reuter 1985; Reuter 1990; Halsall 2003: 71–110.
212 An interesting form of tribute, which illustrates the semi-permanence of at least some Scandinavian warbands in Francia.
213 The reference to the size of Whrwant's entourage must be regarded with caution, coming as it does in the midst of a story that looks to have been passed on orally. Nonetheless, it offers a rare clue to the size of military entourages and thus the size of armies: cf. Reuter 1997; Reuter 1999a.
214 Rivers were often used as meeting places (symbolic neutral ground) for political negotiations: see for example Barrow 2001.

BOOK II   173

forded the stream and without restraint approached the enemy. The Northmen, astonished at the man's daring and courage, backed down and did not dare challenge him to battle. He waited undaunted until the sixth hour and when he realised that nobody from the opposing party was coming he took his men and went home.

His spirit was no less invincible in death than in war. For after accomplishing this victory he was oppressed by illness and dragged into extreme danger. When Pacsweten had heard about his illness, he had regathered his forces and prepared to wage war against Wrhwant's supporters. They were very frightened and fled to their leader; they tearfully recounted to him Pacsweten's threats, asking his counsel against the imminent danger. And he urged them to proceed fearlessly against the enemy carrying his own banner, and promised them victory. When they replied that they did not dare to face their adversaries without him being there he regained his spirit, which had almost slipped away already along with the strength of his body, and because he could not travel on foot or by horse he ordered that he be carried on a bier and put in front of the enemy's battle-line, and in this way he would go into battle. When his followers carried this out, soon the enemy turned in flight. After achieving this victory, when they wanted to carry him back to his house, in the arms of the warriors he breathed out his spirit, which had only just been beating in his chest. A few days later Pacsweten himself died as well.[215] After the successive deaths of these two, Judicael, a son of King Erispoë's daughter, and Alan, the foresaid Pacsweten's brother, divided Brittany between them. There were many disputes and wars between them as well. But when Judicael was killed in a battle he was waging against the Northmen with more daring than foresight, all of Brittany went over to Alan's authority, and he governs it vigorously up to the present day.[216]

In that same year Charles [the Bald] went to Rome and after giving great gifts to the apostolic John and the Romans he was made emperor.[217]

215 Both men probably died in 876: see above, n. 208.
216 Judicael held office in Cornouaille (western Brittany) under Salomon, while Alan was count of Vannes and had influence in the county of Nantes as well: Smith 1992: 121–2. Their subsequent rivalry was not absolute, and they seem to have cooperated against the Vikings at least. Judicael died in 890 (see below, 890), after which Alan became sole ruler, taking the royal title after 897: Smith 1992: 192; Pettiau 2004: 173, 178. Regino's statement that he was alive at the time of writing hints that Alan did not die until 908; although the later *Annales Rotonenses* put his death in 907, the first reference to the next ruler of Brittany does not come until November 908: Pettiau 2004: 173–4.
217 Charles's coronation in Rome, Christmas Day 875, may have been recorded in the *AP*. For the event itself see Nelson 1992: 238–44.

876[218]

In the year of the Lord's incarnation 876, King Louis [the German] ended his final day in the palace of Frankfurt on 28 August and was buried in the monastery of St-Nazarius, which is called Lorsch.[219] He was a most Christian ruler, Catholic in faith, who was not only sufficiently learned in the secular disciplines, but also in the ecclesiastical. He was a most ardent practitioner of those things required by religion, peace and justice. He was most wise by nature, very far-sighted in counsel, and in the granting and removing of public offices he was controlled by the guide of discretion. He was most victorious in battles, and more devoted to the equipment of battle than the splendour of banquets; his greatest treasures were the instruments of war and he loved the hardness of iron more than the glitter of gold.[220] Nobody who was useless had influence with him, and a useful man very seldom displeased his eyes. Nobody could corrupt him with gifts and nobody obtained from him any ecclesiastical or worldly dignity through money. Rather, ecclesiastical positions were acquired by upright behaviour and a holy way of life, and worldly dignity through devoted service and sincere fidelity. Moreover, this very glorious king of blessed memory had joined to himself in marriage a queen named Emma, who was not only noble by birth but, what is more praiseworthy, much more outstanding in the nobility of her mind.[221] By her, Louis had three sons of most excellent character, namely Karlmann, Louis [the Younger] and Charles [the Fat], who by happy destiny managed the government of the empire after their father's death.[222]

When Charles [the Bald] heard that his brother had departed from this world he was, so they say, overwhelmed with great joy since he expected that the portion of Lothar's kingdom which the same brother had held would fall into his hands. So, he gathered an army as quickly as he could and with all his forces he entered the kingdom and came to the palace of Aachen. After delaying there a few days he set out for Cologne.[223]

218 There is no entry for 875.

219 Regino got the date from the *AP*. Louis's middle son Louis the Younger orchestrated the funeral at Lorsch, which was in his main power base: *AF* 876: 79.

220 From 'more devoted' to 'instruments of war' this is almost identical to Justin's description of Philip of Macedon: *Epitome*, 9.8.4: 74 (Yardley 1994: 91).

221 On Emma see Goldberg 2006b. She also died in 876: *AF* 876: 78.

222 'Empire' here may refer to the east Frankish kingdom alone, as eastern writers sometimes characterized Louis as an emperor.

223 *AB* 876: 195–6 says that Charles's initial plan was to go to Metz and receive the

While all these things were going on in the said kingdom, Louis's firstborn son Karlmann had crossed the borders of Italy, desiring to subordinate it to his and his father's rule.²²⁴ For, as we have mentioned, the emperor Louis [II] had already been taken from this life and Charles had withdrawn from Italy carrying back the name of emperor.²²⁵ Meanwhile, Karlmann's brother Charles [the Fat] remained in Alemannia.²²⁶ Louis [the Younger], moreover, who had been present at his father's death and had celebrated his funeral ceremonies with fitting honour, was residing at Frankfurt, the main seat of the eastern kingdom.²²⁷ When it was announced to him that his uncle Charles had already invaded the frontiers of his paternal kingdom and pitched his camp near the River Rhine, Louis was incensed with a great rage and immediately sent legates to him begging him to remember their brotherhood and common blood, and to be mindful of the name of our Lord Jesus Christ, which he himself and his brother had invoked before many witnesses when they divided the kingdom between them and were promising peace to each other with terrible assurances.²²⁸ He said Charles should be very frightened about taking such a great name in vain, that he should render account to the Lord for his oaths, and that the treaty which they agreed between them should remain inviolable; he should restrain his sword and shudder with horror at the terrible desire to spill human blood that had corrupted him in so frightful a manner. He ought to be content with his lot and enjoy in peace what God had given him through the line of heredity and not invade, steal or disturb what by

---

bishops before he changed his mind and made for Aachen and Cologne; *AF* 876: 79–80 suggests that this was part of Charles's plan to annex the significant east Frankish cities that lay west of the Rhine (Mainz, Speyer and Worms) as well as eastern Lotharingia. Earlier disputes over eastern Lotharingia had also centred on Cologne: see above, 869. *AV* 875: 41 also highlights the visit to Cologne.

224 This refers to the events of 875, when Karlmann and Charles confronted each other in Italy. Despite what Regino says, Karlmann withdrew, though the sources disagree on whether this was the result of a retreat or a truce: *AF* 875: 77–8; *AB* 875: 188; *AV* 875: 40; Andrew, *Historia*, c. 19: 230. Karlmann had probably been accepted as his heir by the heirless Louis II in the negotiations described by *AB* 872: 179; D K 4 refers to this designation. On the politics of the succession see Nelson 1992: 238–9; Goldberg 2006a: 328–31; MacLean 2007.

225 Regino mentions Charles's imperial coronation above, 875.

226 Alemannia was the central part of Charles's sphere of influence during his father's reign: MacLean 2003a: 83–91. However, *AB* 875: 188 and Andrew, *Historia*, c. 19: 230 both say he went to Italy in advance of Karlmann after Louis II's death.

227 Louis's orchestration of his father's funeral in his own power base helped establish his authority after his succession: Fried 1984.

228 A reference to the Treaty of Meersen: see above, 870.

right belonged to others.²²⁹ In such a man there should not be the pride of vainglory, nor the arrogance of pride, nor the ambition to usurp the lands of another. Instead, justice, charity and unity should rule, and the peace between him and his nephews should hold the highest dignity of all. But Charles scorned such warnings, claiming that he had made the deal with his brother, not with his nephews.²³⁰

Meanwhile, Louis [the Younger] gathered an army from Saxony, Thuringia and east Francia and, so that one might recognize the son's paternity not so much by his looks as by his perspicacity and ingenuity, he pitched a very well equipped camp opposite Charles's on the bank of the river near Cologne, and he himself crossed the Rhine between Koblenz and Andernach with the whole force of his army. The man who brought this to Charles's attention did not neglect to mention that his nephew had crossed the Rhine with all his forces. That was when Charles first realized he had been duped by Louis's camp. Without delay he moved his army and with more than 50,000 men, or so they say, he advanced to the Maienfeld not far from the fortress of Andernach to engage Louis in battle. However, 'there is no king saved by the multitude of a host ... A horse is a vain thing for safety'.²³¹ When the battle had begun, Count Reginar, who was carrying the royal banner, was killed in the first charge.²³² The tightly-packed battle formation was penetrated by Louis's men and, just as fire rages through stubble and devours it all in an instant, so they destroyed the enemy forces with the sword and laid them out on the earth. Having been violently cut apart, Charles's army turned to flee and the victory was Louis's. When he saw his men running away Charles saved his own life through flight, reflecting too late on how dangerous it is to want, through the desires of unlimited greed, to violate the commandments of justice which are reinforced by the dispositions of divine and human laws. This slaughter took place on 8 October.²³³

229 The language of inheritance used here echoes that of Deuteronomy 32:9: cf. above, 866, n. 125.
230 The fact that Charles sought to manipulate the situation in this way shows how seriously oaths were taken in Carolingian politics: Becher 1993. Carolingian division plans sometimes included 'next-generation' clauses that anticipated these problems: MacLean 2001.
231 Psalms 33:16–17, though Regino's deployment of the quote is slightly baffling.
232 *AB* 876: 197 also records his death; on standard-bearers see Halsall 2003: 199–200.
233 Regino knew the date from the *AP*. The Battle of Andernach decisively established Louis the Younger's rule and ended Charles the Bald's ambitions in the east. Detailed accounts of the battle are also given by *AB* 876: 196–8 and *AF* 876: 80–2,

After this, the three aforementioned brothers met in the place called Schwalfeld, and there they divided the paternal kingdom.[234] Karlmann received Bavaria, Pannonia and *Carnutum* [Carinthia], which in bad style is called *Carantanum*,[235] and also the realms of the Slavs, Bohemians and Moravians. Louis got east Francia, Thuringia, Saxony, Frisia and part of Lothar's kingdom. To Charles's portion fell Alemannia and some cities in the kingdom of Lothar.[236]

877

In the year of the Lord's incarnation 877, the elder Charles [the Bald] set out for a second time to Rome, where already previously he had bought the name of emperor from John, bishop of the apostolic see, for a huge price.[237] And he saw more of the kingdom of Italy in passing than he actually controlled.[238] When he had returned to Lombardy from the city of Rome, he joined Irmingarde, daughter of Emperor Louis, in marriage to Boso, brother of Queen Richildis.[239] The wedding day was celebrated with such splendour and magnificent entertainments that the delights of this festive day are considered to have exceeded every limit. Charles also gave Provence to the foresaid Boso and, placing a crown on top of his head, ordered him to be called king so that he himself would be seen

---

both of which say that Charles attempted a surprise attack at night. *AV* 876: 41 has a shorter notice. For context see Nelson 1992: 244–6; Goldberg 2006a: 336.

234 This took place in November: *AF* 876: 82, which also says that vernacular copies of the oaths sworn were distributed around the realm; these have not survived. Regino's is the most detailed account of the terms, and it accords broadly with what is known about Louis's own plans for the succession: Borgolte 1977; W Hartmann 2002: 70–1; Goldberg 2006a: 275–6.

235 On contemporary names for Carinthia see Bertels 1987. Regino's wording on this point is almost identical to a comment in Paul the Deacon, *Historia*, V.22: 194 (Foulke 2003: 230).

236 The location of Charles's share of Lotharingia is not clear. Most likely this referred to the 'cities' or 'bishoprics' (*civitates*) of Transjurane Burgundy and Alsace, which had in the past belonged to Lothar's kingdom but in recent years had come under the influence of Louis the German and his sons.

237 *AF* 875: 78 also reports Charles to have bribed John. However, the other sources (such as *AB* 876: 189) mention this as no more than the gifts to St Peter expected from an emperor-elect. John VIII, *Fragmenta*, no. 59 suggests that the pope had already declared for Charles the Bald soon after the death of Louis II.

238 There is some truth in this, as the allegiances of the leading Italian aristocrats were split between Charles and Karlmann: Delogu 1968; MacLean 2007.

239 Regino is explicitly referring back to the events of early 876. Boso held a succession of very high offices late in Charles the Bald's reign: see Airlie 1985; Nelson 1992: 221–2, 231–4. *AF* 878: 85 claims that Boso poisoned his first wife before abducting Irmingarde, but Regino's attribution of agency to Charles is much more plausible.

to rule over kings after the fashion of ancient emperors.²⁴⁰ Then, after a few days, he entered Pavia.²⁴¹ While he was concerning himself there with the disposition of public affairs it was suddenly announced to him that Karlmann had invaded the frontiers of the Lombards with a great multitude of armed men.²⁴² Dissolving into panic, he soon crossed the Ticino and the Po and strove with a great effort to return to Gaul. But before he reached the high summits and narrow passes of the Alps he was struck by a fatal illness, and death immediately followed. It is rumoured, however, that a goblet of death had been given him by a certain Jew called Zedechias, who was greatly trusted by him because he was said to have unique experience in treating bodily illnesses. But he was a trickster and had deceived the minds of men with magic tricks and spells.²⁴³ Charles died, then, on 6 October.²⁴⁴ His body was lifted onto a bier and carried out of Italy by his men. But because the intolerable stench coming from the putrid corpse aggravated the bearers, they were forced to commit it to the earth. After a few years his bones were transported from there and interred with honour at the monastery of St-Denis in Paris.²⁴⁵ His son Louis [the Stammerer] succeeded him in the kingdom.

240 *AB* 876: 189–90 more correctly records that Boso was given a 'ducal crown' and established as Charles's representative (*dux*) in Italy; it is in this capacity that he subscribed the record of Charles's election (MGH Capit. 2, no. 220). Boso was also count of Vienne, but the idea that Charles gave him Provence suggests that Regino collapsed into this event Boso's later attempt to seize a crown there: see below, 879. Boso was certainly never king of Italy, nor was he seen as a candidate for the imperial title: Fried 1976. The idea of an emperor as a ruler over multiple kingdoms was one nurtured at times by Charles the Bald: Nelson 1992: 163, 219–20; however, Regino seems to parody this idea, perhaps coloured by his own experience of living in the age of the *reguli*, over whom Arnulf tried to assert overlordship by giving crowns. The reference to ancient emperors may allude to Ptolemy's crowning of his sister as queen in Justin, *Epitome*, 24.3.1: 161 (Yardley 1994: 185), whose wording Regino closely echoes.

241 Charles was in fact already at Pavia when he promoted Boso: *AB* 876: 189.

242 Karlmann's campaign into Italy is described by *AF* 877: 83; *AF* 877: 201–2; *AV* 877: 42. Rumours and counter-rumours about the sizes of each others' forces seem to have been the main factors in keeping the armies apart.

243 *AB* 877: 202–3 and *AV* 877: 42 also say Charles was poisoned by Zedechias, while *AF* 877: 82–3 says he caught dysentery. Kings often had doctors in their entourages, and their arcane knowledge and intimate access to the ruler could attract suspicion, especially if they were also religious outsiders like Zedechias. Royal illnesses and deaths frequently gave rise to accusations of witchcraft and poison, often against the kings' wives and others close to them: Reuter 2006a: 227–9.

244 Regino got this information from *AP*. He died near Maurienne, after crossing the Alps.

245 Similar stories of Charles's death and putrefaction are offered by *AB* 877: 202–3; *AF* 877: 83; *AV* 877: 42. None of them, nor Regino, draws a negative conclusion (in contrast to the case of Lothar II). Charles's first place of burial was at Nantua, west of Geneva. For discussion see Nelson 1996.

878

In the year of the Lord's incarnation 878, there was a great eclipse of the moon on the 16th day of October. On the 29th day of that same month there was an eclipse of the sun around the ninth hour.[246] After only a short time had passed, Charles's son King Louis, who was called 'the Stammerer' because he was somewhat impeded and slow in speech, was taken from this life.[247] That ruler was was a mild and honest man, a lover of peace, justice and religion.[248] When he was still flourishing in the prime of his youth, he had joined to himself in bonds of marriage a certain noble girl called Ansgard, by whom he had two children who were distinguished by their handsome appearance and their great strength of spirit: of these, one was called Louis, the other Carloman.[249] But because he had admitted her to his embraces without the knowledge or consent of his father, he was later forbidden from being with her by his father, and by the imposition of sworn oaths he was forever separated from her side.[250] His father then gave him Adelaide in matrimony, and she was pregnant by him when the king died. And when the time for her to give birth arrived a boy was brought forth. She gave him the name of his grandfather, and ordered that he be called Charles.[251]

879

In the year of the Lord's incarnation 879, Boso, whom we mentioned a little earlier,[252] heard about Louis's death and after leaving Provence tried to take over all of Burgundy. Partly by persuasion and partly

---

246 This information is from the *AP*.

247 Louis died on 10 April, 879, after a reign of less than two years. For details of his reign see *AB* 877–9: 203–16.

248 Honest = *simplex*: see above, 874, n. 203.

249 Louis III (879–82) and Carloman II (879–84). Contemporaries had high opinions of both of them: see Werner 1979; MacLean 2001.

250 Ansgard was a daughter of Harduin, a Neustrian count: *AB* 862: 100. Pope John VIII refused to crown Adelaide as queen, probably because of the repudiation of Ansgard: *AB* 878: 210. Adelaide was the daughter of a Burgundian aristocrat called Adalard: Nelson 1992: 232. For a genealogical discussion see Werner 1967: 432–3, 437–9.

251 Regino's careful account of these circumstances seems designed to endorse the legitimacy of Charles the Straightforward, who was king of west Francia when he was writing.

252 Surely a reference to the information recorded under 877 and not, as argued by Staab 1998, that under 866: see above, 866, n. 92.

through threats he rallied several bishops to make alliance with him and after he had entered Lyon he was anointed as king of Burgundy by Aurelian, metropolitan of that same city, and some other bishops.[253] He disregarded the adolescent sons of Louis [the Stammerer], disdaining them as if they were of inferior birth because on Charles's order their mother had been spurned and repudiated.[254] However, this affair brought him an unremitting series of disasters and the injury of danger rather than the reward of glory and status. By the industry and diligence of Hugh the Abbot and others among the leading men, the said youths Louis and Carloman were raised to the kingdom and they persecuted that same Boso without letting up for the rest of their lives.[255] In the time that followed not only they, but also the other kings of the Franks found his name so unbearable and hated him so much that with oaths and curses they charged not only the leading men and *duces*, but even their lesser followers, with his irrevocable removal and death.[256] However, he was a man of such perspicacious character that although he was, as has been said, doggedly pursued by many kings and kingdoms, none of them could ever capture or outflank him. He was a man of such moderation that, although his supporters were condemned as outlaws and deprived of all their goods, he was never ambushed by his own soldiers or deceitfully betrayed by treachery, even though the enemy often put both to the test.[257]

253 Boso was count of Vienne and one of the most powerful men in the west Frankish kingdom: see above, 877. His decision to have himself crowned king at Mantaille on 15 October 879 (MGH Capit. 2, no. 284), and his subsequent consecration by Aurelian, was probably a first step toward filling the west Frankish power-vacuum created by the death of Louis the Stammerer and the minority of his sons. He presented himself as a pseudo-Carolingian by stressing that his brother-in-law and father-in-law were both emperors. *AB* 879: 219 suggests he was egged on by his wife, a typical stereotype. For discussion see Bautier 1973; Airlie 2000; Bougard 2000; MacLean 2001.

254 See above, 878.

255 Gauzlin of St-Denis and Conrad of Paris led a party supporting the succession of both Louis III and Carloman II; another party, led by Hugh the Abbot (on whom see above, 867, n. 139), pushed for the sole succession of Louis, the elder: Werner 1979; Werner 1984: 418. Both were made kings at Ferrières in September 879: *AB* 879: 218; *AV* 879: 44–5. Despite Regino's ordering, Boso's coronation postdated this event.

256 Boso was besieged in Vienne and his support quickly collapsed under coordinated pressure from the four surviving Carolingian kings: see the works listed above, n. 253.

257 This last sentence is almost identical to Justin's description of Hannibal, whom he identifies as one of 'the three greatest generals in the world': *Epitome*, 32.4.12: 197–8 (Yardley 1994: 222). Boso remained at large until his death in 887: *AF* (B) 887: 113. Boso's son, Louis 'the Blind', became king of Provence in 890, and was crowned

BOOK II   181

At that same time Louis [the Younger], who ruled the Austrasians, learned of the death of his namesake and planned to invade his kingdom. Crossing the Meuse, he occupied the boundaries of the realm. The two above-mentioned brothers [Louis III and Carloman II] rushed to meet him with a strong force. However, by the toing and froing of emissaries, battle was avoided and peace was strengthened. So that Louis would leave them as their ally, the young men conceded to him the part of Lothar's kingdom which their grandfather and father had held, along with the monastery of St-Vaast in Arras.[258] After this agreement had been completed and oaths had been given, Louis was heading back to his own kingdom when, at Thiméon near the Charbonnière forest, he unexpectedly encountered a countless multitude of Northmen returning to their fleet with prodigious booty. Without delay he clashed with them and by God's favour struck most of them down with the sword. The remainder, who had scattered in flight, regrouped at the aforementioned royal estate. Here Hugh, the king's son by a concubine, because he fought carelessly, was seriously wounded and dragged away by the enemy; he gave up his soul in the hands of his adversaries. Believing that his son was being kept alive by the enemy, Louis ordered his army to hold off from the thick of the fighting so he could get Hugh back safely by some kind of deal. In the meantime, the onset of night forced the king and his men back to their camp. The Northmen fled during the night, setting alight the bodies of their dead and beating a path to their fleet. When the king rose at first light and found his son dead, he was afflicted by great sadness; he had the body placed in a coffin and ordered it to be carried to the monastery of Lorsch and there buried.[259]

---

emperor in 901. He was blinded in 905. Regino's positive view of Boso is unusual: Staab 1998. Perhaps it reflects a contemporary debate about Louis the Blind's status prompted by his recent adventures in Italy.

258 Louis came to west Francia on the invitation of Gauzlin and his allies, who feared political exclusion in the prospective dynastic settlement: *AB* 879: 216–18. The concession of eastern Lotharingia was sealed by the Treaty of Ribemont in February 880, and the west Frankish kingdom was divided between the two sons of Louis the Stammerer in March 880 at Amiens. Louis took Francia and Neustria, while Carloman received Burgundy and Aquitaine, a north-south split: *AB* 880: 220; *AF* 880: 88; *AV* 880: 46–7. St-Vaast had earlier been given to Charles the Bald by Lothar II: see above, 866, n. 99. The Treaty of Ribemont ushered in a period of cooperation between the surviving Carolingian rulers: MacLean 2001.

259 The Battle of Thiméon took place as Louis was returning from Ribemont in early 880. See also *AF* 880: 88 (which says that Louis killed over 5,000 of the Vikings, who were based on the River Scheldt); *AB* 880: 220; and *AV* 880: 46–7 (which says that Hugh the Abbot fought there). Louis the Younger seems to have regarded Lorsch as something of a dynastic mausoleum.

880

In the year of the Lord's incarnation 880, King Karlmann ended his last day on 22 March after a decline into paralysis.[260] He was buried with due honour in Bavaria, in the place called Altötting.[261] That most excellent king was learned in letters, dedicated to the Christian religion, just, peace-loving, and in all of his habits adorned with probity. The beauty of his body was extraordinary, and his strength too was remarkable; no less so was the greatness of his spirit.[262] In fact he fought very many battles together with his father, and still more without him, in the lands of the Slavs and always brought back the triumph of victory.[263] He added to and extended thus the borders of his kingdom with the sword.[264] He appeared mild to his own people, terrible to his enemies. He was affable in speech, decorated with humility, and unusually gifted in ordering the affairs of the realm. In short, nothing which was appropriate to royal majesty seemed to lack in him.[265]

No offspring were born to him from legitimate marriage due to his wife's barrenness, but by a certain noble woman he had a son of most elegant appearance.[266] Karlmann ordered him to be called Arnulf [of Carinthia] in remembrance of the most revered Bishop Arnulf of Metz, from whose sainted line his own family and those of the other Frankish kings had sprouted forth.[267] This appears not to have been a coincidence, but rather a clear premonition and portent of what would come

---

260 Regino got this date (which is corrupted in the manuscripts, but is presumed to have been 22 March) from the *AP*. However, the most trustworthy sources suggest that he died on 22 September: *AF* 880: 89, n. 8; Fuchs 2002: 420. Karlmann appears to have suffered a stroke: see *AF* 879: 85–6.

261 Altötting, a monastery in eastern Bavaria, had been rebuilt by Karlmann and dedicated to the Virgin Mary in imitation of Aachen, Frankfurt and Regensburg for use as his main seat: D K 2.

262 Goldberg 1999: 50–1 discusses the admiration of male physical strength and beauty in Carolingian annals.

263 For Karlmann's battles against the Slavs see *AF* 858, 868, 869, 870, 871, 872: 41, 58–62, 65–8; Bowlus 1995: 128–33, 175–85, 197–208; Goldberg 2006a: 279–85.

264 Here Regino seems to contradict his earlier statement (above, 841) that the extensive casualties at the Battle of Fontenoy ended Frankish expansion and even effective defence.

265 The vocabulary used to praise Karlmann draws on a passages of Justin's concerning King Hiero: *Epitome*, 23.4.14: 159 (Yardley 1994: 183).

266 Karlmann's concubine was called Liutswind: on her see Notker, *Continuatio*: 329, and DD AC 87, 136.

267 Early-medieval family consciousness was often focused on the person of a semi-legendary ancestor: Airlie 1995: 438–9. On the historical Arnulf of Metz, see Fouracre 2000: 33–4, 43–4 and above, 517–537, 546–571.

about in the future, seeing that with him [Arnulf of Metz] the royal house began, thanks to divine providence, to proliferate in a favourable ascent over the course of time, until under the great Charles [Charlemagne] it reached the highest peak of authority not only over the Franks, but indeed over various other peoples and kingdoms as well. After Charles's death fortunes changed, such that the worldly glory which had previously flowed beyond everything they had prayed for, began to gradually drain away in the same way it had risen, until not only the kingdoms came to an end, but so did the royal family itself. It withered away partly because of the delicate youth of those kings who died,[268] and partly due to the sterility of their wives, so that from such a numerous royal line he [Arnulf of Carinthia] alone was found suitable to take up the sceptre of the realm of the Franks.[269] This will be shown more clearly below, in its own place.[270]

When Louis [the Younger] heard that his brother had died, he went to Bavaria and came to Regensburg, where all the leading men of the kingdom flocked to him and put themselves under his command.[271] The king conceded Carinthia[272] to Arnulf because his father had already conceded it to him; there lies the very well defended stronghold of Moosburg, so called because of the impenetrable bog which surrounds it and offers very difficult entry to those who approach it.[273]

881

In the year of the Lord's incarnation 881, Charles [the Fat] came from Alemannia and took possession of Lombardy; and within a few days he

---

268 A reference to the unprecedented death rate among Carolingian males in the last years of the empire: eight ruling kings died in the period 875–885.
269 Cf. above, 866, where Regino quotes a letter of Pope Nicholas I in which sterility is equated with sinfulness. Airlie 2006a illuminates the significance of hindsight in the *Chronicle*, as well as this story's value for understanding Regino's perception of the sins of the Franks. Arnulf was already seen as the coming man by authors in the early 880s such as Notker, *Continuatio*.
270 See below, 888.
271 Louis had already intervened in Bavaria during the final illness of Karlmann, who initially tried to arrange for Arnulf to succeed him but eventually abdicated in his brother's favour: *AF* 879: 85–7; MacLean 2003a: 134–5.
272 *Carantanum*: Bertels 1987: 165–8 discusses Regino's use of this unusual form, suggesting that it implicitly included Pannonia as well. Cf. above, 876, n. 235.
273 Arnulf appears to have maintained a high position under Louis the Younger: *AF* 879: 87, n. 9; MacLean 2003a: 135–6. On the Moosburg see Bowlus 1995: 201; Dopsch 2002: 144–59.

received the whole of Italy into submission.²⁷⁴ Coming to Rome, he was favourably received by John, the bishop of the apostolic see, and by the Roman senate, and he was made emperor with great glory.²⁷⁵ At the same time a fleet of Northmen entered the River Waal and landed next to the royal palace of Nijmegen, where they built their camp.²⁷⁶ When this event was brought to Louis [the Younger]'s attention he came without delay with an army and besieged them in their fortification. Although they struggled for several days Louis could still not fully prevail, because the palace's great size and wonderful fortifications provided the enemy with a very secure refuge.²⁷⁷ In this engagement Eberhard Saxo, son of Count Meginhard, was caught by the enemy and taken hostage; his mother Evesa later got him back unharmed by paying a large ransom.²⁷⁸ The king finally retreated with all his troops after accepting the Northmen's promise that, if he raised the siege, they would immediately leave his kingdom. After Louis withdrew, the pagans set the palace on fire along with their fortification, boarded their ships and returned to the mouth of the Rhine.

In the same year in the month of November two kings of the Northmen, Godafrid and Sigfrid, camped at Asselt by the Meuse with an innumerable multitude of men on foot and horseback.²⁷⁹ On their first raid they

274 Cf. Regino's much more negative evaluation of the extent of Charles the Bald's control in Italy: above, 877. Regino's positive view of Charles the Fat's influence there may be more than hyperbole, to judge by the charter evidence: MacLean 2007.

275 The imperial coronation was probably in *AP*. However, Regino here conflates the events of 879–881: Karlmann abdicated in 879 and Charles's first Italian charter was issued on 15 November of that year: D CIII 12. He was crowned king at Ravenna in early January 880, and made emperor in Rome on 12 February 881. Neither of these events is recorded in the *AF*, which at this point is pro-Louis the Younger and consequently passes silently over Charles the Fat's achievements. For details see *AB* 880: 222 (wrongly dating the imperial consecration to Christmas 880); Notker, *Continuatio*: 329–30; Brühl 1962: 325; MacLean 2003: 146–7. The reference to the Roman senate is an anachronistic but common rhetorical flourish in Carolingian historiography.

276 The siege of Nijmegen is also described by *AF* 880: 89–90, which confirms that Louis was rebuffed by the fortifications. Cf. *AV* 881: 49–51. On the Viking campaigns of this period see Vogel 1906: 275–80.

277 The Vikings were extremely adaptable fighters, and particularly accomplished at siege warfare: Leyser 1994f.

278 On the family of Evesa and Eberhard, who was count of Hamaland in Frisia, see further below, s.a. 885 and 898; Hlawitschka 1968: 160; van Winter 1980; Althoff 1992: 166–85; and above, Introduction, pp. 36–7.

279 This encounter is also described by *AB* 882: 224–5; *AF*(M) 882: 92–3; *AF*(B) 882: 104–5; *AV* 882: 51–2. The older identification of the site as Elsloo is mistaken: *AF*(M) 882: 92, n. 7.

laid waste to the surrounding places and burned the city of Liège, the fort of Maastricht and the town of Tongres. On their second incursion they streamed into the lands of the Ripuarians and devastated everything with murder, pillage and fire, ruining with fire the cities of Cologne and Bonn together with the nearby strongholds of Zülpich, Jülich and Neuss. After these things they reduced the palace of Aachen, and the monasteries of Inden [Cornelimünster], Malmedy and Stavelot to ashes.[280]

882

In the year of the Lord's incarnation 882, the Northmen advanced through the Ardennes and entered the monastery of Prüm on the very day of the Lord's epiphany [6 January].[281] They stayed there for three days and pillaged the whole of the surrounding region. In that place a countless multitude from the fields and farms gathered together on foot as one crowd and approached the Northmen as if they were going to fight them. But when the Northmen saw that this crowd of common people was not so much unarmed as bereft of military training, they rushed upon them with a shout and cut them down in such a bloodbath that they seemed to be butchering dumb animals rather than men.[282] With these things achieved, they returned to their camp loaded with plunder. After they had dispersed, the fire which still burned in various buildings consumed the monastery, since there was nobody to put it out.

While these things were going on, King Louis [the Younger] died of an illness at Frankfurt on 20 January and was buried next to his father

280 *AF* 881: 90 also describes these raids, including the detail that the Vikings stabled their horses in the royal chapel at Aachen. The monks of Stavelot-Malmedy rescued the royal relic collection and brought it to Charles the Fat: D CIII 64. A similar trail of destruction is noted by *AV* 881, 882: 50–1.

281 This must have been recorded in *AP*, though Regino may very well have been present himself as well. Epiphany, a Christological feast, was a significant day in the religious identity of Prüm, which was dedicated to the Saviour: Haubrichs 1979: 77–8. This shows the forward planning and local knowledge employed by the Vikings to achieve maximum impact. Airlie 2006a: 121 argues that Regino is here highlighting the inversion of religious norms which revealed 'a society under judgement'. The destruction of Prüm by the Vikings is also alluded to by Notker, *Gesta Karoli*: 74.

282 'Common people' = *ignobile vulgus*. This is rare evidence for the self-mobilisation of the non-noble classes. Carolingian capitularies condemned such horizontal associations, and after a similar band of commoners organised themselves to resist the Vikings on the Seine in 859, they were slaughtered by members of the aristocracy: *AB* 859: 89. Serious military training was generally the preserve of the male secular aristocracy: Halsall 2003: 111–19.

in the monastery of Lorsch.²⁸³ He had taken to himself in marriage Queen Liutgard, by whom he had only one son, to whom he gave his own name, Louis. But when, as we have related, after the death of his brother he entered Bavaria to take up his brother's kingdom and was staying in Regensburg, that same little boy fell out of the window of the palace and died instantly from a broken neck. This led not only the king and queen but also the whole royal house[hold] into great mourning, not just because the death was premature, but also because of its unworthiness.

When the Northmen heard about the king's death they gave themselves over to great rejoicing and thought no longer of combat, but only of booty. Therefore they burst forth from their camp with all their forces and, on 5 April, Maundy Thursday, they seized Trier, the most noble city of the Gauls.²⁸⁴ Here, weary from the journey, they rested their bodies until the holy day of Easter, and razed the whole area around the town right down to the ground. Then they set the town ablaze and led their host to Metz. When the bishop of the same town learned about this he got together with [arch]Bishop Bertulf and Count Adalhard and, taking the initiative, advanced to engage the enemy.²⁸⁵ Battle was joined and the Northmen were the victors. The same bishop Wala [of Metz] died in the battle, and the rest fled.²⁸⁶ The pagans abandoned the journey which they had begun and with immense booty returned to their fleet with the greatest speed.

At that time Emperor Charles [the Fat] was staying in Italy, where he was urged by various embassies from Germany and Gaul to come quickly to take up the kingdoms which were his by hereditary right, and to help the endangered empire which, having lost its leader, was being mocked by the enemy. Without any delay he came to Francia with all his forces and began to besiege the Northmen in the said place [Asselt]

283 Regino found the date in *AP*. The manuscripts have 20 August, presumably a slip of a copyist's pen. Louis put some energy into cultivating Lorsch as a dynastic mausoleum for the east Frankish Carolingians, and probably intended that he would be buried there. See Fried 1984: 13–14; Innes 1998: 319–21. *AF* 882: 91 says that Louis's death caused the army to call off their attack on the Vikings.

284 The date was probably in *AP*. Regino wrote his *Chronicle* in Trier.

285 Bertulf was archbishop of Trier (870–83) (on him see above, 869); Adalhard was count of Metz and the Moselgau, and lay abbot of Echternach: *AF* 880: 89; Hlawitschka 1969: 162.

286 The battle was fought on the Moselle, near Remich, on 10 April: see *AF* 882: 91; *AB* 882: 224; *AV* 882: 51. *AF* says that Wala acted 'rashly'; Regino's reference to the bishop's taking the initiative may imply a similar sentiment. Hincmar, author of the *AB*, criticized Wala for bearing arms. Wala was bishop from 876 to 882.

with the Lombards, Bavarians, Alemans, Thuringians, Saxons, Frisians and all of the kingdoms under his command.[287] But his efforts achieved too little, even though, as we have said, an innumerable multitude had come together from various kingdoms and peoples. This was because the anger of heaven raged against the people who were profaning the Christian religion.[288] Finally Godafrid, the Northmen's king, promised he would become a Christian on condition that he was given the province of Frisia by royal grant, and if he was given Lothar [II]'s daughter Gisela as his wife.[289] When Godafrid had got what he wanted, he was baptised and was raised from the holy font by the emperor. Sigfrid and the rest of the Northmen were given access to an immense amount of gold and silver and, under this arrangement, they left the frontiers of the kingdom.[290]

883

In the year of the Lord's incarnation 883 King Louis [III] the brother of Carloman [II] died at St-Denis and was buried there with honour.[291] All the people of the Gauls lamented him with great wailing. For he was a man of courage and he defended the kingdom placed under him from the infestation of the pagans powerfully and manfully. Among the other things which he vigorously accomplished, particularly noteworthy was

287 In fact, Charles took several months to arrive in Francia: Louis the Younger died in January, but Charles was still in Italy on 17 April and did not receive the leading men at Worms until the second half of May (DD CIII 56–8). The list of Charles's forces highlights the regional organization of Carolingian armies: see especially Reuter 1985. It also demonstrates the extent of the emperor's support at this point in his reign, and shows that the empire could still function as a unit, with aristocrats from one region willing to go to war in another.

288 Perhaps another reference to the curse of Pope Nicholas I against Lothar II and his kingdom for perceived transgressions during that ruler's divorce case: see above, 866 and 869, and below, 883.

289 On Gisela see further below, 885. She was a daughter of Lothar and Waldrada, and married Godafrid in 883. *AF*(M) 883: 94 suggests that the marriage was arranged by Hugh rather than by Charles.

290 The siege of Asselt is described in more detail by *AB* 882: 224–5 (which also says that Charles gave Hugh lands belonging to the church of Metz); *AF*(M) 882: 92–3; *AF*(B) 882: 104–6; *AV* 882: 51–2. The sources disagree on some of the details, including the names of the Viking leaders. Despite the disapproval of Regino and others, grants of land to seal such treaties were a standard and relatively successful feature of Franko-Viking negotiations in the second half of the ninth century: see Coupland 1998; Coupland 1999. On baptism and godfathership see Angenendt 1984 and Lynch 1986.

291 Louis's death was recorded by *AP*, though in fact the date was 5 August 882. *AV* 882: 52 says that he died in a riding accident while chasing a girl into a house.

that outstanding battle which he fought with the greatest strength against the Northmen in the place called Saucourt. In this engagement, so they say, he cut down more than 8,000 of the enemy with the sword.[292] His brother Carloman received his kingdom.

At that same time [arch]bishop Bertulf of Trier went to the Lord on 10 February, and was succeeded on the episcopal throne by the most revered [arch]bishop Ratbod on 8 April through the election of the clergy and all the people.[293] In these days Robert was consecrated bishop for the church of Metz by the same archbishop Ratbod, on 22 April.[294]

Around this time, Hugh the son of Lothar [II] was led into the hope of regaining his father's kingdom by some devotees of discord and quarrelling. Everyone who hated peace and justice flooded to him so that in a few days a countless multitude of bandits had placed themselves under his command. Seduced by vain hope, several of the kingdom's leading men joined them by offering their hands, namely Counts Stephen,[295] Robert,[296] Wigbert,[297]

292 The Battle of Saucourt, 3 August 881, was fought by Louis after he encountered a group of Vikings by chance, and is recorded as a great victory by several sources: *AV* 881: 50; *AF* 881: 90 (which says that he killed 9, 000 horsemen); and the Old High German poem *Ludwigslied* (Dutton 2004: 512–14). *AB* 881: 222 depicts it as a defeat for Louis, apparently because Hincmar was angry at having been excluded from the king's inner circle. For discussion see Fouracre 1985.

293 *AP*. On Bertulf see also above, 869, 882. Ratbod (883–915) was Regino's patron in Trier; on him see Schieffer 1958.

294 Bishop Robert of Metz (883–916).

295 Stephen, brother of Walaho, is named as count in the Bidgau, around Trier, in a charter of 895 (D Z 5); he was also count in the Chaumontois and held significant quantities of property in the middle Rhine and Moselle areas. See also below, 896, 897, 900, 901, where he is identified as an ally of Regino's enemies, counts Gerard and Matfrid (the 'Matfridings'). On Stephen see Hlawitschka 1968: 165–6; Innes 2000: 228–9, 232. Family ties between Stephen and the Matfridings are plausible, though not certain: Hlawitschka 1969: 169, n. 69. Stephen and Wigbert appeared together in a charter of 882 from Verdun: Parisot 1898: 443–4; Hope 2005: 107.

296 This man is hard to identify: Robert/Rupert was a common name among the aristocracy of the middle Rhine. A Robert/Rupert was a relative of Megingoz, the powerful Lotharingian aristocrat murdered in 892, and another succeeded count Adalbert of Metz as lay abbot of Echternach around 889 – these two may even have been the same man. See Hlawitschka 1969: 162; Innes 2000: 226; and above, 882, n. 285.

297 Wigbert was seemingly Hugh's 'nutritor' ('nourisher'; 'foster-father'), which accords with Regino's description of him in the next paragraph: see further Airlie 1985: 153, 171–2, 179–82. He seemingly acted as the emperor's go-between with Godafrid at Asselt in 882, which led one observer to describe him as 'most treacherous': *AF*(M) 882: 92. His role in brokering that deal suggests that Hugh was already on terms with Godafrid at that time. He was associated with Stephen in a charter of 882: see above, n. 295.

BOOK II   189

Theutbald,²⁹⁸ and Alberic²⁹⁹ and his brother Stephen.³⁰⁰ Such plunder and violence was committed in the kingdom by these people that there was no difference between their wickedness and that of the Northmen, except that they refrained from murder and burnings. Thus almighty God was enraged at the kingdom of Lothar and began to act against and to utterly destroy the strength of that same kingdom by increasing disasters of such a kind that the prophecy of the most holy Pope Nicholas, and also the curse which he had pronounced over this kingdom, was fulfilled.³⁰¹

About this time Lothar's son Hugh killed Count Wigbert, who had been close to him since his youth.³⁰² A few days after that, he deceitfully ordered the murder of Bernarius, a noble man who was most faithful to him, because he was captivated by the beauty of his wife, whom he married without delay. The woman was called Friderada. Before she was joined to Bernarius, she had been married to Engelram, a powerful man; she bore him a daughter who was later taken in marriage by Count Richwin, and whom the same count ordered to be beheaded for committing a disgrace.³⁰³

298 Theutbald was the son of Hubert, Theutberga's brother (on whom see above, 859, 864, 866), and was married to Hugh's sister Bertha, thus uniting the families of Lothar II's two women in the generation after his death. It has been suggested that his alliance with Hugh represented the triumph of Lotharingian regnal togetherness over family squabbles (Parisot 1898: 444–6), but it is just as likely that more immediate political concerns were paramount – kinship was only one factor in deciding political allegiance. *AF* 880: 89 describes him as 'the leader of Hugh's army' and records a battle he fought against Henry, who was acting on behalf of Louis the Younger. *AB* 880: 89 and *AV* 880: 47 mention the same engagement; the latter seems to imply he was offering support to Boso's rebellion. Theutbald was subsequently count in Arles.

299 Alberic later killed count Megingoz and was himself killed by Stephen, brother of Walaho, his erstwhile comrade (below, 892 and 896). He belonged to one of the middle Rhine's most prominent families: Le Jan 1995b: 77; Innes 2000: 227.

300 This Stephen is identified in the older literature as count in the Chaumontois. However, Regino does not give him a comital title, and the Stephens referred to in the sources as counts in the Chaumontois and the Bidgau (see above, n. 295) are convincingly demonstrated to be one and the same man by Hlawitschka 1968: 166, n. 27.

301 See above, 856, 866, 869. The 'strength of the realm' (*vires regni*) is a phrase used frequently by Regino to describe the aristocracy: see Hope 2005: 103–7.

302 Wigbert had apparently been responsible for Hugh's upbringing: see above, n. 297.

303 Engelram was count in Flanders and Charles the Bald's chamberlain, though he seems to have fallen from that king's favour sometime in the 870s: Nelson 1992: 213–14, 224, 240. Richwin was count of Verdun in the early tenth century: Hlawitschka 1968: 196; Hlawitschka 1969: 54, 126. He was associated with the Conradines in a memorial book entry from the first decade of the tenth century: Althoff 1992: 258–9. See also above, Introduction, pp. 37–8.

884

In the year of the Lord's incarnation 884, the Northmen, who had retreated from Asselt, entered the River Somme and set up camp there. Because Carloman [II] could not contain their very frequent incursions, he promised them money if they would withdraw from his kingdom. Soon the hearts of this greedy people were inflamed with desire for money and they demanded 12,000 pounds of pure and inspected silver, promising an equal number of years of peace. Having accepted such a large amount of money they untied their ropes from the bank, boarded their ships and returned to the sea coast.[304]

Meanwhile Carloman went on the hunt, where he was seriously injured by a boar; after a short time he lost his life and his kingdom. He was buried at St-Denis. Some say, however, that he was wounded by one of his men using his weapon carelessly and, because he committed this crime accidentally and not deliberately, it was kept secret by the king so that an innocent man would not be put to death.[305]

When the Northmen learned of the king's death, they immediately returned to the kingdom.[306] So, Hugh the Abbot and the other leading men sent legates to them, protesting that the faith and promise they had given had been violated.[307] To this they responded that they had made the treaty with King Carloman, not with anyone else. Whoever succeeded him would have to give the same amount and weight of treasure if they wanted to hold the kingdom in peace and quiet.[308] Scared by demands of this sort, the leading men of the kingdom sent legates to Emperor Charles and voluntarily invited him to take over the kingdom. They came before him at the royal residence of Gondreville

304 *AV* 884: 55 and *AF*(M) 884: 96–7 tell similar stories. All three agree on the amount of tribute, though *AF*(M) wrongly places the tribute after Carloman's death (when it was collected), and *AV* mentions that the Franks used a Christian Dane as their go-between with the Vikings, and that the period of respite lasted from February until October.

305 Carloman died on 12 December, aged 18. *AV* 884: 56 and *AF*(M) 884: 96 offer similar accounts of Carloman's death; the former names the hapless killer as Bertold. Regino seems less sure than other authors that the boar was not responsible.

306 *AF*(M) 885: 97 says they invaded the Hesbaye and were defeated by Liutbert and Henry; *AV* 885: 56–7 says that Carloman's men went out to find and fight the Vikings at Leuven, though without much success.

307 Hugh the Abbot (see above, 866, 867) took a prominent role among the magnates who took charge after Carloman's death: see also *AV* 885: 56.

308 This story suggests a common understanding and observation of political norms between Franks and Vikings, although the latter were obviously trying to manipulate them. Cf. Halsall 1992.

and, giving him their hands and oaths according to custom, placed themselves under his command.³⁰⁹

In that same year the Northmen who had come to Kennemerland from Denmark travelled up the Rhine by boat with the approval of Godafrid and besieged the stronghold of Duisburg.³¹⁰ There, as they are accustomed to do, they constructed a fortification and stayed in it all winter. The *dux* Henry pitched a camp against them and completely stopped them from plundering. At the return of spring they burned their camp and went back to the coastal regions.³¹¹

In those days the Northmen also left the Somme and returned once more to Lothar's kingdom. They pitched camp at the place called Leuven on the edge of the same realm, and wearied both kingdoms with the unremitting infestations of their raids. To contain their malice the emperor sent out his army time and again, but nothing worthy of commemoration was achieved against the great rapacity of these thugs.³¹²

885

In the year of the Lord's incarnation 885, Hugh planned to rebel against the emperor and secretly sent messages to Godafrid in Frisia because he was related to him by marriage through his sister, whom Godafrid had married, urging him to send to his homeland and gather from all sides a strong force of auxiliaries and to bring them to his aid with all their power, so that he would be able to claim by arms his paternal kingdom.³¹³ And if he achieved a happy outcome in this through Godafrid's effort and manful support, he promised half of his kingdom as a

---

309 Charles was the only adult male legitimate Carolingian available, though it is significant that the west Franks invited him in rather than electing one of their own number as king. He was probably inaugurated in early 885 at the Roman amphitheatre of Grand, not far from Gondreville, by a northern Frankish aristocratic group centred on Hugh the Abbot and Gauzlin of St-Denis: *AV* 884: 56; MacLean 2003a: 124–9.

310 Kennemerland, the part of the modern Dutch coast around Harlem, was part of the area given to Godafrid in 882: *AF*(M) 882: 93; Coupland 1998.

311 The encounter with Henry (and Liutbert of Mainz) is also mentioned by *AF*(M) 885: 97, which says that these Vikings were from Leuven.

312 Charles sent forces against the Leuven Vikings as soon as he arrived in 885: *AV* 885: 56. On Viking movements in this period see Vogel 1906.

313 Regino's perception that the Vikings were in touch with their homelands is interesting. Maund 1994 discusses some of the connections. Hugh's alliance with Godafrid went back at least to 882: see above, 882, 883.

reward. Godafrid was corrupted by these persuasive promises as if by a poison, and sought a pretext by which he could remove himself from the fidelity he owed to the emperor while making it seem as if he was justified. Immediately he sent the Frisian counts Gerulf and Gardulf as legates[314] to the emperor to tell him that if he wanted him to stay faithful as he had promised, and to defend the borders of the kingdom that had been committed to him from the attacks of his own people, he would have to give him Koblenz, Andernach, Sinzig and various other estates dedicated to imperial use, because of the abundance of vines that flourished there; for the land which he had obtained through the emperor's generosity was too infertile for growing vines.[315] He asked for this harbouring the intention, if he got what he asked for, of infiltrating his men into the heart of the kingdom and watching to see how things turned out. If, on the other hand, he were denied, then, offended by the refusal, he would have better grounds to complain as if he had justification, and he could use this as the basis of a rebellion.

When the emperor became aware of the cunning machinations and conspiracies of this faction, he had detailed discussions with Henry, a very clever man, as to what stratagem he could use to destroy the enemy which he had allowed into the furthest reaches of the kingdom. Knowing that those places were inaccessible for an army due to the countless watercourses and impenetrable marshes, he decided that it would be better to attempt a trick than to use force. Therefore he dismissed the legates with a vague answer and allowed them to return to Godafrid, assuring them that he would give him a mutually satisfactory response through his own ambassadors concerning all the matters his men had raised, as long as he continued in his fidelity. Then he sent Henry to Godafrid; and, so that the trap he was setting would be concealed, he sent with him Willibert, the venerable bishop of Cologne. Henry secretly ordered his men to travel through Saxony, not in a troop but spread out, and to hurry to meet him at the place and time he had agreed with them. He himself came with a very few men to Cologne, collected the said bishop, and set off immediately to Betuwe.

When he heard they had arrived, Godafrid proceeded to the place called Herispich, where the Rhine and the Waal separate from their common

---

314 Gerulf was a count in Frisia and later an ally of Arnulf of Carinthia: Hlawitschka 1968: 109. *AV* 885: 57 describes him as Godafrid's faithful man and 'crafty helper'.

315 Regino also refers to this region's viticulture above, 842. Desire for wine was given by Paul the Deacon *Historia*, II.23: 101–2 (Foulke 2003: 77–8) as the motive for Brennus' ancient invasion of Italy, a story which Regino knew and referred to obliquely below, 896.

BOOK II   193

course and diverge far from each other to surround the province of Betuwe with their waters.³¹⁶ When they had stepped onto this island, the bishop and the count heard many things from Godafrid and responded with many things on behalf of the emperor. As the day drew to a close the meeting was closed and they left the island, returning to their lodgings planning to resume in the morning. Henry urged the bishop that on the next day he should summon Gisela, Godafrid's wife, off the island, and busy himself with winning her support for peace. In the meantime, he himself would raise with Godafrid the case of Count Eberhard, whose possessions had been violently seized from him.³¹⁷ Then he convinced the same Eberhard to stand up in the middle shouting about the injustice he was suffering and, when harsh and abusive talk was hurled at him by this man of such a primitive and barbarous people, immediately to draw his sword and with great force to strike him on the head before he had a chance to get up off the ground. What more need be said? After being first struck by Eberhard and then stabbed by Henry's companions, Godafrid died; and all the Northmen who were found in Betuwe were massacred.³¹⁸

Only a few days later on the advice of that same Henry, Hugh was enticed to the royal residence of Gondreville with promises and taken prisoner by a trick.³¹⁹ On the orders of the emperor his eyes were put out by that same Henry, and all his followers were deprived of their offices.³²⁰ After these things Hugh was sent into the monastery of St-Gall in Alemannia, whence he was later recalled to his homeland. Finally, in the time of King Zwentibald he was was tonsured by my own

316 Herispich was probably near Rindern, below Kleve (Cleves) on the Rhine. Frankish peace negotiations were often conducted on islands, which symbolized neutral ground, so this meeting suggests the Vikings had become familiar with these norms.

317 On Eberhard, a count in Frisia who had evidently lost out under Godafrid's lordship, see also 881, 898, and above, Introduction, pp. 36–7.

318 Other sources recount this incident in less detail. *AV* 885: 57 notes that Henry killed Godafrid because he was planning to break his allegiance with the help of Gerulf; *AF*(M) 885: 97 says that he was preparing to advance up the Rhine with an army, and that he was killed at a meeting with Henry and other men whom he had angered with abusive talk; *AF*(B) 885: 111 just says that he was killed after being accused of plotting against 'the kingdom of the Franks'.

319 *AV* 885: 57 also states that Henry was involved; *AF*(M) 885: 98 says he was accused of having collaborated with Godafrid; and *AF*(B) 885: 111 refers to Hugh having 'acted unwisely'.

320 'Deprived of their offices' = *dehonestantur*, literally 'dishonoured'. However, by the later Carolingian period this term carried the more precise meaning of deprivation of *honores* (public offices): Zotz 1993b; Airlie 1995: 443–8. *AF*(M) 885: 98 says that his men were 'stripped of their horses, arms and clothing, and scarcely escaped naked'.

hand in the monastery of Prüm (for at the time I was in charge of the Lord's flock there, despite my unsuitability), where after a few years he died and was buried.³²¹

886

In the year of the Lord's incarnation 886, the Northmen left the River Somme and once more returned to Lothar's kingdom, and set up a camp and base on the edge of both realms at the place called Leuven, and they wearied both kingdoms by the unremitting infestations of their raids. To contain their native malice the emperor repeatedly sent his army, but nothing worthy of mention was achieved against the great rapacity of their violence.³²²

In that same year Ansbald, abbot of the community of Prüm, who was a man of very great piety and sanctity, crossed to the heavenly homeland on 12 July. He was succeeded in charge by the venerable father Farabert on 6 August.³²³

887

In the year of the Lord's incarnation 887, the Northmen left Leuven and entered the Seine. After landing by Paris, they set up camp and besieged the city. In the spring the emperor sent the *dux* Henry against them with an army, but he achieved very little. For there were, so it is said, more than 30,000 of the enemy, almost all of them sturdy warriors.³²⁴

In summer, before the corn was bundled up and brought in, that same Henry came once more to Paris with armies from both kingdoms.³²⁵ While his horde was surrounding the fortification, he himself with a few

---

321 Zwentibald reigned 895–900. Taken together, the sources suggest that Hugh was tried at Frankfurt rather than Gondreville, and that he was first incarcerated in St-Boniface at Fulda: MacLean 2003a: 144–60.

322 This paragraph is almost identical to the last paragraph of the 884 entry. Although it is possible that Regino deliberately repeated it in order to return the thread of his narrative to the Vikings, it seems much more likely that this was an error introduced early in the process of the text's transmission.

323 Regino got this information from the *AP*.

324 The siege began in November 885, and Henry arrived in early 886: *AV* 886: 59 says that he was asked to come by Bishop Gauzlin of Paris. Further details are given by *AF*(M) 886: 100 and Abbo, *Bella Parisiacae Urbis*: 66–9. Although the number of 30,000 is implausible, it is interesting that Regino implies there were non-combatants there as well as warriors: cf. above, 873.

325 Abbo, *Bella Parisiacae Urbis*: 90–1 also suggests that the army was multi-regnal.

companions went nearer and walked round it, surveying the lie of the land and looking for the safest place for his army to engage the enemy. However, when they had heard of the army's approach, the Northmen had dug pits one foot across and three feet deep around their camp and had covered them with reeds and refuse, leaving only enough space in between for paths going in and out. On seeing Henry approaching, a few of the brigands who were lurking in the hollows of the paths quickly sprang from their hiding places and challenged the man with their spears and harrassed him verbally. Henry, whose great spirit would not allow him to put up with such unworthy treatment, charged at them; and soon the horse he was riding fell into the concealed pits, toppling to the ground taking Henry with it. The enemy rushed toward him with great speed and, before he could get up, they impaled him on the earth. Without delay they put him to death in the sight of the whole army, and took away his arms and seized some trophies. His troops, however, launched an attack and barely managed to recover the lifeless body. His men carried it to Soissons, where Henry was buried in the church of St-Médard. Deprived of its leader, the army returned home.[326]

At that same time Hugh the Abbot, a man of great power and intelligence, died at Orléans and was buried at St-Germain in Auxerre. The command [*ducatus*] which he had held and governed strenuously was given by the emperor to Robert's son Odo, who at that time was count of Paris, and who along with Gauzlin, bishop of the same town, had defended the city with all his strength against the unremitting assault of the Northmen. In those days, during the oppressions of that very siege, the said bishop Gauzlin departed from the world, and the emperor appointed Bishop Askericus in his place.[327]

After this the emperor passed through the peoples of Gaul and came with an immense army to Paris, and there he set up camp against the enemy.[328] But he achieved nothing worthy of his imperial majesty in that

---

326 Henry was killed on 28 August. *AV* 886: 61–2 gives a very similar account of his death; see also *AF*(M) 886: 100–1; *AF*(B) 886: 112; Abbo, *Bella Parisiacae Urbis*: 82–3. Henry's epitaph survives in an eleventh-century hand (see Schleidgen 1977: 20) and is printed on p. 126 of Kurze's edition of the *Chronicle*. On his family and career see Becher 1996: 161–4, 167–70.

327 Hugh the Abbot died on 12 May 886, and Gauzlin of St-Denis on 16 April. They had been the most important magnates in west Francia since the late 870s: MacLean 2003a: 103–8. On their deaths see also *AF*(M) 886: 100 ('the leading generals of Gaul'); *AV* 886: 59–60; Abbo, *Bella Parisiacae Urbis*: 70–6.

328 Charles finally reached Paris in October, having sent Henry ahead in July: *AF*(M) 886: 100–1. His presence had been requested by count Odo of Paris after the deaths of Hugh and Gauzlin: *AV* 886: 59–60; Abbo, *Bella Parisiacae Urbis*: 78–9. Most

place. In the end he conceded the lands and regions beyond the Seine for the Northmen to plunder because the inhabitants of those regions did not want to obey him.[329] Charles withdrew and went directly back to Alemannia.

The first thing he did there was expel from his side in disgrace a certain Liutward, the bishop of Vercelli, a man who was very dear to him and his only adviser in the administration of affairs of state, accusing him of the crime of adultery because he was mixed up with the queen's secrets more intimately than was appropriate. After a few days he summoned his wife Richgard (for that was the empress's name) before an assembly concerning the same matter and, amazingly, he testified in public that he had never joined with her sexually, although she had been bound as his partner by a contract of legitimate marriage for more than ten years.[330] She for her part declared that she remained untouched not only by him, but by all male union, and that she prided herself on the integrity of her virginity.[331] She confidently asserted that if it pleased her husband she would prove herself by the judgement of almighty God, either through trial by combat or hot ploughshares, for she was a pious woman.[332] After the divorce was completed she retired to a monastery which she had constructed on her own land in order to serve God.[333]

---

contemporary commentators were unimpressed with Charles's efforts, as they usually were when kings paid off Vikings: Abbo, the only eyewitness, is an exception (MacLean 2003a: 55–64).

329 Probably a reference to Burgundy, as suggested by *AF*(M) 886: 101; *AV* 886: 62. The identity of the Burgundian malcontents is not clear – possibly the remaining supporters of Boso, possibly those of his brother Richard 'the Justiciar': see now Koziol 2006b: 365, n. 25.

330 In fact, the couple had married in 861/2: Borgolte 1977.

331 Non-consummation could be grounds for legitimate annulment: Bishop 1985; Regino, *De synodalibus causis*, II.243–5: 362–3. Chastity within marriage after the couple had passed child-bearing age was, however, idealised, and may have been practised by Charles's parents: Goldberg 2006b: 76–9. The implications of this passage for Charles's sexuality are discussed by Nelson 1999 and MacLean 2006.

332 The use of ordeals in matters of sexual politics is discussed by Bartlett 1986.

333 This was the monastery of Andlau in Alsace, on which see MacLean 2003b. The other sources tend to stress Charles's over-reliance on Liutward: *AF*(M) 887: 101–2; *AF*(B) 887: 113. However, this is something of a literary cliché: Bührer-Thierry 1987. For the argument that the divorce and the expulsion of Liutward were orchestrated by Charles, with references to further literature, see MacLean 2003a: 185–91. Regino's story echoes, consciously or not, Bede's account of Queen Aethelthryth (mentioned above, 605–611), who remained a virgin throughout 12 years of marriage and then retired to a monastery she had founded. The legal process described here (proclamation of virginity – ordeal – divorce) closely resembles the canon cited by Regino in *De synodalibus causis* II.244: 363.

After these events the emperor began to grow ill in body and mind. Therefore in the month of November around the time of the feast of St Martin [11 November], he came to Tribur and there summoned a general assembly. When the leading men of the kingdom realized that not only the strength of his body but also the faculty of the mind were slipping away from him, of their own accord they called Karlmann's son Arnulf to [rule] the kingdom, in no time at all formed a conspiracy to defect from the emperor, and crossed eagerly to the said man so that in the space of three days hardly anyone remained who would even show Charles basic human kindness.[334] He was given only food and drink by the hospitality of [arch]bishop Liutbert.[335] It was an affair worthy of note, and for the evaluation of human fate through the fickleness of things remarkable.[336] For just as before, while everything was abundant beyond anything he could imagine, a favourable fortune had given him so many and such great kingdoms of the empire without the sweat of hard work or the conflict of wars, so that in majesty, power, and riches he seemed second to none of the kings of the Franks since the great Charles [Charlemagne], so now an adverse fortune, as if to highlight human frailty, destroyed what he had accumulated and shamefully took away from him in a moment everything that, smiling on his fortunate success, it had once gloriously given him.[337] Made from an emperor into a beggar, and thinking in his desperate situation not about the imperial dignity but daily survival, he sent to Arnulf and asked him imploringly for enough provisions to sustain him in the present life.[338] He also sent to him with gifts his son Bernard, who had been born to

---

334 Charles's deposition is described in several sources: *AF*(M) 887; *AF*(B) 887: 114; *AV* 887: 64; *AH* 887: 19. Triggered by the emperor's failing health, it was ultimately a result of his failure to organise his succession in a way that included the powerful Arnulf: see Keller 1966; Reuter 1991: 115–20; MacLean 2003a: 191–8. On the consequent break-up of the empire see Airlie 1993; Airlie 2006b.

335 Liutbert of Mainz (on whom see above, 869) became Charles's archchancellor in 887 after the disgrace of Liutward of Vercelli.

336 Regino's wording is almost identical to Justin's comment about the troubles of Xerxes: *Epitome*, 2.13.10: 29 (Yardley 1994: 42). It also echoes a comment of Augustine's about 'the mutability of human affairs': Airlie 2006a: 119.

337 Regino's wording in this passage is clearly based on Justin, *Epitome*, 23.3.12: 158 (Yardley 1994: 182), on Pyrrhus I of Epirus. On Regino's view of 'fortuna' see above, Introduction, pp. 14–15.

338 Wealth as a sign of imperial dignity is a well-established motif in Carolingian historiography, including Regino's work. The pathos of Charles's reduced circumstances is also stressed by *AF*(M) 887: 103; and echoes the description of the defeated Xerxes in Justin, *Epitome*, 2.13.10–12: 29 (Yardley 1994: 42).

him by a concubine, and commended him to Arnulf's fidelity.³³⁹ It was a miserable spectacle to see the most opulent emperor not only forsaken by the trappings of fortune but even left wanting for human help.³⁴⁰ King Arnulf conceded to him several royal estates in Alemannia from which his nourishment would be supplied.³⁴¹ He himself, after he had arranged things felicitously in Francia, returned to Bavaria.

In that same year Bishop Witgar of Augsburg died and Adalbero, a man of noble family and of great intelligence and talent, took his seat and succeeded him in the episcopate.³⁴²

888

In the year of the Lord's incarnation 888, the emperor Charles, the third of that name and dignity, died on 12 January and was buried in the monastery of Reichenau.³⁴³ He was, truly, a most Christian ruler, who feared God and observed his commandments with all his heart. He was devotedly obedient to ecclesiastical laws, generous in almsgiving, unceasingly occupied in prayers and the melodies of the psalms, and untiringly dedicated to praising God.³⁴⁴ He committed all his hope and purpose to divine dispensation, whence all things happily turned out for the best for him, to the extent that he understood how to take hold of all the kingdoms of the Franks (which his predecessors had acquired not without bloodshed and with great effort) easily, quickly and without conflict or opposition.³⁴⁵ That toward the end of his life he was stripped of dignities and deprived of all his goods was, so we believe, a trial which was meant not only to purify him but also, more importantly, to test him. Since he bore this, so it is said, with great patience, offering prayers of thanks in adversity just as in prosperity, he has already received (or

339 Bernard had been born to Charles by a concubine *c.*875; he later raised an unsuccessful rebellion against Arnulf and was killed in 891 or 892: Borgolte 1986: 226–7, 263.
340 This sentence seems to reflect Regino's internalisation of several passages in Justin: *Epitome*, 8.5.8, 2.13.10, 23.4.7, 25.3.7: 67, 29, 159, 168 (Yardley 1994: 84, 42, 183, 192). See Manitius 1900: 196–7.
341 Charles's pension in Alemannia is also mentioned by *AF*(M) 887: 103 and *AF*(B) 887: 113. One of the estates in question may have been Neudingen: Borgolte 1977.
342 On Witgar see Goldberg 2006b; Adalbero was the dedicatee of Regino's chronicle: see above, Preface.
343 *AP. AF*(B) 887: 114 has 13 January. *AV* 887: 64 says that he was strangled by his own men.
344 Charles's interest in religious music is also mentioned by a later author: Ekkehard, *Casus S. Galli*, c. 46.
345 Cf. above, 887, for Regino's description of the same events in terms of *fortuna.*

doubtless will receive) the crown of life, which God has promised to those who love him.[346]

After his death the kingdoms which had obeyed his authority, just as though a legitimate heir were lacking, dissolved into separate parts and, without waiting for their natural lord, each decided to create a king from its own guts.[347] This was the cause of great wars; not because the Franks lacked leaders who by nobility, courage and wisdom were capable of ruling the kingdoms, but rather because the equality of descent, authority and power increased the discord among them; none so outshone the others that the rest deigned to submit to his rule.[348] For Francia would have produced many leaders capable of controlling the government of the kingdom, had not fortune equipped them to destroy each other in the competition for power.[349]

Therefore one part of the Italian people made Berengar the son of Eberhard, who held the command [*ducatus*] of Friuli, into their king; while another part decided to raise a certain Guy son of Lambert, *dux* of the Spoletans, to the royal dignity in the same way.[350] As a result of

346 James 1:12: 'Blessed is the man who perseveres under trial, because when he has stood the test, he will receive the crown of life that God has promised to those who love him.' Charles's posthumous reputation for great holiness is also attested to by *AF*(B) 887: 114; *AV* 887: 64.

347 It has been argued (most recently by Kortüm 2002: 70) that Regino did not mean to refer to Arnulf with the phrase 'natural lord', and that he was instead drawing attention to the complete absence of 'legitimate heirs'. The passage would then be translated: 'because [the kingdoms] lacked a legitimate heir ... they no longer expected a natural lord'. The problem turns on whether the kingdoms acted *because* they lacked a legitimate heir, or *as though*. The Latin ('veluti') appears to favour the latter.

348 The last sentence is closely based on Justin, *Epitome*, 13.2.3: 103 (Yardley 1994: 124): 'The equality among the officers actually served to increase their discord since none was so preeminent that anyone else would submit to him.' Justin is here discussing the competition for power among the officers after the death of Alexander the Great. On the resonances of this story for the aristocracy after the death of Charles the Fat see Airlie 2006a: 119–20.

349 Justin, *Epitome*, 13.1.15: 103 (Yardley 1994: 124): 'Such men would never have met their match had they not clashed among themselves, and the province of Macedonia would have produced many Alexanders if fortune had not armed them to destroy each other by making them equals in merit.' Regino's is regarded as the classic account of the disintegration of the empire, for reasons elucidated by Airlie 2006a. Versions of what follows are also offered by *AF*(B) 888: 115–16; *ASC* 887: 199; *AV* 888: 64–6. *AF*(B) 888: 115 describes the new rulers as 'kinglets' (*reguli*), on which term see now Kortüm 2002.

350 Berengar was *marchio* (a regional magnate with responsibility over multiple counts) of Friuli c. 874–888, king (intermittently) 888–924, and emperor from 915: Hirsch 1910; Fasoli 1949: 1–16; Rosenwein 1996. His mother was a daughter of Louis the Pious. Guy (or Wido) was *dux* of Spoleto and Camerino near Rome: *AF*(M) 883,

this discord such a slaughter on both sides afterward took place, and so much human blood was spilled, that, as the word of the Lord says: 'the kingdom divided against itself will all but meet with the misery of desolation'.[351] In the end Guy emerged victorious, and he expelled Berengar from the realm. Thus ejected, Berengar went to King Arnulf and requested his protection against his enemy.[352] What Arnulf did, however, and how he invaded the kingdom of Italy twice with an army, will be recorded in its own place.[353]

Meanwhile the people of Gaul gathered together as one and with Arnulf's consent made the *dux* Odo, the son of Robert whom we mentioned a little earlier, a vigorous man who exceeded the others in beauty of form, stature of body and greatness of power and wisdom,[354] into their king by unanimous counsel and will.[355] He governed the

---

884: 94–6; *AF*(B) 884, 885: 108, 111; Hlawitschka 1983. His initial bid for a throne was in west Francia, where he had strong connections: *AV* 888: 64–5; Hlawitschka 1968: 73–4.

351 Matthew 12:25. The original wording ('regnum divisum contra se desolatur') is slightly different from that cited, suggesting Regino was quoting from memory. He was presumably referring to the Battle of the Trebbia in 889: Dümmler 1888: 365–6.

352 Guy's victory at the Trebbia meant that he became sole king until his death in 894. Berengar was forced to retreat to Verona. A meeting between Berengar and Arnulf in late 888 at which the former sought the latter's endorsement and persuaded him not to enter Italy with an army is mentioned by *AF*(B) 888: 117. The pope was not keen on Guy or Berengar, and shortly afterward tried to get Arnulf to revive his plans to come to Rome, at least according to *AF*(B) 890: 119.

353 See below, 894 and 896.

354 Justin, *Epitome*, 13.1.10–11: 103 (Yardley 1994: 123), which praises Alexander's friends by listing the qualities that made them king-like: '... all of them possessed handsome features, a fine physique and great powers of body and mind alike'. Regino's quotation here is direct, though the translations differ slightly. Justin is known to have had readers among the secular aristocracy: McKitterick 2004: 43–4; Airlie 2006a: 119–20. Cf. *AF*(B) 888: 116, which calls Odo a usurper; and *AV* 888: 64. Odo was count of Paris and son of Robert the Strong: see above, 867 and 887.

355 Odo was anointed on 29 February by Archbishop Walter of Sens. In fact his election was, as with those of Berengar and Guy, partial and factional, as made clear by *AV* 888: 65, which says that Archbishop Fulk of Rheims, count Baldwin of Flanders and Abbot Rudolf of St-Bertin and St-Vaast invited Arnulf to take the throne (he refused). For discussion see Hlawitschka 1968: 73–7; Schneider 1973. Odo also faced major opposition in Aquitaine, where count Ranulf was harbouring the young Charles the Straightforward, son of Louis the Stammerer: *AV* 889: 67. *AF*(B) 888: 116 says that Ranulf had himself crowned king, though this is doubtful. Odo was crowned with Arnulf's approval in November, after which the opposition to him calmed down: *AF*(B) 888: 116; *AV* 888: 66–7. Regino's reference to Arnulf as the empire's 'natural lord' may imply that he attempted to maintain a pseudo-imperial overlordship; but cf. *AV* 888: 66, which says that the two kings 'made friends'. On friendship as a political and social bond see Epp 1999; Althoff 2004.

kingdom manfully and showed himself to be an indefatigable champion against the continuous plundering of the Northmen.[356] At that same time Rudolf, the son of Conrad and nephew of Hugh the Abbot, whom we mentioned above, seized the province between the Jura and the Pennine Alps. At St-Maurice [d'Agaune], having brought in certain leading men and several priests, he placed a crown on his own head and ordered that he should be called king. After this he sent legates through the whole of Lothar's kingdom and by persuasion and promises he beguiled the minds of the bishops and noble men to favour him. When this was announced to Arnulf, he immediately attacked him with an army. Rudolf turned in flight through the narrowest passes and sought to save his life in very well-protected places among the crags. For all the days of their lives, Arnulf and his son Zwentibald pursued Rudolf. However, they could never harm him because, as has been set out above, the inaccessible places, many of which could only be reached by mountain goats, kept the massed ranks of the pursuers well away from gaining entry.[357]

In that same year the Northmen who were besieging the town of Paris achieved an amazing feat unheard of not only in our times, but also in past ages.[358] For when they realised that the town could not be taken, they began to prepare with all their strength and cunning to leave the city behind them and move their fleet with all their troops up the Seine and so, by entering the River Yonne, cross the frontiers of Burgundy unobstructed. However, because the citizens made every effort to stop them going upriver, they dragged their ships across dry land for more than two miles, and having thus avoided all danger they plunged them once more into the waters of the Seine. After a short distance they left the Seine and, as they had planned, navigated the Yonne with all speed, landing at Sens. There they made camp and for six continuous months they blockaded the same town with a siege and laid waste to almost the whole of Burgundy with murder, pillage and fire. But because the citizens, protected by God, bravely fought them off, they

356 Odo was an extremely vigorous ruler, though Regino somewhat exaggerates his record against the Vikings. On Odo's reign see Bautier 1961; Werner 1984: 417–22, 436–41; Koziol 2006b. The main source is *AV* 888–898.

357 Rudolf and before him Conrad had risen to power in Transjurane Burgundy since the 870s, so did not belong to a family with very old connections in the area. On him, and the debate about whether or not his ambition was, as Regino suggests, to resurrect Lotharingia, see *AF*(B) 888: 115–16; *AV* 888: 64–5; Parisot 1898: 261–4; Hlawitschka 1968: 79–83, 94–6; MacLean 2003a: 67–79; Hope 2005: 111–22.

358 In fact, this story must refer to the aftermath of the peace treaty concluded by Charles the Fat in 886: above, 887 and *AV* 886: 63.

were completely unable to take the said city, although they attempted it repeatedly with all the sweat of their labour and using all their trickery and tools.[359]

During the anguishes of that very siege Eberhard, the metropolitan of that place, who was a man of total sanctity who shone with the splendour of wisdom, was released from his bodily chains and passed to the heavenly homeland. Walter, a nephew of bishop Walter of Orléans, was raised to his seat; a man far inferior to his predecessor in habits, piety and the pursuit of wisdom.[360]

889

In the year of the Lord's incarnation 889, the Hungarian people, who were extremely warlike and more savage than any beast, and who were unheard of in previous centuries because they were not named [in the sources], emerged from the Scythian kingdoms and the immense marshes created by the floods of the River Don.[361] But before we follow the cruel deeds of this people with our pen, it does not seem superfluous for us to record something about the location of Scythia and the customs of the Scythians according to the words of the historiographers.[362]

Scythia, so they say, stretches to the east and is enclosed on one side by Pontus, on another by the Riphean mountains, and at the back by Asia

---

359 Tools = *machinamenta*, which could also be translated as 'siege-engines'. The attack on Sens and the death of the bishop (see next paragraph) are reported in similar though briefer terms by *AV* 886, 887: 63, though that source states that Eberhard paid a ransom for the town's relief.

360 Regino's ordering of events is again wrong, since Walter of Sens was already archbishop in time for Odo's consecration in early 888. *Annales sanctae Columbae Senonensis* 886: 104 says that the Vikings arrived from Paris on 30 November 886, that Eberhard died on 1 February and that Walter took over on 2 April 887. Walter later became Odo's archchancellor: Hlawitschka 1968: 139–41.

361 From what follows it seems that Regino, not having found mention of the Hungarians (or Magyars) in his sources, concluded that they and the Scythians were the same people. The Hungarians/Magyars are mentioned very sporadically before the 890s, when Arnulf's use of them as mercenaries established their role in western Europe; their settlement of the Carpathian basin was under way by 896: Reuter 1991: 127–31. Classic studies include Büttner 1956; Fasoli 1949 and de Vajay 1968. More recently see Bowlus 1995; Dopsch 2002: 173–83; Bowlus 2006. Regino's account of them, much the fullest of the contemporary sources, had a lasting influence, not least on later Hungarian chroniclers: Silagi 1988.

362 The following two paragraphs are drawn directly from Justin and Paul the Deacon respectively. Regino makes some grammatical alterations; I will note only changes of substance.

BOOK II   203

and the River Ithasis.³⁶³ In both length and breadth it is an extensive land. The people who live there have no frontiers between themselves. They very rarely³⁶⁴ engage in agriculture, and they have no houses or shelters or residences; for they constantly pasture their cattle and flocks and are accustomed to roaming the uncultivated wilderness. They transport their wives and children with them in wagons which they use as houses by covering them with hides as protection against the rain and cold of winter.³⁶⁵ No crime is for them more serious than theft since, as they have no buildings to protect their cattle, sheep and food, what would be left among the forests if theft were allowed? They do not desire gold and silver in the same way as other mortals, but are devoted to hunting and fishing and feed on milk and honey.³⁶⁶ They know nothing about the uses of wool and clothing and although they are constantly afflicted by the cold they wear only the skins of wild animals and rodents.³⁶⁷ The Scythians tried to conquer Asia three times, while they themselves always remained untouched and unconquered by foreign powers.³⁶⁸ The feats of the women were no less famous than those of the men, for while the men founded the Parthian and Bactrian kingdoms, their women established the Amazonian kingdom, so that in considering the deeds of the men and the women it is hard to decide which of the two sexes is more illustrious among them.³⁶⁹ They drove the Persian king Darius from Scythia in shameful flight, and butchered Cyrus with his entire army. In the same way they annihilated Alexander the Great's general Sopyrion with all his forces. They had heard about the arms of Rome, but not felt them. Hardened by war and by hard work, they have immensely strong bodies.³⁷⁰

363 Pontus is part of Anatolia bordering the Black Sea, the Riphean mountains are the Urals and the Ithasis is the Itz in Germany. Justin has the river's name as Phasis (the Rioni in the Caucasus). Regino here and elsewhere reproduces errors in his manuscript of Justin.
364 Justin says never.
365 Here Regino drops a line: 'Their justice derives from the natural bent of their race rather than from codified law.' (Yardley 1994: 27).
366 The references to hunting and fishing are not in Justin's account.
367 All the above, except where noted, comes from Justin, *Epitome*, 2.2.1–9: 15–16 (Yardley 1994: 27). Justin goes on to explain that their simple lifestyle gives the Scythians a refined, moderate and morally admirable lifestyle. By omitting this, Regino turns Justin's celebration of the simplicity of an ancient civilization into revulsion at a backward people.
368 Justin, *Epitome*, 2.3.1: 16 (Yardley 1994: 27).
369 Justin, *Epitome*, 2.1.2–4: 14 (Yardley 1994: 25). Again, Regino omits Justin's context, which is an explanation of the antiquity and greatness of the Scythians.
370 Justin, *Epitome*, 2.3.2–5, 7: 16 (Yardley 1994: 27–8). Regino cuts two sentences from

They overflowed with such a huge population, however, that the land they already had was not enough to feed them.[371] This is because the further the lands of the north are removed from the warmth of the sun, and the more they are frozen by icy snow, the healthier they are for human bodies and the more suitable for propagation of peoples. Conversely, all the southern regions, which are closer to the sun's heat, always abound in illness and are less well adapted to the rearing of humans. This is why such great numbers of peoples spring up under the northern skies, so that it is quite correct to call that entire region from the Don to the west by the general name of Germany, though individual places within it also have their own names.[372] Because Germany is so populous, innumerable groups of captives are often taken from there and sold to southern peoples for money. Peoples have frequently left this region because it produces so many human beings that there are barely enough resources to feed them. These groups have afflicted Asia, but mainly they have troubled adjacent parts of Europe. Ruined cities throughout Illyricum and Gaul testify to this, but above all unhappy Italy has experienced the savagery of almost all of these peoples.[373]

The Hungarians were thus driven from their home in these lands by a neighbouring people called the Petchenegs, because they were superior to them in strength and number and because, as we said before, their own country was not sufficient to accommodate their swelling numbers.[374]

---

this section. One, stating that the Scythians had founded the Parthian and Bactrian empires, was superfluous given that he had already pasted this information in from an earlier part of his source. The other, at the end of the passage, stated that the Scythians (unlike the Magyars, needless to say) were not acquisitive and that they fought for nothing other than glory. Both omissions highlight Regino's very deliberate editing of his sources.

371 This is similar to Justin, *Epitome*, 9.2.7: 69 (Yardley 1994: 86), but it is more likely to be an editorial intervention by Regino based on a sentence from Paul the Deacon in the following paragraph. The idea that invaders were motivated by land pressure was often used by early medieval authors to explain the sudden appearance of new groups.

372 This is a pun in the Latin: Germany/germination (of peoples). Here, Regino drops a sentence from Paul about the Romans' division of *Germania* into two provinces.

373 Paul the Deacon, *Historia*, I.1: 52–3 (Foulke 2003: 1–2). Paul offered this as an explanation for the appearance of the Goths, Vandals, Lombards and others, while Regino appropriates it for the Scythians/Hungarians. Regino uses this section from Paul to explain the aggression of the Scythians/Hungarians in preference to Justin, *Epitome*, 2.1.5–21: 14–15 (Yardley 1994: 25–6), which uses the same climate theories to argue for the antiquity and robustness of the Scythians. The Hungarians were very active in Italy from 899, but their attacks were highly political and often carried out on behalf of rulers like Arnulf: Reuter 1991: 128–9; Bowlus 2006: 73–95.

374 For discussion of these developments see now Curta 2006.

After they had been forced to flee by the violence of the Petchenegs, they said goodbye to their homeland and set out to look for lands where they could live and establish settlements. First they roamed the wildernesses of the Pannonians and the Avars, and sought their daily food by hunting and fishing. Then they attacked the lands of the Carinthians, Moravians and Bulgars with the infestation of constant raids, killing a very few with the sword and many thousands with arrows, which they fire from their bows made of horn with such skill that it is almost impossible to avoid being hit by them.[375]

But they know nothing about fighting hand-to-hand in formation or taking besieged cities.[376] They fight by charging forward and turning back on their horses, often indeed simulating flight. Nor can they fight for a long time; but they would be irresistible if their perseverance were as strong as their charge. Mostly they leave the battle at the height of the fighting and soon afterward come back from their retreat to fight again, so that just when you think you have won, the critical moment has to be faced.[377]

Their way of fighting is all the more dangerous in that other peoples are not used to it.[378] The one difference between their way of fighting and the Bretons' is that they use arrows while the Bretons throw missiles. They do not live like humans, but like beasts. For, so it is rumoured, they eat their meat raw, drink blood, chop up the hearts of captives and swallow them bit by bit just as if they were medicine; and they are not swayed by any compassion nor moved by any stirrings of pity. They cut their hair down to the skin with their knives.[379]

---

375 Bowlus 2006: 19–44 offers a detailed analysis of Hungarian equipment and warfare which was, as described by Regino, dominated by mounted archers.

376 This paragraph is from Justin, *Epitome*, 41.2.7–9: 229 (Yardley 1994: 254–5). Justin is here discussing the Parthians rather than the Scythians, though as noted above he does see them as linked.

377 Regino drops some of Justin's information about the Parthians' use of drums for battle-signals and about their armour; presumably these were irrelevant to Hungarian practice.

378 In fact, Nithard, *Historia*, 3.6: 110–13 describes two Frankish armies practising feigned retreats at Worms in 842 (discussed by Nelson 1989; Halsall 2003: 116–18). To judge by his own descriptions of Frankish warfare, however, Regino regarded the close-formed battle-line as typical, as indeed it was of much early medieval fighting whether on foot or horseback: Halsall 2003: 194–204.

379 On this passage's discussion of warfare see Leyser 1982a: 27–9. Regino seems keen here to help his audience understand an 'unknown' people with reference to one that was familiar to them. For Regino, the cultural otherness of the Hungarians (nomadic non-Christians) evidently mattered more than his observation that their way of fighting was in fact not that different from the Bretons' (a group he described

They ride their horses all the time; they are accustomed to travel, halt, think and talk on them.[380] They put a lot of effort into teaching their children and slaves horse-riding and archery.[381] By nature they are puffed up, quarrelsome, deceitful and insolent, as is to be expected from people who attribute the same fierceness to women as to men. They are always restless and inclined to make trouble either at home or abroad. They are inherently taciturn, and more given to action than to words.[382] By their savagery, this abominable people devastated not only the regions already mentioned, but also most of the kingdom of Italy.[383]

In that same year the Northmen left the town of Sens and once more reached Paris with all their troops.[384] And because the citizens completely prevented them from proceeding downriver, they once again pitched camp and assailed the city with all their might; but they could not prevail against the help offered by God. After a few days had passed, they again went up the Seine with their fleet and, after entering the River Marne, they destroyed the city of Troyes with fire and pillaged the whole area as far as the towns of Verdun and Toul.[385]

In those days Liutbert, [arch]bishop of the town of Mainz, was lifted from human affairs. With the agreement of Poppo, *dux* of the Thuringians, and King Arnulf, Sunderolt was elected in his place: he was a devout and honest man, adequately instructed in sacred texts, who had

---

as culturally similar to the Franks). On the cultural categories used to define groups in the early Middle Ages see Pohl and Reimitz 1998; Corradini, Diesenberger and Reimitz 2003.

380 Justin, *Epitome*, 41.3.4: 229 (Yardley 1994: 255). The opening clause of this sentence is missing from all Regino manuscripts, presumably due to a scribal error, and is supplied from Justin.

381 Justin, *Epitome*, 41.2.5: 229 (Yardley 1994: 254). This is Justin's discussion of the Parthian army, which he says was made up almost entirely of slaves.

382 Justin, *Epitome*, 41.3.7–8: 230 (Yardley 1994: 255). This paragraph sees Regino picking out sections from Justin that he sees as relevant to the Hungarians, and leaving much out. Regino alters Justin's statement that the Parthians consider violence more appropriate to men than to women, not just to emphasise the alterity of the Hungarians, but also to make this section consistent with his earlier citation of Justin concerning Scythian women.

383 In the light of contemporary Hungarian attacks on Italy (see above, n. 373), this line seems to confirm that Regino saw the Hungarians as the same people as those he found in the pages of Justin and Paul.

384 Probably a reference to the events of 887, in May of which year the Vikings returned to Paris to collect the tribute that had been promised them by Charles the Fat: *AV* 887: 63–4.

385 *AV* 887: 64 also says that they left the Seine and entered the Marne. In fact, Troyes is on the Seine, Verdun on the Meuse and Toul is near the Moselle.

from infancy been raised and had lived according to the Rule in the monastery of Fulda under the direction of the abbot.[386]

890

In the year of the Lord's incarnation 890, King Arnulf gave the command [*ducatus*] of the Bohemians to King Zwentibald of the Moravian Slavs. Hitherto, the Bohemians had rulers from among their own kind and people, and had kept the fidelity they promised to the kings of the Franks by inviolable agreement.[387] Arnulf did this because, before he had been raised to the throne of the kingdom, he had been joined to Zwentibald in close friendship.[388] In fact, he raised from the holy font Arnulf's son, who was born to him by a concubine, and named him Zwentibald after him.[389] This matter [the granting of Bohemia to Zwentibald of Moravia] provided a considerable stimulus for discord and defections. For the Bohemians, on the one hand, withdrew the fealty that they had long kept, and Zwentibald, on the other, believing himself to have gained considerable strength through the acquisition of another realm and puffed up with the arrogance of pride, rebelled against Arnulf. When Arnulf learned about this he invaded the Moravian realm and razed everything outside the cities to the ground. Finally, because even the fruit trees were being uprooted, Zwentibald asked for peace and, having given his son as a hostage, belatedly gained it.[390]

386 Liutbert died on 17 February 887. Poppo was a brother of the *dux* Henry killed at the siege of Paris; their family had long been among the most pre-eminent in Thuringia and had close ties to Fulda: on him see *AF* 880: 89; *AF*(M) 883: 94; *AF*(B) 882, 883: 106–7; Becher 1996: 167–70; Innes 2000: 230; and below, 892.

387 This story is unique to Regino, but plausible. Arnulf is known to have held talks with Zwentibald in March 890, at which they discussed the state of affairs in Italy: *AF*(B) 890: 119–20. The Bohemians seem to have been under Bavarian influence since their submission to Louis the German in 845, and after 890 are described as being under Moravian hegemony: *AF*(B) 895, 897: 131, 137. It seems likely that the deposition of Charles the Fat had disrupted relationships across the frontier. For discussion of Franko-Bohemian relations see Třeštík 1995; Bowlus 1995; Goldberg 2006a: 139–45.

388 *Gratia familiaritatis*. Friendship could refer to solemn and important relationships in this period: Epp 1999; Althoff 2004.

389 Arnulf's son Zwentibald had been born *c*.870. Arnulf's alliance with the Moravians may explain why he was reported to have had Slav allies in his deposing of Charles the Fat: *AF*(M) 887: 103; *AF*(B) 888: 115. Such alliances between Frankish factional leaders and groups across frontiers were a perennial feature of Carolingian politics: Reuter 1991: 77–84; Smith 1995.

390 Zwentibald's withdrawal from Arnulf's hegemony took place in 892. The king invaded with a very large army, among which was a group of Hungarians, and tried to outflank Zwentibald politically by renewing his alliance with the Bulgarians and

At the same time, the Northmen left the River Marne and returned to Paris. Since their way downstream was completely blocked by the bridge, they pitched camp for the third time and once again assailed the city. But because they were resisted so fearlessly by the citizens, who had been hardened by the constant effort of defence and vigilance, and had become practised in the unremitting fighting, the Northmen gave up. They dragged their ships overland with great effort and, having regained the river in this way, they moved their fleet to the frontiers of Brittany.[391] They besieged a certain fortress in the area of Coutances which is called St-Lô. They cut off all access to the water source and, when the townspeople dried up with thirst, terms of surrender were arranged: the Northmen would leave them with their lives but take away everything else. When the inhabitants emerged from the stronghold these treacherous people profaned the faith and the promise they had given, and butchered them all without a second thought. Among those they killed was the bishop of the church of Coutances.[392]

At that time there was a serious dispute between the leaders [*duces*] of the Bretons, Alan and Judicael, concerning the division of the realm.[393] Finding the Bretons thus split and divided, not so much in terms of territory as in their minds, the pagans confidently attacked them. For as long as they considered the war to be a private one for each of them rather than a communal struggle, they refused to bring help to each other, as if a victory for one were not a victory for all, and they were deeply harmed by the enemy.[394] Everywhere they yielded, and all their possessions were plundered up to the River Blavet. Then for the first

---

asking them not to sell salt to the Moravians. He invaded again the following year, and in 894 peace was restored after Zwentibald died: *AF*(B) 892, 893, 894: 123–5, 129. See Bowlus 1995; Innes 1997b; Dopsch 2002 (the latter two express significant reservations about Bowlus's arguments concerning the location of Moravia).

391 Regino apparently conflates two phases of Viking activity. In 888 Odo set up a camp at Paris to defend against the probability that the Vikings would return from the Marne, only for them to bypass the city by setting up a base on the Loing: *AV* 888: 67. Then in autumn 889 they returned to Paris and were bought off by Odo before moving to Brittany: *AV* 889: 67–8. Bridges had proved to be an effective way of restricting the movement of Viking fleets since the 860s: Coupland 1991; Nelson 1992: 206–7, 213, 218–19.

392 *AV* 890: 68 names the bishop as Lista, and confirms that the Vikings killed the inhabitants of St-Lô. From this source it seems that the siege began in late 889 and was lifted in 890. For context see Price 1989. Contemporary charters support the chronology presented by Regino: Chédeville and Guillotel 1984: 364.

393 See above, 874.

394 This is based closely on Justin, *Epitome*, 15.2.15: 117 (Yardley 1994: 139–40), which describes the fight against Antigonus led by Ptolemy and Cassander.

time they understood how much damage was being done to them by their discord, and how much strength it gave to their opponents. Reassuring each other through the exchange of embassies, they agreed a time and place to meet, and planned to wage war with joined forces.³⁹⁵ Then Judicael, who was the younger, desiring to increase the glory of his own reputation, joined battle without waiting for Alan and his men. He killed many thousands of the enemy and forced the rest to flee to a certain village. But when he rashly pursued them further than he should have, he was killed by them, because he did not know that while it is good to win, it is not good to push your victory too far; for [the enemy's] desperation is dangerous. After this Alan, when he had united all of Brittany in this way, vowed that if he could overcome his enemies through divine power he would send to Rome a tenth part of all his goods for God and St Peter.³⁹⁶ When all the Bretons had given sureties for the same vow he advanced to war and, engaging in battle, routed the enemy with such a slaughter that barely 400 men out of 15,000 returned to their fleet.³⁹⁷

At that time Bishop Willibert, who was very holy and very learned in divine and human affairs, was withdrawn from the light of this world and the venerable man Hermann was put in charge of the church of Cologne by the election of the clergy and people.³⁹⁸ Also around this time Salomon [II], who was bishop of the church of Constance, departed from this world. He was succeeded by Salomon [III], who at this time was holding the abbacy of St-Gall and was a man distinguished not only by his nobility, but also by the virtues of wisdom and intelligence. He is recognized as the third bishop of Constance to have that name.³⁹⁹

395 This sentence draws on Justin, *Epitome*, 15.2.16: 117 (Yardley 1994: 140). See previous note.

396 Direct links between Brittany and Rome had been established by the translation of relics of St Marcellinus to Redon in 848–9: *GSR* II.10: 174–82; Smith 2000: 333, 337. Alan's appeal to St Peter is echoed in a charter of 889: Chédeville and Guillotel 1984: 365–7.

397 On Judicael and Alan see above, 874; Smith 1992: 121–2; Pettiau 2004: 173–4, 178. Regino's account of these events is by far the most detailed. *AV* 890: 68 refers briefly to the Bretons' 'manful' defence of their realm after the siege of St-Lô, which forced the Vikings to return to the Seine. The numbers of men given by Regino, as in most early medieval histories, are to be read as indications of orders of magnitude rather than reliable figures.

398 Willibert died 11 September 889, and Hermann gained the pallium in May 890. The latter's family had close links to Prüm: MUB 120; Kuchenbuch 1978: 350.

399 Salomon II died 23 December 889, and Salomon III succeeded him in 890, while keeping control of St-Gall. They belonged to an episcopal dynasty of some pedigree: *AF*(B) 890, n. 7; Reuter 1991: 107.

891

In the year of the Lord's incarnation 891, the Northmen, badly weakened by two consecutive battles in Brittany, moved their fleet to Lothar's kingdom where, after pitching camp, they engaged in plunder.[400] King Arnulf sent an army against them and ordered tents to be pitched by the Meuse to stop the enemy crossing the river. But before the army was assembled at the appointed place near the fortress of Maastricht the Northmen, staying upstream, crossed the Meuse near Liège, left their enemies behind, and dispersed in the forests and swamps around the palace of Aachen. They killed whomever they encountered and captured many wagons and carts in which provisions were being carried to the army. When the report reached the army, which had almost fully gathered by the day of the nativity of St John the Baptist [24 June], the minds of all of them were seized not so much by fear as by stupefaction. The leaders convoked a meeting at which they discussed not so much the danger as the uncertainty of the situation. They were not sure whether the Northmen would enter the land of the Ripuarians and make for Cologne, or go via Prüm and march to Trier, or even cross the Meuse and hurry to their fleet in fear of the multitude assembled against them. While these things were going on, night fell and stopped the assembly. The next day, when dawn displayed the rays of its light, they all took up their arms and marched downriver, banners raised and ready for battle. And when they had crossed a brook called the Geul, their battle-lines stopped together. Then they decided, so that the whole army would not become fatigued needlessly, that each of the leaders should dispatch 12 of his men who, combined into a single group, would track down the enemy.[401] While they were discussing this, scouts of the Northmen suddenly appeared. Without consulting their leaders, the whole host chased them in ragged disorder; and in a certain little village they stumbled on a crowd of foot-soldiers who were massed together and so easily repelled the scattered attackers and forced them to retreat. Then, as is their custom, the Northmen rattled their quivers, raised their war cry to the sky, and joined battle. When they heard the shouting, the Northmen's horsemen rushed in with great haste. As the fighting got worse the army of the Christians (oh the shame of it!) committed a sin and retreated. In this battle

---

400 *AV* 890, 891: 68–70 describes Viking movements in some detail. Their activity was focused around Noyon, Leuven and Arras (where the *AV* was being written), thus around the frontier between the western and middle kingdoms.

401 This passage seems to support the view of Carolingian armies as dominated by lords' military entourages: see above, 874, n. 211.

[arch]Bishop Sunzo [Sunderolt] and Count Arnulf were killed, along with a countless multitude of noblemen.[402] Having achieved victory, the Northmen took the camp, which was filled with all kinds of riches. After butchering those whom they captured during the battle, they returned to their fleet weighed down with booty. This bloodbath took place on 26 June.[403]

While this was going on, King Arnulf was staying in the furthermost parts of Bavaria, restraining the insolence of the Slavs. When the massacre of his men and the victory of the enemy were announced to him he was at first greatly saddened at the loss of his faithful men and lamented with a sigh that the Franks, who were previously undefeated, should have shown their backs to their adversaries.[404] But then, turning the shamefulness of the affair over in his noble breast, he grew angry at the enemy. Gathering an army from the eastern realms, he soon crossed the Rhine and established a camp near the banks of the Meuse. After a few days the Northmen, elated by the previous battle, set out to plunder with all their might. The king moved to engage them with his lightly-armed troops. When the Northmen saw that the battle-lines were approaching alongside the River Dyle, they fortified their position with a pile of wood and earth in the usual way and taunted the army with jeers and abuse, launching repeated insults and mocking them that they should remember the Geul, their shameful flight and the slaughter that had been inflicted on them, because they were about to suffer the same fate again. His bile rising, the king ordered his army to dismount and engage the enemy on foot.[405] As soon as he had said this they leapt off their horses, let out yells of encouragement, broke into the enemy's stronghold and, given strength by God in heaven, hewed them to death with their swords and laid them out on the ground, in such a way that out of a countless multitude, barely anyone was left to report the bad

---

402 Sunderolt was archbishop of Mainz. An Arnulf is recorded as having held counties in Alemannia: DD AC 129, 159.

403 *AF*(B) 891: 121 reports this battle in passing, and mentions that Sunderolt was killed because he had acted rashly. *AV* 891: 69 also refers to the Vikings dispersing into the woods in the same region, but in order to escape Odo rather than Arnulf. The battle on the Geul is discussed by Halsall 2003: 187–90, 214.

404 Presumably Regino means that the Franks were undefeated in Arnulf's reign.

405 The decision to fight on foot was important in this battle, whose site was hemmed in by marshes, and probably represents Arnulf's determination to fight to the death. It has, however, in light of the detailed account in *AF*(B) 891: 121–3, been used as evidence that the Franks were unused to fighting while dismounted. In reality, Frankish forces used a combination of fighting styles, including combat on horseback and on foot: see above all Bachrach 1970: 51–3; Halsall 2003: 186–8.

news to the fleet.[406] With the matter thus concluded satisfactorily, Arnulf returned to Bavaria.

In that same year the venerable abbot Hatto, who had up till then been the father [abbot] of many monks at the monastery of Reichenau, was consecrated metropolitan of the church of Mainz.[407]

892

In the year of the Lord's incarnation 892, in the month of February, the Northmen who had remained with their ships crossed the Meuse, entered the country of the Ripuarians and, devouring everything according to their natural savagery, they came as far as Bonn. Leaving there, they seized a certain village called Lannesdorf. There an army of Christians met them, but it did nothing worthy of being described as courageous. When night fell the Northmen left the said village and, fearing an enemy attack, did not dare at all to venture onto the flatlands and fields but kept constantly to the woods. They left the army behind them to the left and moved their troops as fast as they could to the monastery of Prüm. The abbot and the community of brothers barely managed to escape just as they were breaking in. The Northmen entered the monastery, pillaged everything, killed some of the monks, butchered most of the servants and led the rest away as captives. After leaving there they entered the Ardennes, where they attacked and quickly conquered a certain stronghold that had recently been built on a certain prominent mountain, where a countless multitude of the common people had fled for refuge.[408] After all had been killed, they went back to their fleet with great booty and, on their heavily laden ships, they returned to the lands across the sea with all their forces.[409]

---

406 *AV* 891: 70 also mentions the battle of the Dyle, and says that after Arnulf had gone home the Vikings regrouped at the same camp, i.e. Leuven. The scarcity of survivors to tell the tale is an image also used by Justin, *Epitome*, 1.8.12: 11 (Yardley 1994: 21).

407 The exact date of Hatto's accession is unknown. He was one of the men responsible for guiding the court of Louis the Child and was the dedicatee of Regino's *De synodalibus*. On him see *AF*(B) 893, 894, 895: 125, 127, 130; and below, 899.

408 On the development of such refuge-fortresses in this period see Jäschke 1975.

409 Regino is the only source for this story, which presumably represents local knowledge. *AF*(B) says nothing about the Vikings after the battle of the Dyle. *AV* 892: 72 says that the Vikings based at Leuven returned to Odo's kingdom but after finding the kingdom 'weakened by famine' they put to sea and left in autumn. This ended the activities of the so-called Great Army on the continent, which had been active since 879: MacLean 1998; Abels 2003.

BOOK II   213

At that same time Farabert, abbot of the community of Prüm, set aside his pastoral office voluntarily and with the king's permission; and I, although unworthy, succeeded him in charge by the brothers' election, as stipulated by the authority of the Rule.[410] However, I did not remain in that position for very long because at the instigation of my rivals I had to put up with Richar, the brother of Gerard and Matfrid, becoming the hateful successor to my job.[411] I pray that the reader will not find it burdensome if I go back to the beginnings of the matter and set out in plain language how this affair was brought through to its conclusion. For it seems absurd that I, who have set out to explain the actions of others and the causes of events, should pass over in silence a matter that relates to me ...

[MISSING SECTION][412]

... in particular I ask on bended knee for the reader's pardon since in this account I have been more verbose than is proper.[413] For necessity dictated that I set down in the right order not only what was said but also what was done, because of the scurrilous complaint of those who envy and oppose me.[414]

Let it suffice that I have recorded just a few things of the many that relate to the preceding case and the passing of time. For we have decided

410 *AP* reveals this happened in May. Regino may have commissioned the famous Prüm estate survey after the sack of 892: Kuchenbuch 1978; Schwab 1983. For arguments against Regino's involvement see Wisplinghoff 1999.

411 This sentence does not appear in Kurze's B manuscripts: see below, n. 414. Richar succeeded Regino in 899: see below. Gerard, Matfrid and Richar had their main power base around Metz and held significant properties in a number of surrounding areas; they came from a family of longstanding prominence and were related to the Engiltrude discussed by Regino above, 866. For detailed analysis see Hlawitschka 1968: 166–74, 188–92; Hlawitschka 1969: 154–71, who argues that the three men's father was the count Adalhard of Metz mentioned by Regino above, 882. The identity of Regino's unnamed 'rivals' has been the subject of much debate: see MacLean forthcoming.

412 The explanation introduced by Regino is missing in all manuscripts. This implies that a considerable amount of text was excised from the original manuscript, most likely by the author himself: see above, Introduction, pp. 48–51.

413 Regino uses the word 'relatio' to refer to his (self-)censored account, which has overtones of making a formal case.

414 The section from 'I pray that the reader ...' to the end of the paragraph is omitted in all of Kurze's A manuscripts, in other words those that are supposed to represent the version edited by Adalbert. Schleidgen 1977: 88–96 highlights the problems with Kurze's edition at this point, where he included both this section and the sentence about Gerard and Matfrid, although these never appear together in the manuscripts. Despite this, it is still possible that both sections were written by Regino: see above, Introduction, pp. 48–51.

to keep quiet concerning the present age because if we write down in clear unclouded fashion the truth about what was done then without doubt we will incur the hatred and displeasure of certain people who are still alive.[415] If, on the other hand, we hold back from the truth and write about the case other than it really was, we will incur a reputation as a flatterer and liar, since the affair is known to almost everyone. We therefore leave this to posterity to be explained more fully.[416] But so that we may not be accused of having left it completely untouched, we will undertake to record only some of the events, and in summary.[417]

So, in the above-mentioned year, in the month of July, Count Waltgar, a cousin of King Odo – he was a son of Odo's uncle Adalelm – raised arms in rebellion against that king with the help of certain others and, taking himself to Laon, strove to oppose the king's power with every effort. When Odo heard this he laid siege to the city and he received its surrender very quickly. Then he ordered the same Waltgar to be beheaded, by the judgement of all the leading men who were there at the time, because he had drawn his sword against his lord and king in a public assembly.[418] After that he set out for Aquitaine against Ranulf, his brother Gauzbert, Abbot Ebolus of St-Denis and several others who had refused to obey his commands, in order to curb their insolence.[419]

In the same year on 28 August, Count Megingoz, a cousin of the King Odo mentioned above, was treacherously killed by Alberic and his accomplices in the monastery of St-Sixtus which is called Rethel.[420]

415 Cf. above, Preface.
416 Cf. above, Preface.
417 Regino seems to imply that the rest of his text is somehow relevant to the events surrounding his deposition. In keeping with his promise, the entries from this point on become much briefer: MacLean forthcoming.
418 Adalelm was count of Laon, a brother of Robert the Strong, and held high office under Charles the Bald: Werner 1960: 159; Nelson 1992: 228, 247–50. The execution of Waltgar (who was abbot of St-Peter in Ghent: Le Jan 1995a: 51) at Odo's command is also recorded by *AV* 892: 71–2, which says that the king had given Laon to him and suggests that his crime was to have made an alliance with Baldwin of Flanders, who had resumed his opposition to Odo earlier in the year after a dispute about the distribution of abbacies. Regino's detail that he drew his sword in an assembly reflects the tight rules that governed aristocrats' behaviour at such occasions: see Reuter 2001.
419 The account of these events given by *AV* 892: 72–3 suggests that these men were part of a wider conspiracy against Odo, and says that Ranulf (on whom see above, 888, n. 355) was already dead. For discussion see Brunterc'h 1997.
420 Adalbert adds: 'his body was carried to Trier and buried at St-Maximin'. Megingoz was a powerful count whose power bases were in the Maienfeldgau and at the monastery of St-Maximin in Trier, where he was lay abbot. His career in east Francia goes back to 858 and by 892 he was the key figure in Lotharingia with

At that same time Arn, the venerable bishop of Würzburg, set out to fight the Slavs at the urging and encouragement of Poppo *dux* of the Thuringians, and was killed in the battle.[421] Count Conrad's brother Rudolf gained his seat and succeeded him as bishop.[422]

Arnulf granted some of Count Megingoz's offices to his son Zwentibald.[423]

Poppo *dux* of the Thuringians was stripped of his offices, and the command which he had held was entrusted to Conrad; he held it for a short time and then gave it back voluntarily. Then it was given to Count Burchard, who rules it vigorously to this day.[424]

While King Odo was staying in Aquitaine, most of the great men of the Franks defected from him and at the urging of Archbishop Fulk [of Rheims] and Counts Herbert and Pippin [of Vermandois], Charles, who was the son of Louis by Queen Adelaide as we mentioned earlier, was raised to the kingship in the city of Rheims.[425]

---

the ability to act as the main middle-man between the king and regional elites. On Megingoz's relationship to Odo (Regino's word is 'nepos') see Ewig 1980: 181. It is likely that Megingoz brokered Arnulf's recognition of Odo's kingship. His murder sparked off a series of further disputes and political violence in the kingdom (see also below, 896). Alberic was named by Regino as one of Hugh's supporters (above, 883) and belonged to a family with a history of opposition to Megingoz's. The murder is best explained as the result of Megingoz's eclipsing of Alberic's access to royal patronage: see Hlawitschka 1968: 110–13; Althoff 1992: 219–23; Innes 2000: 225–7. Rethel is on the Moselle. 28 August was the anniversary of Louis the German's death; perhaps the murder was planned to coincide with its commemoration for maximum impact.

421 Arn died on 13 July; he had been bishop since 855: see *AF* 855, 871, 872, 884: 37, 66–8, 95. On Poppo see above, 889, n. 386.

422 Adalbert glosses Rudolf's name thus: 'although he was a noble man, he was nonetheless very stupid; he was the brother of Counts Conrad and Gebhard'. On this family, see below, n. 424.

423 Zwentibald received the lay abbacy of St-Maximin at Trier: Innes 2000: 227.

424 Poppo's removal is also reported by *AF*(B) 892: 124. Burchard was an ally of Conrad, and perhaps his kinsman. Along with the grant of the bishopric of Würzburg to his brother Rudolf, this act represented a clear policy decision on Arnulf's part to dispossess the Babenbergers, Poppo's family (which was related to Megingoz's), and install Conrad's: Geldner 1971: 15–20; *AF*(B) 892: 124, n. 9; Innes 2000: 230. Poppo was later restored (D AC 174), though the bad blood created by the events of 892–893 must have been what caused the feud between the families described by Regino below, 897, 902, 903, 906. Conrad and his family thereafter dominated the court circles of Arnulf and Louis the Child: Althoff 1992: 240–63; Innes 2000: 230–3. There is a vast literature on the 'Conradines', much of it concerned with a controversy over their genealogy: see Jackman 1997; Hlawitschka 2003. It is often argued that Arnulf's wife (and Louis's mother) Uota (or Oda) was a Conradine, though for reservations see Reuter 2006a: 220–3.

425 Charles the Straightforward, aged 13, was crowned in opposition to Odo on 28

893

In the year of the Lord's incarnation 893, Arnulf left Bavaria, came to Frankfurt, and after crossing the Rhine he travelled round most of the cities in Lothar's kingdom; during this trip prodigious gifts were given to him by the bishops.[426]

After settling matters in Aquitaine Odo returned to Francia. With the help of his brother Robert he put Charles to flight and pursued the rebels.[427]

While Abbot Ebolus of St-Denis was storming a certain fortress in Aquitaine too eagerly, he died from a blow by a rock.[428] Odo recalled the monastery of St-Denis to his own service.[429]

Charles, who was unable to resist Odo's forces, requested Arnulf's protection as a suppliant. Since it was summer the said king was celebrating a general assembly at the city of Worms.[430] Charles came there and acquired Arnulf's favour with great gifts, and received from his hand the kingdom which he had usurped. The command was also given that the bishops and counts who lived around the Meuse should give him help and after leading him into the kingdom should place him on the royal throne.[431] But neither of these things was of any help to him. When King Odo finally heard about this he set up camp with his army on the bank of the Aisne and completely prevented Arnulf's

---

January 893, the anniversary of Charlemagne's death: Koziol 2006b. *AV* 893: 73–4 names Fulk and Herbert as Charles's main supporters. On Fulk, one of Odo's keenest antagonists, see Schneider 1973; on Herbert and Pippin see above, 818. Regino's cross-reference here is to 878.

426 Arnulf's tour of Lotharingia in the first two months of the year is also mentioned by *AF*(B) 893: 124; DD AC 110–14. Arnulf needed to smooth out the disruption caused by recent events, and to convince the nobility to accept Zwentibald as king: Innes 2000: 227. The ruler's formal circuit of the kingdom became a central institution of politics in east Francia during the tenth century: Müller-Mertens 1999.

427 Odo returned from Aquitaine in late summer 893, forcing Charles to flee. However, he returned in September and the two sides agreed a truce until Easter: *AV* 893: 74.

428 *AV* 892: 73 confirms the manner of Ebolus's death, but places it at the same time as Odo's campaign into Aquitaine in late 892: above, 892.

429 That is to say, he himself became lay abbot, as had Charles the Bald before him: Koziol 2006b: 374.

430 Note Regino's reference to the regularity of Arnulf's itinerary, which took him between the two east Frankish royal heartlands of Bavaria and the middle Rhine: Eibl 1984.

431 *AV* 894: 74–5 says that the men sent by Arnulf to help Charles were 'friends' with Odo. This probably refers to the circles around the late Megingoz, which included the Matfridings: Ewig 1980: 191.

forces from entering the kingdom. The king's generals, realising that Odo had been manfully prepared for battle, turned aside from there and went back to their own lands. Charles withdrew to Burgundy, and when Odo had returned to Paris he once more attacked the realm and pursued Odo's faithful men. And in such a way many died on each side in turn, and prodigious evils, countless acts of rapine and continuous plunder were done.[432]

894

In the year of the Lord's incarnation 894, Arnulf crossed the frontiers of the Lombards with a strong army and around the Purification of the Virgin Mary [2 February] he took by arms the fortress of Bergamo and hanged Ambrose, count of that city, from a certain tree in front of the town gates. Because of this act, such fear fell over the other cities that nobody dared to speak against him, but they all came out to meet him. He then came right up to Piacenza; and from there he crossed the Pennine Alps, entered Gaul and came to St-Maurice [d'Agaune].[433] He was not able to harm Rudolf, whom he was after, because he had gone up to the mountains and was hiding in very secure places. The army did serious damage to the region between the Jura and Mons Iovis [Great St. Bernard].[434]

After this he came to Worms and there held an assembly, desiring to put his son Zwentibald in charge of Lothar's kingdom. However, the leading men of that kingdom showed no consent to his succession.[435] When he came to Lorsch after dissolving the assembly, Arnulf gave Boso's son Louis, on the intervention of his mother Irmingarde, certain cities with their hinterlands which were held by Rudolf. But this was an

---

432 Charles's family relationship with Arnulf is mentioned by *AF*(B) 894: 128 as the basis of their alliance, though it is hard to see this, with Hlawitschka 1968: 115–32, as evidence for a renewed Carolingian family settlement against outsiders. *AV* 894: 74–5 also reports the confrontation across the Aisne, though it attributes the absence of conflict simply to God's mercy. This text also refers obliquely to the blinding of Bishop Theutbold of Langres by a follower of Richard the Justicier, which may also have been connected to the dynastic dispute since Theutbold was a relative of Fulk of Rheims (Flodoard, *Historia*, IV.6: 395).

433 A much longer account of these events is given by *AF*(B) 894: 126–8, which recounts Ambrose's fate and the effects of the victory in terms consistent with Regino's report. On Ambrose and the siege of Bergamo see Hlawitschka 1960a: 123–4; Jarnut 1979.

434 *AF*(B) 894: 128 also mentions that Arnulf forced Rudolf to flee. Cf. above, 888.

435 Regino is the only source for this attempt. However, *AF*(B) 894: 128 suggests that this assembly was the same one at which Arnulf recognised Charles as king of west Francia.

empty grant, because he did not succeed at all in wresting them from Rudolf's control.[436]

In the same year Guy, who ruled Italy and held the name of emperor, died. His son Lambert acquired the kingdom and, coming to Rome, had the imperial diadem conferred on him by the bishop of the apostolic see.[437]

During that same time Hildegard, the daughter of King Louis [the Younger], the brother of Karlmann and Charles [the Fat], having been accused by certain people before Arnulf, was deprived of her royal possessions and thus deprived was sent into exile in the monastery of nuns called Chiemsee. But not long afterward she returned to favour and received back the greater part of her property.[438]

Also around this time Zwentibald king of the Moravian Slavs, a man most prudent among his people and very cunning by nature, ended his final day. His sons held his kingdom for a short and unhappy time, because the Hungarians utterly destroyed everything in it.[439]

895

In the year of the Lord's incarnation 895, a great synod was celebrated at Tribur against the very many laypeople who were trying to diminish episcopal authority. 26 bishops together with the abbots of monasteries gathered there and made strong in writing many decrees concerning

436 On Louis and Irmingarde see above, 877. Again, Regino is the unique source for this story. *AF*(B) 894: 128 reports that Arnulf sent Zwentibald against Rudolf with an army of Alemans, though to no avail. Arnulf had long been a supporter of Louis. It would seem therefore that at this assembly Arnulf (unsuccessfully) attempted to establish the royal credentials of no fewer than three candidates: Zwentibald, Charles and Louis. See Hlawitschka 1968: 125–6.

437 Guy died near Parma and Lambert was raised to the kingship in December 894: Liutprand, *Antapodosis*, I.37: 26 (Wright 1993: 27). *AF*(B) 894: 129 says Guy had a fever and characterizes both him and Lambert as tyrants.

438 This happened in 895. *AF*(B) 895: 129–30 implicitly connects her disgrace (she 'was accused of acting contrary to her fidelity to the king') with the fall of Engildeo, *marchio* of Bavaria, who was replaced by Arnulf's relative Liutpold. D AC 132 (5 May 895) mentions that the pair had unlawfully taken lands from a vassal of the bishop of Eichstätt. See also Reindel 1953: 2–4; Becher 2002: 102–5, 114–16; Reuter 2006a: 221.

439 *AF*(B) 894: 129 is similarly satisfied at Zwentibald's death. His sons, Moimir and Zwentopulk, later engaged in a feud for control that was intimately connected with Bavarian factional politics: *AF*(B) 898, 899: 138–9. *AF*(B) 901: 142 records a Hungarian attack on the Moravians. By 906 the Hungarians, encouraged by the Franks, had effectively destroyed Moravian power: Reuter 1991: 128–9; Bowlus 1995; Dopsch 2002.

the state of the Holy Church.⁴⁴⁰ After this Arnulf came to Worms and there held a public assembly with leading men who came to him from all the kingdoms which were under his command; in this assembly he set his son Zwentibald over the kingdom of Lothar with the consent and praise of all.⁴⁴¹

At the same assembly King Odo came to Arnulf with great gifts, for which reason he was received with honour.⁴⁴² And after he had achieved everything for which he had come and was returning to his own kingdom, his *mansionarii* came across [arch]Bishop Fulk and Count Adalung in the middle of the road, en route to Arnulf with gifts sent by Charles. Odo's men charged at them with a great cry: the bishop slipped away in flight, Adalung was mortally wounded, and their luggage was taken away. The said count was buried in the Trechergau, at the estate [*villa*] called Beltheim.⁴⁴³

In the same year Zwentibald, wishing to extend the boundaries of his kingdom, gathered a huge army, came to Laon and laid siege to the city, as if to bring help to Charles against Odo. But he was not at all able to capture it, although he struggled for many days with great force. On hearing that Odo, who was staying at that time in Aquitaine, was approaching with his army, he withdrew with his whole army and retreated to his own realm.⁴⁴⁴

440 This synod, which discussed a wide variety of topics including marriage law, was one of the greatest Frankish church councils of the ninth century: *AF*(B) 895: 130; Carroll 2002.

441 This event may have been recorded in *AP*. *AF*(B) 895: 130 says that Zwentibald was also made king in Burgundy, presumably against Rudolf. Arnulf had been trying to establish his son in the middle kingdom for some time: see above, 892, 894. The synod of Tribur and the assembly at Worms, both held in May, were clearly connected, and represented part of Arnulf's attempt to consolidate the dynastic constellation: Innes 2000: 227, and see next note. On Zwentibald's reign see Kasten 1997: 547–57; M. Hartmann 2002.

442 Odo's attendance is also mentioned by *AF*(B) 895: 130. According to *AV* 895: 75, Arnulf had summoned both Charles and Odo to attend, but Charles was dissuaded from attending by his own men and sent legates instead. Among Arnulf's motivations may have been a desire to conform to a tradition of shared east and west Frankish involvement in the destiny of the middle kingdom.

443 *AV* 895: 75–6 tells a very similar version of the story, also naming Adalung and Fulk. Beltheim is on the left bank of the Rhine between Bacharach and Koblenz. 'Mansionarii' were officials involved in the provisioning of royal residences. Prüm had landed interests at Beltheim: Schwab 1983: 248.

444 Zwentibald's offer of aid to Charles suggests that his aims diverged somewhat from those of his father, who was apparently on good terms with Odo at this point. *AV* 895: 76 says that Zwentibald's siege of Laon was carried out in response to an invitation from Charles, who offered him part of 'his' kingdom and reminded him of their family relationship. See Hlawitschka 1968: 137–9.

At that time the venerable man Ludelmus was consecrated bishop in the church of Toul by the metropolitan Ratbod [of Trier] and his suffragans.[445]

896

In the year of the Lord's incarnation 896, Arnulf entered Italy for the second time and came to Rome, and with the consent of the supreme pontiff he took the city by force. This had been unheard of in previous centuries, because it had never happened except a single time when, a long time before the birth of Christ, the Galli Senones had done it under their leader Brennus.[446] Lambert's mother, who had been left behind by her son for protection, fled in secret with her men. After entering the city Arnulf was received with great honour by Formosus, the bishop of the apostolic see, and was crowned emperor before the altar of St. Peter. Returning from there, he was troubled by a paralysing illness which weakened him for a long time.[447]

In the same year Guy's son Lambert, of whom we made mention a little earlier, left this life, and Louis the son of Boso left Provence and entered Italy on the invitation of the Lombards.[448]

At that same time around the feast of St Andrew [30 November], Count Alberic, who had killed Megingoz, was murdered by Stephen, the brother of Walaho.[449]

445 Ludelmus's predecessor Arnold died on 4 December 894, so his own accession presumably took place in early 895.

446 Brennus is mentioned in three of Regino's sources: Bede, *DTR*, c. 66: 487 (Wallis 2004: 186); Paul the Deacon, *Historia*, II.23: 101–2 (Foulke 2003: 77–8); Justin, *Epitome*, 24.6–8, 32.3.6: 163–6, 195–6 (Yardley 1994: 188–90, 220). None of them was particularly flattering. Regino overlooks Alaric the Goth, whose sack of Rome he mentioned above, 364–369.

447 According to *AF*(B) 893 and 895: 125–6, 131–2, Formosus was persistent in his attempts to entice Arnulf to Rome. He was evidently no fan of Guy and Lambert, though according to letters recorded by Flodoard, *Historia*, IV.3, 5: 376, 385–6, he was on good terms with the latter – presumably the pope was not averse to playing different rulers against each other. Arnulf's coronation was recorded in *AP* and *AF*(B) 896: 132–5, which offers a detailed account of the king's troubled journey, the resistance mounted by Ageltrude (Lambert's mother), Arnulf's triumphant coronation and the arrangements he made for the government of Italy before illness forced him to leave.

448 Lambert was killed while hunting on 15 October 898. After his death Berengar ruled alone for nearly two years: Louis was only summoned by elements among the aristocracy in September 900: BZ no. 1110.

449 On Alberic and Stephen see above, 883 and 892. Stephen's aim in committing this murder in such a public way (choosing a religious festival for maximum impact)

897

In the year of the Lord's incarnation 897, Counts Stephen, Odacar, Gerard and Matfrid lost the offices and dignities which they had received from the king. Zwentibald came to Trier with his army and divided the lands which these men had held among his own men, reserving for himself the monastery at the grain stores [*ad Horrea*, i.e. Oeren] and the monastery of St-Peter which is in Metz.[450] After this he consulted his father through legates about the wife whom he desired to take. At his urging he sent a representative to Count Otto, asking for his daughter Oda in marriage. Otto happily agreed to Zwentibald's petitions and handed over his daughter to him. He celebrated his wedding after Easter, and united her with him in matrimony.[451]

In that same year Arnulf came to Worms and there held an assembly. Zwentibald came to this meeting and, on the emperor's intervention, Stephen, Gerard and Matfrid were reconciled with his son.[452]

At that time a great dispute of discords and implacable controversy of hatreds arose, from the smallest and most trivial matter, between Bishop Rudolf of Würzburg and the sons of *dux* Henry, namely Adalbert, Adalard and Henry; and, just as a great fire rises from the tiniest spark, so, growing day to day, the dispute expanded to immense proportions. And while they were growing too proud of the nobility of their blood,

---

seems to have been to revenge Megingoz and so lay claim to his political position. At around the same time, Megingoz's widow Gisela married Burchard, Walaho's son and so Stephen's nephew: Wolfhard, *Miracula S. Waldburgis*, III.5: 268–70. For full discussion see Hlawitschka 1968: 110–11, 164; Innes 2000: 228.

450 Zwentibald started to move against the four counts in late 896 (*AF*(B) 897: 137), and his march on Trier took place in late January/early February 897: Hlawitschka 1968: 164, n. 23. Innes 2000: 228–9 sees the conflict as the result of competition between the king and the counts over the legacy of Megingoz; for more detail see Hlawitschka 1968: 164–71. Oeren was a monastery in Trier dedicated to St Mary: D Z 4. On Stephen, Gerard and Matfrid, see above, 883 and 892. Odacar was count in the Bliesgau and the Ardennes, but unlike the others appears not to have been a member of a top-level aristocratic family: Hlawitschka 1968: 166, 168; Nonn 1983: 242.

451 Otto 'the Illustrious', father of the future king Henry I (919–936), was a leading Saxon noble and an ally of Arnulf's great favourite Conrad. The marriage was intended to seal Zwentibald's position in Lotharingia and to help balance the positions of the major aristocratic families in the realm: Hlawitschka 1968: 34; Becher 1996: 169–73; Innes 2000: 228; Becher 2002: 117–18.

452 The reconciliation took place in May 897: *AF*(M) 897: 137. The counts were not restored to all their former properties and offices (Stephen, for instance, seems to have lost the Bidgau), and they were subsequently overshadowed in Zwentibald's regime by count Reginar: Hlawitschka 1968: 170–2. It is presumably no accident that Odacar's name was missing from the list of those reconciled, as he is found in rebellion again below, 898.

the numerous multitude of their relatives and the magnitude of their earthly power, they burst forth in mutual slaughter. A countless number on each side perished by the sword, hands and feet were lopped off, and the regions subjected to them were completely devastated by plunder and burning.[453]

898

In the year of the Lord's incarnation 898, King Odo was struck by an illness and on the third day of January he ended his final day.[454] He was committed to burial with due honour at St-Denis. The leading men gathered as one and by their common counsel and will they made Charles their king.[455]

In the same year Zwentibald, I know not on whose instigation, cast from his side *dux* Reginar, who was his most faithful and only counsellor and, after prohibiting him from the offices and hereditary possessions which he held in his kingdom, he ordered him to leave the realm within 14 days.[456] He joined Count Odacar and certain others to him, and along with their wives and children and all their household possessions entered a certain heavily fortified place called *Durfos*, and there barricaded themselves in.[457] When the king learned of this he

453 On the origins of this feud (often called the 'Babenberger feud' after the main fortress of one of the families involved) see above, 892, n. 424; Becher 1996: 173–81; Innes 2000: 230–1.

454 Regino presumably got this date from *AP*, though other sources say Odo died on 1 January, including *AV* 898: 79.

455 Odo and Charles had struck a deal in 897 by which Charles was promised the succession (Odo was sonless) and received a portion of the kingdom to hold, probably centred on Laon: *AV* 897: 78–9; Koziol 2006b: 371–4.

456 On Reginar 'Longneck', count in the Hennegau and Haspengau, lay abbot of Echternach and sometime partisan of Charles the Straightforward, see *AV* 895, 898: 76, 80; DD Z 7 and 17; Hlawitschka 1968: 172–80, 188–90; Barth 1990: 15–38; Hope 2005: 188–233. His mother was a daughter of Lothar I, he was closely related to Charles the Straightforward by marriage, and later (by 911) he was to become the pre-eminent figure in the Lotharingian aristocracy. Regino's coyness about the instigator of Reginar's fall may be diplomatic since the count's rise to prominence at Zwentibald's court had taken place partly at the expense of Archbishop Ratbod of Trier, Regino's own patron. On their rivalry see Beumann 1966/7 (with commentary by Hlawitschka 1968: 175, n. 60). On the rhetorical accusation of 'unique counsellor', see Bührer-Thierry 1987, and cf. Regino's evaluation of Liutward of Vercelli above, 887.

457 The identification of *Durfos* as either Doveren or Dordrecht in Holland is common, but significant doubts are raised by Hlawitschka 1968: 175, n. 58 and Nonn 1983: 226. *Durfos* was later associated with Reginar's son Giselbert: Flodoard, *Annals*, 931: 48 (Fanning and Bachrach 2004: 20). On Odacar see above, 897, nn. 450, 452.

gathered an army and tried to storm the stronghold, but he had little success because of the marshes and numerous flooded areas which the River Meuse creates in that place.[458] After the king raised the siege the said counts went to Charles and led him into the kingdom with an army. Zwentibald, albeit too late, realised he was surrounded and slipped away in flight with a few men; Charles made straight for Aachen, and then moved on to Nijmegen. Meanwhile Zwentibald went to Bishop Franco[459] and, taking him with him with all his men, crossed the Meuse and came to Flörchingen, where all the leading men of the kingdom who were in those parts flocked to him.[460] Rejoicing that he had recovered his strength after having been in such a desperate situation, he regained his confidence and set out to fight his rival. Charles turned back from Nijmegen and came to Prüm, and from there he sent his forces against Zwentibald.[461] But although the armies approached each other from either side, battle was not joined; peace was established by legates going back and forth and oaths were sworn. Charles crossed the Meuse and returned to his own kingdom.[462]

While this was happening in Francia, there were very many encounters between Louis and Berengar in Italy, and many dangerous struggles followed one after the other. In the end Louis put Berengar to flight and advanced to Rome, where he was crowned by the supreme pontiff and called emperor.[463]

At that time *dux* Eberhard, the son of Meginhard, was treacherously murdered during the hunt by Waltgar the Frisian, the son of Gerulf. The command [*ducatus*] he had held was entrusted by the emperor to his brother Meginhard.[464]

458 The wording here is very similar to that used by Regino to describe the floods of the Don in the Hungarians' homeland: above, 889.
459 Bishop of Liège, 855–901.
460 Flörchingen, near Thionville, was in a heartland of Gerard and Matfrid's power: Hlawitschka 1968: 173. Zwentibald was there in October: D Z 23.
461 This is a tantalizing clue that Regino gave help to Zwentibald's opponents.
462 *AV* 898: 80–1 gives a much briefer account of these events, simply stating that Charles and Zwentibald exchanged embassies before the former returned home 'with the matter still unresolved'. Flörchingen lay in the heartlands of Gerard, Matfrid and Stephen, suggesting that they may have returned to support Zwentibald after the fall of Reginar: Hlawitschka 1968: 173.
463 Louis went to Italy in 900 and was crowned emperor in February 901. Berengar forced him out of the kingdom in summer 902. On Italian politics in this period see Fasoli 1949; Rosenwein 1996.
464 On Eberhard, count of Hamaland, see above, 881 and 885. His 'ducal' title probably refers to a general responsibility for defending the coast against the Vikings: van

899

In the year of the Lord's incarnation 899, Zwentibald held an assembly with the leading men of Arnulf, Charles, and his own men, at St-Goar. Taking part from Arnulf's realm were Archbishop Hatto and the counts Conrad and Gebhard, and from that of Charles Bishop Askericus and Count Odacar. The outcome of the matter afterward showed more clearly to the light what was discussed at that meeting in private and outwith the king's presence.[465]

In that same year Richar was made abbot of the monastery of Prüm. However, I have refrained from recording here the manner in which this was done against me, lest I appear, perhaps exasperated by injustices beyond the limits allowed by Christian patience, to have exaggerated the causes of my persecution; and lest an account of wordy reasoning which is intricate and complicated inspire contempt in my audience. For, as we set out above, we have decided to record the course of events and not to explain their causes in detail by indicating the reasons explicitly. Those of us who strive for brevity in [describing] the affairs of other people must guard against the vice of verbosity in [describing] our own.[466]

Zwentibald came to *Durfos* for a second time with his army and made an effort to conquer the stronghold with all his forces. But when his attempt met with no success, he commanded the bishops to excommunicate Reginar and Odacar and their associates; but when they refused to pass a sentence of anathema, he used threats, accusations and insults, and after the siege was thus lifted, each went back to his homeland.[467]

Winter 1980: 26. Gerulf is mentioned above, 885, as one of the partisans of Godafrid who had been opposed to Eberhard. On Gerulf and Waltgar see Nonn 1983: 62–3, 217. See also Dümmler 1888: 465–6.

465 St-Goar, on the Rhine southeast of Koblenz, was a dependency of Prüm. Hatto was archbishop of Mainz: see above, 891, n. 407. On Conrad see above, 892, n. 424; Gebhard was his brother: they are further discussed below, 902, 903, 906. Askericus was bishop of Paris: see above, 887, and *AV* 886, 887: 62–3. On Odacar, see above, 897, nn. 450, 452. Since Arnulf was very ill by this point (*AF*(B) 899: 139), Hatto, Conrad and Gebhard were probably representing the group of magnates who hoped to influence the prospective regime of the young Louis the Child, and the secret talks were therefore meant to broker a deal for Louis to succeed at Zwentibald's expense: Hlawitschka 1968: 179; *AF*(B) 900: 140, n. 3; Althoff 1992: 65–6; Innes 2000: 229; M Hartmann 2002: 136–7; MacLean forthcoming. *AV* 899: 81 has an oblique reference to Charles making peace with Zwentibald, which probably refers to the St-Goar summit.

466 Cf. above, 892, where Regino (as stressed by Lintzel 1937) expresses rather different sentiments regarding the proper amount of detail.

467 This was probably when Zwentibald hit Archbishop Ratbod of Trier over the head with his own episcopal staff: *AF*(B) 900: 140. For discussion see Hlawitschka 1968: 179. On *Durfos* see above, 898, n. 457.

BOOK II   225

At that time the holy man Odilbald, bishop of the church of Utrecht, was taken from human affairs and crossed to the heavenly kingdom. The venerable Bishop Ratbod was put in his place.[468]

Toward the close of the year Emperor Arnulf left this world on 29 November and was buried with honour in Altötting, where his father also lay entombed.[469]

900

In the year of the Lord's incarnation 900, the magnates and leading men who had obeyed Arnulf gathered as one at Forchheim and made Louis, his son by a legitimate marriage, into their king; and when he was crowned and had assumed the royal trappings they raised him to the pinnacle of the kingdom.[470]

While this was going on in Germany, an irreconcilable conflict rose up between Zwentibald and the magnates of the kingdom because of the continuous plundering and pillaging being carried out in the realm; and because by running the affairs of the realm with women and the lesser-born he was deposing all the more honourable and noble people whom he kept stripping of offices and dignities. For this reason he became hated by everyone.[471] Therefore they eagerly went over to Louis, brought him into the realm, and at the residence of Thionville they subjected themselves to his authority by giving their hands. While Louis was going across the Rhine, Zwentibald, when he had gathered together whomever he could, went round the cities of the kingdom and destroyed everything with fire and plunder, believing that he could win back those people who had abandoned him on account of his prodigious malice and arrogance even while he was doing things that were even more brutal and wicked.[472] Louis was summoned into the kingdom again, and Zwentibald was killed in battle by Counts Stephen, Gerard

468 Odilbald had been bishop since 870 and Ratbod died in 917. Ratbod of Utrecht was a relative of Gunther of Cologne: M Hartmann 2002: 139–40.
469 Regino's source for the date was probably *AP*. In fact, Arnulf died on 8 December and was buried at St-Emmeram in Regensburg: *AF*(B) 900: 140; BM 1955b; Fuchs 2002. Given his interest in marital affairs, it is surprising that Regino does not mention the accusations made against Arnulf's wife Uota: *AF*(B) 899: 138–9; Reuter 2006a.
470 This took place on 4 February. *AF*(B) 900: 140 stresses the legitimacy of Louis's birth.
471 *AF*(B) 900: 140 also refers to Zwentibald's cruelty and the opposition it inspired.
472 Regino describes Zwentibald's tour of the kingdom as an inversion of Arnulf's regal circuit: see above, 893.

and Matfrid on 13 August near the Meuse. In that same year Count Gerard took to himself in marriage Oda, Zwentibald's wife.[473]

901

In the year of the Lord's incarnation 901, the Hungarian people entered the lands of the Lombards and savagely destroyed everything with murder, fire and plunder. When the inhabitants of that land endeavoured to resist their violence and their bestial frenzy in a concerted group, a countless number perished from arrow strikes, and very many bishops and counts were slaughtered.[474] When Liutward, bishop of the church of Vercelli and formerly the closest friend and private counsellor to Emperor Charles [the Fat], had taken with him his wealth and incomparable treasure, in which he abounded beyond all estimation, and strove with it to escape their bloodthirsty ferocity, he happened upon them unaware and was soon killed; the wealth which he carried with him was plundered.[475]

In the same year Count Stephen, the brother of Walaho, was sitting on the toilet clearing his bowels one night when he was seriously wounded by a poisoned arrow fired by someone through the window of the room. He died of his wound that same night.[476]

902

In the year of the Lord's incarnation 902, Adalbert along with his brothers Adalard and Henry gathered a strong force and, pouring out of the fortress called Babenberg, they set out to wage war against the brothers Eberhard, Gebhard and Rudolf, of whom we made mention a little earlier.[477] They courageously fought off the attack, charged into their battle-lines with their swords, struck down everyone who got in

---

473 The date of Zwentibald's death was recorded in the *AP*. Regino's is the most detailed account of this event; cf. *AF*(B) 900: 140. The *AF* has no further notices on Lotharingian events, and stops completely in 901. On Zwentibald's fate see Hlawitschka 1968: 179–84; Ewig 1980: 195–200; Innes 2000: 229; M Hartmann 2002: 137–42. On Stephen, Gerard and Matfrid see above, 883, 892, 896.

474 This presumably refers to Berengar's battle with the Hungarians on 24 September 899: *AF*(B) 900: 140–1; Liutprand, *Antapodosis*, II.13–15: 40–2 (Wright 1993: 43–4).

475 Regino is the sole source for this story, which is cast as a parable about wealth. On Liutward see above, 887.

476 On Stephen see also above, 883, 896, 900.

477 See above, 892, 897, 899.

their way and did not stop until they had forced their enemies' troops to take flight. In this battle Henry was killed and Adalard was taken prisoner, and after a while he was beheaded on the orders of Gebhard. Eberhard too had fallen in battle punctured by many wounds. When the fighting had stopped he was found by his men among the dead bodies and carried home, where after a few days he too died.[478]

903

In the year of the Lord's incarnation 903, Adalbert forced Bishop Rudolf to flee from the church of Würzburg and most barbarously destroyed the church's properties and possessions. He also forced the sons of Eberhard together with their mother to leave their own hereditary lands and the offices they held by royal permission, and compelled them to withdraw beyond the Spessart.[479]

Around this time Archbishop Fulk of Rheims was murdered by a certain Winemarus, a member of Count Baldwin's entourage.[480] The cause of this killing is remembered to have been as follows. The said Baldwin invaded the fortress of Arras, that is to say the abbey of St-Vaast, which had not been given to him by anyone. King Charles took it away from him and awarded it to [arch]Bishop Fulk as a benefice. Baldwin took this badly and sent Winemarus to the aforementioned bishop, requesting that he would not, led by greed, usurp the offices which hitherto he himself had held and possessed. In addition he offered him prodigious gifts if by his help and intervention Baldwin could obtain the possessions concerned. But when the bishop did not agree, and replied with something more harsh and bitter than he ought to have, Winemarus was inflamed at the devil's instigation to a great rage and, after leaving Fulk, he entered a certain wood with his men. When Fulk was returning from seeing the king at the palace of Compiègne, he fell

---

478 On the feud between the Babenberger and the Conradines, see above, 897, n. 453; Becher 1996: 173–81; Innes 2000: 230–1.

479 The plundering of Würzburg's properties is also mentioned in D LC 23 (9 July 903), in which Louis the Child compensated the church with estates confiscated from Adalbert and Henry. The properties granted were in Conrad's county and the charter was issued at the Babenberger stronghold of Theres, both of which helped drive the point home. Rudolf's brother Gebhard was given the exalted title '*dux regni Hlotharii*' in another royal charter issued only weeks earlier at an assembly where the magnates met to organise resistance to the Babenberger: D LC 20. The timing of this acknowledgement of his pre-eminence in the middle kingdom is telling, but the nature of his supremacy was fluid and not constitutionally defined. See now Hope 2005: 217–19.

480 Fulk died on 16 June 900. Baldwin II was count of Flanders (879–918).

on him and butchered him without delay. Heriveus was raised up to the see of Rheims, and along with many other bishops he excommunicated this Winemarus and condemned him to eternal anathema for such an unheard-of crime.[481]

905[482]

In the year of the Lord's incarnation 905, Boso's son Louis, whom we mentioned above had been given the name of emperor, expelled Berengar from Italy and subjected the whole of that kingdom to his authority.[483] Realising moreover that there was nobody who could or would dare to resist him, he misguidedly took his security for granted and began to think of peace and rest. Therefore he dissolved his army and went with a very few men to Verona at the urging of Adalard, bishop of the town. With the greatest speed, however, the townspeople sent word of this to Berengar, who was in exile in Bavaria at this time.[484] Without waiting he gathered forces from all sides, came to Verona, treacherously seized the unwary man and in captivity deprived him of his eyes. For the townspeople who supported his faction opened up the city gates to him and received him within the walls at night. And thus, unexpectedly and without premeditation, Louis was deprived not only of his kingdom, but also his sight. And so at last Berengar acquired the kingdom of Italy, bloodstained by many slaughters, sought for a long time by disastrous and unfortunate battles, with this sort of triumph.[485] In that same year in the month of May a comet appeared, and this change in the kingdom happened in August.[486]

906

In the year of the Lord's incarnation 906, Count Conrad sent his son Conrad with a considerable force of armed men to attack Gerard and his brother Matfrid, because they had violently seized his offices and those of his brother Gebhard by taking possession of St-Maximin and

481 A similar but more detailed account is given by *AV* 899: 81–2. This is the *AV*'s final entry.
482 There is no entry for 904.
483 See above, 898.
484 Verona was Berengar's main stronghold.
485 Regino's tone here seems sarcastic.
486 On these events, which indeed took place in August 905, see also Liutprand, *Antapodosis*, II.35–41: 50–2 (Wright 1993: 52–4).

St-Mary at Oeren.[487] An army from Lothar's kingdom joined them. They came as far as the Bliesgau, destroying the hereditary lands and possessions of the said brothers and their followers with plunder and burning. Then Gerard and Matfrid petitioned for peace, sending a legation from the fortress in which they had barricaded themselves. After this request had been granted until the octave of Easter through the swearing of mutual oaths, the army returned home.[488]

While this was going on in Lothar's kingdom, the elder Conrad was in Hesse in the place called Fritzlar with a great crowd of foot- and mounted soldiers, mistrusting Adalbert's constant raiding.[489] Meanwhile his brother Gebhard was in the Wetterau with everyone whom he could gather to him, ready for a surprise attack by the same Adalbert.[490] The way things turned out showed that they were completely right. Since Adalbert knew that the forces of his enemies were stretched, because they were divided into three parts, he rejoiced that a long-awaited opportunity had arrived and, after his men had been gathered, he soon took up arms. At first he made as if he wanted to send his forces against Gebhard, so that he would both frighten him with the prospect of war and make his brother feel more secure. Then, as quickly as he could, he directed the army toward Conrad. When Conrad realised this too late, he divided his men into three troops and without hesitation went out to meet him. And when battle was joined two of the divisions, one of foot-soldiers and the other of Saxons, immediately turned and fled, though Conrad exhorted them in vain with a great yell that they should never yield to the enemy and should fight with all their might for the safety of their wives and children and the defence of the homeland. He himself, inspiring his men, charged the enemy with the third group, but soon in that very first assault he was punctured with many wounds and killed. Adalbert had the victory and with his men chased those who were

---

487 On Oeren's name see above, 897. These key Trier institutions had supported the power of Megingoz and then Zwentibald: Innes 2000: 229. Gerard and Matfrid had established themselves as prominent figures with the marriage of the former to Zwentibald's widow: above, 900, and Hlawitschka 1968: 188–9. For the Matfridings at St-Maximin see Nightingale 2001: 196. For Gebhard's dominant position in Lotharingia see above, 903, n. 479.

488 For commentary see Hlawitschka 1968: 191, suggesting that the fortress in question was Blieskastel.

489 Regino refers to the 'elder' Conrad (brother of Rudolf, Eberhard and Gebhard) to distinguish him from his own son Conrad (later King Conrad I, 911–18).

490 The Wetterau is north of Würzburg, the city whose bishopric was claimed by both the Conradines and the Babenberger. The count in the Wetterau was Gebhard: D LC 71.

fleeing, putting to the sword a countless multitude, most of them on foot.[491] Thus he traversed that whole region for three consecutive days, destroying everything with slaughter and pillage. With these things accomplished, he returned to the fortress of Babenberg with his men loaded down with booty and prodigious plunder. This massacre took place on 27 February. The sons who came with their mother took up Conrad's corpse and entombed it in the stronghold called Weilburg.[492]

In the same year, around the month of July, King Louis celebrated a general assembly at the royal estate of Tribur.[493] He ordered the oft-mentioned Adalbert to attend, so that in the presence of the great men of the kingdom he could explain himself and, setting aside his tyrannical cruelty, finally undertake to live in a condition of peace, which up to now he had regarded as hateful; and at least, though it was a bit late in the day, stop murdering, pillaging and burning. But he showed absolutely no compliance with these salutary admonitions. Thus the king, observing that his heart was stubborn and fixed on the wickedness of the rebellion that he had started, gathered an army from all sides and besieged him in the fortress which is called Theres.[494]

In the meantime Egino, who had been his inseparable companion in every depravity, defected from his alliance and crossed to the king's camp with all his men.[495] When the siege had therefore been dragged out a little bit longer, since Adalbert's spirit had been broken, he resorted to sneaky tricks and with all his ingenuity began to ponder by what stratagem he could get the siege lifted so that, after he had gained his longed-for liberty through the army's departure, he along with his partisans could spread far and wide the treachery he was nurturing in his heart.[496] So, after the gates were opened, he left the fortification with a few men and voluntarily presented himself before the king; as a suppliant he begged pardon for the things he had done, and promised to

---

491 The danger of flight without horses was one reason why Arnulf was apparently quite reluctant to tell his men to fight on foot at the battle of the Dyle: above, 891, and Halsall 2003: 187–8.

492 Conrad's sons were Conrad and Eberhard. Weilburg was a central place for the Conradines and King Conrad I later fostered the growth of a monastery there.

493 He issued D LC 46 there at the end of June.

494 Theres was on the River Main, and lay in the heart of Babenberger territory. *AA* 905, 906 records 2 separate attacks on Adalbert.

495 Egino was a count with close links to the monastery of Fulda; he died in 908 fighting the Hungarians alongside the Conradine bishop Rudolf and *dux* Burchard of Thuringia: Althoff 1992: 66, 270–2.

496 Regino's language here recalls his description of Adalgis's treachery: above, 871.

BOOK II

make amends. But when the deception he had contrived was revealed by the betrayal of his own men, he was taken into custody and led into the presence of the whole army with his hands tied. By the judgement of everyone he received capital punishment on 9 September. His resources and possessions were given over to the fisc, and by the king's gift they were distributed among some more noble men.[497]

After thus setting in order matters in east Francia, the king came to Metz and at a public assembly there condemned Gerard and Matfrid to confiscation [of property].[498] After leaving there he went to the town of Strasbourg, and there he reconciled the bishop and the people, who were fighting among themselves. And so crossing the Rhine he made straight for Alemannia.

At that time the bishops Baltram of Strasbourg and Ludelm of Toul left this world; they were succeeded on their episcopal thrones by Otbert in Strasbourg and Drogo in Toul.[499]

HERE ENDS THE CHRONICLE OF ABBOT REGINO.[500]

---

497 Some of Adalbert's property had been redistributed in 903: see above, 903, n. 479. Archbishop Hatto of Mainz and the defector Egino were among those who benefited: D LC 60 (8 June 908). Later sources are much more flattering about Adalbert than was Regino: BM 2037a.

498 DD LC 49–50 were issued there in October. D LC 51 (4 November 906) grants some of Matfrid's properties to St-Cyriacus, a dependency of the bishopric of Worms; and D LC 57 (18 January 908) confirms some of Gerard's ('former count') in the hands of Bishop Stephen of Liège, described as his relative. Eberhard, Conrad the Elder's son, became lay abbot of St-Maximin in Trier sometime before 909: MUB nos 153–4; Hlawitschka 1968: 191. The facts that Gerard probably died alongside Gebhard while fighting the Hungarians in 910, and that Matfrid was called count in a charter of 911, suggest that they were eventually reconciled with the Conradines and the king, though in reduced circumstances: Hlawitschka 1968: 191–2 with n. 21.

499 Baltram died on 12 April, Ludelm on 11 September.

500 This explicit is only in Kurze's B manuscripts. This suggests that Regino himself wrote it and that Adalbert left it out when writing his continuation.

ADALBERT'S CONTINUATION

Thus far Regino. That which follows, we have added.

907

The Bavarians fought the Hungarians, and many were cut down with a great slaughter. In this battle *dux* Liutpold [of Bavaria] was killed. His son Arnulf succeeded him in the command [*ducatus*].[1]

908

The Hungarians came across the frontiers again, and devastated Saxony and Thuringia.[2]

909

The Hungarians entered Alemannia.[3]

910

The Franks fought the Hungarians on the frontier between Bavaria and Francia, and pitiably they either fled or were defeated. In this battle Count Gebhard [of Lotharingia] died, leaving behind his two sons Udo and Hermann. They were still children, and later became famous nobles in Francia.[4]

---

1 The Battle of Bratislava (Preßburg) was a major defeat and claimed the lives of several leading aristocrats: Reuter 1991: 129–30; Bowlus 2006: 83–4. On its significance see Hiestand 1994. On Arnulf see Airlie 2000. Adalbert's sources here were versions of *AnnAug* 907: 68 and *AL* 908: 54.

2 Based on *AnnAug* 908: 68. Several leading aristocrats were killed in this raid, including Bishop Rudolf of Würzburg (see above, 897, 902, 903), count Egino (above, 906), and *dux* Burchard of Thuringia (above, 892): BM 2052a.

3 Based on *AnnAug* 909: 68. They were engaged by *dux* Arnulf on their way back through Bavaria: Reindel 1953: 93–4; Bowlus 2006: 84.

4 Liutprand, *Antapodosis*, II.3–4: 35–7 (Wright 1993: 37–9) attributes the Hungarians' victory to their successful execution of a feigned retreat. See Reuter 1991: 129; Bowlus 2006: 85 and, on the Hungarians' fondness for this tactic, above, 889. *AL*

911

King Louis [the Child], son of the emperor Arnulf, died.⁵ Conrad, son of the Conrad killed by Adalbert, succeeded to the kingdom because the royal line had now failed.⁶

912

Once again the Hungarians ravaged Francia and Thuringia without resistance. Archbishop Hatto [of Mainz] died, a man of great vigour and intelligence, and he was succeeded by Heriger.⁷ Otto *dux* of the Saxons died.⁸

913

Winter was very harsh. The Hungarians laid waste to areas of Alemannia and they were cut down by the Bavarians and Alemans next to the River Inn.⁹

In the same year Einhard the bishop of Speyer was blinded by Counts Bernard and Conrad.¹⁰

910: 54–5, one of Adalbert's sources (the other being *AnnAug* 910: 68), distinguishes two separate engagements. Adalbert generally uses 'Francia' to refer to Franconia, the region focused on the middle Rhine valley. On Gebhard see above, 906. Udo (d. 949) was count of the Rheingau and Wetterau and married a daughter of count Herbert of Vermandois, while Hermann (d. 949) was made *dux* of Alemannia by Henry I after marrying the widow of the former *dux* Burchard in 926. See Reuter 1991: 141–2; Althoff 1992: 241–5, 254–6. This entry makes it clear that Adalbert is writing with hindsight.

5 Based on *ASGM* 911: 77. Louis died on 24 September, aged 18.

6 Adalbert's cross-reference to the death of Conrad the Elder (above, 906) suggests that he saw his text as a seamless continuation of Regino's. His reference to the failing of the royal line, one of Regino's main themes, points in the same direction: Airlie 2006a: 110–11. On Conrad I's reign see Goetz 1980; Reuter 1991: 126–37; Goetz 2006.

7 Adalbert's main source here was probably *AL* 926 (912): 55. On Hatto, see above 891, 899.

8 Otto died on 30 November 912: he was the father of Henry I, the first king of the Ottonian dynasty. On Otto see Reuter 1991: 130–1 and above, 897, n. 451.

9 Taken directly from *AnnAug* 913: 68 which, however, places the Hungarian raid before the bad winter. The Bavarians seem to have realised that the Hungarians were easier to defeat when they were withdrawing from their raids, laden with booty: Bowlus 2006: 85. *ASGM* 913: 77 claims that all but 30 of them were slaughtered. This source also credits the Alemans Erchangar, Bertold and Udalrich with the victory, along with Arnulf of Bavaria: Adalbert's omission of this information may be a result of these men's subsequent disgrace (see below, 917).

10 Einhard was bishop by 903 and died in 918. On the basis of variants in the way

Otbert bishop of Strasbourg was killed.[11]

914

Bishop Salomon [of Constance] was taken prisoner.[12]

915

The Hungarians laid waste the whole of Alemannia with fire and sword; indeed, they overran the whole of Thuringia and Saxony and came as far as the monastery of Fulda.[13]

916

[no entry]

917

The Hungarians came through Alemannia to Alsace as far as the borders of the Lotharingian kingdom. Erchangar and Bertold were beheaded. Arnulf *dux* of the Bavarians rebelled against the king.[14]

---

his name is spelled by the manuscripts, Bernard is probably to be identified with Werner, count in the Wormsgau and Speyergau. Conrad may have been Conrad 'Kurzbold', son of the Eberhard killed in 902 and Werner's brother-in-law: Jackman 1997: 72–4, 171. The case was discussed in 916 at the Synod of Hohenaltheim, which instructed Bishop Richgowo of Worms to investigate and bring the guilty parties to justice: Fuhrmann 1987, c. 31: 35.

11 This information is from *ASGM* 913: 77. The appointment of Otbert's successor became a focus for competition between Conrad I and Charles the Straightforward: Bührer-Thierry 1997: 192–6.

12 Based on *ASGM* 914: 77. Salomon III's succession was mentioned above, 890. He was taken captive by the Alemannian counts of the palace Erchangar and Bertold, who were brothers. Their sister Cunigunde was married to Liutpold of Bavaria, whose son, *dux* Arnulf of Bavaria, was therefore their nephew. After Liutpold's death at Bratislava in 907, Cunigunde married Conrad I himself. The precise circumstances of the counts' dispute with Salomon is not clear, but was probably connected with the struggle for power in Alemannia between the families of Erchangar and the *dux* Burchard who had been executed in 911: Reuter 1991: 131. The outcome was that Conrad exiled Erchangar and invaded Arnulf's Bavaria. See Borgolte 1984: 205–7; Borgolte 1986: 81–2, 85–7, 110–11; Althoff 1992: 329–38.

13 Adalbert's account of the raid on Alemannia is from *AnnAug* 915: 68. Following Conrad's invasion of Bavaria, Arnulf found sanctuary among the Hungarians, with whom he subsequently kept an alliance: Bowlus 2006: 85–6.

14 The first two sentences are from *AnnAug* 917: 68; the third is similar to *AA* 917: 56. On Erchangar and Bertold see above, 914, n. 12. Erchangar had returned from exile in 915, defeated his rivals in battle and was elected *dux*: *AA* 915: 56; Reuter 1991: 131. He and Bertold were then condemned to lifelong penance at the Synod

918

King Conrad celebrated the nativity of St John [the Baptist, 24 June] at the monastery of Hersfeld.[15]

919

King Conrad died.[16] He was in everything a mild and judicious man, and a lover of divine religion. When he sensed the day of his death was at hand, he called to his side his brothers and kinsmen, that is the great men of the Franks; he foretold that death was close to him and admonished them in a paternal voice that in choosing his successor there should be no division in the kingdom.[17] But he also urged them to choose Henry *dux* of the Saxons, the son of Otto, who was a vigorous and determined man and a most distinguished adherent of peace. Since he attested that no other man could be found who was as suitable for this office, he transmitted to him, through them, the sceptre and the crown and the other ornaments of royal dignity, in return for an assurance about the protection and preservation of the kingdom. He himself, though, withdrew from this life and was buried in a fitting grave in the monastery of Fulda. In the few years that he reigned, he was tired out by his many labours, because the Bavarians, Alemans and Saxons kept rebelling against him; but with God's favour he overcame them before his death.[18]

---

of Hohenaltheim in 916: Fuhrmann 1987, c. 21: 29. *AA* adds that a certain Liutfrid was also beheaded in 917. In common with all the pro-Ottonian histories of the period, Adalbert characterises Arnulf as a rebel, when in fact he may well have been regarded as a quasi-regal figure, or even as a king, in Bavaria: Reuter 1991: 130; Airlie 2000. Tension between Conrad and Arnulf had been escalated by the former's marriage to the latter's mother and his attempts to intervene directly in Bavaria: Hiestand 1994: 16–17. Adalbert uses the term 'regnum Lothariense' for Lotharingia rather than the 'regnum Lotharii' found in most ninth-century sources including Regino: see Anton 1993 for a discussion of terminology.

15 Hersfeld is in Thuringia, north of Fulda.

16 Adalbert got Conrad's death notice from *AnnAug* 919: 68. In fact, he died on 23 December 918. According to Widukind, *RGS*, I.25: 37, Conrad was mortally wounded on campaign against Arnulf.

17 'Discidium regni', which could be (and often is) translated as 'division of the kingdom'. However, the context suggests that Adalbert was referring to general disharmony in the political community rather than paraphrasing a principled statement about territorial indivisibility.

18 Similar accounts of Conrad's deathbed request are offered by Widukind, *RGS*, I.25: 37–8; Liutprand, *Antapodosis*, II.20: 43–4 (Wright 1993: 45–6); Thietmar, *Chronicon*, I.8: 72–3 (which is based on Widukind). Hauck 1974 argued that Adalbert's account was based on Liutprand's (they met at Otto I's court: see below, 965). Frase 1990:

920

Dux Henry was chosen as king with the consent of the Franks, Alemans, Bavarians, Thuringians and Saxons.[19] He entered upon his reign by training [people] to keep the peace. For at that time many men, even nobles, were intent on brigandage.[20]

921

In upper [west] Francia serious civil discord seethed between Robert, who was a usurper of the kingdom, and King Charles [the Straightforward].[21]

Meanwhile King Henry strongly persisted in stabilising peace and restraining the savagery of the Slavs.[22]

922

At Soissons, so great a battle took place between Robert and Charles that it almost seemed as if both sides had won. But Charles drove his lance so hard into Robert's sacrilegious mouth that it split his tongue and came out the back of his neck.[23]

51–6 contends that the similarities identified by Hauck are too general to convince; and Fried 1995 draws into question the veracity of all the accounts by invoking a process of fictionalisation through oral transmission. Meanwhile, Althoff 2000: 29–46 advocates accepting the sources as plausible. Buc 2004 summarises the debate and makes a strong case that a literary source (the account of Charles the Fat's deathbed in the 'Panegyric of Berengar', c. 915) was the ultimate model for the accounts of both Liutprand and Adalbert. See also Bagge 2002: 30–43.

19 May 919, in Fritzlar. Widukind, *RGS*, I.26: 39 famously says that he rejected the offer of royal anointing: see Weiler 2000. Adalbert overstates the extent of Henry's support: the Alemans and Bavarians are not known to have attended, and the latter elected Arnulf as a king at around this time: Reuter 1991: 137–40; Airlie 2000; Deutinger 2002. Widukind attributes the new king's election only to the Franks and Saxons.

20 Adalbert may refer to Henry's policy of founding his authority on horizontal bonds of 'amicitia' (friendship) as opposed to Conrad I's more authoritarian style: Reuter 1991: 141–2; Althoff 1992; Althoff 2004. The rhetoric of brigandage and peace was an important component of royal ideology in this period: Reuter 2006b.

21 Robert, the brother of Odo (king 888–898) and son of Robert the Strong, had been made king on 29 June 922. The tension between him and Charles is described by Flodoard, *Annals*, 920, 921: 2–6 (Fanning and Bachrach 2004: 3–7). For discussion see Felten 1996; Koziol 2006a; Koziol 2006b.

22 Henry consistently attempted to impose overlordship on the Slavs: Reuter 1991: 143–4.

23 The battle took place on 15 June 923. Flodoard, *Annals*, 923: 13–14 (Fanning and Bachrach 2004: 8) says that Charles fled in defeat despite Robert's death.

923

The most precious treasure of the Lord's blood came to Reichenau on 8 November.[24]

Haicho the abbot of Fulda died, and Hildebert succeeded him.

Charles [the Straightforward] wanted to usurp for himself Alsace and that part of Francia next to the Rhine as far as Mainz, so he advanced with hostile intent as far as the estate of Pfeddersheim by Worms. From there, since King Henry's faithful men had gathered at Worms, he fled in a manner not fitting for a king.[25]

In the same year King Henry joined to himself Archbishop Roger and *dux* Giselbert to besiege the town of Metz; and he forced Witgar, who had long resisted, to obey him.[26]

The very holy man Hermann, [arch]bishop of Cologne, died, and Wigfrid succeeded him.[27]

924

The Hungarians laid waste to eastern Francia.

Kings Charles and Henry met at the fortress of Bonn and, making peace between them, entered into a treaty; and Charles withdrew, never again to usurp for himself the Lotharingian kingdom.[28]

---

24 Taken from *AnnAug* 923: 68.

25 These events belong to 920: Flodoard, *Annals*, 920: 3 (Fanning and Bachrach 2004: 4). Charles's attempt to claim the areas of the eastern kingdom that lay west of the Rhine was characteristic of a period in which various parties sought to gain footholds on the peripheries of Henry's influence.

26 Roger was archbishop of Trier (915–30) and Witgar (in some sources Wigeric) was bishop of Metz (917–27). Giselbert was son of Reginar 'Longneck' (see above, 898, 899) and the leading Lotharingian magnate. In 920 he seemingly planned to set himself up as an independent ruler: Hlawitschka 1968: 203–4; Reuter 1991: 140–1. The events described here relate to the aftermath of Robert's death; his erstwhile supporters, including Roger and Giselbert, called Henry into the middle kingdom to resist the claims of Raoul of Burgundy, who had been elected king after the battle of Soissons: Flodoard, *Annals*, 923: 18 (Fanning and Bachrach 2004: 10); Hlawitschka 1968: 205.

27 Hermann died 11 April 924.

28 Adalbert's chronology is out: the Treaty of Bonn, by which Henry and Charles swore mutual friendship and recognized each other's kingdoms, was sealed on 7 November 921 on a ship on the Rhine. See MGH Constitutiones, vol. 1, no. 1; Flodoard, *Annals*, 921: 6 (Fanning and Bachrach 2004: 5); Althoff 1992: 23–5.

In the same year he was captured by Herbert and imprisoned.[29]

925

While King Henry was holding the unified and stabilised Lotharingian kingdom in his own power, King Charles died in the prison where he was held.[30] It is said that he was a man of dull character, and ill-suited to the usefulness of the kingdom. Everyone also defected from his son, seeing as he had gone into exile in Ireland when his father was imprisoned, and chose a certain Raoul to be king over them.[31]

In the same year Bishop Witgar died and Benno, who had formerly led the life of a hermit in the Alps, was chosen to be his successor from among those who were in orders in Strasbourg.[32]

926

The Hungarians laid waste to the whole of Francia, Alsace, Gaul and Alemannia with fire and sword. Burchard *dux* of Alemannia was killed in Italy.[33]

Heriger [of Mainz], a bishop worthy of God, died and Hildebert the abbot of Fulda succeeded him.[34]

29 In fact, this took place in 923: Flodoard, *Annals*, 923: 14–15 (Fanning and Bachrach 2004: 8). Herbert II was count of Vermandois: see Werner 1984; Schwager 1994. He was the leader of the party which had asked Raoul to take the throne after the battle of Soissons; he was directly descended from Louis the Pious (see above, 818) and in the 920s was one of the most powerful men in west Francia.

30 In fact, Charles died in 929. By telescoping and juxtaposing the Treaty of Bonn and Charles's capture and death, Adalbert reinforces the impression that the fate of Lotharingia was definitively settled in favour of the eastern kings. Flodoard, *Annals*, 925: 33 (Fanning and Bachrach 2004: 15) says that toward the end of the year 'all the Lotharingians committed themselves to Henry'.

31 Charles's son, still an infant at the time of his capture, was the later Louis IV (936–54), nicknamed d'Outremer; he went into exile in England, not Ireland. Louis's mother Eadgifu was a daughter of Edward the Elder (899–924) and a sister of Athelstan (924–39), kings of Wessex. Raoul, or Rudolf (this is what Adalbert calls him), was *dux* of Burgundy, and had been made king at Soissons in July 923.

32 The bishopric in question was Metz: see also 923, 927.

33 All this was taken from *AnnAug* 926: 68, though Adalbert inserts the words 'in Italy'. Hungarian depredations in the west are recorded by Flodoard, *Annals*, 926: 34 (Fanning and Bachrach 2004: 15). Henry sealed a nine-year truce with the Hungarians around this time: Reuter 1991: 143. Henry had attacked Burchard ('bellator intolerabilis') early in his reign and gained his submission: Widukind, *RGS*, I.27: 39–40. He died while supporting an expedition for the Italian crown mounted by Rudolf II of Burgundy, his son-in-law: Liutprand, *Antapodosis*, II.60, III.13–15: 59, 73–4 (Wright 1993: 60, 76–7). On Burchard see Althoff 1992: 273–8.

34 December 927.

The *ducatus* of Alemannia was entrusted to Hermann, who took Burchard's widow as his wife.[35]

927

Benno, who was also called Bishop Benedict, was blinded by the people of Metz. A synod was held at Duisburg and there all the perpetrators of this deed were excommunicated; and the noble Adalbero was installed as bishop in his place.[36]

928

King Henry attacked the Bohemians with hostile intent and with God's aid he courageously conquered them.[37] At that time a son named William was born to the same king's son Otto.[38]

Winter was very harsh.[39]

Roger archbishop of Trier died, and Robert succeeded him.[40]

929

Dux Giselbert took King Henry's daughter Gerberga as his wife.[41]

---

35 Hermann was a cousin of Eberhard of Franconia, and hence a Conradine. He was therefore an outsider in Alemannia, and the marriage was intended to boost his legitimacy. This shows that Henry was to some extent able to treat the office of *dux* as a royal office: Reuter 1991: 141–2. The grant was made at a major assembly at Worms in November 926: BO no. 13a.

36 Little else is known about the synod of Duisburg: Hehl 1987, no. 6; Bührer-Thierry 1997: 75. Flodoard, *Annals*, 927, 928, 929: 37, 43–4 (Fanning and Bachrach 2004: 16, 18) reveals that Benno had been given the bishopric by Henry although another candidate was elected by the people, that he was castrated as well as blinded, and that he was given an abbey in compensation.

37 The re-establishment of Saxon hegemony over the Bohemians in 929 was a high-point of Henry's eastern campaigns: Widukind, *RGS*, I.35: 50–1; Reuter 1991: 144.

38 William, an illegitimate son, became archbishop of Mainz in 955 and had a material influence on Adalbert's career: see below, 961, 962.

39 *AnnAug* 927: 68.

40 Robert succeeded in 931.

41 Probably 928. The marriage helped seal a bond of friendship between Henry and Giselbert, who was referred to henceforth as *dux* of Lotharingia. On Giselbert and Gerberga see Hlawitschka 1960b; Schmid 1960; Althoff 1992: 235–9; Le Jan 2001a.

930

King Henry's son Otto took as his wife Edith, the daughter of the king of the English.[42]

931

King Henry made the king of the Abodrites and the king of the Danes into Christians.[43]

In the same year the king was summoned to Francia by Eberhard and the other counts and bishops of Francia; and by each of them in turn, in their residences and the seats of their churches, he was honoured with feasts and gifts that befitted a king.[44]

932

The Hungarians, after destroying many cities in eastern Francia and Alemannia with fire and sword and crossing the Rhine next to Worms, devastated Gaul as far as the ocean before returning through Italy.[45]

934

King Henry cut the Hungarians down with a great slaughter, and took even more prisoner.[46]

42 Edith was a daughter of Edward the Elder (899–924) and sister of Athelstan (924–939), kings of Wessex. Her marriage to Otto is recorded in numerous sources; for discussion of these see above all Leyser 1994a.

43 *AnnAug* 931: 69. Similar claims are made (about the Danes) by Widukind, *RGS*, I.40: 59; Liutprand, *Antapodosis*, III.21, 48: 76, 93 (Wright 1993: 78, 93–4).

44 This refers to Henry's visit of 930: he was at Frankfurt in April and Aachen in June (DD HI 22–3). Henry's willingness to venture out of Saxony to meet these powerful men on their home patch underlines that his regime was built on relatively horizontal bonds of friendship that constructed his royal persona as a kind of first among equals. This tour helped underline Henry's claims to royal status on these terms, and may also have been the occasion for the recognition of his son Otto as king: Schmid 1960; Reuter 1991: 139–41, 144–5; Innes 2000: 234. Eberhard, *dux* of Franconia, was brother of Conrad I and so a son of Conrad the Elder killed in 906 (see above).

45 This is taken directly from *AnnAug* 932: 69.

46 This is based closely on *AnnAug* 934: 69. The engagement in question (the Battle of Riade, somewhere in Thuringia) took place in 933: see Widukind, *RGS*, I.38: 55–7 (Bowlus 2006: 186–8); Liutprand, *Antapodosis*, II.31: 48–9 (Wright 1993: 50–1; Bowlus 2006: 182–3); and Flodoard, *Annals*, 933: 55 (Fanning and Bachrach 2004: 23), who claims that 36,000 died. Following an interpretation of Widukind's account, the battle was traditionally seen as the result of military reforms instituted

In that same year he attacked the Slavs called Vucrani with hostile intent; he defeated them and made them his tributaries.[47]

The church of St-Maximin [in Trier] collapsed in a storm. By the king's mercy the [right of] election was returned to the monks and Hugh, formerly prior, was chosen as abbot of that place; and the monks who were following an irregular way of life were expelled.[48]

935

King Henry was struck down by paralysis.[49]

936

A synod was celebrated at Erfurt in Thuringia by a good many bishops.[50]

King Henry, the most distinguished adherent of peace and vigorous persecutor of pagans, ended his final day on 2 July, after winning in a strong and manly fashion many victories which extended the frontiers of his realm on all sides. His son Otto was chosen as his successor with the consent of the leading men of the kingdom.[51]

Archbishop Hildebert [of Mainz] died, and Frederick succeeded him.[52] Archbishop Unni [of Hamburg-Bremen] died, and Adaldag succeeded him.[53]

---

by Henry I, though this has been disputed: see Leyser 1982a; Reuter 1992: 142–4; Bowlus 2006: 66–71.

47 Adalbert is the main source for this: BO 46a.

48 This refers to the beginnings of the so-called Lotharingian or Gorze reform, which called for a return to rigorous observation of the Benedictine Rule. However, the rhetoric often masked underlying continuities in the essential social role of monasteries: Nightingale 2001. The reform of St-Maximin, Adalbert's own monastery, was carried through by *dux* Giselbert of Lotharingia: Hlawitschka 1960b.

49 Henry grew ill while hunting at Botfeld: *Later Life of Queen Mathilda*, c. 7 (Gilsdorf 2004: 97–8); cf. Widukind, *RGS*, I.40: 59.

50 1 June 932: Hehl 1987, no. 8. Adalbert apparently confused this synod with the royal assembly held at Erfurt in 936: Hehl 1987: 100; BO 52a.

51 More detailed accounts of Henry's death and Otto's succession are given by Widukind I.41, II.1: 60–1, 63–6; Liutprand, *Antapodosis*, IV.15–16: 105–7 (Wright 1993: 109–10); Thietmar, *Chronicon*, II.1: 89–90. For context see Reuter 1991: 148–50, and for discussion of the sources see Bagge 2002.

52 Hildebert died 31 May 937.

53 Unni died 17 September 936. An eleventh-century account of the bishops of Hamburg-Bremen in this period is provided by Adam of Bremen (Tschan 2002).

937

The monastery of St-Gall and the monastery of St-Boniface [Fulda] were consumed by flames. Rudolf king of the Burgundians and Arnulf *dux* of the Bavarians died.[54]

There arose serious civil discord between the king's brother Henry and Eberhard *dux* of the Franks, because of hostilities that arose between their vassals.[55]

938

The sons of *dux* Arnulf rebelled against the king with the ambition of gaining the *ducatus* [of Bavaria].[56] Intending to fight them to the end, Otto himself went to Bavaria; but not being strong enough to pacify them as he had wished, he turned back. Meanwhile the king's brother Henry was captured by Eberhard at the fortress of Belecke. But after he was quickly freed, Eberhard was sent into exile at Hildesheim.[57] The king returned to Bavaria once again and subjected everyone to him; and he sent Arnulf's son Eberhard, who was more rebellious than

---

Adaldag was a relative of the powerful Saxon noble Hermann Billung who had been promoted to a key frontier command in 936: BO 63a; and see also Althoff 1992: 158–63.

54 Drawn from *AnnAug* 937: 69. There were two regions known as Burgundy: the kingdom of Burgundy was focused on Transjurane Burgundy around Lake Geneva, while the duchy of Burgundy was further west and south: Bouchard 1999. Rudolf II was king of the former and is not to be confused with Raoul, *dux* of the latter and king of west Francia. On Arnulf see Reuter 1991: 130–46; Airlie 2000.

55 The early years of Otto's reign were marked by internal unrest. Widukind, *RGS*, II.6: 71–2 describes Eberhard attacking a Saxon vassal of his who was refusing to obey him on the grounds that it was not fitting for Saxons to commend themselves to non-Saxons; on Eberhard see also above, 931. Despite the fact that Otto had probably been designated heir in 930, he had to fight to turn this promise into reality: Flodoard, *Annals*, 936: 64 (Fanning and Bachrach 2004: 28). Widukind, *RGS*, II.1: 67 implies that Henry had to be kept out of the way during Otto's coronation; see Reuter 1991: 149–50. This entry is also interesting for its explicit description of how political conflict between great lords could be driven by the demands and expectations of their followers.

56 Widukind, *RGS*, II.8: 72 says that Arnulf's sons disobeyed an order to accompany the king, probably meaning a demand that they perform military service or that they come and submit to Otto publicly (Reuter 1991: 151).

57 In fact the attack on Henry was led by Thankmar, Otto's half-brother, who felt himself slighted in the king's distribution of high offices and allied himself with the disgruntled Eberhard and the Saxon noble Wichmann Billung: Widukind, *RGS*, II.11: 74–8 (who gives a full account of Thankmar's rebellion); cf. Liutprand, *Antapodosis*, IV.20: 108–9 (Wright 1993: 111–12). For discussion see Leyser 1979: 13–14; Frase 1990: 149–54; Reuter 1991: 152.

the others, into exile.[58] The Hungarians were once again defeated with great bloodshed by the Saxons.[59]

939

Eberhard was allowed back from exile, and the whole kingdom was disturbed by hostililties and rebellions.[60] For Eberhard and Giselbert conspired against the king with the king's brother Henry; indeed, even some churchmen, worthless and hateful to God, made common cause with their faction, and everywhere they threw into disorder every law of peace and concord.[61] Then, while the king advanced on the Lotharingians, where the heart of the rebellion then lay, Giselbert with the king's brother, having not been strong enough to stop the king crossing the Rhine, engaged the king's men, to whom God granted victory, near Birten.[62] After many of Giselbert's men were killed and others fled, he himself and the king's brother sought the refuge of flight. Pursuing them, the king came as far as Chèvremont and encircled the stronghold there on all sides with a solid siege.[63] Meanwhile Louis [IV], king of Roman Gaul and son of Charles [the Straightforward], invaded Alsace on the advice of the king's enemies, on the pretext of gaining the kingdom of the Lotharingians, which his father had lost; there he did whatever he could, acting more like an invader than a king.[64] King Otto did not tolerate this patiently; he lifted the siege of Chèvremont and, heading into Alsace, he ejected King Louis. After expelling Louis,

---

58 Otto installed Arnulf's brother Bertold as *dux* on this occasion: Widukind, *RGS*, II.34: 94; Reuter 1991: 151–2.

59 Widukind, *RGS*, II.14: 78–9 describes this raid in more detail. This whole annal is closely based on *AnnAug* 938: 69. The naming of the fortress of Belecke is Adalbert's addition; as is the line about sending Arnulf's son Eberhard into exile (which replaces the original's more pessimistic statement that Otto had defeated everyone 'except one of Arnulf's sons').

60 Eberhard of Franconia, not Eberhard of Bavaria. His return to Otto's favour is described by Widukind, *RGS*, II.13: 78. Widukind, *RGS*, II.15: 79 makes Henry the revolt's prime mover, and does not make the same direct link as Adalbert between Eberhard's forgiveness and the resumption of hostilities.

61 On Giselbert see above, 929; and on Henry see above, 938.

62 The Battle of Birten (near Xanten) is described in detail by Widukind, *RGS*, II.17: 81–3 and Liutprand, *Antapodosis*, IV.24: 110–11 (Wright 1993: 113–14).

63 Chèvremont was one of Giselbert's main seats: Flodoard, *Annals*, 922: 11 (Fanning and Bachrach 2004: 7).

64 In 939 Giselbert allied himself with Louis against Otto, as did counts Otto of Verdun, Isaac of Cambrai and Theoderic of Holland and, later in the year, the Lotharingian bishops: Flodoard, *Annals*, 939: 71–5 (Fanning and Bachrach 2004: 31–2).

Otto besieged the very secure fortress of Breisach. How many heroic and warlike deeds were done there by both sides will not be forgotten by the future succession of generations.[65] Frederick archbishop of Mainz and Ruodhard bishop of Strasbourg, having pitched their tents among the besiegers and left behind the packs of supplies they had brought with them, fled secretly from there by night and approached the city of Metz hoping that they were about to meet Giselbert and Henry, as they had conspired. Yet things turned out completely differently, since their most foolish hope deluded them.[66] For when Giselbert and Eberhard with their men were about to cross the Rhine by the fortress of Andernach, they were prevented by Counts Udo and Conrad and the other men faithful to the king, who met them with war and a swift, quick death. For Eberhard was killed and Giselbert drowned after plunging into the Rhine. Most of their allies were killed and the rest either fled or were captured.[67] When they heard about this, the castellans of Breisach placed themselves under the power of the king and the siege was lifted.

Then the king came to the Lotharingians again and subjected all of them to his rule.[68] But he also received his brother with his accustomed mercy, after he had come to him and cast aside his arms.[69] For Otto forgave everything which his brother had done against him, and kept

65 On the sieges of Chèvremont and Breisach, which had been occupied by Eberhard and his men, see also Widukind, *RGS*, II.22–4: 85–7; Liutprand, *Antapodosis*, IV.27, 30, 34: 115–16, 119–21 (Wright 1993: 118–23); BO 78b. Adalbert omits to mention that Otto and Henry both returned to Saxony at least once in the midst of all this action, though the precise chronology is hard to determine: BO 76n–78.

66 The two bishops' defection is also described by Widukind, *RGS*, II.24–5: 87–8 (who refrains from giving a full explanation); and, in terms quite similar to Adalbert's, by Liutprand, *Antapodosis*, IV.27, 32: 115–16, 120 (Wright 1993: 118–19, 122–3).

67 Similar accounts are given by Widukind, *RGS*, II.26: 88–9; Flodoard, *Annals*, 939: 73–4 (Fanning and Bachrach 2004: 32); Liutprand, *Antapodosis*, IV.29: 118–19 (Wright 1993: 120–1). Widukind names Hermann, *dux* of Alemannia, as Otto's military leader at Andernach; Liutprand also gives Udo and Conrad. Udo was Hermann's brother and Conrad 'Kurzbold' was their cousin: Althoff 1992: 240–1. All three were thus Conradines, as was their victim Eberhard of Franconia: family was not the only determinant of political allegiance. On Udo see also 910, 944, 949; on Conrad see 913, 948. Eberhard's death was important in hindering the development of a Franconian 'duchy': Reuter 1991: 153–4.

68 Flodoard, *Annals*, 939: 74–5 (Fanning and Bachrach 2004: 32) agrees, though says that before this happened Louis IV made another journey to Lotharingia and married Gerberga, Giselbert's widow and Otto's sister.

69 These two sentences are substantially drawn from *AnnAug* 939: 69. Liutprand, *Antapodosis*, IV.34–5: 121 (Wright 1993: 123) says that before he surrendered, Henry tried to take refuge in Chèvremont but was chased off by his sister Gerberga (Giselbert's widow).

him at his side in brotherly love. However, even though all the Lotharingians had been subdued, the bishop of Metz tried to hold out for a time.[70] Otto destroyed the chapel of the the lord emperor Louis the Pious at the estate of Thionville, which had been begun in the likeness of Aachen, so that it could not be completed or used as a fortification.[71] Nevertheless he did not last very long in this rebellion since immediately the whole kingdom came over to the king by God's favour, as if out of the very guts of faith, and with [Otto's] enemies extinguished, peace and concord were renewed.[72] Archbishop Frederick was sent to the monastery of Fulda and Ruodhard of Strasbourg was despatched to the monastery of Corvey.[73]

While all the things we have been talking about were going on, the lady queen Edith remained at the monastery of Lorsch.[74] At this same time Thankmar, the brother of the king born to a concubine, was killed at the fortress of Eresburg while in rebellion, and his other followers were mutilated or hanged. This storm whirled here and there not just in one but in every province of Saxony and Francia. The Saxon rebel Wichmann was reconciled.[75]

King Louis took Giselbert's widow Gerberga as his wife.[76]

---

70 This is also mentioned by *AnnAug* 939: 69. Adalbero I (929–64) was a partisan of Giselbert, and may have been related to him: Hlawitschka 1960b: 428.

71 The palace of Nijmegen had been used as a fortified camp by the Vikings in 881: see above. On Ottonian architectural imitation of Aachen see Zotz 1993a.

72 This is an unusual way of describing the end of the rebellion, clearly attributing it to God's favour. On the rhetoric of peace-making in various accounts of this rebellion see Frase 1990: 154–77, who argues that this theme had a particular interest for Adalbert. Against the argument that such accounts of divine intervention contributed to a conscious political ideology of Ottonian sacrality (Leyser 1979: 75–107), Körntgen 2001 argues for this discourse as an expression of authorial piety.

73 Widukind, *RGS*, II.25: 88 says that Frederick's destination was Hamburg rather than Fulda.

74 Lorsch, near Frankfurt, was in the heart of Eberhard's power base. For commentary on this story see Leyser 1994a: 90–1.

75 Adalbert was here describing the end of the rebellion alluded to above, 938, and these events properly belong to that year. After Thankmar was killed, his allies Eberhard and Wichmann made peace with Otto: Widukind, *RGS*, II.11: 77–8. Eberhard's exile (above, 938) in fact came after this submission.

76 Flodoard presents this marriage as part of Louis's attempt to assert himself in Lotharingia before Otto had triumphed: see above, n. 68. Adalbert's ordering gives the impression that Otto arranged the union after securing victory. On the significance of the marriage for Louis IV see Le Jan 2001a.

940

The Lotharingian *ducatus* was entrusted to the king's brother Henry, who was soon expelled by the Lotharingians in the same year; Count Otto succeeded him in the *ducatus*.[77] Bishop Frederick was released from Fulda.

941

The king's brother Henry conspired against the king with certain of the Saxons, and the king ordered that those who seemed to be the most distinguished [*maiores*] should be beheaded. He sent his brother, on the other hand, into custody at Ingelheim.[78] Archbishop Frederick, because he seemed to have taken part in this conspiracy, absolved himself through a public test, by taking the body and blood of the Lord in church before the people.[79]

942

The king celebrated Christmas at Frankfurt, where his brother, secretly escaping from custody at night with the help of Robert, deacon of the church of Mainz, threw himself at the king's feet as he was entering the church in the time before daybreak and, after forgiveness was granted, he obtained the mercy for which he pleaded.[80]

A very distinguished synod was held in the fortress of Bonn by 22 bishops.[81] In Trier, the church of St-Maximin was dedicated.[82] A comet-

---

77 Otto was a son of count Richwin of Verdun (on whom see above, 883), and was simultaneously made the guardian of Giselbert's son, whose name was Henry: see Widukind, *RGS*, II.26: 88–9; Flodoard, *Annals*, 940: 77–8 (Fanning and Bachrach 2004: 33). Widukind says that the king's brother Henry withdrew from Lotharingia to the 'regnum Karoli'; in II.29: 91 he reports that the king gave his brother some towns and properties in Lotharingia for his upkeep, but this may also be a reference to his earlier installation as *dux*.

78 Widukind, *RGS*, II.31: 92–3 says that Henry's supporters were 'milites' from the eastern parts of Saxony and that their plan was to kill Otto during the Easter celebrations (which took place at Quedlinburg). Widukind also claims that Henry fled the realm. For more detail see BO 94b.

79 Cf. Regino's account of the ordeal to which Lothar II was subjected: above, 869.

80 A version of this story is also told by Liutprand, *Antapodosis*, IV.35: 121 (Wright 1993: 123), who nonetheless collapses the events of 939–42 into one continuous narrative, with Henry's request for clemency as the conclusion. On rituals of submission like this one see Althoff 1997: 21–56, 99–125; Reuter 2006c; Reuter 2006d. The date was Christmas 941: BO 102a.

81 Hehl 1987, no. 10.

82 13 October. The old church had been damaged by a storm: above, 934.

like star was seen for 14 nights, and a vast mortality among cattle followed.[83]

943

Dux Otto died, and he was succeeded in the *ducatus* [of Lotharingia] by Conrad, son of Werner.[84]

944

The king held an assembly at Duisburg during the Rogations with the leading men of the Lotharingians and the Franks. There, at the behest of *dux* Conrad, Archbishop Robert of Trier and Richar bishop of Tongres[-Liège] were accused of infidelity before the king; but they were quickly absolved of the offences attributed to them.[85] The body of St Servatius was also taken there by the clerics of Maastricht, on account of the many injuries done to it by Count Immo.[86]

The Hungarians were destroyed by the Carinthians with such a great slaughter that they were never weakened by our men in such a way before.[87] Count Adalbert, the son of Matfrid, was killed by Udo.[88]

83 The comet was reported by a variety of sources, including Widukind, *RGS*, II.32: 93.

84 Conrad 'the Red' came from a family with interests along the west bank of the Rhine, though his spectacular career was based more on royal patronage: Barth 1990: 105–29; Innes 2000: 235, 265. He is mentioned by Widukind, *RGS*, II.31: 92 as one of the men consulted by Otto over the fates of Henry and his supporters. Flodoard, *Annals*, 944: 91 (Fanning and Bachrach 2004: 39) places Otto's death a year later; Widukind, *RGS*, II.33: 94 says that Conrad succeeded because the young Henry, the king's nephew and Giselbert's son, had also died.

85 12–14 May 945: BO 123a. Adalbert is the only narrative source for this incident; Robert was the king's uncle; Richar was the nemesis of Regino (above, 892, 899).

86 Immo was mentioned in a charter issued on 15 May: D OI 66. He had been a supporter of Giselbert: Widukind, *RGS*, II.23, 37: 86, 89.

87 *ASGM* 943: 78 attributes this victory to the Bavarians, as do some manuscripts of Adalbert's work. No doubt both groups were involved, led by *dux* Bertold: Widukind, *RGS*, II.34: 94; Bowlus 2006: 145.

88 Adalbert was count of Metz, and his father was none other than the persecutor of Regino: above, 892, 899, 906. Richar bishop of Liège, accused of infidelity in the same year (above, n. 85), was therefore Adalbert's uncle. The accusation and the murder were thus likely connected, and presumably related to a renewed struggle for power in Lotharingia after the elevation of Conrad the Red by Otto. The aristocratic group surrounding Adalbert's family had been allied to the eastern kings since the reign of Henry I and were powerful in Verdun, where Conrad's predecessor Otto had been count. See Hlawitschka 1969: 71–4; though for some doubts on the prosopography see Althoff 1992: 210–17. The most prominent Udo active at this time was the

945

Bishop Richar [of Liège] died, and Hugh abbot of Trier succeeded him in the bishopric.[89] *Duces* Hermann and Conrad, who had certain enmities between them, were reconciled in the presence of the most pious king at Cassel.[90]

The Bavarian *dux* Bertold died, and the king's brother Henry succeeded him in the *ducatus*.[91]

946

King Louis [IV], having been expelled from the kingdom by his own men, came to King Otto asking for help and got what he wanted. For the king entered Gaul with a strong force and made the towns of Rheims and Laon and many other sturdy and well-defended strongholds return to Louis; and he himself advanced with hostile intent as far as Rouen. From there he returned to the homeland, after almost all of the greater men, with the exception of Robert's son Hugh [the Great], had been subjected to their king.[92]

Conradine count who was the brother of *dux* Hermann of Alemannia (see also 910, 939, 949). Widukind, *RGS*, II.31: 92 associates this Udo closely with Conrad the Red in 941.

[89] Richar, formerly abbot of Prüm, was bishop from 922–45. Hugh had become abbot of St-Maximin, Adalbert's monastery, in the reform of 934: see above. According to Flodoard, *Annals*, 945: 99–100 (Fanning and Bachrach 2004: 43), Hugh at first ran away and had to be forced into becoming bishop.

[90] Cassel (Kastel) is near Mainz. Hermann was *dux* of Alemannia. Adalbert is the only narrative source for the dispute, so it is not clear exactly how it relates to the events mentioned in the previous annal.

[91] Bertold died in November 947. Henry's position was cemented by marriage to the daughter of the late *dux* Arnulf: Widukind, *RGS*, II.36: 95.

[92] Louis struggled throughout his reign to impose obedience on the leading west Frankish magnates, in particular Herbert II of Vermandois and Hugh the Great, *dux* of the Franks: on his reign see Lauer 1900; McKitterick 1983: 305–40; Brühl 1996. Louis had been captured by the Northmen at Rouen in 945 and handed over to Hugh the Great, who then tried and failed to make a deal with Otto. After an appeal from Edmund king of Wessex, Hugh restored Louis in 946, but kept hold of Laon, the king's main power base. Otto invaded after an appeal from his sister Gerberga, Louis's wife, and travelled as far as Normandy, retaking Rheims en route. Laon was not recaptured until 948. See Flodoard, *Annals*, 946, 947: 97–103 (Fanning and Bachrach 2004: 42–5); Widukind, *RGS*, III.2–4: 104–7. Flodoard's account is more reliable than Widukind's, which like Adalbert's talks up Otto's military successes. Louis's relationship with Hugh and the other great men remained volatile.

947

The lady queen Edith died and was buried at Magdeburg, to the great grief of the king and all his men.[93] *Dux* Conrad, who was at that time dear to the king above almost all others, took the king's daughter Liutgard in marriage.[94] The king's son Liudolf married Ida, the daughter of *dux* Hermann, with fitting pomp.[95]

948

A synod was held by 34 bishops in Ingelheim. It was presided over by Bishop Marinus, legate of the church of Rome, and the renowned kings Otto and Louis were there. Many things of use to the Church were promulgated. The case of Herbert's son Hugh, who had invaded the see of the church of Rheims and expelled Archbishop Artald, was also aired; and he was condemned by the judgement of all the bishops who were there.[96] Count Conrad, who was the son of Eberhard and was known as Kurzbold, died; he was a wise and judicious man.[97]

---

93 26 January 946. See also Widukind, *RGS*, II.41: 99–100; Flodoard, *Annals*, 946: 101 (Fanning and Bachrach 2004: 44); BO 131a. Magdeburg was part of Edith's dower.

94 Widukind, *RGS*, II.33: 94 places the marriage at the same time as Conrad's appointment as *dux* in Lotharingia (above, 943). Adalbert's description of Conrad the Red as the king's closest adviser is borne out by the huge number of charters in which his intervention is mentioned, suggesting that he, even more than Megingoz in the early 890s, was able to dominate access to royal patronage in Lotharingia at least: Innes 2000: 235.

95 Otto had endorsed Liudolf, his eldest son, as his heir after the death of Edith: Widukind, *RGS*, III.1: 104. The marriage to Ida was evidently intended to establish him as heir to the sonless Hermann's position in Alemannia in the meantime. Liutprand, *Antapodosis*, V.1: 123–4 (Wright 1993: 129) suggests that the marriage was Hermann's idea; Widukind, *RGS*, III.6: 108 says that it was arranged by Otto once Liudolf had come of age.

96 Herbert was count of Vermandois and had been at the centre of a dispute over the see of Rheims ever since he had had his infant son made archbishop in 925: Flodoard, *Annals*, 925: 32 (Fanning and Bachrach 2004: 14). Artald was one of Louis IV's main supporters, and the condemnation of his enemies by this synod and a subsequent council held at Trier went a long way to re-establishing the king's authority. For detailed accounts see Flodoard, *Historia*, IV.35: 428–36; Flodoard, *Annals*, 948: 107–21 (Fanning and Bachrach 2004: 46–51), who lists only 31 bishops; Hehl 1987, no. 13; and analysis by Bührer-Thierry 1997: 103–4. For a recent discussion of the Rheims dispute see Glenn 2004: 215–34. Otto's rulership began to take on a more imperial tone after Ingelheim: Reuter 1991: 167.

97 That is, the Conradine Conrad rather than Conrad the Red: see above, 913, 939. His nickname may refer to a religious vow of celibacy: Jackman 1997: 207–8.

949

Bishop Waldo of Chur died, and Hartbert succeeded him.[98] Count Udo died. He, with the permission of the king, had divided whatever benefices and prefectures he held, as if they were hereditary, among his sons.[99] *Dux* Hermann, the wisest and most judicious among his own men, died on 10 December.[100] In the same year a daughter, Mathilda, was born to the king's son Liudolf.[101]

950

The king celebrated the Purification of St Mary [2 February] at Frankfurt, and from there he went to Worms.[102] *Dux* Hermann's widow came to him there and he received her favourably. He entrusted the dukedom of Alemannia to his own son Liudolf.[103] There also Conrad, son of Count Gebhard, since he claimed to have slept with a certain niece [*neptis*] of the king and was defeated in single combat by a certain Saxon called Burchard, revealed that he had lied.[104]

In the same year Boleslaw, ruler of the Bohemians, rebelled against the king, who went against him with a very strong force and enforced his lordship completely.[105]

---

98 The careers of these men are discussed by Bührer-Thierry 1997: 47–8, 50–2, 222–4.

99 On Udo, who had married a daughter of Herbert of Vermandois, see also 910, 939, 945. He was count in the Rheingau and the Wetterau. Jackman 1997: 19–21 argues that Adalbert's report is a simile: that is, that Udo's permission was to distribute his benefices to people who were not his sons, *as if* they were.

100 Hermann was *dux* of Alemannia and brother of Udo: see also 910, 926, 945, 947.

101 Mathilda later became abbess of Essen.

102 Since Otto was in Worms in early February 950, Adalbert is usually thought to be referring here to a visit in 949, though the rest of the annal probably does belong in 950: BO 174, 182b.

103 Liudolf had been lined up for this position for some time: see above, 947.

104 A Gebhard son of Udo was killed in the rebellions of 938–939: Widukind, *RGS*, II.11: 75. However, Jackman 1997: 25 identifies the Gebhard mentioned here as count of Ufgau-Ortenau who died 947/9. Thietmar, *Chronicon*, II.39: 120–1, written in the early eleventh century, offers a more coherent but slightly different version of this story in which a certain Cono (i.e. Conrad) claims to have slept with Otto's daughter, who was married to Conrad the Red. If Adalbert's word 'neptis' is translated as 'female descendant' rather than 'niece', then his account could be made to fit Thietmar's – it is possible that he was being evasive due to the sensitivity of the affair. See also Jackman 1997: 25–6, 55–7, 60–1; Innes 2000: 235–6.

105 Also mentioned by Widukind, *RGS*, III.8: 108–9; Flodoard, *Annals*, 950: 127–8 (Fanning and Bachrach 54–5). For context Reuter 1991: 161–2; Bowlus 2006: 110–12.

Ruodhard bishop of Strasbourg died, and Udo the son of Count Udo succeeded in the bishopric.[106] Rihgowo bishop of Worms died, and Anno succeeded him.[107]

Archbishop Robert [of Trier] expended much labour for the sake of acquiring the abbey of St-Maximin, but with God's approval he did not succeed.[108]

951

King Otto, wanting to go to Italy, made many preparations for this journey since he planned to free Adelheid, the widow of the Italian King Lothar and daughter of King Rudolf, from the chains and imprisonment in which she was being held by Berengar [II]; and to take her in marriage and acquire at the same time the Italian realm.[109] His son Liudolf went on ahead with the Alemans, desiring to please his father by performing some act of bravery for his own entrance. But he achieved nothing of the kind that he had hoped: instead, by offending his father by failing to consult him, he sowed the seeds of thoroughgoing rebellion and discord. For his uncle, *dux* Henry, envious of all his offices and successes, sent his legates from Bavaria via Trent to Italy and turned against him the minds of all the Italians that he could, to

---

106 15 April. The count Udo here is probably the count of the Rheingau whose death Adalbert recorded in 949: Jackman 1997: 23.

107 Anno had been abbot of Magdeburg (937–950) and remained bishop of Worms until 978.

108 Robert (931–956) was probably not, as earlier scholarship presumed, the brother of Queen Mathilda, but may instead have been the brother of Queen Frederun of west Francia (wife of Charles the Straightforward): Hlawitschka 1987; Gilsdorf 2004: 152–3. On events at St-Maximin see Nightingale 2001: 169–260. Given the strategic importance of this monastery for Lotharingian politics, this incident may have been connected with the ordeal at Worms involving Conrad the Red.

109 Berengar was the margrave of Ivrea who with his wife had visited Otto's court and perhaps received the Saxon ruler's endorsement for his claim to the Italian throne (via his grandfather Berengar I) against the current incumbent Hugh of Arles (926–947): see Liutprand, *Antapodosis*, V.11–13, 26: 129–30, 138–9 (Wright 1993: 133–5, 143). Berengar became sole ruler after the deaths of Hugh (947) and his son Lothar (950). Rudolf was Rudolf II of Burgundy (d. 937), who had briefly aspired to the Italian throne before being ejected in 926 and renouncing his claim in 933 in return for concessions north of the Alps from Hugh. Marriage to Adelheid (whose brother Conrad III of Burgundy had been taken to Otto's court in 937 while still a child) could thus bring great legitimacy to Otto, she being the widow of one Italian ruler and the daughter of another. Her treatment at Berengar's hands seems to have been used by Otto as his pretext for invasion: see also Widukind, *RGS*, III.7: 108 (which also characterises Berengar as a usurper); Reuter 1991: 168–9; Sergi 1999.

the extent that not a town or fortress which subsequently stood open to the king's cooks and bakers was opened to the king's son, and he was subjected there to every inconvenience and copious annoyances.[110] Soon afterward the king entered the Italian kingdom and with the assistance of God he was made the possessor of the whole of Italy. Not only that, but the lady Adelheid, a queen beloved of God, was liberated from custody by her own cleverness and God's favour; and under God's auspices she was united with King Otto in happy marriage.[111] Then *dux* Liudolf, distressed at that which we wrote about earlier, returned to his homeland along with Archbishop Frederick [of Mainz], without consulting his father.

952

After expelling Berengar, the king with his faithful men wintered in Italy and celebrated Christmas at Pavia. And after ordering the affairs of the realm in such a way he returned to his homeland in spring, leaving *dux* Conrad in Italy to pursue Berengar.[112] *Dux* Liudolf, after returning from Italy with royal bombast, celebrated Christmas at Saalfeld, where he kept with him Archbishop Frederick and all the greater men of the kingdom who were present.[113] This feast began to be regarded with suspicion by many people; and it was being said that the talk there was more of destruction than of profit. Because *dux* Conrad had been left to chase Berengar, on the advice of that same *dux* Berengar came voluntarily to the king in Saxony.[114] But from these things he got nothing that he wanted; instead, by the machinations of *dux* Henry, the king's

110 Liudolf's raid is mentioned briefly by Widukind, *RGS*, III.6: 108, who agrees that he acted rashly but suggests that he was relatively successful. In addition to his desire to impress his father, Liudolf may have been underlining his new status by continuing the tradition of semi-autonomous intervention in Italy that was characteristic of the southern duchies in the tenth century: Reuter 1991: 169. As *dux* of Bavaria, his uncle Henry may have had something similar in mind.

111 Otto marched to Pavia and received the leading men in September, then married Adelheid, while Berengar fled: Flodoard, *Annals*, 951: 132 (Fanning and Bachrach 2004: 56). Widukind, *RGS*, III.9: 109 has a different emphasis from those of Adalbert and Flodoard by presenting the marriage as the key to Otto's success. See also BO 196c, 201a. See also the 'Epitaph of Adelheid' (Gilsdorf 2004: 128–43).

112 That is, Conrad the Red. Otto returned in February 952. He seems not to have arranged a coronation for himself: his rule south of the Alps was only referred to in the formulas of charters actually issued in Italy.

113 Widukind, *RGS*, III.9: 109 confirms this, and glosses that this was a place of evil counsel (in reference to Henry's visit there in the rebellion of 939). See Althoff 1982.

114 At Easter, in Magdeburg: Widukind, *RGS*, III.10: 109–10.

brother, he returned to Italy having barely been allowed his life and homeland. Because of this *dux* Conrad was also very offended, and withdrew from the fidelity due to the king. Then Archbishop Frederick and *dux* Conrad became friends; for previously they had been mutual enemies.[115] However, in that same year, in the middle of August, a public assembly of the Franks, Saxons, Bavarians, Alemans and Lombards was held in the town of Augsburg in the province of Rhaetia, where the said Berengar gave himself, with his son Adalbert, into the king's power as his vassal in everything; and he received back Italy to rule by the gift and grace of the king. However, the march of Verona and Aquileia were excepted, and committed to the king's brother Henry.[116] Berengar, however, returned to Italy and twisted all this against the bishops and counts and the other leading men of Italy, assailed them with every hatred and enmity, and thus made them his mortal enemies.[117]

953

The king celebrated Christmas at Frankfurt.[118] Going from there into Alsace, he gave the abbey of Erstein to his mother-in-law Bertha, mother of the lady Queen Adelheid.[119] Then the animosities and plots already made against him in secret began to emerge openly, and one and all

---

115 Adalbert's account of events at Magdeburg differs from Widukind's (see previous note). Widukind says that Berengar was received honourably and agreed to formally submit to Otto later in the year; but that Conrad was offended by the fact that Berengar was made to wait three days to meet the king, and so made common cause with Liudolf, suspecting that Henry was to blame for the loss of face. See also Thietmar, *Chronicon*, II.5: 93–4. The line about the friendship between Conrad and Frederick draws on Luke 23:12.

116 The assembly, held 7 August, was accompanied by a synod and was mentioned in several sources: see Flodoard, *Annals*, 952: 133 (Fanning and Bachrach 2004: 56–7); Widukind, *RGS*, III.11: 110; Hehl 1987, no. 18. Adalbert is the main source for the grant to Henry (also alluded to by Ruotger, *Vita Brunonis*, c. 17: 260), though he seems not to have effectively exercised the claim: BO 217a. This was the first common action by Italian and east Frankish bishops since the Carolingian period.

117 Moral condemnation of Berengar was the norm in most Ottonian texts; underlying their hostility was the fact that he was able to conduct himself as a more or less autonomous ruler: Reuter 1991: 170; Sergi 1999: 355–8.

118 It was probably here that Adelheid gave birth to the couple's first son, Henry, who died in either 953 or 954: Flodoard, *Annals*, 953: 135 (Fanning and Bachrach 2004: 57–8); Widukind, *RGS*, III.12: 110.

119 Bertha was the daughter of Burchard, *dux* of Alemannia and the widow of two Italian kings: Rudolf II of Burgundy (d. 937) and Hugh (d. 947). Erstein was an important royal nunnery in Alsace that had been founded by Empress Ermengard (d. 851), wife of Lothar I: see Hummer 2006: 228, 232, 235. Otto made the grant while holding court at Erstein: BO 227.

uncovered what they concealed in their hearts. While he was returning from Alsace to celebrate Easter at Ingelheim, his son Liudolf and the vile *dux* Conrad had conspired with their mostly youthful supporters who had joined them from Francia and from Saxony and from Bavaria, and they began to fortify whichever fortresses and strongholds they could for the coming strife. For now they did not even keep their plans secret, but openly displayed the banners of rebellion.[120]

When the king therefore came to Ingelheim with a small number of his faithful men, he reckoned it too unsafe to celebrate Easter in the midst of his enemies, so he went from there to Mainz. There he waited outside the gates longer than befits a king and, because Archbishop Frederick was already conspiring with those men, he scarcely gained entry to the town. Then Liudolf and Conrad, coming to him there with a humility which later turned out to be feigned, said that they had done nothing of this sort against him; but they did not deny that if his brother Henry came to Ingelheim for Easter, they were going to capture him. The king took this calmly and moderately, then went by ship to Cologne and thence proceeded to the settlement of Dortmund, where he celebrated Easter.[121]

After Easter he gathered a multitude of his faithful men and went back again to Cologne; and there he held a meeting with the bishop of Metz, in whom Liudolf and Conrad seemed to have the greatest hope and faith, as well as all the Lotharingians, except for a few who were bandits and plunderers at heart. And with kindness and charity he received those who defected to him from his enemies, bringing them into his fidelity firmly and stably. With these things arranged he returned to Saxony and, once he had similarly established and stabilised his affairs there,

120 Conrad the Red and Liudolf had seemingly become allies during the assembly at Magdeburg the previous Easter. Otto's marriage to Adelheid and the birth of their son Henry were a threat to Liudolf's position especially as, according to Flodoard, the king designated Henry as his heir: see above, n. 118. On descriptions of Ottonian assemblies as secret or public see Althoff 1997: 157–84.

121 The account of Widukind, *RGS*, III.13–15: 111–12, is different in detail but broadly consistent: Otto went to Mainz because he had heard rumours of rebellion and wanted Frederick to broker a settlement; after meeting Conrad and Liudolf there he agreed to their terms because of the danger he was in and then went to Aachen (in the heart of Conrad's territory) for Easter, where he found nothing prepared for him; he returned to Saxony where he was fittingly received and he declared that he would not be sticking to the agreement made at Mainz, to which Frederick objected and thereby earned the king's suspicion. Cf. Thietmar, *Chronicon*, II.6: 95; and for commentary Reuter 1998. Flodoard, *Annals*, 953: 135–6 (Fanning and Bachrach 2004: 57–8) claims that Otto had removed Lotharingia from Conrad's control. However, Adalbert's implication that the main target of the rebels was Henry rather than Otto is supported by other sources: BO 227a-b; Reuter 1991: 155.

he returned again to Francia with a hostile force.[122] When he heard about this, Archbishop Frederick left Mainz and entrusted the city to the protection of the king's enemies. He himself went to the fortress of Breisach, which is always a refuge for those who rebel against king and God, and remained there for almost the whole summer waiting to see how things turned out.[123]

When the king heard that Mainz, which was the metropolitan of Francia and a royal city, had been given to his enemies he came as quickly as he could and, after gathering a multitude of his faithful men from among the Franks and Saxons as well as the Lotharingians, he surrounded it with a firm siege.[124] But his brother Henry came from Bavaria to bring help to the king, although by this he acquired more inconvenience than advantage for himself. For in the meantime Liudolf turned the Bavarians from him by the plotting of Arnold, brother of his wife Judith, and after being admitted to Regensburg he stole all of his treasure there and distributed the plunder among his own men.[125] Putting Henry's troubles before his own, the king raised the siege of Mainz, directed his course to Bavaria, and besieged Regensburg; and he remained in this siege almost up until Christmas.[126]

In that same year Archbishop Wigfrid of Cologne died. The king's brother Brun succeeded him and along with the bishopric received the *ducatus* and rule over the whole of the Lotharingian kingdom.[127] The king's daughter Liutgard died.[128]

---

122 The specific details of Otto's itinerary are explored by BO 231c.
123 Widukind, *RGS*, III.17: 113 says that 'the Lotharingians' were ready to oppose Conrad because he had been made *dux* against their will. The bishop of Metz was Adalbero, who had earlier opposed the king in Lotharingia: see above, 939, n. 70. On Breisach as a place known for its association with rebellion see Althoff 1990; Zotz 1992; and, in general, Leyser 1994b.
124 This was in July: Widukind, *RGS*, III.18: 113, who also says that Liudolf had occupied the city with an army and gives an account of the fighting.
125 Arnold/Arnulf, count palatine of Bavaria, and Judith, Henry's wife, were children of *dux* Arnulf of Bavaria: their involvement can be seen as an attempt to restore the position of the Liutpolding family which had been excluded from the highest office since the death of *dux* Bertold in 947. A similar account is given by Widukind, *RGS*, III.20–1: 115; cf. Thietmar, *Chronicon*, II.6: 96.
126 Otto went to Bavaria in September: see Widukind, *RGS*, III.26–8: 116–17.
127 Brun became even more powerful when, after the death of Louis IV of west Francia in 954, he formed something like a regency council with his sister Gerberga for her son Lothar: see Le Jan 2001a.
128 This is the Liutgard who was married to Conrad the Red of Lotharingia.

954

The king stopped the siege and celebrated Christmas in Saxony, returning again to Bavaria as Lent approached.[129] There, Archbishop Herold [of Salzburg] was blinded by the king's brother.[130] With God's favour the forces of his enemies were diminished and in a short time the might of Bavaria and Alemannia was converted to him, to the extent that the city of Regensburg was given back to the king and the rebels themselves professed themselves unwilling and unable to do anything against him.[131] Even Frederick agreed that he was going to purge himself with an oath that he had not done anything that broke his fidelity to the king; but the king, full of every piety, absolved him of this oath.[132]

In that same year *dux* Conrad was going to meet [in battle] the Lotharingians under *dux* Brun the archbishop at the estate [*villa*] of Rümlingen in the Bliesgau, but at the last minute he stayed where he was, because it was against the king and God did not wish it to be done. During Lent the Hungarians, led by the king's enemies, after they had crossed the Rhine, invaded Gaul and committed unheard-of evils against God's churches, and returned through Italy.[133]

Archbishop Frederick died. He was vigorous in holy religion and very praiseworthy, if only he had not seemed so reprehensible in this alone:

129 Apparently because he had heard that his enemies had recruited Hungarian forces, as Adalbert mentions in the next paragraph: Widukind, *RGS*, III.30: 117–18; BO 237c.

130 This took place in April 955 (cf. Widukind, *RGS*, III.43: 123). Herold, bishop since 938 and another member of the Liutpolding family, had supported the rebels, though despite his injuries he was not pressured into abdication until 958: Bührer-Thierry 1997: 199–205; Thietmar, *Chronicon*, II.40: 121, n. 146. Prior to Herold's defection Otto had worked hard to entice him to stay loyal: Bowlus 2006: 91.

131 Adalbert's phrasing here is interesting in that God is depicted as having agency, and the king as being the passive recipient of his favour. Otto besieged Liudolf in Regensburg in June after some of the Bavarians had sued for peace: Widukind, *RGS*, III.31–8: 118–21 gives a detailed account; see also Thietmar, *Chronicon*, II.8: 97. However, the final submission of Regensburg and the reinstallation of Henry only took place in April 955: Widukind, *RGS*, III.43: 123.

132 Liudolf's public display of contrition is described by Widukind, *RGS*, III.40: 122. The final truce was not sealed until the meeting at Arnstadt in December: see below. Adalbert does not mention the Saxon arm of the rebellion of 953–4, where various parties took the opportunity to settle old scores: Widukind, *RGS*, III.25, 29: 116–17; Thietmar, *Chronicon*, II.6: 95–6; Leyser 1979: 23–31; Reuter 1991: 155.

133 It was probably Liudolf's Bavarian allies who got the Hungarians involved, and their raid took them as far west as Rheims: Widukind, *RGS*, III.30: 117–18; BO 237b; Bowlus 2006: 91–5. Flodoard, *Annals*, 954: 137–8 (Fanning and Bachrach 2004: 58), claimed that Conrad brought them in to attack Brun.

that wherever even a single enemy of the king sprang up he immediately placed himself at his side. The king's son William succeeded him, after he was harmoniously elected by the clergy and people at Arnstadt.[134] At that time Liudolf was restored to the king's favour and surrendered to his father the vassals he had as well as his *ducatus*. Burchard succeeded him in the *ducatus*.[135] Conrad, stripped of all the riches he had and having lost his *ducatus*, was also admitted to the king's favour, since he had been content with his life, homeland and property.[136] A son called Otto was born to Liudolf.[137]

955

The Hungarians came forth with such a great multitude that they said they could not be defeated by anyone unless the earth swallowed them up or the sky fell and crushed them. With God's support they were defeated at the River Lech by the army of the king with so great a slaughter that never before among our people was such a victory heard of or accomplished.[138] Conrad, the former *dux*, was killed there.[139] When he had returned from there the king sent his army against the Slavs, where he won a similar victory and struck them down with a

---

134 Frederick died on 25 October. At Arnstadt on 17 December Otto finally made peace with Liudolf and Conrad, and it was on this occasion, according to Widukind, *RGS*, III.41: 122, that Mainz and Franconia finally returned to the king. All the sources are listed by BO 239b. William was Otto's eldest son, but he was illegitimate. Adalbert's source for the change of archbishop was probably *AnnAug* 954: 69.

135 Burchard, who remained *dux* of Alemannia until his death in 973, was probably a member of the Hunfriding family and may have been the son of Burchard II of Alemannia, whose death is recorded above, 926. This would have made him a close relative of the Empress Adelheid, Burchard II's granddaughter. Burchard was given in marriage Hadwig, Henry of Bavaria's daughter: Widukind, *RGS*, III.44: 125. See also Reuter 1991: 159; Bührer-Thierry 1997: 35, 257.

136 Conrad remained in high enough favour to be involved in the royal army at the Lech the following year: see below, 955. Adalbert's account of the rebellion of 953–4 is analysed in detail by Frase 1990: 177–279.

137 Otto (d. 982) was later *dux* of Alemannia and Bavaria.

138 The Battle of the Lech (10 August 955) is regarded as vital in limiting the Hungarian impact on western Europe, and was commemorated by contemporaries as a turning point in Otto's reign (which may have caused historians to over-rate its significance). Widukind, *RGS*, III.44, 47–9: 123–5, 128–9 gives the most detailed account. See also Thietmar, *Chronicon*, II.9–10: 97–9 (with Warner's analysis at 58–9); Flodoard, *Annals*, 955: 140–2 (Fanning and Bachrach 2004: 61); BO 240g. For discussion see Leyser 1982b; Reuter 1991: 160–2; Bowlus 2006.

139 This line seems to have been a marginal addition to the original manuscript, though Conrad the Red's death is also mentioned in Widukind, *RGS*, III.47: 128 and Flodoard, *Annals*, 955: 141 (Fanning and Bachrach 2004: 61).

great massacre.[140] Wichmann was expelled.[141] The king's brother Henry, after recovering from his desperate situation and receiving the dukedom of Bavaria, died.[142] The pious king gave the *ducatus* and the march to Henry's son Henry.[143] The king's son Otto was born.[144]

956

The king, while living in peace and quiet, held a royal assembly with most of his faithful men at Cologne.[145] At that time a grave sickness prowled through all parts of the kingdom, and killed a countless multitude of people everywhere. Archbishop Robert of Trier and Hadamar abbot of Fulda died from it. Henry succeeded to the bishopric and Hatto to the abbacy.[146]

In that same year Liudolf was sent to Italy to suppress the tyranny of Berengar and after he had quickly expelled Berengar he became the possessor of almost all of Italy.[147]

The abbey of St-Nazarius in Lorsch was restored to election.[148]

---

140 The Battle of the Recknitz (16 October), at which Otto defeated the Abodrites and their allies: Widukind, *RGS*, III.53–5: 132–5.

141 Wichmann Billung 'the Younger', a prominent Saxon noble, had been involved in the rebellion of 953–954: see above, 954, n. 132 for references. He had co-opted elements among the Slavs to his cause, and after being ejected across the Elbe (he was not included in the settlement at Arnstadt) he continued to attack Saxony with Slav support: Widukind, *RGS*, III.50–6: 129–35; Thietmar, *Chronicon*, II.12: 99–100; Reuter 1991: 160.

142 Henry had been re-installed as *dux* earlier in 955: see above, 954, n. 131.

143 Henry 'the Wrangler' or 'the Quarrelsome', *dux* of Bavaria (955–976, 985–995). In 955 he was only 4, so his Liutpolding mother Judith (daughter of *dux* Arnulf) acted as regent: Reuter 1991: 159. His sister Hadwig was married to Burchard of Alemannia.

144 The future Otto II.

145 In May: BO 246a.

146 These events are also datable to May: BO 246a. The plague and the deaths of various bishops are also mentioned by Flodoard, *Annals*, 956: 142 (Fanning and Bachrach 2004: 61–2), who says that Henry was a relative of the king. On him see also below, 961, n. 162.

147 Liudolf's expedition was probably undertaken in September. Widukind, *RGS*, III.57: 135–6 says that he went 'because he wanted to keep faith with his friends'. Thietmar, *Chronicon*, II.12: 100 thought, wrongly, that he was mounting a new rebellion. According to Flodoard, *Annals*, 957: 144 (Fanning and Bachrach 2004: 62) he 'gained almost all of Italy'. Further details are only available from later sources: BO 252a.

148 In other words it was reformed: see above, 934, n. 48.

957

The king attacked the Slavs again.[149] Liudolf died in Italy, and his body was brought from there and buried honourably at St-Alban in Mainz by his brother, the venerable Archbishop William.[150] Willerus, abbot in Trier, died, and Wikerus succeeded him.[151] At that time the most clement king, out of zeal for holy religion, restored to its original dignity the abbey of St-Peter in Wissembourg, which in much earlier times under his predecessors had been deprived of the gift of free election, and of its privileges. He made Geilo, a venerable man, into the abbot of that same monastery.[152]

958

The king celebrated Easter [11 April] at Ingelheim and from there he went to Cologne by boat, planning to hold an assembly there. In that same year, by the doing of Archbishop Brun's faction, Count Reginar was captured and sent into exile among the Slavs.[153] With the consent of Herold, Frederick was ordained archbishop of Salzburg in the king's presence at Ingelheim during a synod of 16 bishops held on the octave of Easter [18 April].[154]

Alewic, abbot of the monastery of Reichenau, died; Ekkehard succeeded him. Gralo abbot of St-Gall died and Burchard succeeded him.[155]

---

149 The Slavs in question were the Redarii: Widukind, *RGS*, III.58: 136. Widukind places this campaign after Liudolf's death, thus later than September.
150 6 September: Widukind, *RGS*, III.57 135–6; Flodoard, *Annals*, 957: 144 (Fanning and Bachrach 2004: 62); Thietmar, *Chronicon*, II.12: 100.
151 7 October, referring to Adalbert's home monastery of St-Maximin.
152 Adalbert became abbot of Wissembourg himself in 964, and was probably in that position at the time of writing. In 968 the monastery was placed under the control of the bishop of Magdeburg, to which position the historian was then appointed. On Ottonian patronage of monastic reform in Alsace see Hummer 2003; Hummer 2006: 229–33.
153 Reginar [III] was the nephew of the Giselbert killed in 939. He and his family retained considerable power in Lotharingia and had made trouble for both Conrad the Red and Brun: Flodoard, *Annals*, 951, 953, 954, 956, 957: 131, 136–7, 143–4 (Fanning and Bachrach 2004: 56, 58, 62); Le Jan 1995a: 369–70, 417–20, 453.
154 Details of the synod, whose *acta* do not survive, are provided by Hehl 1987, no. 20. Herold had been blinded by Henry of Bavaria: see above, 954.
155 13 May and 26 February respectively.

959

The king invaded the Slavs again, and Thietmar was killed there.[156] Legates of Helen, queen of the Rus', who had been baptized in Constantinople under the Constantinopolitan emperor Romanus, came to the king and asked (falsely, as became clear later) that a bishop and priests be appointed to that people.[157]

In that same year Hagano abbot of Hersfeld was struck by paralysis.[158]

960

The king celebrated Christmas at Frankfurt, where Libutius from the monks of St-Alban [in Mainz] was appointed bishop to the Rus' people by the venerable archbishop Adaldag [of Hamburg-Bremen]. Gunther was made abbot [of Hersfeld] at the request of Hagano.

In that same year the king proceeded against the Slavs again.[159]

John the deacon and the *scrinarius* Azo, legates from the apostolic see, also came.[160] They called upon the king to defend Italy and the Roman state from Berengar's tyranny. Waltbert archbishop of Milan, Waldo bishop of Como and the *marchio* Otbert also approached the king in Saxony as fugitives from Berengar. But almost all the other counts and bishops in Italy sent letters or messengers to Otto, entreating him to come and liberate them.[161]

Geilo abbot of Wissembourg died and Gerric succeeded him.

---

156 This must refer to Otto's battle against Slavs led by Wichmann the Younger during the previous year: Widukind, *RGS*, III.60: 136; Flodoard, *Annals*, 958: 146 (Fanning and Bachrach 2004: 63) (who calls the Slavs 'Sarmatae'); BO 263a. Thietmar was a count under the influence of Hermann Billung: Becher 1996: 287.

157 Helen was the baptismal name of Olga, queen of the Kievan Rus'; Romanus was Romanos I Lekapenos (920–944, d. 948). See Franklin and Shepard 1996: 135–7; Noonan 1999: 508–10. Adalbert was to become missionary to the Rus', an enterprise about which he was somewhat bitter: see below, 961, 962.

158 He died in 960.

159 Probably in July or August: BO 289a.

160 The *scrinarius* was an official of the papal writing office.

161 A similar account is offered by Liutprand, *Historia Ottonis*, c. 1: 169 (Wright 1993: 159). Lintzel 1933 argued that Adalbert's account of Otto's invitation to Italy was based on Liutprand's. Frase 1990: 50–6 admits that some details, particularly the identity of the five people named here, are consistent with this theory, but argues that the texts are dissimilar in other respects. The matter would benefit from renewed investigation in light of Buc 2004: see also BO 289b and above, 919, n. 18. On the legates see Hlawitschka 1960: 140, 244–5.

961

The king celebrated Christmas at the city of Regensburg, where Bishop Poppo of Würzburg, who was very dear to the king, ended his final day on 14 February. His kinsman Poppo followed him in the bishopric.[162] Libutius, whom certain delays had prevented from travelling in the previous year, died in the present year on 15 February. By the contrivance and counsel of Archbishop William [of Mainz], Adalbert from the monks of St-Maximin [in Trier] was appointed to be sent abroad in his place, even though he expected better from William and had never done anything to offend him. With his accustomed mercy, the most pious king equipped him with all the supplies he needed and sent him with honour to the people of the Rus'.[163]

The king, deciding to go to Italy, brought together a great multitude of his faithful men at Worms, where, with the consent and unanimity of the leading men of the kingdom and of all the people, his son Otto was elected king.[164] Moving on from there, he was also made king at Aachen with the agreement and election of all the Lotharingians.[165] With his son appointed, the father returned to Saxony, arranged the affairs of the kingdom, entrusted his son to Archbishop William for protection and nourishment, and in such a way let himself into Italy via Bavaria and Trent.[166] There he met almost all the counts and bishops of Italy and, having been received by them with honour, as was fitting, he entered Pavia forcefully and without any resistance and ordered them to rebuild the palace that had been destroyed by Berengar. Berengar, Willa and

162 Poppo I (941–961); Poppo II (961–983). They are usually identified as descendants of the Babenberger family who fought with the Conradines in the first years of the tenth century (see above, 906). Both were also related to the Ottonians (Otto II referred to Poppo II as his *nepos*); and Poppo I's brother was archbishop Henry of Trier: Althoff 1992: 264–9; and above, 956, n. 146.

163 This is a key passage for establishing Adalbert as the author of the present text. Little else is known about the mission: see Franklin and Shepard 1996: 135–7; Shepard 1999: 612; Wood 2001: 207–8.

164 May 961: BO 297a. The impetus for Otto's decision to go to Italy was an appeal for help from Pope John XII: Reuter 1991: 170; Müller-Mertens 1999: 250–1; Sergi 1999: 356–7.

165 26 May 961. Cf. Ruotger, *Vita Brunonis*, c. 41: 270, which also implies two separate ceremonies (an election and an anointing, the latter administered by Brun). Liutprand, *Historia Ottonis*, c. 2: 169–70 (Wright 1993: 160) points out that anticipatory succession was 'contrary to custom'; in 930, Otto I had probably been recognised as heir, but not formally made king (see above, 931 and Georgi 1995). Coronation of sons as kings was, however, standard practice in the Carolingian period.

166 Briefly mentioned by Widukind, *RGS*, III.63: 137. Widukind is, however, comparatively uninterested in Otto's Italian exploits.

their children, however, hid themselves away in whatever fortifications and strongholds they could, and never ventured out of doors while daring anything against the king.[167] In the same year Godfrid bishop of Speyer died; Otger succeeded him.[168] There was an eclipse of the sun on 17 May. The king sent Abbot Hatto of Fulda ahead to arrange lodgings for him in Rome.

962

The king celebrated Christmas in Pavia. Proceeding from there he was favourably received in Rome and by the acclamation of all the Roman people and clergy he was called emperor and augustus and ordained by Pope John, son of Alberic.[169] The pope also kept Otto with him in great love and promised never to defect from him during all the days of his life. However, the outcome of this promise was far different from what had been made out.

After the august emperor had returned from Rome and was celebrating Easter in Pavia, Berengar attracted very many forces from all over and fortified himself on a certain mountain called San Leo, and Willa barricaded herself on a certain island called San Giulio, in Lago Maggiore.[170] Their sons Adalbert and Guy wandered aimlessly here and there, but they along with their followers still possessed certain fortifications, namely the strongholds at Garda and Val Travaglia, and an island in Lake Como.[171] Willa was first to be attacked, and after every exit from the lake had been blocked she was worn down by the daily

---

167 See also Liutprand, *Historia Ottonis*, c. 2: 169–70 (Wright 1993: 160); BO 307e. Benedict, *Chronicon*, c. 36 mentions Hubert of Tuscany as an ally of Berengar.

168 Godfrid was probably elected in 951, and died 16 May.

169 Alberic was a prominent Roman aristocrat. The imperial coronation took place on 2 February 962. Adelheid was crowned empress at the same time. John also agreed to the establishment of the missionary bishopric of Magdeburg, though internal opposition meant that this project remained dormant until 968. In return for the pope's oath of fidelity, Otto, acting consciously in the tradition of his Carolingian predecessors, confirmed the rights and privileges of the papacy. See also Liutprand, *Historia Ottonis*, c. 3: 170 (Wright 1993: 160); Flodoard, *Annals*, 962: 151 (Fanning and Bachrach 2004: 66); BO 309c–311; Reuter 1991: 170–1; Müller-Mertens 1999: 251.

170 A synod was held at Pavia while Otto was there, dealing with a variety of important west Frankish and Italian issues: Flodoard, *Annals*, 962: 153–4 (Fanning and Bachrach 2004: 66); BO 316a. San Leo (Montefeltro) is near San Marino; San Giulio is actually in Lago di Orta (near Novara). Adalbert is the main source for Otto's campaigns against Berengar and his family.

171 Val Travaglia is on the eastern shore of Lago Maggiore; Garda is on Lake Garda in the province of Verona.

bombardments from catapults, bowmen and other instruments of war. Before two full months of the siege had passed she was captured, but in the end she was freed by the emperor's clemency and allowed to go where she wanted. She went to Berengar as quickly as she could and in every way persuaded him not to give himself up to the emperor.[172]

In the same year Adalbert, who had been ordained as bishop of the Rus', returned, realising that he could not accomplish any of the things that he had been sent to do and that he was tiring himself out in vain; some of his men were killed on the way home, and he himself only just escaped with great effort. When he came to the king he was received with love and embraced and supported like a brother with all good things and comforts by Archbishop William, beloved of God, to make up for the very troublesome pilgrimage that he had engineered for him. A letter was sent to the emperor on his behalf, and he was ordered to await the emperor's return in the palace.[173]

In that same year Adalbero bishop of Metz, a venerable man, died; and Bishop Theoderic, the emperor's cousin, was chosen in his place.[174]

963

The king again celebrated Christmas and Easter at Pavia. In the meantime Adalbert [son of Berengar] hurried to and fro and gathered to himself whomever he could from all sides; and he even went to Corsica in a bid to defend himself.[175] He also asked the Roman pontiff to come to his aid many times. While these things were going on, the emperor left Pavia and besieged Berengar on the mountain of San Leo; and he stayed there the whole summer with the mountain often surrounded on all sides, and completely prevented free entry and exit. In the meantime Pope John cast to oblivion the promises he had made to the emperor, defected from him and, favouring the parties of Berengar or Adalbert, allowed Adalbert into Rome.[176]

---

172 Adalbert is the main source for these events: BO 320a–b.

173 For Adalbert's mission see above, 961.

174 Adalbero had been bishop since 929 and died on 26 April: see above, 939, 953. Theoderic (Dietrich) was a nephew of Otto's mother Queen Mathilda: Althoff 1992: 168–71; Gilsdorf 2004: 147–53.

175 According to Liutprand, *Historia Ottonis*, c. 4: 170–1 (Wright 1993: 160), in the aftermath of Otto's coronation Adalbert had gone to Fraxinetum in Provence, a Muslim base, and put himself under Muslim protection.

176 Liutprand, *Historia Ottonis*, cc. 4–6: 170–2 (Wright 1993: 160–3) gives a longer account of these events, dwelling on the pope's sexual immorality and Otto's moral

When the emperor heard about the fraud of the pope's deceit, he abandoned the siege around the mountain and moved towards Rome with his army. They [supporters of Adalbert and the pope], fearing Otto's arrival, pillaged most of the treasure of St Peter and sought refuge in flight. Then the Romans split into factions, some favouring the emperor (for they complained that the said pope had oppressed them with many injuries), and others who flattered the pontiff. But although they saw things differently they nonetheless allowed the emperor into the town with due honour and subjected themselves to his authority in everything by giving hostages.[177] After bringing together a great number of bishops, the emperor convoked a synod; and on their advice he sent a legation and recalled the fugitive pope with canonical authority to the pontifical and apostolic see. But when the pope completely refused, the Roman people by common consent elected and ordained in his place the *protoscrinarius* Leo, who was a vigorous and determined man.[178] At this synod there were present almost all the bishops of Romania and Italy,[179] as well as Angelfredus the patriarch of Aquileia, who died there at that very time. But some of our people were also present, namely Archbishops Adaldag [of Hamburg-Bremen] and Henry [of Trier]; and Bishops Lantward [of Minden] and Otger [of Speyer].[180]

Afterward John, also called Octavian, seeing that he had been deposed, distanced himself from Adalbert, led by a repentance that came too late.[181] Adalbert, however, went back to Corsica. In that same year the fortress of Garda in Italy was captured.

Back home the Slavs called Lausitzer were also subdued.[182]

---

probity. According to Liutprand, John asked Adalbert to come to Rome and tried to turn the tables on Otto by accusing him of violating his oath to the pope. DD OI 253–60 were issued during the siege, which lasted from May to September.

177 Liutprand, *Historia Ottonis*, c. 8: 173 (Wright 1993: 163) is similar, though he puts more stress on the Romans' pledge of support for Otto and makes clear that John and Adalbert had both fled.

178 The *protoscrinarius* was the head of the papal scribes.

179 Romania refers to the bishops directly subject to Rome; Italy to the 'regnum Italiae', roughly the northern half of the peninsula.

180 Liutprand, *Historia Ottonis*, cc. 9–16: 173–80 (Wright 1993: 164–70), who was a participant in the synod, offers a detailed account of the proceedings, including a list of those present and the moral and legal arguments used to justify the pope's replacement. The synod convened in 3 sittings across November and December: BO 348e–350a.

181 Adalbert's reference to John's pre-papal name underlines his implication of illegitimacy.

182 Widukind, *RGS*, III.66–7: 141–2 describes these campaigns, led by the margrave Gero.

964

The emperor celebrated Christmas in Rome. Berengar, besieged with his men on the mountain of San Leo, was defeated. The fortress itself was subjected to the emperor's power and Berengar was sent with Willa to Bavaria.[183] The Romans, according to their custom, again defected from the emperor and, after joining to themselves many other castellans from outside through a sworn conspiracy, they tried to kill Otto. But their treachery was revealed and on the very day that they were setting in motion the attempt to kill him – 3 January – he anticipated the death that had been prepared for him. He attacked them with a very few of his own men and killed a not inconsiderable number of them within the walls of the city. On the next day, however, the Romans came back and gave him 100 hostages, and on the body of St Peter they promised fidelity to emperor and pope under oath.[184]

Then the emperor, having stayed among them for a full week, left to set in order the *ducatus* of Spoleto and Camerino.[185] On Pope Leo's petition, he sent the hostages back to the Romans.[186] But the Romans were ungrateful for his favours and, although the emperor had not yet got far from the city, they admitted John, also called Octavian, into the city and were not afraid to disregard their promise of faith to emperor and pope. Pope Leo was stripped of all his wealth and barely escaped with a few of his men. He came to the emperor who was staying in Camerino and celebrated Easter there. John, also called Octavian, cruelly mutilated John the deacon and Azo the *scrinarius*, and kept Bishop Otger of Speyer with him against his will for some time, after arresting and whipping him. But he afterward sent him back at once in the hope of receiving the emperor's pardon. In this hope, by divine ordination, he was disappointed, for on 14 May he departed from human affairs. Then the Romans, fearing greatly the emperor's arrival and heedless of their faith and of the election of the lord Leo, elected Benedict, a certain deacon of the Roman church, and, after he was ordained, set him on the apostolic throne.[187]

183 Widukind, *RGS*, III.63: 137–9 mentions Berengar's exile in passing. Thietmar, *Chronicon*, II.13: 100–1 (whose chronology is wrong) adds that Berengar was sent to Bamberg, where he died.

184 Liutprand, *Historia Ottonis*, cc. 17–18: 180–1 (Wright 1993: 170–1) gives a more detailed account, placing the battle on a bridge over the Tiber.

185 Liutprand, *Historia Ottonis*, c. 18: 181 (Wright 1993: 171) says that Otto had heard Adalbert was there.

186 This detail is also in Liutprand, *Historia Ottonis*, c. 18: 181 (Wright 1993: 171).

187 Liutprand, *Historia Ottonis*, cc. 19–21: 181–2 (Wright 1993: 171–2) gives a similar

When he heard about this, the emperor gathered a multitude of his faithful men from all sides and advanced on Rome. He laid siege to the city firmly and on all sides, so that nobody could get out. But the aforementioned Benedict, falsely called pope, encouraged the Romans to hold out longer against the emperor. He himself, threatening the emperor and his faithful men with excommunication, climbed up on the walls of the city and behaved with greater arrogance than befits a pope. In the end, forced by hunger and the siege and regretting that they had erred and unlawfully offended the emperor, the Romans opened the gates of the city on the vigil of the Precursor [John the Baptist], that is 23 June.[188] When the emperor had been admitted with the appropriate honour, they delivered Benedict, the impious perjurer, into his power and restored the lord Leo to the apostolic throne. Then the apostolic Leo summoned a synod of many bishops and by the judgement of all he deposed that Benedict, invader of the see of Rome, from the rank which he had usurped. In front of everyone, he ripped off the pontifical pallium that Benedict had placed upon himself, snatched the pastoral staff from his hand, and broke it into pieces. At the request of the emperor he allowed Benedict to enjoy merely the rank of deacon.[189]

After celebrating the nativity of the blessed John [the Baptist, 24 June] and the feast of the holy apostles [Peter and Paul, 29 June], the emperor returned from Rome and on the way enjoyed a less auspicious omen than he had hoped. For his army was attacked by so deadly an illness that a healthy man hardly had any hope that he would live from morning to evening or from evening to morning. Among those who died from this pestilence were Henry archbishop of Trier, Gerric abbot of Wissembourg and Godfrid *dux* of the Lotharingians, and a countless multitude of others, noble as well as non-noble. Finally, when by divine mercy the pestilence had ended, the emperor arrived in Liguria and passed a peaceful and leisurely autumn there, going hunting frequently.[190]

In that same year the palace chaplain Duodo was captured by Adalbert

---

sequence of events. He adds that John the deacon had had his right hand cut off, and that Azo had lost his tongue, two fingers and his nose. Liutprand also claims to have heard from eyewitnesses that Pope John refused the last sacraments while on his deathbed. The new pope was Benedict V.

188 Liutprand, *Historia Ottonis*, c. 21: 181–2 (Wright 1993: 171–2) is a parallel account of the siege, with some different details.

189 Liutprand, *Historia Ottonis*, c. 22: 182–3 (Wright 1993: 172–3) is longer, but similar in structure and detail. This is the end of Liutprand's text.

190 Otto's hunt, an archetypal masculine elite activity, was probably less to do with leisure than with advertising the fact that recent events had not diminished his status or health.

[son of Berengar] and after being flogged he was taken away to Corsica; but he was released not long after.[191] At that time Waldo bishop of Como seized the island in Lake Como and completely destroyed the fortifications there. This was the beginning of troubles for Count Udo. For he received into his fidelity Atto, defender of that island, and after its destruction he could not reconcile him with the emperor as he had wished. He took this badly and twisted the whole thing against Bishop Waldo, and decided to take revenge on him through acts of enmity if he could.[192] Erchanbert was made abbot of the monastery of Wissembourg in place of his brother Gerric.

965

The emperor celebrated Christmas at Pavia and after the feast was finished and the affairs of the kingdom of Italy were put in order, he immediately went home. His sons King Otto and Archbishop William rushed to meet him at the estate of Heimsheim on the frontier between Francia and Alemannia, and received him there with great eagerness.[193] From there he moved on to Worms and met with his brother Archbishop Brun on the Purification of St Mary [2 February]. And so he remained in Francia throughout Lent and celebrated Easter with great joy at Ingelheim. From there he reached Cologne by boat, and there he called before him with fitting love and honour his mother the lady Mathilda, his sister Queen Gerberga and her son King Lothar.[194] Then he directed his course to Saxony. He also brought with him to Francia from Rome the deposed Benedict, whom he entrusted to Archbishop Adaldag [of Hamburg-Bremen] for safekeeping.[195] He also detained Berengar's two daughters in the palace with the lady empress, with the proper honour.[196]

191 Duodo was perhaps the Liudolf *cancellarius* who worked in Otto's chancery between 953 and 967, and then became bishop of Osnabruck.
192 Atto was the count of Lecco charged by Berengar II with the defence of the island, which had been fortified since the days of the Byzantines and Lombards. Despite this incident, Atto remained powerful until his death in 975: Hlawitschka 1960a: 138–42. Udo had come to Italy with Otto and is probably to be identified as count of Maienfeld: Jackman 1997: 62–5, 79–80, 227.
193 Heimsheim is west of Stuttgart.
194 This was also presented as a major family and political assembly by Ruotger, *Vita Brunonis*, c. 42: 271; see also BO 386b for other sources. Lothar's marriage to Emma (see below) was doubtless one of the items on the agenda.
195 Cf. Adam, *History*, II.12.10 (trans. Tschan 2002).
196 The daughters were Gisela and Gerberga.

In that same year some of the Lombards defected from the emperor, as they usually do, and brought Adalbert back into Italy. Then the emperor sent Burchard *dux* of the Alemans to Italy. He set out to do battle with Adalbert wherever he might be found, sailing down the Po with the Alemans and the Lombards who were loyal to the emperor, and landing the ships in the places where he had heard Adalbert might be. As soon as they left the river Adalbert attacked them, and on this occasion his brother Guy and many others were killed.[197] Adalbert himself scarcely slipped away and escaped and went to a certain mountainous area where he could be hidden from the emperor. Therefore, rejoicing in his victory, the *dux* went home and told the emperor what had happened to him. In the meantime Bishop Guy of Modena approached the emperor in Saxony on a mission for Adalbert, pretending with fox-like cunning to be loyal to the emperor and boasting that he would betray those who were unfaithful. But he did not share in the emperor's presence or conversation. Instead, after he had been allowed to return home in shame, he was arrested in the Alps on the other side of Chur and, after being sent back to Saxony, was placed in custody among the Slavs.[198]

Udo bishop of Strasbourg died; Erchanbold succeeded him.[199]

Also in that year, the lord Pope Leo died. Then legates of the Romans, namely Azo the *protoscrinarius* and Marinus, bishop of the church of Sutri, approached the emperor in Saxony for the sake of installing whom he wanted as Roman pontiff. They were received honourably and sent home.[200] And Otger bishop of Speyer and Liuzo bishop of Cremona were sent with them by the emperor to Rome.[201] Then John, bishop of Narni, was elected by all the Roman people and enthroned as pope on the apostolic seat. He immediately persecuted the greater Romans with

197 The engagement took place on 25 June. Margrave Guy, Berengar's son, had previously had properties confiscated by Otto: Hlawitschka 1960a: 287.

198 Guy became bishop in 943 and was Berengar's archchancellor until *c.*962, when he became Otto's chancellor for Italy. The lands confiscated in 963 from Margrave Guy, Berengar's son, were given to him: D OI 260 (issued during the siege of San Leo). His support for Adalbert caused his fall from grace, but he later returned to the emperor's good books: Sergi 1999: 354–9.

199 Udo, who had accompanied Otto to Italy, died on 26 August. Aspects of both men's careers are discussed by Bührer-Thierry 1997: 51, 76–7, 195, 219.

200 The emperor's right to supervise the selection of popes had been established in the Carolingian period and was one of the points at issue in the disputes of the early 960s.

201 On Otger's previous role in Italy see above, 963, 964. Liuzo is Liutprand of Cremona, the historian whose work Adalbert may have known (see above, 919, n. 18 and 960, n. 161). He was bishop 961–*c.*971. On him see Sutherland 1988; Leyser 1994c; Leyser 1994d.

a more arrogant spirit than was fitting, and soon he had to endure these men as his greatest and most dangerous enemies. For he was captured by the prefect of the city and a certain Rotfred, and after being ejected from the town he was put in custody in Campania.[202]

Finally in this year, on the emperor's return from Italy, Theoderic, a deacon of that church, was installed as successor to Archbishop Henry of Trier; and the emperor's cousin Theoderic replaced Bishop Adalbero of Metz.[203]

Archbishop Brun, the emperor's brother, a man extremely worthy of the *ducatus* and the episcopate alike, died on 11 October.[204] Folcmar succeeded him as bishop.

In the same year Gero, the best and most distinguished of the *marchiones* of our times, died.[205] King Lothar [of west Francia] joined to himself in marriage the lady Emma.[206]

966

The emperor celebrated Christmas at Cologne and there he arranged all the affairs of the Lotharingian kingdom as he deemed suitable.[207]

Erchanbert abbot of Wissembourg died and after an election by the monks, the emperor put Adalbert, who had been ordained bishop to the Rus', in charge of that monastery.[208]

Bishop Starkand of Eichstätt died, and Reginold succeeded him as bishop.[209]

202 On Otto and John XIII (October 1, 965 – 972) see Müller-Mertens 1999: 252–3; Sergi 1999: 360. Rotfred was count in Campania. Benedict, *Chronicon*, c. 39 also describes his imprisonment.

203 Adalbero had died in 962, in which annal Adalbert had already reported the succession, which was presumably formalised in 965.

204 Ruotger, *Vita Brunonis*, cc. 44–8: 272–4 recounts the end of his life and gives his burial date as 19 October.

205 Gero was one of the most prominent war-leaders of his age: Reuter 1991: 165–6; Becher 1996: 258–9, 275–6; Althoff 1999: 272–3, 282–5.

206 Emma was a daughter of Adelheid by her earlier marriage to King Lothar of Italy, so the marriage strengthened the hegemonial position of Otto's family, which had been weakened by Brun's death. On east-west Frankish dynastic links in this period see Ehlers 1992; Le Jan 2001a; Le Jan 2001b.

207 He issued three diplomas for St-Maximin, Trier: DD OI 313–15.

208 Erchanbert died 9 February. This Adalbert is the author of the present text.

209 11 February. Starkand had been bishop since 933 and was close to Brun of Cologne: Bührer-Thierry 1997: 227–8.

Because Count Udo was engaged in a conspiracy with Berengar's son Adalbert and decided to go to Italy to blind Bishop Waldo of Como, he was convicted of treason against the emperor and after swearing that he would never presume to enter any part of the kingdom again, he was expelled from the realm.[210]

Wikerus, abbot of the monastery of Trier, died, and Asolf succeeded him in the abbacy.[211]

Deciding to go to Italy again, the emperor celebrated the Assumption of St Mary [15 August] at Worms, and there he took counsel with all the greater men of the kingdom.[212] From there he went through Alsace, crossed the Alps via Chur, and entered Italy. He sent Bishop Sigolf of Piacenza and certain of the counts of Italy, who had defected from him in the previous year because of Adalbert, into custody in the transalpine regions of Francia and Saxony.[213] Then the Romans, fearing the emperor's arrival, released Pope John from the captivity in which he had been held by Rotfred, who was now dead, and after asking forgiveness for the evils they had done him they restored him to his place and seat.[214]

In the same year Count Eberhard died.[215]

In that same year Berengar, former king of Italy, died as an exile and was buried in Babenburg in royal fashion.[216] Before he was buried, his widow Willa took the veil as a nun.[217]

Forgetful of his oath, Count Udo entered Francia, but he left there again without having gained anything.[218]

---

210 On Udo and Waldo see above, 964.
211 8 May. Adalbert is referring to St-Maximin in Trier.
212 Widukind, *RGS*, III.73: 150 says that he left his son William, archbishop of Mainz, in charge in his absence.
213 Sigolf was later pardoned: Sergi 1999: 359; BO 437c.
214 Benedict, *Chronicon*, c. 39 suggests John escaped. See also above, 965.
215 Probably count of the Lahngau and brother of the Udo exiled earlier in the year; he was prominent in Otto's entourage during the early 960s: Jackman 1997: 60–6, 194–5, 227, who also summarises contrary views.
216 Babenburg was a fortress in Bamburg.
217 High-status widows often became dedicated religious on the deaths of their husbands.
218 On Udo see above, n. 210 and 964.

967

The emperor celebrated Christmas at Rome and except for the prefect of the city, who had fled, he ordered that 13 leading Romans who appeared to have been the ringleaders of the expulsion of the lord Pope John be killed by hanging.[219] Advancing from there through Spoleto, he came to Ravenna and after celebrating Easter there with the lord Pope John he gathered a greater number of bishops there from Italy and Romania. They held a synod and he devised many things of advantage to the Holy Church, and returned to the apostolic John the town and territory of Ravenna and a great many other things that had been taken away from the Roman pontiffs in much earlier times.[220] He himself withdrew to the regions of Tuscany and Lucania.[221]

In the meantime, Pope John and Emperor Otto sent a letter of invitation to King Otto [II] and ordered that he should hurry to Rome to celebrate Christmas with them. Then, in order to arrange the affairs of the realm before his trip to Italy, the king came to Worms and there in his first assembly, with God's favour, he gave many indications of his future judiciousness and clemency. And so, after celebrating the nativity of the Precursor [24 June] and the feast of the apostles [Peter and Paul, 29 June] at Frankfurt, he returned to Saxony in order to hasten his journey.[222]

At that time Abbot Asolf of Trier was taken from the present life, and Thietfrid was elected his successor.[223] Also at that time the lord archbishop William was inconvenienced by a minor illness, but by God's mercy he soon recovered.[224]

While the lord emperor was residing in Italy, legates of Nicephorus emperor of the Greeks came to him at Ravenna, bringing with them honourable gifts and asking him for peace or friendship.[225] Having received them honourably and sent them back properly, the lord

---

219 BO 439a.
220 The popes' authority over Ravenna had been a bone of contention for centuries. Otto's intervention in the city in 967 (recorded also in DD OI 339–341) was not regarded by everyone as positively as by Adalbert: Warner 2006.
221 Lucania refers to the territory of Lucca.
222 Adalbert is the only source for these events.
223 18 May.
224 Though he died in March 968.
225 Nikephoros II Phokas (963–969). The envoys probably arrived in April, when Otto is known to have been in Ravenna: BO 450a.

emperor sent his envoy to the emperor of the Greeks in Constantinople for the sake of arranging the joining in marriage of his son King Otto with the stepdaughter of Nicephorus himself, that is the daughter of the emperor Romanus.[226] He returned to the emperor again before Christmas in the same year.[227]

At the beginning of September in the same year King Otto celebrated the commemoration of St Michael [29 September] in the city of Augsburg as he was about to set out for Rome with a suitable entourage.[228] From there he travelled through the valley of the Trent and met his father at Verona. And after celebrating there the festival of all saints [1 November] they departed, and from there went by boat via Mantua to Ravenna. After spending a few days there, heading to Rome, they arrived on 21 December, and at the third milestone from the city they met a very great crowd of senators with crosses and banners and acclamations. The lord pope, moreover, received them with honour on the steps of St Peter's, and on the following day he ordained King Otto [II] as caesar and augustus before the *confessio* of St Peter with the acclamation of all the Roman people. And there was no little joy among our own people and the Romans at this most pleasing meeting of the two emperors with the lord pope.

---

226 Romanos II (959–963). The bride who arrived, Theophanu, was a Byzantine princess (probably the niece of the Emperor John I Tzimiskes, 969–976) but was not the daughter of Romanos. After marrying Otto II in 972 she became a very powerful figure, particularly during the minority of her son Otto III: see von Euw and Schreiner 1991; Davids 1995. The negotiations between Otto and the Byzantines turned on their rivalry for hegemony in southern Italy and the Ottonian desire for recognition of their imperial title: Reuter 1991: 173–4; Müller-Mertens 1999: 253–4.

227 The legate was Domenic of Venice: Liutprand, *Relatio*, c. 31: 200–1 (Wright 1993: 191–2).

228 The rest of this paragraph only survives in a twelfth-century chronicle by the Saxon Annalist, a connoisseur of Regino and his continuator, and has generally not been regarded as part of Adalbert's original work: Frase 1990: 38–42. Although the matter is hard to resolve definitively, Nass 1996: 264–6 shows that the passage was known by another later author independently of the Saxon Annalist, and makes a persuasive case for accepting it as genuine.

BIBLIOGRAPHY

Primary sources

Abbo, *Bella Parisiacae Urbis*, ed. H. Waquet, *Abbon. Le Siège de Paris par les Normands* (Paris, 1942).

Adalbert of Magdeburg, *Continuation of Regino's Chronicle*, ed. F. Kurze, *Reginonis abbatis Prumiensis Chronicon cum continuatione Treverensi*, MGH SRG (Hanover, 1890).

Adam of Bremen, *History*: see Tschan 2002.

Ado of Vienne, *Chronicon* (extracts), ed. G. Pertz, MGH SS 2 (Hanover, 1829), pp. 315–23.

Ado of Vienne, *Martyrologium*, ed. G. Renaud and J. Dubois, *Le Martyrologe d'Adon* (Paris, 1984).

Andrew of Bergamo, *Historia*, ed. G. Waitz, MGH SRL (Hanover, 1878), pp. 220–31.

Anglo-Saxon Chronicle, trans. M. Swanton (London, 1996).

Annales Alammanici, ed. G. Pertz, MGH SS 1 (Hanover, 1826), pp. 22–60.

Annales Augienses, ed. G. Pertz, MGH SS 1 (Hanover, 1826), pp. 67–9.

Annales Bertiniani, ed. F. Grat, J. Vielliard, S. Clémencet and L. Levillain, *Annales de Saint-Bertin* (Paris, 1964).

Annales Engolismenses, ed. O. Holder-Egger, MGH SS 16 (Hanover, 1859), p. 486.

Annales Fontanellenses, ed. J. Laporte (Rouen and Paris, 1951).

Annales Fuldenses, ed. F. Kurze, MGH SRG (Hanover, 1891).

Annales Hildesheimenses, ed. G. Waitz, MGH SRG (Hanover, 1878).

Annales Laubacenses, ed. G. Pertz, MGH SS 1 (Hanover, 1826), pp. 52–5.

Annales Prumienses: see Boschen 1972.

Annales Regni Francorum, ed. F. Kurze, MGH SRG (Hanover, 1895).

Annales Rotonenses, ed. B. Bischoff, *Anecdota Novissima: Texte des vierten bis sechzehnten Jahrhunderts* (Stuttgart, 1984), pp. 103–5.

Annales Sanctae Columbae Senonensis, ed. G. Pertz, MGH SS 1 (Hanover, 1826), pp. 102–9.

Annales Sancti Amandi, ed. G. Pertz, MGH SS 1 (Hanover, 1826), pp. 3–14.

Annales Sangallenses Maiores, ed. G. Pertz, MGH SS 1 (Hanover, 1826), pp. 72–85.

Annales Xantenses et Annales Vedastini, ed. B. von Simson, MGH SRG (Hanover, 1909).

Bede, *De Temporum Ratione*, ed. C.W. Jones, *Bedae opera didascalia* 2, Corpus Christianorum Continuatio Medievalis 123B (Turnhout, 1977).

Benedict of St-Andrea, *Chronicon*, ed. G. Zuchetti, *Il Chronicon di Benedetto* (Rome, 1920).

Beyer, H. (ed.), *Urkundenbuch zur Geschichte der Mittelrheinischen Territorien*, vol. 1 (Koblenz, 1860).

Böhmer, J.F. and Mühlbacher, E., *Regesta Imperii. Die Regesten des Kaiserreichs unter den Karolingern, 751–918* (Innsbruck, 1908).

Böhmer, J.F. and Ottenthal, E., *Die Regesten des Kaiserreichs unter den Herrschern aus dem sächsischen Hause 919–1024* (Innsbruck, 1893).

Böhmer, J.F. and Zielinski, H., *Die Regesten des Regnum Italiae und der burgundischen Regna 840–926 (962) Teil 2: Das Regnum Italiae in der Zeit der Thronkämpfe und Reichsteilungen* (Cologne, Weimar and Vienna, 1998).

Collectio canonum hispaniae, ed. G. Martínez Díez et al., *La colección canónica Hispana* (Madrid, 1966–).

Das Prümer Urbar, ed. I. Schwab (Dusseldorf, 1983).

Davis, R. (trans.) 1992. *The Lives of the Eighth-Century Popes*. Liverpool.

Davis, R. (trans.) 1995. *The Lives of the Ninth-Century Popes*. Liverpool.

Davis, R. (trans.) 2000. *The Book of Pontiffs (Liber Pontificalis)*. Liverpool.

De abbatia Sancti Martini, ed. G.H. Pertz, MGH SS 8 (Hanover, 1848), pp. 208–9.

Dutton, P.E. 2004. *Carolingian Civilization: A Reader*. 2nd edn, Peterborough, Ontario.

Ekkehard, *Casus S.Galli*, ed. H.F. Haefele, *St.Galler Klostergeschichten* (Darmstadt, 1980).

Epistolae ad divortium Lotharii II regis pertinentes, ed. E. Dümmler, MGH Epistolae 6 (Berlin, 1925), pp. 207–40.

Erchempert of Monte Cassino, *Historia Langobardorum Beneventanorum*, ed. G. Waitz, MGH SRL (Hanover, 1878), pp. 231–64.

Ermold, *Ad eundem Pippinum*, ed. E. Farals, *Ermold le Noir. Poème sur Louis le Pieux et épîtres au roi Pépin* (Paris, 1964), pp. 218–32.

Fanning, S. and Bachrach, B.S. (trans.) 2004. *The Annals of Flodoard of Reims, 919–966*. Peterborough, Ontario.

Flodoard, *Annales*, ed. P. Lauer, *Les annales de Flodoard* (Paris, 1906).

Flodoard, *Historia Remensis Ecclesiae*, ed. M. Stratmann, MGH SS 36 (Hanover, 1998).

Foulke, W.D. (trans.) 2003. *Paul the Deacon, History of the Lombards*. Philadelphia.

Frechulf of Lisieux, *Histories*, ed. M. Allen, *Frechulfi Lexoviensis episcopi opera omnia*, Corpus Christianorum Continuatio Mediaevalis 169–169A (Turnhout, 2002).

Fuhrmann, H. (ed.) 1987. 'Hohenaltheim, 20. September 916', in Hehl (ed.) 1987, pp. 1–41.

Gesta Dagoberti, ed. B. Krusch, MGH SRM 2 (Hanover, 1888), pp. 396–425.

Gesta sanctorum Rotonensium, ed. C. Brett, *The Monks of Redon: Gesta sanctorum Rotonensium and Vita Conuuoionis* (Woodbridge, 1989).

Gilsdorf, S. (trans.) 2004. *Queenship and Sanctity: The Lives of Mathilda and the Epitaph of Adelheid*. Washington.

Hartmann, W. (ed.) 1998. *Die Konzilien der karolingischen Teilreiche 860–874*, MGH Concilia 4. Hanover.

Hehl, E.D. (ed.) 1987. *Die Konzilien Deutschlands und Reichsitaliens 916–1001*, MGH Concilia 6. Hanover.

Heito of Reichenau, *Visio Wettini*, ed. H. Knittel, *Heito und Walahfrid Strabo* (Heidelberg, 2004).

John VIII, *Fragmenta*, ed. E. Caspar, MGH Epistolae 7 (Berlin, 1928), pp. 273–312.

Jonas, *Vita Columbani*, ed. B. Krusch, *Vitae sanctorum Columbani, Vedastis, Iohannis*. MGH SRG (Hanover, 1905).

Jonas of Orléans, *De institutione regia*, ed. A. Dubreucq, *Jonas d'Orléans. Le métier du roi* (Paris, 1995).

Justin, *Epitome*, ed. O. Seel, *Epitoma historiarum Philippicarum* (Stuttgart, 1972).

Kehr, P. (ed.), *Die Urkunden Arnulfs*. MGH Diplomata regum Germaniae ex stirpe Karolinorum 3 (Berlin, 1940).

Kehr, P. (ed.), *Die Urkunden Karls III*. MGH Diplomata regum Germaniae ex stirpe Karolinorum 2 (Berlin, 1936–7).

Kehr, P. (ed.). *Die Urkunden Ludwigs des Deutschen, Karlmanns und Ludwigs des Jüngeren*, MGH Diplomata regum Germaniae ex stirpe Karolinorum 1 (Berlin, 1932–4).

King, P.D. (trans.) 1987. *Charlemagne. Translated Sources*. Kendal.

Liber Historiae Francorum, ed. B. Krusch, MGH SRM 2 (Hanover, 1888), pp. 215–328.

Liutprand of Cremona, *Antapodosis*, ed. P. Chiesa, *Liudprandi Cremonensis Opera Omnia*, Corpus Christianorum Continuatio Medievalis 156 (Turnhout, 1998), pp. 3–150.

Liutprand of Cremona, *Historia Ottonis*, ed. P. Chiesa, *Liudprandi Cremonensis*

Opera Omnia, Corpus Christianorum Continuatio Medievalis 156 (Turnhout, 1998), pp. 167–83.

Liutprand of Cremona, *Relatio de legatione Constantinopolitana*, ed. P. Chiesa, *Liudprandi Cremonensis Opera Omnia*, Corpus Christianorum Continuatio Medievalis 156 (Turnhout, 1998), pp. 185–218.

Lupus of Ferrières, *Letters*, ed. L. Levillain, *Loup de Ferrières. Correspondance* (Paris, 1927 and 1935).

Mühlbacher, E. (ed.), *Die Urkunden Pippins, Karlmanns und Karls des Grossen*, MGH Diplomata Karolinorum 1 (Hanover, 1906).

Nelson, J.L. (trans.) 1991. *The Annals of St-Bertin: Ninth-Century Histories*, Vol. 1. Manchester and New York.

Nicholas, *Epistolae*, ed. E. Perels, MGH Epistolae 6 (Berlin, 1925), pp. 257–690.

Nithard, *Historia*, ed. P. Lauer, *Nithard. Histoire des fils de Louis le Pieux* (Paris, 1964).

Notker, *Erchanberti Breviarium Continuatio*, ed. G. Pertz, MGH SS 2 (Hanover, 1829), pp. 329–30.

Notker, *Gesta Karoli Magni*, ed. H.F. Haefele, *Notker der Stammler, Taten Kaiser Karls des Großen*, MGH SRG NS (Berlin, 1959).

Paul the Deacon, *Historia Langobardorum*, ed. G. Waitz, MGH SRG (Hanover, 1878).

Rau, R. (trans.) 1960. *Quellen zur Karolingischen Reichsgeschichte*, Vol. 3. Berlin.

Regenos, G.W. (trans.) 1966. *The Letters of Lupus of Ferrières*. The Hague.

Regino, *Chronicle*, ed. F. Kurze, *Reginonis abbatis Prumiensis Chronicon cum continuatione Treverensi*, MGH SRG (Hanover, 1890).

Regino, *De synodalibus causis*, ed. W. Hartmann, *Das Sendhandbuch des Regino von Prüm* (Darmstadt, 2004).

Regino, *De Harmonica institutione*, ed. M.P. LeRoux, 'The *De harmonica institutione* and *Tonarius* of Regino of Prüm', PhD dissertation, Catholic University of America (Washington DC, 1965); see also www.chmtl.indiana.edu/tml/9th-11th/9TH-11TH_INDEX.html.

Reuter, T. (trans.) 1992. *The Annals of Fulda: Ninth-Century Histories*, Vol. 2. Manchester.

Revelatio Stephani Papae, ed. G. Waitz, *Ex Hilduini abbatis libro de Sancto Dionysio*, MGH SS 15 (Stuttgart, 1887), pp. 2–3.

Ruotger, *Vita Brunonis*, ed. G. Pertz, MGH SS 4 (Hanover, 1841), pp. 252–75.

Schieffer, T. (ed.), *Die Urkunden Zwentibolds und Ludwigs des Kindes*, MGH Diplomata Regum Germaniae ex Stirpe Karolinorum IV (Berlin, 1960).

Schieffer, T. (ed.), *Die Urkunden Lothars I. und Lothars II.*, MGH Diplomata Karolinorum 3 (Berlin, 1966).

Scholz, B. and Rogers, B. (trans.) 1970. *Carolingian Chronicles*. Ann Arbor.

Sickel, T. (ed.), *Die Urkunden Konrad I., Heinrich I. und Otto I.*, MGH Diplomata regum et imperatorem Germaniae, Vol. 1 (Hanover, 1879–84).

Swanton, M. (trans.), *The Anglo-Saxon Chronicle* (London, 1996).

Thegan, *Gesta Hludowici imperatoris*, ed. E. Tremp, MGH SRG (Hanover, 1995).

Thietmar of Merseburg, *Chronicon*, trans. D. Warner, *Ottonian Germany: the Chronicon of Thietmar of Merseburg* (Manchester, 2001).

Tschan, F. (trans.) 2002. *Adam of Bremen, History of the Archbishops of Hamburg Bremen*. New York.

Vita Arnulfi, ed. B. Krusch, MGH SRM 2 (Hanover, 1888), pp. 426–46.

Wallis, F. (trans.) 2004. *Bede: the Reckoning of Time*. 2nd ed., Liverpool.

Widukind of Corvey, *Rerum Gestarum Saxonicarum Libri Tres*, ed. P. Hirsch, MGH SRG (Hanover, 1935).

Wolfhard, *Miracula S. Waldburgis Monheimensis*, ed. A. Bauch, *Ein bayerisches Mirakelbuch aus der Karolingerzeit* (Regensburg, 1979).

Wright, F.A. (trans.) 1993. *Liudprand of Cremona. The Embassy to Constantinople and Other Writings*. London.

Yardley, J. (trans.) 1994. *Epitome of the Philippic History of Pompeius Trogus*. Atlanta.

Secondary sources

Abels, R. 2003. 'Alfred the Great, the *micel hæthen here* and the Viking Threat', in T. Reuter (ed.), *Alfred the Great: Papers from the Eleventh-Centenary Conferences*. Aldershot, pp. 265–79.

Airlie, S. 1985. 'The Political Behaviour of Secular Magnates in Francia, 829–79', unpublished D.Phil. thesis. University of Oxford.

Airlie, S. 1993. 'After Empire: Recent Work on the Emergence of Post-Carolingian Kingdoms', *Early Medieval Europe* 2, pp. 153–61.

Airlie, S. 1995. 'The Aristocracy', in McKitterick (ed.) 1995, pp. 431–50.

Airlie, S. 1998. 'Private Bodies and the Body Politic in the Divorce Case of Lothar II', *Past and Present* 161, pp. 3–38.

Airlie, S. 1999. 'Narratives of Triumph and Rituals of Submission: Charlemagne's Mastering of Bavaria', *Transactions of the Royal Historical Society*, 6th series, 9, pp. 93–119.

Airlie, S. 2000. 'The Nearly Men: Boso of Vienne and Arnulf of Bavaria', in A. Duggan (ed.), *Nobles and Nobility in Medieval Europe*. Woodbridge, pp. 25–41.

Airlie, S. 2001. 'True Teachers and Pious Kings: Salzburg, Louis the German, and Christian Order', in R. Gameson and H. Leyser (eds), *Belief and Culture in the Middle Ages*. Oxford, pp. 89–105.

Airlie, S. 2006a. '"Sad stories of the deaths of kings": Narrative Patterns and Structures of Authority in Regino of Prüm's *Chronicon*', in E.M. Tyler and R. Balzaretti (eds), *Narrative and History in the Early Medieval West*. Turnhout, pp. 105–31.

Airlie, S. 2006b. 'Les élites en 888 et apres, ou comment pense-t-on la crise carolingienne?', in F. Bougard, L. Feller and R. Le Jan (eds), *Les Elites au Haut Moyen Age. Crises et Renouvellements*. Turnhout, pp. 425–37.

Airlie, S. forthcoming. 'Un roi et son royaume destinés à l'effrondrement? La Francia Media dans l'ombre de Lothaire II (855–885)'.

Allen, M.I. 1998. 'The Chronicle of Claudius of Turin', in A.C. Murray (ed.), *After Rome's Fall. Narrators and Sources of Early Medieval History. Essays Presented to Walter Goffart*. Toronto, pp. 288–319.

Allen, M.I. 2003. 'Universal History, 300–1000: Origins and Western Developments', in Deliyannis 2003a, pp. 17–42.

Althoff, G. 1978. *Das Necrolog von Borghorst. Edition und Untersuchung*. Münster.

Althoff, G. 1982. 'Zur Frage nach der Organisation sächsischer coniurationes in der Ottonenzeit', *Fruhmittelalterliche Studien* 16, pp. 129–42.

Althoff, G. 1990. 'Breisach: ein Refugium für Rebellen im frühen Mittelalter?', in H. Nuber, K. Schmid, H. Steuer and T. Zotz (eds), *Archäologie und Geschichte des ersten Jahrtausends in Südwestdeutschland*. Sigmaringen, pp. 457–72.

Althoff, G. 1992. *Amicitiae und Pacta: Bündnis, Einung, Politik und Gebetsgedenken im beginnenden 10. Jahrhundert*. Hanover.

Althoff, G. 1997. *Spielregeln der Politik im Mittelalter: Kommunikation in Frieden und Fehde*. Darmstadt.

Althoff, G. 1999. 'Saxony and the Elbe Slavs in the Tenth Century', in Reuter 1999b, pp. 267–92.

Althoff, G. 2000. *Die Ottonen. Königsherrschaft ohne Staat*. Darmstadt.

Althoff, G. 2001. 'Geschichtsschreibung in einer oralen Gesellschaft. Das Beispiel des 10. Jahrhunderts', in B. Schneidmüller and S. Weinfurter (eds), *Ottonische Neuanfänge. Symposion zur Ausstellung 'Otto der Große, Magdeburg und Europa'*. Mainz, pp. 151–69.

Althoff, G. 2004. *Family, Friends and Followers: Political and Social Bonds in Medieval Europe*. Cambridge.

Angenendt, A. 1984. *Kaiserherrschaft und Königstaufe. Kaiser, Könige und Päpste als geistliche Patrone in der abendländischen Missiongeschichte*. Berlin and New York.

Anton, H. 1993. 'Synoden, Teilreichsepiskopat und die Herausbildung Lotharingiens (859–870)', in G. Jenal (ed.), *Herrschaft, Kirche, Kultur. Beiträge zur Geschichte des Mittelalters. Festschrift für Friedrich Prinz.* Stuttgart, pp. 83–124.

Arnold, D. 2005. *Johannes VIII. Päpstliche Herrschaft in den karolingischen Teilreichen am Ende des 9. Jahrhunderts.* Frankfurt.

Bachrach, B.S. 1970. 'Charles Martel, Mounted Shock Combat, the Stirrup and Feudalism', *Studies in Medieval and Renaissance History* 7, pp. 49–75.

Bagge, S. 2002. *Kings, Politics and the Right Order of the World in German Historiography, c. 950–1150.* Leiden, Boston and Cologne.

Barford, P. 2001. *The Early Slavs.* London.

Barrow, J. 2001. 'Chester's Earliest Regatta? Edgar's Dee-Rowing Revisited', *Early Medieval Europe* 10, pp. 81–93.

Barth, R. 1990. *Der Herzog in Lotharingien im 10. Jahrhundert.* Sigmaringen.

Bartlett, R. 1986. *Trial by Fire and Water. The Medieval Judicial Ordeal.* Oxford.

Bauer, T. 1994. 'Rechtliche Implikationen des Ehestreites Lothars II.', *Zeitschrift der Savigny-Stiftung für Rechtsgeschichte: Kanonistische Abteilung* 80, pp. 41–87.

Bauer, T. 1997. *Lotharingien als historischer Raum: Raumbildung und Raumbewusstsein im Mittelalter.* Cologne.

Bautier, R.H. 1961. 'Le règne d'Eudes (888–898) à la lumière des diplômes expédiés par sa chancellerie', *Comptes rendus de l'académie des inscriptions et belles-lettres*, pp. 140–57.

Bautier, R.H. 1973. 'Aux origines du royaume de Provence: de la sédition avortée de Boson à la royauté légitime de Louis', *Provence historique* 23, pp. 41–68.

Becher, M. 1993. *Eid und Herrschaft: Untersuchungen zum Herrscherethos Karls des Grossen.* Sigmaringen.

Becher, M. 1996. *Rex, Dux und Gens. Untersuchungen zur Entstehung des sächsischen Herzogtums im 9. und 10. Jahrhundert.* Husum.

Becher, M. 2002. 'Zwischen König und "Herzog". Sachsen unter Kaiser Arnolf', in Fuchs and Schmid 2002, pp. 89–121.

Bernhard, M. 1979. *Studien zur Epistola de armonica institutione des Regino von Prüm.* Munich.

Bertels, K. 1987. 'Carantania. Beobachtungen zur politisch-geographischen Terminologie und zur Geschichte des Landes und seiner Bevölkerung im frühen Mittelalter', *Carinthia I* 177, pp. 87–196.

Beumann, H. 1966/67. 'König Zwentibolds Kurswechsel im Jahre 898', *Rheinische Vierteljahrsblätter* 31, pp. 17–41.

Bishop, J. 1985. 'Bishops as Marital Advisers in the Ninth Century', in J. Kirshner and S.F. Wemple (eds), *Women of the Medieval World.* Oxford, pp. 53–84.

Boncella, P. 1995. 'Regino Prumiensis and the Tones', in G. Hair (ed.), *Songs of the Dove and the Nightingale: Sacred and Secular Music c.900–c.1600*. Sydney, pp. 74–89.

Borgolte, M. 1977. 'Karl III. und Neudingen. Zum Problem der Nachfolgeregelung Ludwigs des Deutschen', *Zeitschrift für die Geschichte des Oberrheins* 125, pp. 21–55.

Borgolte, M. 1984. *Geschichte der Grafschaften Alemanniens in fränkischer Zeit.* Sigmaringen.

Borgolte, M. 1986. *Die Grafen Alemanniens im merowingischer und karolingischer Zeit. Eine Prosopographie.* Sigmaringen.

Borst, A. 1973. *Lebensformen im Mittelalter.* Frankfurt.

Borst, A. 1993. *The Ordering of Time. From the Ancient Computus to the Modern Computer.* Chicago.

Boschen, L. 1972. *Die Annales Prumienses. Ihre nähere und ihre weitere Verwandtschaft.* Dusseldorf.

Bouchard, C. 1999. 'Burgundy and Provence, 879–1032', in Reuter 1999b, pp. 328–45.

Bougard, F. 1998. 'La Cour et le gouvernement de Louis II (840–875)', in Le Jan 1998, pp. 249–67.

Bougard, F. 2000. 'En marge du divorce de Lothaire II: Boson de Vienne, le cocu qui fut fait roi?', *Francia* 27, pp. 33–51.

Bowlus, C. 1995. *Franks, Moravians and Magyars. The Struggle for the Middle Danube, 788–907.* Philadelphia.

Bowlus, C. 2006. *The Battle of Lechfeld and its Aftermath, August 955: the End of the Age of Migrations in the Latin West.* Aldershot.

Boynton, S. 1999. 'The Sources and Significance of the Orpheus Myth in *Musica Enchiriadis* and Regino of Prüm's *Epistola de harmonica institutione*', *Early Music History* 18, pp. 47–74.

Brown, G. 1994. 'The Carolingian Renaissance: an Introduction', in McKitterick 1994, pp. 1–51.

Brühl, C. 1962. 'Fränkischer Krönungsbrauch und das Problem der "Festkrönungen"', *Historische Zeitschrift* 194, pp. 265–326.

Brühl, C. 1996. 'Ludwig IV. "der überseeische" (936–54)', in Ehlers, Müller and Schneidmüller 1996, pp. 47–59.

Brunterc'h, J.P. 1983. 'Géographie historique et hagiographie: la vie de Saint Mervé', *Mélanges de l'Ecole Française de Rome* 95, pp. 7–63.

Brunterc'h, J.P. 1997. 'Naissance et affirmation des principautés au temps du roi Eudes: l'example de l'Aquitaine', in Guillot and Favreau 1997, pp. 69–116.

Buc, P. 2004. 'Noch Einmal 918–919. Of the Ritualised Demise of Kings and of Political Rituals in General', in G. Althoff (ed.), *Rituale, Zeichen, Werte*. Munster, pp. 151–78.

Bührer-Thierry, G. 1987. 'Le Conseiller du roi: les écrivains carolingiens et la tradition biblique', *Médiévales* 12, pp. 111–23.

Bührer-Thierry, G. 1997. *Évêques et pouvoir dans le royaume de Germanie. Les Églises de Bavière et de Souabe, 876–973.* Paris.

Bührer-Thierry, G. 1998. 'Just Anger or Vengeful Anger? The Punishment of Blinding in the Early Medieval West', in B. Rosenwein (ed.), *Anger's Past. The Social Uses of an Emotion in the Middle Ages.* Ithaca, pp. 75–91.

Bullough, D.A. 1986. 'Ethnic History and the Carolingians: Paul the Deacon's *Historia Langobardorum*' in C. Holdsworth and T. Wiseman (eds), *The Inheritance of Historiography.* Exeter, pp. 85–105.

Büttner, H. 1956. 'Die Ungarn, das Reich und Europa bis zur Lechfeldschlacht des Jahres 955', *Zeitschrift für bayerische Landesgeschichte* 19, pp. 433–58.

Carroll, C. 2002. 'The Last Great Carolingian Church Council: the Tribur Synod of 895', *Annuarium Historiae Conciliorum* 33, pp. 9–25.

Castelnuovo, G. 1998. 'Les élites des royaumes de Bourgogne (milieu IXe – milieu Xe siècle)', in Le Jan 1998, pp. 383–408.

Chédeville, A. and Guillotel, H. 1984. *La Bretagne des Saints et des Rois, Ve–Xe siècle.* Evreux.

Chiesa, P. (ed.) 2000. *Paolo Diacono, uno scrittore fra tradizione longobarda e rinnovamento carolingio.* Udine.

Claude, D. 1972. *Geschichte des Erzbistums Magdeburg bis ins 12. Jahrhundert.* Cologne.

Corradini, R., Diesenberger, M. and Reimitz, H. (eds). 2003. *The Construction of Communities in the Early Middle Ages.* Leiden and Boston.

Corradini, R., Meens, R., Pössel, C. and Shaw, P. (eds) 2006. *Texts and Identities in the Early Middle Ages.* Vienna.

Costambeys, M., Innes, M. and MacLean, S. forthcoming. *The Carolingian World.* Cambridge.

Coupland, S. 1991. 'The Fortified Bridges of Charles the Bald', *Journal of Medieval History* 17, pp. 1–12.

Coupland, S. 1995. 'The Vikings in Francia and Anglo-Saxon England to 911', in McKitterick 1995, pp. 190–201.

Coupland, S. 1998. 'From Poachers to Gamekeepers: Scandinavian Warlords and Carolingian Kings', *Early Medieval Europe* 7, pp. 85–114.

Coupland, S. 1999. 'The Frankish Tribute Payments to the Vikings and their Consequences', *Francia* 26, pp. 57–75.

Curta, F. 2006. *Southeastern Europe in the Middle Ages.* Cambridge.

Davids, A. (ed.) 1995. *Empress Theophano: Byzantium and the West at the Turn of the First Millennium.* Cambridge.

Davies, W. 1988. *Small Worlds: the Village Community in Early Medieval Brittany.* London.

De Jong, M. 2000. 'The Empire as *ecclesia*. Hrabanus Maurus and Biblical *historia* for Rulers', in Y. Hen and M. Innes (eds), *The Uses of the Past in the Early Middle Ages*. Cambridge, pp. 191–226.

De Jong, M. 2001. 'Exegesis for an Empress', in E. Cohen and M. de Jong (eds), *Medieval Transformations: Texts, Power, and Gifts in Contexts*. Leiden, pp. 69–100.

De Jong, M. 2006. '*Ecclesia* and the Early Medieval Polity', in S. Airlie, W. Pohl and H. Reimitz (eds), *Staat im frühen Mittelalter*. Vienna.

De Jong, M. forthcoming. 'Charlemagne's Balcony'.

De Vajay, S. 1968. *Der Eintritt des ungarischen Stämmebundes in die europäische Geschichte (862–933)*. Mainz.

Deliyannis, D.M. (ed.) 2003a. *Historiography in the Middle Ages*. Leiden and Boston.

Deliyannis, D.M. 2003b. 'Introduction', in Deliyannis 2003a, pp. 1–13.

Delogu, P. 1968. 'Vescovi, conti e sovrani nella crisi del regno Italico (ricerche sull'aristocrazia Carolingia in Italia III)', *Annali della scuola speciale per archivisti e bibliotecari dell'Università di Roma* 8, pp. 3–72.

Depreux, P. 1992. 'Das Königtum Bernhards von Italien und sein Verhältnis zum Kaisertum', *Quellen und Forschungen aus italienischen Archiven und Bibliotheken* 72, pp. 1–25.

Deutinger, R. 2002. '"Königswahl" und Herzogserhebung Arnulfs von Bayern. Das Zeugnis der älteren Salzburger Annalen zum Jahr 920', *DA* 58, pp. 17–68.

Devroey, J.-P. 1976. '*Mansi absi*: indices de crise ou de croissance de l'économie rurale du haut moyen âge', *Le Moyen Âge* 82, pp. 421–51.

Diesenberger, M. 2006. 'How Collections Shape the Texts: Rewriting and Rearranging *Passions* in Carolingian Bavaria', in M. Heinzelmann (ed.), *Livrets, collections et textes. Études de la tradition hagiographique latine*. Ostfildern, pp. 195–224.

Dopsch, H. 2002. 'Arnolf und der Südosten – Karantanien, Mähren, Ungarn', in Fuchs and Schmid 2002, pp. 143–86.

Dubois, J. 1978. *Les Martyrologes du moyen âge latin*. Turnhout.

Dümmler, E. 1888. *Geschichte des ostfränkischen Reiches*, Vol. 3. 2nd edn, Leipzig.

Dunbabin, J. 2000. *France in the Making, 843–1180*. 2nd edn, Oxford.

Ehlers, J. 1992. 'Carolingiens, Robertiens, Ottoniens: politique familiale ou relations franco-allemandes', in M. Parisse and X. Barral I Altet (eds), *Le Roi de France et son royaume autour de l'an mil*. Paris, pp. 39–45.

Ehlers, J., Müller, H. and Schneidmüller, B. (eds) 1996. *Die französischen Könige des Mittelalters. Von Odo bis Karl VIII. (888–1498)*. Munich.

BIBLIOGRAPHY

Eibl, E.M. 1984. 'Zur Stellung Bayerns und Rheinfrankens im Reiche Arnulfs von Kärnten', *Jahrbuch für Geschichte des Feudalismus* 8, pp. 73–113.

Epp, V. 1999. *Amicitia: zur Geschichte personaler, sozialer, politischer und geistlicher Beziehungen im frühen Mittelalter*. Stuttgart.

Ermisch, H. 1872. *Die Chronik des Regino bis 813*. Göttingen.

Ewig, E. 1980. *Frühes Mittelalter (Rhenische Geschichte I.2)*. Dusseldorf.

Fasoli, G. 1949. 'Points de vue sur les incursions hongroises en Europe au Xe siècle', *Cahiers de civilisation médiévale* 2, pp. 17–36.

Felten, F.J. 1996. 'Robert I. (922/923) und Rudolf I. (923–936)', in Ehlers, Müller and Schneidmüller 1996, pp. 36–45.

Fentress, J. and Wickham, C. 1992. *Social Memory*. Oxford.

Fouracre, P. 1985. 'The Context of the OHG *Ludwigslied*', *Medium Aevum* 54, pp. 87–103.

Fouracre, P. 2000. *The Age of Charles Martel*. Harlow.

Fouracre, P. 2005. 'The Long Shadow of the Merovingians', in J. Story (ed.), *Charlemagne: Empire and Society*. Manchester, pp. 5–21.

Fouracre, P. and Gerberding, R. 1996. *Late Merovingian France: History and Hagiography, 640–720*. Manchester.

Franklin, S. and Shepard, J. 1996. *The Emergence of Rus: 750–1200*. London and New York.

Frase, M. 1990. *Friede und Königsherrschaft. Quellenkritik und Interpretation der Continuatio Reginonis*. Frankfurt.

Fried, J. 1976. 'Boso von Vienne oder Ludwig der Stammler? Der Kaiserkandidat Johanns VIII.', *DA* 32, pp. 193–208.

Fried, J. 1984. *Könige Ludwig der Jüngere in seiner Zeit*. Lorsch.

Fried, J. 1995. 'Die Königserhebung Heinrichs I. Erinnerung, Mündlichkeit und Traditionsbildung im 10. Jahrhundert', in M. Borgolte (ed.), *Mittelalterforschung nach der Wende 1989*. Munich, pp. 267–318.

Fuchs, F. 2002. 'Arnolfs Tod, Begräbnis und Memoria', in Fuchs and Schmid 2002, pp. 416–34.

Fuchs, F. and Schmid, P. (eds) 2002. *Kaiser Arnolf. Das ostfränkische Reich am Ende des 9. Jahrhunderts*. Munich.

Ganz, D. 2005a. Review of McKitterick 2004, *IHR Reviews in History*. www.history.ac.uk/reviews/paper/ganz.html.

Ganz, D. 2005b. 'Einhard's Charlemagne: the Characterisation of Greatness', in J. Story (ed.), *Charlemagne. Empire and Society*. Manchester, pp. 38–51.

Garipzanov, I. 2005. 'The Carolingian Abbreviation of Bede's World Chronicle and Carolingian Imperial "Genealogy"', *Hortus Artium Medievalium* 11, pp. 291–8.

Geldner, F. 1971. *Neue Beiträge zur Geschichte der 'alten Babenberger'*. Bamberg.

Georgi, W. 1995. 'Bischof Keonwald von Worcester und die Heirat Ottos I. mit Egitha im Jahre 929', *Historisches Jahrbuch* 115, pp. 1–40.

Gerberding, R. 1987. *The Rise of the Carolingians and the Liber Historiae Francorum*. Oxford.

Glenn, J. 2004. *Politics and History in the Tenth Century: the Work and World of Richer of Reims*. Cambridge.

Goetz, H.-W. 1980. 'Der letzte "Karolinger"? Die Regierung Konrads I. im Spiegel seiner Urkunden', *Archiv für Diplomatik* 26, pp. 56–125.

Goetz, H.-W. 1985. 'Die "Geschichte" im Wissenschaftssystem des Mittelalters', in F.-J. Schmale, *Funktion und Formen mittelalterlicher Geschichtsschreibung*. Darmstadt, pp. 165–213.

Goetz, H.-W. 1987. 'Regnum: zum politischen Denken der Karolingerzeit', *Zeitschrift der Savigny-Stiftung für Rechtsgeschichte, Germanistische Abteilung* 104, pp. 110–89.

Goetz, H.-W. 1999. 'Vergangenheitswahrnehmung, Vergangenheitsgebrauch und Geschichtssymbolismus in der Geschichtsschreibung der Karolingerzeit', *Settimane di studio della Fondazione Centro Italia* 46, pp. 177–225.

Goetz, H.-W. (ed.) 2006. *Konrad I. – Auf dem Weg zum "Deutschen Reich"?* Bochum.

Goffart, W. 2005. 'Bede's *vera lex historiae* Explained', *Anglo-Saxon England* 34, pp. 111–16.

Goldberg, E.J. 1999. '"More Devoted to the Equipment of Battle than the Splendor of Banquets": Frontier Kingship, Military Ritual, and Early Knighthood at the Court of Louis the German', *Viator* 30, pp. 41–78.

Goldberg, E.J. 2004. 'Ludwig der Deutsche und Mahren. Eine Studie zu karolingischen Grenzkriegen im Osten', in W. Hartmann (ed.), *Ludwig der Deutsche und seine Zeit*. Darmstadt, pp. 67–94.

Goldberg, E.J. 2006a. *Struggle for Empire. Kingship and Conflict Under Louis the German, 817–876*. Ithaca.

Goldberg, E.J. 2006b. '*Regina nitens sanctissima Hemma*: Queen Emma (827–876), Bishop Witgar of Augsburg, and the Witgar-Belt', in Weiler and MacLean 2006, pp. 57–95.

Goldschmidt, A. 1914. *Die Elfenbeinskulpturen aus der Zeit der karolingischen und sächsischen Kaiser*. Berlin.

Guillot, O. and Favreau, R. (eds) 1997. *Pays de Loire et Aquitaine de Robert le Fort aux premiers Capétiens*. Poitiers.

Halsall, G. 2003. *Warfare and Society in the Barbarian West, 450–900*. London and New York.

Hamilton, S. 2001. *The Practice of Penance, 900–1050*. Woodbridge.

Hartmann, M. 2002. 'Lotharingien in Arnolfs Reich: das Königtum Zwentibolds', in Fuchs and Schmid 2002, pp. 122–42.

Hartmann, W. 1989. *Die Synoden der Karolingerzeit im Frankenreich und in Italien*. Paderborn.

Hartmann, W. 2002. *Ludwig der Deutsche*. Darmstadt.

Hartmann, W. 2003. 'Regino von Prüm', in *Neue deutsche Biographie* 21. Berlin, pp. 269–70.

Hartmann, W. 2004. 'Die Capita incerta im Sendhandbuch Reginos von Prüm', in O. Münsch and T. Zotz (eds), *Scientia veritatis. Festschrift für Hubert Mordek*. Ostfildern.

Haubrichs, W. 1979. *Die Kultur der Abtei Prüm zur Karolingerzeit*. Bonn.

Hauck, K. 1974. 'Erzbischof Adalbert von Magdeburg als Geschichtsschreiber. Mit der Mitteilung von der mikrochemischen Analyse der Heiligen Lanze in Wien von H. Malissa', in H. Beumann (ed.), *Festschrift für Walter Schlesinger*. Cologne, Vol. 2, pp. 276–353.

Hehl, E.-D., Siebert, H. and Staab, F. (eds). 1987. *Deus qui mutat tempora: Menschen und Institutionen im Wandel des Mittelalters. Festschrift für Alfons Becker*. Sigmaringen.

Hennebicque, R. 1981. 'Structures familiales et politiques au neuvième siècle: un groupe familiale de l'aristocratique Franque', *Revue Historique* 265, pp. 289–333.

Herbers, K. 1998. 'Rom im Frankenreich – Rombeziehungen durch Heilige in der Mitte des 9. Jahrhunderts', in D. Bauer, R. Hiestand, B. Kasten and S. Lorenz (eds), *Herrschaft – Kirche – Mönchtum 750–1050, Festschrift Josef Semmler*. Sigmaringen, pp. 133–69.

Herrmann, H.-W. and Schneider, R. (eds). 1995. *Lotharingia. Eine europäische Kernlandschaft um das Jahr 1000*. Saarbrücken.

Hiestand, R. 1994. 'Pressburg 907. Eine Wende in der Geschichte des ostfränkischen Reiches?', *Zeitschrift für bayerische Landesgeschichte* 57, pp. 1–20.

Hlawitschka, E. 1960a. *Franken, Alemannen, Bayern und Burgunder in Oberitalien (774–962). Zum Verständnis der fränkischen Königsherrschaft in Italien*. Freiburg.

Hlawitschka, E. 1960b. 'Herzog Giselbert von Lothringen und das Kloster Remiremont', *Zeitschrift für die Geschichte des Oberrheins* 108, pp. 422–65.

Hlawitschka, E. 1968. *Lotharingien und das Reich an der Schwelle der deutschen Geschichte*. Stuttgart.

Hlawitschka, E. 1969. *Die Anfänge des Hauses Habsburg-Lothringen*. Saarbrücken.

Hlawitschka, E. 1975. 'Regino von Prüm (gest. 915)', *Rheinische Lebensbilder* 6, pp. 7–27.

Hlawitschka, E. 1983. 'Die Widonen im Dukat von Spoleto', *Quellen und*

Forschungen aus italienischen Archiven und Bibliotheken 63, pp. 20–92.

Hlawitschka, E. 1987. 'Kontroverses aus dem Umfeld von König Heinrichs I. Gemahlin Mathilde', in Hehl, Siebert and Staab 1987, pp. 33–54.

Hlawitschka, E. 2003. *Konradiner-Genealogie, unstatthafte Verwandtenehen und spatottonisch-fruhsalische Thronbesetzungspraxis.* Hanover.

Hope, G. 2005. 'The Political Development of the Carolingian Kingdom of Lotharingia, 870–925', unpublished PhD thesis. University of Glasgow.

Hummer, H. 2003. 'Reform and Lordship in Alsace at the Turn of the Millennium', in W. Brown and P. Górecki (eds), *Conflict in Medieval Europe: Changing Perspectives on Society and Culture.* Aldershot, pp. 69–84.

Hummer, H. 2006. *Politics and Power in Early Medieval Europe: Alsace and the Frankish Realm, 600–1000.* Cambridge.

Hümpfner, W. 1924. 'Eine unbeachtete Interpolation zu Reginos von Prüms Chronik', *Historisches Jahrbuch* 44, pp. 65–72.

Hüschen, H. 1962. 'Regino von Prüm, Historiker, Kirchenrechtler und Musiktheoretiker', in H. Hüschen (ed.), *Festschrift Karl Gustav Fellerer zum sechzigsten Geburtstag.* Regensburg, pp. 205–23.

Huschner, W. 2003. *Transalpine Kommunikation im Mittelalter: diplomatische, kulturelle und politische Wechselwirkungen zwischen Italien und dem nordalpinen Reich (9.-11. Jahrhundert).* Hanover.

Innes, M. 1997a. 'The Classical Tradition in the Carolingian Renaissance: Ninth-Century Encounters with Suetonius', *International Journal of the Classical Tradition* 3, pp. 265–82.

Innes, M. 1997b. 'Franks and Slavs c.700–1000: the problem of European Expansion before the Millennium', *Early Medieval Europe* 6, pp. 201–14.

Innes, M. 1998. 'Memory, Orality and Literacy in an Early Medieval Society', *Past and Present* 158, pp. 3–36.

Innes, M. 2000. *State and Society in the Early Middle Ages: the Middle Rhine Valley, 400–1000.* Cambridge.

Innes, M. 2001. 'People, Places and Power in the Carolingian World: a Microcosm', in M. De Jong and F. Theuws (eds), *Topographies of Power in the Early Middle Ages.* Leiden, Boston and Cologne, pp. 397–437.

Innes, M. 2003. '"A Place of Discipline": Aristocratic Youth and Carolingian Courts', in C. Cubitt (ed.), *Court Culture in the Early Middle Ages.* Turnhout, pp. 59–76.

Jackman, D. 1997. *Criticism and Critique: Sidelights on the Konradiner.* Oxford.

Jarnut, J. 1979. *Bergamo 568–1098.* Wiesbaden.

Jäschke, K.U. 1975. *Burgenbau und Landesverteidung um 900.* Sigmaringen.

Karpf, E. 1985. *Herrscherlegitimation und Reichsbegriff in der ottonischen Geschichtsschreibung des 10. Jahrhunderts.* Stuttgart.

Kasten, B. 1997. *Königssöhne und Königsherrschaft. Untersuchungen zur Teilhabe am Reich in der Merowinger- und Karolingerzeit*. Hanover.

Keller, H. 1966. 'Zum Sturz Karls III. Uber die Rolle Liutwards von Vercelli und Liutberts von Mainz, Arnulfs von Kärnten und der ostfränkischen Großen bei der Absetzung des Kaisers', *DA* 34 (1966), pp. 333–84.

Kéry, L. 1999. *Canonical Collections of the Early Middle Ages (c.400–1140): a Bibliographical Guide to the Manuscripts and Literature*. Washington.

Kölzer, T. 1987. 'Adalbert von St. Maximin, Erzbischof von Magdeburg (968–981)', *Rheinische Lebensbilder* 17, pp. 7–18.

Körntgen, L. 2001. *Königsherrschaft und Gottes Gnade: zu Kontext und Funktion sakraler Vorstellungen in Historiographie und Bildzeugnissen der ottonischfrühsalischen Zeit*. Berlin.

Kortüm, H.-H. 'Multi reguli in Europa ... excrevere. Das ostfränkische Reich und seine Nachbarn', in Fuchs and Schmid 2002, pp. 68–88.

Kortüm, H.-H. 1994. 'Weltgeschichte am Ausgang der Karolingerzeit: Regino von Prüm', in Scharer and Scheibelreiter 1994, pp. 499–513.

Kottje, R. 1983. 'Kirchliches Recht und päpstlicher Autoritätsanspruch. Zu den Auseinandersetzungen über de Ehe Lothars II.', in H. Mordek (ed.), *Aus Kirche und Reich. Festschrift für Friedrich Kempf*. Sigmaringen, pp. 97–103.

Koziol, G. 2006a. 'Is Robert I in Hell? The Diploma for Saint-Denis and the Mind of a Rebel King (Jan. 25, 923)', *Early Medieval Europe* 14, pp. 233–67.

Koziol, G. 2006b. 'Charles the Simple, Robert of Neustria, and the *vexilla* of Saint-Denis', *Early Medieval Europe* 14, pp. 355–90.

Kreutz, B. 1996. *Before the Normans: Southern Italy in the Ninth and Tenth Centuries*. Philadelphia.

Krüger, K.H. 1973, 'Königskonversionen im 8. Jahrhundert', *Frühmittelalterliche Studien* 7, pp. 169–222.

Kuchenbuch, L. 1978. *Bäuerliche Gesellschaft und Klosterherrschaft im 9. Jahrhundert. Studien zur Sozialstruktur der Familia der Abtei Prüm*. Wiesbaden.

Kupper, L. 1984. 'Saint Lambert: de l'histoire à la légende', *Revue d'Histoire Ecclésiastique* 79, pp. 5–49.

Kurze, F. 1890. 'Handschriftliche Überlieferung und Quellen der Chronik Reginos und seines Fortsetzers', *Neues Archiv* 15, pp. 293–330.

Lauer, P. 1900. *Le Règne de Louis IV d'Outre-Mer*. Paris.

Le Jan, R. 1995a. *Famille et pouvoir dans le monde Franc (VIIe–Xe siècle). Essai d'anthropologie sociale*. Paris.

Le Jan, R. 1995b. 'L'aristocratie lotharingienne: structure interne et conscience politique', in Herrmann and Schneider 1995, pp. 71–88.

Le Jan, R. (ed.) 1998. *La Royauté et les élites dans l'Europe carolingienne (début IXe siècle aux environs de 920)*. Lille.

Le Jan, R. 2000. 'Frankish Giving of Arms and Rituals of Power: Continuity and Change in the Carolingian Period', in F. Theuws and J. Nelson (eds), *Rituals of Power. From Late Antiquity to the Middle Ages*. Leiden, pp. 281–309.

Le Jan, R. 2001a. 'La Reine Gerberge, entre carolingiens et ottoniens', in Le Jan 2001c, pp. 30–8.

Le Jan, R. 2001b. 'D'une cour à l'autre: les voyages des reines de France au Xe siècle', in Le Jan 2001c, pp. 39–52.

Le Jan, R. 2001c. *Femmes, Pouvoir et Société dans le haute moyen age*. Paris.

Levison, W. 1926. 'Nachrichten', *Neues Archiv* 46, p. 285.

Leyser, K. 1979. *Rule and Conflict in an Early Medieval Society: Ottonian Saxony*. London.

Leyser, K. 1982a. 'Henry I and the Beginnings of the Saxon Empire', in Leyser 1982c, pp. 11–42.

Leyser, K. 1982b. 'The Battle at the Lech, 955', in Leyser 1982c, pp. 43–68.

Leyser, K. 1982c. *Medieval Germany and its Neighbours, 900–1250*. London.

Leyser, K. 1994a. 'The Ottonians and Wessex' in Leyser 1994e, pp. 73–104.

Leyser, K. 1994b. 'Ritual, Ceremony and Gesture: Ottonian Germany', in Leyser 1994e, pp. 189–214.

Leyser, K. 1994c. 'Liudprand of Cremona, Preacher and Homilist', in Leyser 1994e, pp. 111–24.

Leyser, K. 1994d. 'Ends and Means in Liudprand of Cremona', in Leyser 1994e, pp. 125–42.

Leyser, K. 1994e. *Communications and Power in Medieval Europe I. The Carolingian and Ottonian Centuries*. Ed. T. Reuter, London and Rio Grande.

Leyser, K. 1994f. 'Early Medieval Warfare', in Leyser 1994e, pp. 29–50.

Lintzel, M. 1933. *Studien über Liudprand von Cremona*. Berlin. Reprinted in Lintzel 1961b.

Lintzel, M. 1937. 'Zur Chronik Reginos von Prüm', *DA* 1, pp. 499–502. Reprinted in Lintzel 1961b.

Lintzel, M. 1961a. 'Erzbischof Adalbert von Magdeburg als Geschichtschreiber', in Lintzel 1961b, Vol. 2, pp. 399–406.

Lintzel, M. 1961b. *Ausgewählte Schriften*, 2 vols. Berlin.

Lošek, F. 1994. 'Die Spinne in der Kirchendecke – Eine St. Galler Klostergeschichte (Notker, *Gesta Karoli*, 1, 32)', in Scharer and Scheibelreiter 1994, pp. 253–61.

Löwe, H. 1967. 'Geschichtschreibung der ausgehenden Karolingerzeit', *DA* 23, pp. 1–30.

Löwe, H. 1973a. *Von Cassiodor zu Dante*. Berlin and New York.

Löwe, H. 1973b. 'Regino von Prüm und das historische Weltbild der Karolingerzeit', in Löwe 1973a, pp. 149–73.

MacLean, S. 1998. 'Charles the Fat and the Viking Great Army: the Military Explanation for the End of the Carolingian Empire', *War Studies Journal* 3, pp. 74–95.

MacLean, S. 2001. 'The Carolingian Response to the Revolt of Boso, 879–87', *Early Medieval Europe* 10, pp. 21–48.

MacLean, S. 2003a. *Kingship and Politics in the Late Ninth Century. Charles the Fat and the End of the Carolingian Empire*. Cambridge.

MacLean, S. 2003b. 'Queenship, Nunneries and Royal Widowhood in Carolingian Europe', *Past and Present* 178, pp. 3–38.

MacLean, S. 2006. 'Ritual, Misunderstanding and the Contest for Meaning: Representations of the Disrupted Royal Assembly at Frankfurt (873)', in Weiler and MacLean 2006, pp. 97–120.

MacLean, S. 2007. '"After his death a great tribulation came to Italy ..." Dynastic Politics and Aristocratic Factions after the Death of Louis II, *c*.870–*c*.890', *Millennium Jahrbuch* 4, pp. 239–60.

MacLean, S. forthcoming. 'Insinuation, Censorship and the Struggle for Late Carolingian Lotharingia in Regino of Prüm's *Chronicle*', *English Historical Review*.

Magdalino, P. 1999. 'The Distance of the Past in Early Medieval Byzantium (VII–X Centuries)', *Settimane di studio della Fondazione Centro Italia* 46, pp. 115–46.

Manitius, M. 1900. 'Regino und Justin', *Neues Archiv* 25, pp. 192–204.

Maund, K.L. 1994. '"A Turmoil of Warring Princes": Political Leadership in Ninth-century Denmark', *Haskins Society Journal* 6, pp. 29–47.

Mazo Karras, R. 2006. 'The History of Marriage and the Myth of *Friedelehe*', *Early Medieval Europe* 14, pp. 119–52.

McKitterick, R. 1983. *The Frankish Kingdoms under the Carolingians, 751–987*. Harlow.

McKitterick, R. 1989. *The Carolingians and the Written Word*. Cambridge.

McKitterick, R. (ed.) 1994. *Carolingian Culture: Emulation and Innovation*. Cambridge.

McKitterick, R. (ed.) 1995. *The New Cambridge Medieval History II c.700–c.900*. Cambridge.

McKitterick, R. 2004. *History and Memory in the Carolingian World*. Cambridge.

McKitterick, R. 2006. *Perceptions of the Past in the Early Middle Ages*. Notre Dame.

Meens, R. 1998. 'Politics, Mirrors of Princes and the Bible: Sins, Kings and the Well-Being of the Realm', *Early Medieval Europe* 7, pp. 345–57.

Morse, R. 1991. *Truth and Convention in the Middle Ages*. Cambridge.

Müller-Mertens, E. 1999. 'The Ottonians as Kings and Emperors', in Reuter 1999b, pp. 233–66.

Nass, K. 1996. *Die Reichskronik des Annalista Saxo und die sachsische Geschichtsschreibung im 12. Jahrhundert.* Hanover.

Nelson, J.L. 1988. 'A Tale of Two Princes: Politics, Text and Ideology in a Carolingian Annal', *Studies in Medieval and Renaissance History* 10, pp. 103–40.

Nelson, J.L. 1989. 'Ninth-century Knighthood: the Evidence of Nithard', in C. Harper-Bill, C. Holdsworth and J.L. Nelson (eds), *Studies in Medieval History Presented to R. Allen Brown.* Woodbridge, pp. 255–66.

Nelson, J.L. 1992. *Charles the Bald.* London.

Nelson, J.L. 1995. 'The Wary Widow', in W. Davies and P. Fouracre (eds), *Property and Power in the Early Middle Ages.* Cambridge, pp. 82–113.

Nelson, J.L. 1996. 'La mort de Charles le Chauve', *Médiévales* 31, pp. 53–66.

Nelson, J.L. 1999. 'Monks, Secular Men and Masculinity, *c.*900', in D.M. Hadley (ed.), *Masculinity in Medieval Europe.* Harlow, pp. 121–42.

Nicholas, D. 1992. *Medieval Flanders.* London.

Nightingale, J. 2001. *Monasteries and Patrons in the Gorze Reform: Lotharingia c.850–1000.* Oxford.

Noble, T.F.X. 1974. 'The Revolt of King Bernard of Italy in 817: its Causes and Consequences', *Studi Medievali* 15, pp. 315–26.

Nonn, U. 1983. *Pagus und Comitatus in Niederlothringen.* Bonn.

Noonan, T. 1999. 'European Russia, *c.*500–*c.*1500', in Reuter 1999b, pp. 487–513.

Odegaard, C.E. 1951. 'The Empress Engelberge', *Speculum* 26, pp. 77–103.

Offergeld, T. 2001. *Reges pueri: das Königtum Minderjähriger im frühen Mittelalter.* Hanover.

Parisot, R. 1898. *Le Royaume de Lorraine sous les carolingiens (843–923).* Paris.

Parisse, M. 1995. 'La Lotharingie: naissance d'un espace politique', in Herrmann and Schneider 1995, pp. 31–48.

Pettiau, H. 2004. 'A Prosopography of Breton Rulership, AD818–952', *Journal of Celtic Studies* 4, pp. 171–191.

Pizarro, J.M. 2003. 'Ethnic and National History, *c.*500–1000', in Deliyannis 2003a, pp. 43–87.

Pohl, W. 1994. 'Paulus Diaconus und die *Historia Langobardorum*: Text und Tradition', in Scharer and Scheibelreiter 1994, pp. 375–405.

Pohl, W. and Reimitz, H. 1998. *Strategies of Distinction: the Construction of Ethnic Communities, 300–800.* Leiden, Boston and Cologne.

Price, N. 1989. *The Vikings in Brittany.* Lancaster.

Prinz, O. 1973. 'Die Überarbeitung der Chronik Reginos aus sprachlicher Sicht', in A. Önnerfors, J. Rathofer and F. Wagner (eds), *Literatur und Sprache im europäischen Mittelalter. Festschrift für Karl Langosch.* Darmstadt, pp. 122–41.

Rabin, A. 2005. 'Historical Re-collections: Rewriting the World Chronicle in Bede's *De Temporum Ratione*', *Viator* 36, pp. 23–39.

Reimitz, H. 1999. 'Ein fränkisches Geschichtsbuch aus Saint-Amand', in C. Egger and H. Weigl (eds), *Text-Schrift-Codex. Quellenkundliche Arbeiten aus dem Institut für österreichische Geschichtsforschung.* Vienna, pp. 34–90.

Reimitz, H. 2006. 'The Art of Truth. Historiography and Identity in the Frankish World', in Corradini, Meens, Pössel and Shaw 2006, pp. 87–104.

Reindel, K. 1953. *Die bayerischen Luitpoldinger 893–989. Sammlung und Erläuterungen der Quellen.* Munich.

Reuter, T. 1985. 'Plunder and Tribute in the Carolingian Empire', *Transactions of the Royal Historical Society*, 5th series, 35, pp. 75–94.

Reuter, T. 1990. 'The End of Carolingian Military Expansion', in P. Godman and R. Collins (eds), *Charlemagne's Heir.* Oxford, pp. 391–405.

Reuter, T. 1991. *Germany in the Early Middle Ages, 800–1056.* London.

Reuter, T. 1997. 'The Recruitment of Armies in the Early Middle Ages – How Much Can We Know?', in A. Norgard Jorgenssen and B.L. Clausen (eds), *Military Aspects of Scandinavian Society in a European Perspective.* Copenhagen, pp. 32–7.

Reuter, T. 1998. '*Regemque, quem in Francia pene perdidit, in patria magnifice recepit*: Ottonian Rulership in Synchronic and Diachronic Comparison', in G. Althoff and E. Schubert (eds), *Herrscherreprasentation im ottonischen Sachsen.* Sigmaringen, pp. 363–80. Reprinted in Reuter 2006e.

Reuter, T. 1999a. 'Carolingian and Ottonian Warfare', in M. Keen (ed.), *Medieval Warfare: A History.* Oxford, pp. 13–35.

Reuter, T. (ed.) 1999b. *The New Cambridge Medieval History Vol. III 900–1024.* Cambridge.

Reuter, T. 2001. 'Assembly Politics in Western Europe from the Eighth Century to the Twelfth', in P. Linehan and J.L. Nelson (eds), *The Medieval World.* London and New York, pp. 432–50. Reprinted in Reuter 2006e.

Reuter, T. 2006a. 'Sex, Lies and Oath-Helpers: the Trial of Queen Uota', in Reuter 2006e, pp. 217–30.

Reuter, T. 2006b. 'The Insecurity of Travel in the Early and High Middle Ages: Criminals, Victims and their Medieval and Modern Observers', in Reuter 2006e, pp. 38–71.

Reuter, T. 2006c. 'Contextualising Canossa: Excommunication, Penance, Surrender, Reconciliation', in Reuter 2006e, pp. 147–66.

Reuter, T. 2006d. 'Peace-breaking, Feud, Rebellion, Resistance: Violence and Peace in the Politics of the Salian Era', in Reuter 2006e, pp. 355–87.

Reuter, T. 2006e. *Medieval Polities and Modern Mentalities*, ed. J.L. Nelson. Cambridge.

Reynolds, S. 1999. 'Carolingian Elopements as a Sidelight on Counts and Vassals', in B. Nagy and M. Sebok (eds), *The Man of Many Devices who Wandered Full Many Ways ... Festschrift in Honor of Janos M. Bak*. Budapest, pp. 340–6.

Riché, P. 1993. *The Carolingians. A Family Who Forged Europe*. Philadelphia.

Rosenwein, B.H. 1996. 'The Family Politics of Berengar I, King of Italy (888–924)', *Speculum* 71, pp. 247–89.

Rosenwein, B.H. 1999. *Negotiating Space: Power, Restraint and Privileges of Immunity in Early Medieval Europe*. Manchester.

Sanderson, W. 1982. 'Archbishop Radbod, Regino of Prüm and Late Carolingian Art and Music in Trier', *Jahrbuch der Berliner Museen* 24, pp. 41–61.

Scharer, A. and Scheibelreiter, G. (eds) 1994. *Historiographie im frühen Mittelalter*. Vienna.

Schieffer, T. 1958. 'Die lothringische Kanzlei um 900', *DA* 14 (1958), pp. 16–148.

Schleidgen, W.-R. 1977. *Die Überlieferungsgeschichte der Chronik des Regino von Prüm*. Mainz.

Schmid, K. 1960. 'Neue Quellen zum Verständnis des Adels im 10. Jahrhundert', in *Zeitshrift für die Geschichte des Oberrheins* 69, pp. 185–232.

Schmitz, G. 1989. 'Regino von Prüm', *Die deutsche Literatur des Mittelalters, Verfasserlexikon*, 2nd edn, Vol. 7, col. 1115–22.

Schneider, G. 1973. *Erzbischof Fulco von Reims (883–900) und das Frankenreich*. Munich.

Schneidmüller, B. 1978. 'Die "Einfältigkeit" Karls III von Westfrankreich als frühmittelalterliche Herrschertugend. Überlegungen zu den cognomen *simplex*', *Schweizerische Zeitschrift für Geschichte* 28, pp. 62–6.

Schneidmüller, B. 1987. '*Regnum* und *ducatus*. Identität und Integration in der lothringischen Geschichte des 9. bis 11. Jahrhunderts', *Rheinische Vierteljahrsblätter* 51, pp. 81–114.

Schneidmüller, B. 1990. 'Regino von Prüm', in *Handwörterbuch zur deutschen Rechtsgeschichte* 4, col. 492–5.

Schwager, H. 1994. *Graf Heribert II. von Soissons, Omois, Meaux, Madrie sowie Vermandois (900/06–43) und die Francia (Nord-Frankreich) in der 1. Hälfte des 10. Jahrhunderts*. Kallmünz.

Screen, E. 2003. 'The Importance of the Emperor: Lothar I and the Frankish Civil War, 840–843', *Early Medieval Europe* 12, pp. 25–51.

Sergi, G. 1999. 'The Kingdom of Italy', in Reuter 1999b, pp. 346–71.

Shepard, J. 1995. 'Slavs and Bulgars', in McKitterick 1995, pp. 228–48.

Shepard, J. 1999. 'Byzantium and the West', in Reuter 1999b, pp. 605–23.

Silagi, G. 1988. 'Die Ungarnstürme in der ungarischen Geschichtsschreibung', *Settimane di Studio del Centro italiano di studi sull' alto medioevo* 35, pp. 245–72.

Simon, G. 1958. 'Untersuchungen zur Topik der Widmungsbriefe mittelalterlicher Geschichtsschreiber bis zum Ende des 12. Jahrhunderts', *Archiv fur Diplomatik* 4, pp. 52–119.

Simon, G. 1959. 'Untersuchungen zur Topik der Widmungsbriefe mittelalterlicher Geschichtsschreiber bis zum Ende des 12. Jahrhunderts', *Archiv fur Diplomatik* 5, pp. 73–154.

Smith, J.M.H. 1992. *Province and Empire. Brittany and the Carolingians.* Cambridge.

Smith, J.M.H. 1995. '*Fines imperii*: the Marches', in McKitterick 1995, pp. 169–89.

Smith, J.M.H. 2000. 'Old Saints, New Cults: Roman Relics in Carolingian Francia', in J.M.H. Smith (ed.), *Early Medieval Rome and the Christian West. Essays in Honour of Donald A. Bullough.* Leiden, Boston and Cologne, pp. 317–39.

Smith, J.M.H. 2005. *Europe After Rome. A New Cultural History 500–1000.* Oxford.

Sonntag, R. 1987. *Studien zur Bewertung von Zahlenangaben in der Geschichtsschreibung des früheren Mittelalters: die Decem Libri Historiarum Gregors von Tours und die Chronica Reginos von Prüm.* Kallmünz.

Staab, F. 1998. 'Jugement moral et propagande. Boson de Vienne vu par les élites du royaume de l'est', in Le Jan 1998, pp. 365–82.

Stafford, P. 1983. *Queens, Concubines and Dowagers: the King's Wife in the Early Middle Ages.* London.

Stoclet, A. 2000. 'La *Clausula de unctione Pippini Regis*, vingt ans après', *Revue belge de philologie et d'histoire* 78, pp. 719–71.

Story, J. 2005. 'The Frankish Annals of Lindisfarne and Kent', *Anglo-Saxon England* 34, pp. 59–109.

Sutherland, J.N. 1988. *Liudprand of Cremona. Bishop, Diplomat, Historian.* Spoleto.

Tellenbach, G. 1988. 'Der Konvent der Reichsabtei Prüm unter Abt Ansbald (860–886)', in G. Tellenbach, *Ausgewählte Abhandlungen und Aufsätze.* Stuttgart, Vol. 2, pp. 411–25.

Thornton, D.E. 1996. 'Locusts in Ireland? A Problem in the Welsh and Frankish Annals', *Cambrian Medieval Celtic Studies* 31, pp. 37–53.

Tremp, E. 1988. *Studien zu den Gesta Hludowici imperatoris des Trierer Chorbischofs Thegan.* Hanover.

Třeštík, D. 1995. 'The Baptism of the Czech Princes in 845 and the Christianization of the Slavs', in *Historica: Historical Sciences in the Czech Republic.* Prague, pp. 7–59.

Van Houts, E.M. 1999. *Memory and Gender in Medieval Europe, 900–1200*. London.

Van Houts, E.M. 2006. Review of Glenn 2004, *Early Medieval Europe* 14, pp. 332–6.

Van Winter, J.M. 1980. 'Die Hamaländer Grafen als Angehörige der Reichsaristokratie im 10. Jahrhundert', *Rheinisches Vierteljahrsblatter* 44, pp. 16–46.

Vogel, W. 1906. *Die Normannen und das fränkische Reich bis zur Gründung der Normandie (799–911)*. Heidelberg.

Von den Brincken, A.-D. 1957. *Studien zur lateinischen Weltchronik bis in das Zeitalter Ottos von Freising*. Dusseldorf.

Von Euw, A. and Schreiner, P. (eds) 1991. *Kaiserin Theophanu: Begegnung des Ostens und Westens um die Wende des ersten Jahrtausends*. Cologne.

Warner, D. 2006. 'The Representation of Empire: Otto I at Ravenna', in Weiler and MacLean 2006, pp. 121–40.

Wattenbach, W., Levison, W. and Löwe, H. 1990. *Deutschlands Geschichtsquellen im Mittelalter*. Vol. 6, Weimar.

Weiler, B. 2000. 'The *Rex Renitens* and the Medieval Idea of Kingship, *c*.900–*c*.1250', *Viator* 31, pp. 1–42.

Weiler, B. and MacLean, S. (eds) 2006. *Representations of Power in Medieval Germany, 800–1500*. Turnhout.

Werner, K.F. 1959a. 'Zur Arbeitsweise des Regino von Prüm', *Die Welt als Geschichte* 19, pp. 96–116.

Werner, K.F. 1959b, 1959c and Werner, K.F. 1960. 'Untersuchungen zur Frühzeit des französischen Fürstentums (9.–10. Jahrhundert)', *Die Welt als Geschichte* 18, pp. 256–89; 19, pp. 146–93; 20, pp. 87–119.

Werner, K.F. 1967. 'Die Nachkommen Karls des Großen bis um das Jahr 1000 (1.–8. Generation', in W. Braunfels (ed.), *Karl der Grosse. Lebenswerk und Nachleben*. Dusseldorf, vol.4, pp. 403–84.

Werner, K.F. 1979. 'Gauzlin von Saint-Denis und die westfränkische Reichsteilung von Amiens (März 880). Ein Beitrag zur Vorgeschichte von Odos Königtum', *DA* 35, pp. 395–462.

Werner, K.F. 1984. *Les Origines (avant l'an mil)*. Paris.

Werner, K.F. 1987. 'Gott, Herrscher und Historiograph. Der Geschichtsschreiber als Interpret des Wirken Gottes in der Welt und Ratgeber der Könige (4. bis 12. Jahrhundert)', in Hehl, Siebert and Staab 1987, pp. 1–31.

Werner, K.F. 1990. 'Dieu, les rois et l'histoire', in R. Delort (ed.), *La France de l'an mil*. Paris, pp. 264–81.

Werner, K.F. 1997. 'Les premiers Robertiens et les premiers Anjou (IXe siècle–début Xe siècle)', in Guillot and Favreau 1997, pp. 9–67.

Wickham, C. 1981. *Early Medieval Italy: Central Power and Local Society, 400–1000*. London.

BIBLIOGRAPHY

Wickham, C. 2005. *Framing the Early Middle Ages: Europe and the Mediterranean, 400–1000*. Oxford.

Willwersch, M. 1989. *Die Grundherrschaft des Klosters Prüm*, ed. I. Schwab and R. Nolden. Trier.

Wisplinghoff, E. 1999. 'Untersuchungen zur Geschichte des Klosters Prüm an der Wende vom 9. zum 10. Jahrhundert', *DA* 55, pp. 439–75.

Wood, I. 2001. *The Missionary Life: Saints and the Evangelisation of Europe, 400–1050*. Harlow.

Zeller, B. 2006. 'Die Liudolfinger als fränkische Könige? Beobachtungen zur sogenannten Continuatio Reginonis', in Corradini, Meens, Pössel and Shaw 2006, pp. 137–52.

Zielinski, H. 1989. 'Die Kloster- und Kirchengründungen der Karolinger', in I. Crusius (ed.), *Beiträge zu Geschichte und Struktur der mittelalterlichen Germania Sacra*. Göttingen, pp. 95–134.

Zimmermann, H. 1974. 'Imperatores Italiae', in H. Beumann (ed.), *Historische Forschungen für Walter Schlesinger*. Cologne and Vienna, pp. 379–399.

Zotz, T. 1992: 'Est in Alsaciae partibus castellum Brisicau. Breisach als Schauplatz der politischen Geschichte im 10. Jahrhundert', *Zeitschrift des Breisgau-Geschichtsvereins* 111, pp. 9–23.

Zotz, T. 1993a. 'Carolingian Tradition and Ottonian-Salian Innovation: Comparative Observations on Palatine Policy in the Empire', in A. Duggan (ed.), *Kings and Kingship in Medieval Europe*. London, pp. 69–100.

Zotz, T. 1993b. 'In Amt und Würden. Zur Eigenart "offizieller" Positionen im früheren Mittelalter', *Tel Aviver Jahrbuch für deutsche Geschichte* 22, pp. 1–23.

INDEX

Note: 'n.' after a page number indicates the number of a note on that page.

Aachen 4, 43, 129, 140, 142, 160, 162, 174, 182 n.261, 185, 210, 223, 240 n.44, 245, 254 n.121, 261
Abodrites 240, 258 n.140
Adalard, bishop of Verona 228
Adalard, son of *dux* Henry 221–2, 226–7
Adalbero, bishop of Augsburg 2, 7, 9, 16, 39, 48–9, 61–2, 198
Adalbero, bishop of Metz 239, 245, 254–5, 263
Adalbert, count of Metz 247
Adalbert, son of Berengar II 253, 262–70
Adalbert, son of *dux* Henry 221–2, 226–7, 229–31, 233
Adalbert of Magdeburg, as missionary 261, 263, 269
Adaldag, archbishop of Hamburg-Bremen 241, 260, 264, 267
Adalelm, Odo's uncle 214
Adalgis of Benevento 52, 165–7
Adalhard, count of Metz 186
Adalung, count 219
Adelaide, queen 179, 215
Adelheid, empress 251–4, 257 n.135, 262 n.169, 269 n.206
Ado of Vienne, historian 11–12, 14, 20, 23
Adventius, bishop of Metz 160
Aelius Pertinax, emperor 71
Ageltrude, queen 220 n.447
Agilulf, king 99, 101
Alan, Breton leader 10, 35, 41, 173, 208–9
Alberic, count in Lotharingia 48, 189, 214, 220

Alboin, king 88, 92, 93 nn. 256, 258
Albuin, Frankish noble 163
Alemannia 7, 53, 56, 59, 99, 116, 121, 144, 175, 177, 183, 193, 196, 198, 231–4, 238–40, 250, 256, 267
Alewic, abbot of Reichenau 259
Alsace 55, 177 n.236, 234, 237–8, 243, 253–4, 270
Altfrid, bishop of Hildesheim 162
Altötting 182, 225
Altrip 3
Anastasius I, emperor 26, 85
Anastasius II, emperor 22, 114–15, 116 n.398
Andernach, battle 175–6
Andlau 196 n.333
Angelfredus, patriarch of Aquileia 264
Angers, siege 168–9
Anglo-Saxons *see* England
Annales Regni Francorum see Royal Frankish Annals
Anno, bishop of Worms 251
Ansbald, abbot of Prüm 4, 35–6, 40, 136, 194
Ansgard, queen 179
Antoninus Pius, emperor 70
Aquitaine 86, 98, 102, 116–17, 121, 133–4, 152–3, 214–16, 219
Arcadius, emperor 81–3
Arn, bishop of Würzburg 215
Arnold, count in Bavaria 255
Arnstadt 257, 258 n.141
Arnulf, bishop of Metz 17, 43, 101–2, 107, 182–3
Arnulf, count 211
Arnulf, *dux* of Bavaria 232, 233 n.9,

INDEX

234, 242
Arnulf of Carinthia, king of east Francia and emperor 6, 34, 42, 48, 53, 182–3, 197–8, 200–1, 206–7, 210–13, 215–25
Arras 86, 145 n.99, 181, 210 n.400, 227
Arsenius, papal legate 143–5
Artald, archbishop of Rheims 249
Askericus, bishop of Paris 195, 224
Asolf, abbot of St-Maximin 270–1
Asselt, siege 184–7, 190
assemblies 121, 138, 146, 158, 166, 196–7, 210, 214, 216–17, 219, 221, 224, 230–1, 247, 253, 258–9, 271
Astronomer, historian 42
Atto, count of Lecco 267
Augsburg 77, 144, 253, 272
Augustine of Hippo 13–14, 25, 78, 82–3, 116, 197 n.336
Aurelian, archbishop of Lyon 180
Aurelian, emperor 75
Aurelius Alexander, emperor 72
Authari, king 95, 97, 99
Azo, papal legate 260, 265, 266 n.187, 268

Babenberg 226, 230, 270
Babenbergers 215 n.424, 222 n.453, 227 n.479, 229 n.490, 261 n.162
  see also Adalard, son of *dux* Henry; Adalbert, son of *dux* Henry; Henry, *dux*, east Frankish general; Henry, son of *dux* Henry; Poppo *dux* of the Thuringians
Baldwin I of Flanders 130
Baldwin II of Flanders 130, 227
Baltram, bishop of Strasbourg 231
baptism *see* conversion
Bavaria 97, 108, 113, 116, 121, 124–5, 161, 177, 182–3, 186–7, 198, 211–12, 216, 228, 232–6, 242, 248, 251, 253–6, 258, 261, 265

Bede, historian 11–14, 19–23
Belecke 242
Belisarius, Byzantine general 87–8
Beltheim 34, 219
Benedict, bishop of Metz 239
Benedict V, pope 265–7
Benevento 105, 111, 142, 155, 165–7
Beneventum *see* Benevento
Berengar I, king 199–200, 223, 228
Berengar II, king 251–3, 258, 260–3, 265–70
Bergamo 217
Bernard (or Werner), count in the Wormsgau 233
Bernard, son of Bernard of Italy 130
Bernard, son of Charles the Fat 197–8
Bernard of Italy, king 129–30
Bernarius 37–8, 189
Bertha, queen 253
Bertold, count in Alemannia 233 n.9, 234
Bertold, *dux* in Bavaria, son of Arnulf of Bavaria 243 n.58, 247 n.87, 248, 255 n.125
Bertrada, founder of Prüm 4, 13 n.50, 127 n.20
Bertrada, queen 4, 127 n.20, 128
Bertulf, archbishop of Trier 160, 186, 188
Betuwe 192–3
Boethius 15, 87
Bohemians 177, 207, 239, 250
Boleslaw, Bohemian leader 250
Bonn 185, 212, 237, 246
Boris-Michael, Bulgar king 44–5, 157–8
Boso, count in Italy and brother of Theutberga 143–4
Boso, count of Vienne and king 39–40, 177–80, 217, 220, 228
Bratislava, battle 46, 232
Breisach 244, 255
Brennus 220
Bretons *see* Brittany
Brissarthe, battle 38, 153–4
Brittany 5, 9, 31, 33–5, 38, 40, 46–7,

110 n.360, 130, 133, 136–9, 153, 168–73, 205, 208–10
Brun, archbishop of Cologne 255–6, 259, 267, 269
Brunhild, queen 90–2, 99, 100–1
Bulgars 108, 116 n.399, 157–8, 205
Burchard, abbot of St-Gall 259
Burchard, a Saxon 250
Burchard, *dux* in Alemannia 238–9, 268
Burchard, *dux* in Thuringia 10, 215, 232 n.2
Burchard of Worms 7
Burgundy 86, 99, 109, 179–80, 201, 217

Camerino 265
Campania 75, 92, 105, 111, 165, 269
Capua 34, 165, 167 n.192
Carloman, king 128
Carloman, mayor of the palace 32–3, 45, 121, 122–4
Carloman, son of Charles the Bald 45, 163–4
Carloman, son of Louis the German *see* Karlmann of Bavaria
Carloman II, king of west Francia 39, 179–81, 187–90
Carus, emperor 76
Charibert, king 91
Charlemagne, emperor 1, 2, 43, 128, 129, 197
Charles, son of Charles the Bald 52, 163
Charles III the Fat, emperor 1, 5, 42, 45, 174–5, 177, 183–4, 186–7, 190–9, 218, 226
Charles III the Straightforward, king of west Francia 6, 31, 48, 51, 130 n.30, 170 n.203, 179, 215–17, 219, 222–3, 236–8
Charles Martel, mayor of the palace 1, 3, 22, 23, 27, 28, 43, 113, 115, 116, 117, 118, 121
Charles of Provence, king 133–5
Charles the Bald, king of west Francia and emperor 4, 17,
32–3, 45, 52, 131–3, 135–9, 145, 151–3, 160–4, 168–9, 173–9
Chèvremont 243, 244 nn.65, 69
Chiemsee 218
Childebert I, king 88–90
Childebert II, king 95–8
Chilperic I, king 90–4, 98
Claudius, emperor 65–6
Claudius, another emperor 75
Claudius of Turin, historian 11–12
Clodomer, king 90
Clothar I, king 89–90
Clothar II, king 98–9, 101, 104
Clovis, king 26, 28, 86
Cologne 100, 107, 109, 160–2, 174, 176, 185, 192, 209–10, 254, 258–9, 267, 269
Compiègne 138, 227
Conrad, count 152–3, 201
Conrad, count of Paris 180
Conrad I, king of east Francia 53, 228, 233–5
Conradines 53, 189 n.303, 215 n.424, 229 n.490, 230 n.492, 244 n.67
  see also Conrad I, king of east Francia; Conrad the Elder, father of Conrad I; Eberhard, brother of Conrad the Elder; Eberhard, *dux* of Franconia, Gebhard, *dux* in Lotharingia; Herman, son of Gebhard, *dux* in Alemannia; Rudolf of Würzburg; Udo, son of Gebhard
Conrad 'Kurzbold', son of Eberhard (brother of Conrad the Elder) 233, 244, 249
Conrad son of Gebhard 250
Conrad the Elder, father of Conrad I 215, 224, 228–30, 233
Conrad the Red, *dux* in Lotharingia 247–9, 252–7
Constans II, emperor 104, 105
Constantine I, emperor 78
Constantine III, emperor 103
Constantine IV, emperor 106

INDEX

Constantinople 83–5, 88, 92, 94, 96, 100, 102–3, 105–7, 109, 112–13, 116–17, 260, 272
Constantius, emperor 79
conversion 64, 67, 73, 86, 95–6, 101, 103, 107, 157–8, 187, 240, 260
Corsica 167, 263–4, 267
Corvey 245
councils *see* synods
Coutances 208
Cross, True 78, 100–1, 111

Dagobert I, king 94, 101–4, 106–10
Danes 128, 191, 240
Decius, emperor 73
De harmonica institutione 6
Denis, St 127–8
De synodalibus causis 7, 10, 36
Deutz 161
Diocletian, emperor 76, 77
Domitian, emperor 68
Dortmund 254
Drogo, bishop of Metz 42, 134
Drogo, bishop of Toul 231
Duisburg 37, 191, 239, 247
Duodo, palace chaplain 266–7
Durfos 222, 224
Dyle, battle 34, 211–12

Eberhard, archbishop of Sens 202
Eberhard, brother of Conrad the Elder 226–7
Eberhard, count of Lahngau 270
Eberhard, *dux* of Franconia and brother of Conrad I 57, 240, 242–4
Eberhard Saxo, count in Hamaland 36–7, 40, 184, 193, 223
Eberhard, son of Arnulf of Bavaria 242–3
Ebo, archbishop of Rheims 131
Ebolus, abbot of St-Denis 214, 216
Echternach 164
Edith, queen 240, 245, 249
Egino, count 230–1, 232 n.2
Eigil, abbot of Prüm 3, 133, 136
Einhard, bishop of Speyer 233

Ekkehard, abbot of Reichenau 259
Emma, east Frankish queen 174
Emma II, west Frankish queen 269
Engelram, count in Frisia 37, 38, 189
Engiltrude, ex-wife of Count Boso 141 n.82, 143–5, 213 n.411
England 96, 101, 104–5, 108, 114, 240
Erchanbert, abbot of Wissembourg 267, 269
Erchanbold, bishop of Strasbourg 268
Erchangar, count in Alemannia 233 n.9, 234
Eresburg 245
Erfurt 241
Erispoë, Breton leader 137 n.65, 138–9, 153, 170 n.205, 173
Ermengard, empress 133, 253 n.119
Erstein 253
Eusebius of Caesarea, historian 11
Evesa, mother of Eberhard 26, 184

Farabert, abbot of Prüm 194, 213
Flamersheim 163
Flörchingen 223
Folcmar, archbishop of Cologne 269
Forchheim 225
Formosus, pope 220
Franco, bishop of Liège 160–1, 223
Frankfurt 174–5, 185, 194 n.321, 216, 240 n.44, 246, 250, 253, 271
Frechulf of Lisieux, historian 11, 12, 17
Fredegund, queen 91, 94, 98
Frederick, archbishop of Mainz 241, 244–6, 252–7, 259
Frederick, archbishop of Salzburg 259
Friderada 189
Frisia 37–8, 111, 115, 126, 177, 187, 191–2
Fritzlar 229, 236 n.19
Fulda 207, 234–5, 242, 245–6
Fulk, archbishop of Rheims 10, 34, 52, 215, 219, 227–8

Gaius, emperor 65
Gallus, emperor 74
Garda 262, 264
Gardulf, count in Frisia 192
Gauzbert, count in Aquitaine 136
Gauzbert, Ranulf's brother 214
Gauzlin of St-Denis 180 n.255, 181 n.258, 191 n.309, 194 n.324, 195
Gebhard, *dux* in Lotharingia 224, 226–30, 232
Geilo, abbot of Wissembourg 259–60
Gerard, count in Lotharingia 6, 47–50, 188 n.295, 213, 221, 225–6, 228–9, 231
Gerberga, daughter of Berengar II 267
Gerberga, wife of Giselbert then Louis IV 239, 244 n.68, 245, 255 n.127, 267
Germanus, St 165
Gero, *marchio* 264 n.182, 269
Gerric, abbot of Wissembourg 260, 266–7
Gerulf, count in Frisia 192, 223
Gesta Dagoberti 19, 26–7
Geul, battle 34, 210–11
Gewelesdorf 34
Gisela, daughter of Berengar II 267
Gisela, daughter of Lothar II 187, 191–3
Giselbert, *dux* in Lotharingia 237, 239, 243–4, 245 n.70, 246 n.77, 247 n.86, 259 n.153
Godafrid, Viking leader 36–7, 184, 187, 191–3
Godfrid, bishop of Speyer 262
Godfrid, *dux* in Lotharingia 266
Gondreville 190
Gordian, emperor 73
Gralo, abbot of St-Gall 259
Gratian, emperor 81
Gregory I the Great, pope 7, 96, 156
Grimoald, Lombard king 104–8
Gunther, abbot of Hersfeld 260
Gunther, archbishop of Cologne 44, 139–43

Guntram, Frankish king 26, 90, 93, 97–9
Guy, bishop of Modena 268
Guy, son of Berengar II 262, 268
Guy of Spoleto, Italian king 199–200, 218, 220

Hadamar, abbot of Fulda 258
Hadrian, emperor 70
Hadrian II, pope 43, 156, 158–60, 164
Hagano, abbot of Hersfeld 260
Hagano, papal legate 141–2
Haicho, abbot of Fulda 237
Hartbert, bishop of Chur 250
Hasting, Viking leader 154, 172–3
Hatto, abbot of Fulda 258, 262
Hatto, archbishop of Mainz 7, 39, 212, 224, 233
Heimsheim 267
Helen, queen of the Rus' 260
Henry, archbishop of Trier 258, 264, 266
Henry, brother of Otto I 242–6, 251–6, 258
Henry, *dux*, east Frankish general 189 n.298, 191–5, 221
Henry, son of *dux* Henry 221–2, 226–7
Henry I, east Frankish king 53–4, 235–41
Henry the Quarrelsome, *dux* of Bavaria 258
Heracleonas, emperor 102
Heraclius, emperor 101
Herbert I, count of Vermandois 10, 130, 215
Herbert II, count of Vermandois 238, 249
heresy, heretics 24–6, 28, 79, 82–6, 102, 103–4, 106, 109, 112, 114, 117, 142
Heriger, archbishop of Mainz 233, 238
Herispich 192
Heriveus, archbishop of Rheims 228
Hermann, archbishop of Cologne 209, 237

INDEX 301

Hermann, son of Gebhard, *dux* in Alemannia 232, 239, 248, 250
Herod 62–3, 65
Herold, archbishop of Salzburg 256, 259
Hersfeld 235
Herstal 162
Hildebert, abbot of Fulda and archbishop of Mainz 237–8, 241
Hildegard, daughter of Louis the Younger 218
Hildesheim 242
Hilduin, archbishop of Cologne 160–2
Hilduin of St-Denis, abbot 41
Hincmar of Rheims, historian 52
Honorius, emperor 82
Hubert, brother of Theutberga 135, 141, 144 n.92, 145 n.97, 152, 153 n.132, 189 n.298
Hugh, abbot of St-Maximin and bishop of Liège 241, 248
Hugh, archbishop of Rheims 249
Hugh, son of Louis the Younger 181
Hugh of Lotharingia, son of Lothar II 5, 32, 37, 43, 46, 188–9, 191–4
Hugh the Abbot 153 n.132, 154–5, 180, 181 n.259, 190, 191 n.309, 195, 201
Hugh 'the Great', count of Tours 248
Hungarians 46–7, 202–6, 218, 226, 232–4, 237–8, 240, 243, 247, 256–7

Ida, daughter of *dux* Hermann 249
Immo, count in Lotharingia 247
Inden 185
Ingelheim 130–1, 246, 249, 254, 259, 267
Irmingarde, daughter of Louis II 177, 217
Isidore of Seville 11
Italy *see* Benevento; Lombards; Louis II of Italy; Rome

Jengland, battle 33, 47, 136–8

Jerome, historian 11, 13, 31
John VIII, pope 164, 166–7, 173, 177, 184
John XII, pope 262–5
John XIII, pope 268–72
John the deacon, papal legate 260, 265, 266 n.187
Jovian, emperor 80
Judicael, Breton leader 35, 173, 208–9
Judith, empress 17, 131
Judith, wife of *dux* Henry 255
Julian, emperor 80, 164
Jülich 185
Justin, historian 15, 30, 46
Justin I, emperor 86–7
Justin II, emperor 89
Justinian, emperor 87–8
Justinian II, emperor 109–10, 112–13

Karlmann of Bavaria, east Frankish king 174–5, 177, 182, 218
Koblenz 192

Lago Maggiore 262
Lake Como 262, 267
Lambert, count of Nantes 136
Lambert, Italian king 218, 220
Lannesdorf 212
Lantward, bishop of Minden 264
Laon 214, 219, 222 n.455, 248
Lausitzer 264
Lech, battle 54, 257
Leo (Leontios), emperor 110–12
Leo II, emperor 84
Leo III, emperor 116–18
Leo VIII, pope 264–6, 268
Leuven 191, 194
Liber Historiae Francorum 19, 23, 26–7
Liber Pontificalis 20–1, 23
Libutius, missionary 260–1
Liège 112, 185, 210
Liudolf, son of Otto I 249–52, 254–9
Liutbert, archbishop of Mainz 161–2, 164 n.185, 197, 206

Liutgard, daughter of Otto I 249, 255
Liutpold, *dux* of Bavaria 232
Liutpoldings 255 n.125
  see also Arnold, count in Bavaria; Arnulf, *dux* of Bavaria; Judith, wife of *dux* Henry; Liutpold, *dux* of Bavaria
Liutprand, Lombard king 113, 117, 118
Liutprand of Cremona, historian 54, 56, 268
Liutward, bishop of Vercelli 196, 226
locusts 167–8
Lombards 22, 25, 88–90, 92–6, 99, 101–2, 104–5, 107–11, 118, 126, 178, 187, 217, 220, 226, 253, 268
Lorsch 39, 174, 181, 186, 217, 245, 258
Lothar I, king of middle Francia and emperor 4, 5, 14, 32, 33, 39, 40, 41, 52, 129, 131–2, 133–4, 135, 136
Lothar II, king of Lotharingia 5, 25, 27, 30, 39, 43, 44, 45, 133–4, 135, 139–52, 155–60
Lothar, king of Italy 251
Lothar, king of west Francia 267, 269
Lotharingia/Lotharingians 2, 5, 6, 37, 43–4, 48, 53, 59, 132 n.40, 132, 134, 161–2, 174, 177, 181, 189 n.298, 191, 194, 201, 210, 216–17, 229, 234, 237–9, 241, 243–7, 254–6, 261, 266, 269,
Louis, son of Louis the Younger 186
Louis II of Italy, emperor 34, 52, 133–4, 142, 155, 165–7, 170
Louis II the Stammerer, king of west Francia 163, 178–9
Louis III, king of west Francia 39, 179–81, 187–8
Louis IV d'Outremer, king of west Francia 238, 243–5, 248–9
Louis IV the Child, king of east Francia 6–7, 18, 42, 45–7, 51, 53, 58, 225, 230–1, 233

Louis the Blind of Provence, king of Italy 39, 180 n.257, 217–18, 220, 223, 228
Louis the German, king of east Francia 45, 52, 131–2, 136, 144, 151–2, 157, 161–3, 164 n.185, 174
Louis the Pious, emperor 41–2, 52, 129–31, 134, 245
Louis the Younger, king of east Francia 174–7, 181, 183–6
Lucania 165, 271
Lucius Commodus, emperor 71
Ludelmus, bishop of Toul 220, 231
Lupus, abbot of Ferrières 17, 33, 35
Lyon 71, 81, 180

Maastricht 185, 210, 247
Magdeburg 55, 249, 252 n.114, 253 n.115, 262 n.169
Magyars *see* Hungarians
Maienfeld 176, 214 n.420, 267 n.192
Mainz 132 n.39, 174 n.223, 237, 254–5, 257 n.134, 259
Marcian, emperor 83
Marcus Aurelius, emperor 70, 71
Marcward, abbot of Prüm 13, 32–3, 130
Marinus, bishop of Sutri 268
Marinus, papal legate 249
martyrdoms 67–80, 85, 100, 119–20
Matfrid, count in Lotharingia 6, 47–50, 188 n.295, 213, 221, 225–6, 228–9, 231, 247
Matfridings 6, 47–50, 188 n.295, 216 n.431, 229 n.487
  see also Gerard; Matfrid; Richar
Mathilda, daughter of Liudolf 250
Mathilda, east Frankish queen 267
Maurice, emperor 95–6, 99
Maximinus, emperor 73
Meersen 162–3
Megingoz, count in Lotharingia 48, 188 n.295, 189 n.299, 214–15, 216 n.431, 220, 221 n.450, 229 n.487, 249 n.94

INDEX

Meginhard, count in Hamaland 36, 223
Meginhard, father of Eberhard 36, 184
Metz 4, 90, 109, 131, 140, 142, 160, 186, 213 n.411, 221, 231, 237, 239, 244–5
Monte Cassino 32–3, 110, 122–4
Moosburg 183
Moravians 136, 177, 205, 207, 218
Morman, Breton leader 130
Muslims *see* Saracens

Nantes 36, 133, 136 n.63, 137 n.64, 153, 173 n.216
Nero, emperor 67
Nerva, emperor 69
Neuss 185
Nicephorous II, emperor 271–2
Nicholas I, pope 24, 43, 141–51, 155–6, 159, 189
Nijmegen 29, 184, 223
Nominoë, Breton leader 35, 130, 137 n.64, 138
Northmen 5, 133, 153–4, 168–73, 181, 184–96, 201–2, 206, 208–12
Notker of St-Gall, historian 31

oaths 115, 121, 126, 139, 143–6, 151, 158, 165–7, 175, 179–81, 191, 223, 229, 256, 265, 270
Octavian Augustus 62
Oda, Zwentibald's wife 221, 226
Odacar, count in Lotharingia 221–2, 224
Odilbald, bishop of Utrecht 225
Odo, count of Paris and king of west Francia 4 n.6, 6, 34, 39, 41, 51, 130 n.30, 154–5, 195, 200, 214–17, 219, 222
Oeren 221, 229
Orbe 153
Orosius, historian 17
Otbert, bishop of Strasbourg 231, 234
Otbert, *marchio* 260

Otger, bishop of Speyer 262, 264–5, 268
Otto, *dux* in Lotharingia 246–7
Otto, son of Liudolf 257
Otto I, emperor 54–5, 57–8, 239, 241–72
Otto II, emperor 55, 56, 58, 258, 261–2, 267, 271–2
Otto the Illustrious, father of Henry I 221, 233

Pacsweten, Breton leader 35, 170–1, 173
Paris, siege 194–6, 201, 206, 208
Paul, saint 24, 64, 66–7, 127–8, 132, 144, 148
Paul the Deacon, historian 19, 21–4, 27–8, 30, 46
Pavia 178, 252, 261–3, 267
Persians 25, 87, 93, 100–1, 103
Petchenegs 204–5
Peter, saint 24, 65–8, 127–8, 132, 144, 148
Pfeddersheim 237
Philip, emperor 73
Philippicus, emperor 112–14
Phineas 147
Phocas, emperor 100
Piacenza 160, 217
Pippin, son of Bernard of Italy 130, 215
Pippin I of Aquitaine, king 42, 134
Pippin I of Italy, king 130
Pippin II of Aquitaine, king 133–4
Pippin II, *dux* 102, 113
Pippin III, king 1, 117–18, 121–2, 124, 125, 128
Pippin the Hunchback, son of Charlemagne 32
Poppo, *dux* of the Thuringians 206, 215
Poppo I, bishop of Würzburg 261
Poppo II, bishop of Würzburg 261
Pressburg *see* Bratislava
Probus, emperor 76
Prüm 185, 194, 210, 212, 223

Ranulf, count in Aquitaine 214
Ranulf, count of Poitiers 153–4, 168
Raoul, king 238
Rastiz, Moravian leader 136
Ratbod, archbishop of Trier 6–7, 188
Ratbod, bishop of Utrecht 225
Ravenna 68, 83–4, 86, 92, 116–17, 184 n.275, 271–2
Regensburg 183, 186, 225 n.469, 255–6, 261
Reginar, count and standard-bearer 176
Reginar, count in Lotharingia 48, 51, 222, 224
Reginar III, count in Lotharingia 259
Reginold, bishop of Eichstätt 269
Reichenau 198, 212, 237
Rennes 171
Rethel 214
Revelatio Stephani Papae ('Vision of Pope Stephen') 13 n.50, 28, 30, 42, 126–8
Rheims 86, 90, 215, 248–9, 256 n.133
Richar, abbot of Prüm and bishop of Liège 47–8, 50, 213, 247–8
Richard, count 39–40
Richgard, empress 196
Richildis, queen of west Francia 177
Richwin, count of Verdun 37–8, 189, 246 n.77
Rihgowo, bishop of Worms 251
Robert, archbishop of Trier 239, 247, 251, 258
Robert, bishop of Metz 188
Robert, count in Lotharingia 188
Robert, count of Tours and king 154–5, 216, 236, 248
Robertians *see* Odo, Robert the Strong, Robert count of Tours
Robert the Strong, count of Angers 38–9, 41, 138, 153–4, 168, 195, 200
Rodoald, papal legate 141–2
Roger, archbishop of Trier 237, 239
Romanus I, emperor 260
Romanus II, emperor 272
Rome 1, 23–6, 28, 32, 43, 54, 56–8, 66–70, 75–8, 80–2, 85, 88, 92, 94, 99, 105–6, 112, 115, 117, 122, 132, 141–3, 145, 156, 158, 160, 166–7, 173, 177, 184, 203, 209, 218, 220, 223, 262–8, 271–2
Rotfred 269–70
Royal Frankish Annals 2, 16–17, 22, 29, 42
Rudolf, bishop of Würzburg and brother of Conrad the Elder 215, 221–2, 226–7, 232 n.2
Rudolf, count of Cambrai 130
Rudolf I of Burgundy, king 201, 217–18
Rudolf II of Burgundy, king 242, 251
Rümlingen 256
Ruodhard, bishop of Strasbourg 244–5, 251
Rus' 55, 260–1, 263, 269

Saalfeld 252
St-Alban, Mainz 164 n.185, 259–60
St-Denis 19, 30, 41, 110, 178, 187, 190, 216, 222
St-Gall 193, 209, 242
St-Goar 48, 98, 224
St-Lô 208
St-Maurice d'Agaune 201, 217
St-Maximin, Trier 48, 55, 214 n.420, 215 n.423, 228–9, 231 n.498, 241, 246, 251, 259, 261, 270
St-Médard 133, 195
St-Vaast 3, 34, 130 n.30, 145 n.99, 181, 227
Salomon, Breton leader 35, 39, 40–1, 153, 169–72
Salomon II, bishop of Constance 209
Salomon III, bishop of Constance 209, 234
Samnium 165
San Giulio 262
San Leo 262–3, 265, 268 n.198
Saracens 45, 105, 107, 109, 115–18, 155
Saucourt, battle 188

INDEX

Saxony 53, 55, 121, 124–5, 176, 192, 232, 234, 245, 252, 254, 256, 260–1, 267–8, 270–1
Schwalfeld 177
Scythians 46–7, 202–4
Sens 152, 201–2, 206
Severus, emperor 71, 72
Sigibert I, king 90–1
Sigifrid, Viking leader 184, 187
Sigolf, bishop of Piacenza 270
Sinzig 192
Slavs 45, 108, 136, 177, 182, 207, 211, 215, 218, 236, 241, 257, 259–60, 264, 268
see also Abodrites; Bohemians; Lausitzer; Moravians; Vucrani
Soissons 90, 98, 125, 133, 195, 236
Sophia, empress 93, 95
Spain 65, 86, 88–90, 95, 96, 103, 108, 117
Spoleto 265, 271
Starkand, bishop of Eichstätt 269
Stavelot-Malmedy 185
Stephen, brother of Alberic 189
Stephen II, pope 126–8
Stephen, Lotharingian count and brother of Walaho 48, 188, 189 n.299, 220–1, 225–6
Strasbourg 231, 238
Sunderolt, archbishop of Mainz 206–7, 211
Swabia see Alemannia
synods 43, 78, 81, 103, 109, 112, 115, 131, 140–2, 218–19, 239, 241, 246, 249, 259, 264, 266, 271

Tacitus, emperor 75, 76
Tancrad, abbot of Prüm 130
Tassilo I of Bavaria 97
Thankmar, brother of Otto I 242 n.57, 245
Thegan, historian 41, 52
Theoderic, archbishop of Trier 269
Theoderic, bishop of Metz 263, 269
Theodosius I, emperor 81
Theodosius II, emperor 83
Theodosius III, emperor 115

Theophanu 272 n.226
Theres 227 n.479, 230
Theudebert I, Frankish king 89–90
Theudebert II, Frankish king 98–101
Theuderic II, Frankish king 98–101
Theutbald, son of Hubert 189
Theutberga, queen 43, 135, 139–41, 143, 145–50, 152
Theutgaud, archbishop of Trier 44, 139–40, 142–3
Thietmar, Saxon count 260
Thiméon, battle 52, 181
Thionville 126, 225, 245
Thuringia 26, 87, 90, 124, 176–7, 187, 206, 215, 232–4, 236, 241
Tiberius III, emperor 111
Tiberius Constantine, emperor 93–5
Tiberius, emperor 63–4
Titus, emperor 68
Tongres 79, 112, 185
Toul 206
Trajan, emperor 69
Tribur 197, 218, 230
Trier 4, 6–7, 13, 16, 20, 31, 38, 41, 47–8, 55–6, 78–9, 83–4, 89, 98, 160, 186, 210, 214 n.420, 221, 228–9
see also St-Maximin
Troyes 206

Udo, bishop of Strasbourg 251, 268
Udo, count of Maienfeld 267, 270
Udo, son of Gebhard 232, 244, 247, 250
Unni, archbishop of Hamburg-Bremen 241

Valens, emperor 80–1
Valentinian, emperor 80
Val Travaglia 262
Verdun 38, 83–4, 132, 206
Verona 92, 228, 253, 272
Vespasian, emperor 67–8
Vikings see Northmen
Villance 39
Vivian, count of Tours 136

Vucrani 241

Wala, bishop of Metz 186
Walaho, brother of Stephen 188
    n.295
Waldo, bishop of Chur 250
Waldo, bishop of Como 260, 267, 270
Waldrada, mistress or wife of Lothar
    II 139–41, 143, 145–51, 159
Waltbert, archbishop of Milan 260
Walter, archbishop of Sens 202
Walter, bishop of Orléans 202
Waltgar, cousin of Odo 214
Waltgar the Frisian 223
Wandalbert of Prüm 13–14
Wanger, lover of Engiltrude 144
warfare *see* Andernach; Angers;
    Asselt; Bratislava; Brissarthe;
    Brittany; Dyle; Geul;
    Hungarians; Jengland; Lech;
    Northmen; Paris; Saucourt;
    Thiméon
Weilburg 230
Wichmann, Saxon noble 242 n.57,
    245, 258, 260 n.156
Widukind of Corvey, historian 54, 56
Wigbert, count in Lotharingia 188–9

Wigfrid, archbishop of Cologne 237,
    255
Wikerus, abbot of St-Maximin 270
Wikerus, archbishop of Mainz 259
Willa, queen 261–2, 265, 270
William, archbishop of Mainz 55,
    239, 257, 259, 261, 263, 267,
    271
Willibert, archbishop of Cologne
    161–2, 192–3, 209
Winemarus, follower of Baldwin II
    227–8
Wissembourg 55, 259
Witgar, bishop of Augsburg 198
Witgar, bishop of Metz 237
Worms 216–17, 219, 221, 250, 261,
    267, 270–1
Wrhwant, Breton leader 15, 35, 44,
    170–3

Zedechias, doctor 178
Zeno, emperor 85
Zülpich 87, 100, 185
Zwentibald, king of Lotharingia 6,
    10, 38, 48, 51, 130 n.30, 193,
    201, 215, 217, 219, 221–6
Zwentibald, Moravian leader 207,
    218

EU authorised representative for GPSR:
Easy Access System Europe, Mustamäe tee 50,
10621 Tallinn, Estonia
gpsr.requests@easproject.com